SOCIETY AND CULTURE IN RAJASTHAN

SOCIETY AND CULTURE IN RAJASTHAN

c. AD 700–900

SHANTA RANI SHARMA

Pragati Publications
1996

PRAGATI PUBLICATIONS
9926 Library Road,
Azad Market, Delhi 110006

First Published 1996

ISBN: 81-7307-037-7

The publication of this book has been financially supported by the Indian Council of Historical Research and the responsibility for the facts stated and all opinions expressed is entirely of the author and not of the Council.

Published by Vinod Kapoor for Pragati Publications
9926 Library Road, Azad Market, Delhi 110006

Typeset and Printed by Vikas Print Communication Services
New Delhi 110026

Dedicated to
the memory of my father
Professor Dasharatha Sharma

Contents

Foreword

The period between the eighth and the twelfth centuries in Northern India, which was once considered a 'dark period', has now become one of the most exciting and rewarding periods of Indian history—exciting because despite its outer appearance it is a period of change and flux, rewarding because it helps us to understand the processes at work during the earlier period of Indian history, as also the one that succeeded it namely, the period of Sultanat rule. It is thus a link period in more than a chronological sense.

While a number of scholarly studies have enabled us to understand better the period between the eighth and the twelfth centuries, it still remains a challenging period because of the vast variety of sources—Sanskrit, Apabhramsha, Arabic as well as numismatic, epigraphic, literary and archaeological. Because of the vast range of these sources, it has been difficult for an individual scholar to use all of them. In the present work, which deals with society and culture in Rajasthan during the eighth and ninth centuries, Dr Shanta Sharma has drawn extensively on the Prakrit sources comparing them critically with archaeological and literary data. She has thus continued her family tradition of working in Apabhramsha and Prakrit languages, familiarity with which is unfortunately declining in our universities. Critically examining the thesis of the Supervisor of her Ph.D. thesis, Professor R.S. Sharma, characterising the period as one of 'feudalism' in which there was a decline of long distance trades, absence of gold and silver coins and a decentralisation of government authority to the local landed elites, Dr Shanta Sharma gives evidence of extensive and lively domestic and foreign trade during the period. The foreign trade included import of horses from Central and West Asia, and different kinds of linen, silk and woollen fabrics from these countries as well as from China, as well as other commodities, and Indian traders being active in overseas trade. She also gives evidence regarding continuation and even revival of towns and town life, and the use of gold and silver coins—Dinar, Suvarana and Rupak. At the same time, she gives evidence of the growing power and authority of the local landed elites.

Dr Shanta Sharma's work will therefore lead to a lively controversy among scholarly circles. It is however necessary to say that a feudal order of society was by no means a society based on a natural economy in which only relations of barter existed. In other words, domestic and foreign trade and the circulation of coins were not precluded from a feudal society. The question is of quantum, as also the actual relations of production including forms of state power. Hence, more detailed work would be needed to clarify these aspects.

Dr Shanta Sharma has given evidence to show that some of the Shudras participated in trade, and at the religious level, tantrism and a form of Bhakti provided them greater freedom. At the same time, there were efforts in some other sections, specially among the commentators of the Dharma Shastras, to further increase their disabilities. Similarly, a section of the Vaishyas participated in warfare, while many tribes were being absorbed into Hinduism.

Thus, Dr Shanta Sharma's work presents us a fascinating picture of a society and a culture in flux which would be found rewarding both by the scholars and the general reader.

SATISH CHANDRA

Preface

The eighth and ninth centuries represent a significant epoch in the history of Rajasthan, marked by the establishment of a territorial polity and the ascendancy of the Rajputs. The socio-cultural life of the people is amply reflected in the extensive *Prākrit* literature during the period. Yet a systematic, detailed and satisfactory use of this valuable material is not found in most of the research publications on the subject.

General books on Indian society and culture fail to do adequate justice to the region. The large time span and wide scope of *Rajasthan Through the Ages* by my father, Professor Dasharatha Sharma, naturally precluded a detailed study of the period. Independent studies based on Prākrit works of the period by Jhinkoo Yadava, Prem Suman Jain and A.P. Jamkhedkar lack historical sense and fail to identify trends of change and continuity. The present work aims at filling this lacuna and is a carefully revised version of my thesis approved by the University of Delhi in 1993. It attempts to correlate changes in the social structure of early medieval Rajasthan with distinctive economic, political and religious developments during this period there—especially rural prosperity and urbanism with its industrial and mercantile base; a territorial polity with wide-ranging feudal ties; and emerging new trends in Jainism as well as Purāṇic Hinduism with emphasis on charity, pilgrimage and practice of rituals.

I express my gratitude to Professor R.S. Sharma, former Head of the Department of History, Delhi University, for his able guidance and supervision of my work. I am particularly grateful to Dr Vivekanand Jha, Director, Journal, Publications and Library, ICHR, for his help and keen interest in the publication of this work. I am deeply indebted to my mother Malathi Sharma for her constant encouragement, my daughter Jaya for her help in typing and correction of proofs and my colleague Dr Kush Satyendra for his consistent assistance.

I offer my sincere thanks to the Indian Council of Historical Research for grant of a publication subsidy and to Shri Vinod Kapoor of Pragati Publications for his whole-hearted cooperation in the speedy publication of my work. My thanks are also due to Shri S.P. Das for preparing the index.

3 January 1996
Delhi

Shanta Rani Sharma

Abbreviations

ABORI	*Annals of the Bhandarkar Oriental Research Institute*
AIOC	*Proceedings and Transactions of the All-India Oriental Conference*
ASIR	*Annual Report of the Archaeological Survey of India*
CII	*Corpus Inscriptionum Indicarum*
Dh.S.	*Dharmasūtra*
Dhū.	*Dhūrtākhyāna*
ECD	*Early Chauhan Dynasties* by D. Sharma
ED	Elliot and Dowson's *The History of India as Told by Its Own Historians*
EI	*Epigraphia Indica*
HD	*History of the Dharmaśāstra* by P.V. Kane
IA	*Indian Antiquary*
IHC	*Proceedings of the Indian History Congress*
IHR	*The Indian Historical Review,* ICHR, New Delhi
JRASB	*Journal of the Royal Asiatic Society of Bengal*
JNSI	*Journal of the Numismatic Society of India*
JRAS	*Journal of the Royal Asiatic Society of Great Britain and Ireland*
Kām. Nīti.	*Kāmandakīya Nītisāra*
Karpūra.	*Karpūramañjarī*
KM	*Kuvalayamālā*
Manu	*Manusmṛti*
Mbh.	*Mahābhārata*
PRAS, WC	*Progress Report of the Archaeological Survey of India,* Western Circle
RTTA	*Rajasthan Through the Ages* by D. Sharma
SK	*Samarāiccakahā*
Upamiti.	*Upamitibhavaprapañcākathā*
Yājña	*Yājñavalkyasmṛti*
ZDMG	*Zeitschrift der Deutschen Morgenlandischen Gesellschaft*

1

Introduction

RAJASTHAN—ITS GEOGRAPHICAL FEATURES

RAJASTHAN IS ROUGHLY rhombic in shape, with an area of about 1,32,147 square miles. It is bounded by Pakistan on the west and north-west, by Punjab and Haryana on the north and north-east, by U.P. on the east, by Madhya Pradesh on the south-east and Gujarat on the south-west. The most striking topographical feature of Rajasthan is the Aravalli range of hills, which running from north-east to south-west, divides it into two distinct 'natural regions'. To its west and north-west lie Bikaner, Jaisalmer, Marwar and Shekhavati region of the former Jaipur state, mostly arid and sandy desert. On the east and south-east are the alluvial plains and plateau region covering Mewar, Kota, Bundi and Jaipur excluding Shekhavati. The main range of the Aravallis widens out south of Ajmer, spreads to Dungarpur and Banswara districts, and rises towards Sirohi and Pali districts, its highest peak at Gurushikhara on Mount Abu (Sirohi), 5,650 feet above sea level. An important branch runs from Mandalgarh in Udaipur through Bundi, Kota and Jhalavad. There are more or less continuous ranges in Jaipur and Alwar districts. Several small off-shoots appear in Jodhpur.

The sandy desert to the west of the Aravallis can be classified under four physiographic divisions, the Thār desert, the Pāṭ, the Ghaggar area and steppe desert. The Thār desert lies in Jaisalmer and Barmer districts and joins with Sind (Pakistan), in which its major portion is situated. The Pāṭ includes parts of Sind, Khairpur (both in Pakistan), Jodhpur and Bikaner, the land here more rugged but flatter (pāṭ) than the Thār. The Ghaggar area, composed of the dry beds of the rivers Sarasvatī and Dṛṣadvatī, has firm and loamy soil. The steppe desert is an arid waste land, about one-third sandy and two-thirds rocky.

To the east of the Aravallis, the plateau region spreads from Chittor to Bijolia, Mandalgarh, Bundi and Kota. Locally known as the Uparmāl, this area is comparatively well watered and fertile, with fertile black soil on flat hill tops. Then there are the fertile plains of Central Mewar, watered by the Banas and Berach rivers, and Jaipur, its territory eastwards along the Banganga valley and southern portion enclosed by the bend of Banas consisting of a rich alluvial loam.

The Sarasvatī, the modern Ghaggar river, which once flowed through the northern part of the former Bikaner state and is said to have joined the Indus, dried up by the time of the Mahābhārata, which speaks of Vinaśana as the place where it disappeared underground, but leaves behind a fertile area in the desert, the dry bed sometimes getting filled up in the rains. The most important river in western Rajasthan is the Luni, which flows for about 200 miles from the Pushkara valley into the Rann of Kutch, a veritable blessing to the southern parts of the Jodhpur division. The Lilri, Rajpur Luni, Guhiya, Bandi, Sukri, Jawai and Jojri are its tributaries, but they are mere rain gutters. The Chambal flows out from Indore in Madhya Pradesh and entering Rajasthan passes by Bhainsarodgarh (in Mewar), Kota and Dholpur and falls into the river Yamuna 25 miles south-west of Etawah in Uttar Pradesh. Banas originates from the mountain range three miles away from the Kumbhalgarh fort and passing through Udaipur, Jaipur, Bundi, Tonk and Karauli joins the Chambal at Rameshwar (M.P.). Kalisindh originates in Central India, runs through Jhalawad and Kota and falls into the Chambal. Parbati also originates in Central India, runs through Tonk and Kota and joins the Chambal at Palighat (in Kota). The Mahi passes through Dungarpur and Banswara districts. Its chief tributary is the Son. There are three important salt lakes at Sambhar, Didwana and Pachbhadra.[1]

These distinctive features of Rajasthan exercised a profound influence on its history. The arid and dreary Thār desert served as an effective obstacle to invasions from the western side. But the regions east of the Aravallis were easily approachable, no natural barriers standing on the way, and hence fell successively under the sphere of Śaka, Kuṣāṇa and Gupta political influence.[2] The influence of Kuṣāṇa and Gupta art can be seen in the terracottas and sculptures of Rajasthan.[3] The inaccessible hills and sands provided a means of defence which was lacking in the plains and after their defeat by Alexander various indigenous tribes such as the Mālavas, Śibis and Arjunāyanas migrated to Rajasthan, where they valiantly kept up their struggle for freedom against the Śakas and Kuṣāṇas.[4] The heroic resistance put up by the

Rajputs against the Muslim rulers of Delhi was possible as much due to the nature of the land they inhabited as their fighting capabilities. The secluded mountain fastnesses also enabled wild primitive tribes like the Bhillas and Mers to survive and retain their primitive culture. The portion of the Aravalli chain between Kumbhalmer and Ajmer is termed Merwārā and is inhabited by the Mers.[5] Due to its rugged terrain and scant means of subsistence offered by it, large portions of the mountainous region remained sparsely populated. But in places like Udaipur, Dungarpur, Banswara, Bundi and Kota the Aravallis are clad with fairly thick forests which abound in trees of mango, mahuā, sāgwān, vaṭa, pīpal, nīm, gūlar, jāmun, khejdā, sālar etc.[6] Here existed picturesque spots endowed with charming scenic surroundings which provided secluded retreats conducive to undisturbed religious reflection and developed into holy places like Ekaliṅgajī and Nāgdā.

Quite appropriately termed 'region of death', *Marusthalī*, the waterless and inhospitable desert, extremely difficult to traverse, offered little temptation to an invader. Shershāh after his victory over Māldeo (the ruler of Marwar) declared that he had come very near losing an empire for a handful of millets.[7] The desert also provided shelter to many a fleeing monarch. The Waṇī and Rādhanpur grants state that Dhruva caused Vatsarāja 'to enter upon the path of misfortune in the centre of (the deserts of) Maru' which indicates that Vatsarāja took refuge in the desert.[8] The area also provided refuge to Rao Jodhā who successfully carved out a mighty kingdom in Marwar.[9] The rigours of the climate, precarious and scanty rainfall, and meagre agricultural resources of the desert in most parts, made its inhabitants hardy and instilled in them the virtues of industry, frugality, perseverance and fortitude. In response to the challenge of nature, they became daring and adventurous. The enterprising Mārwārī traders are well known now and that even in early days they were not deterred by the desert is known from Jātaka references to caravans crossing the desert.[10] Some parts of the desert are quite fertile. The extensive western divisions of Jalor, Sanchor and Bhīnmāl possess an excellent soil. Pali and Sojat, fertilised by numerous streams flowing from the Aravallis also produce abundantly a variety of grains. Marwar is well endowed with natural wealth, with its salt lakes, marble quarries of Makrana, limestone quarries near Jodhpur and Nagor, tin and lead at Sojat, alum about Pali, and iron at Bhīnmāl.[11] It was in these centres, where agricultural produce and mineral resources conducive to the growth of urbanisation were available, that the first important cities of the desert arose.

Bhīnmāl and Sanchor are reputed to have gained a commercial celebrity from ancient times because they lay on the high road to Cutch and Gujarat.[12]

The agricultural productivity of the plains encouraged settlements and therefore they became centres of culture and civilisation from early times. Here the harvests were rich and means of communication easy, which provided time for leisure and cultural advancement. Rivers too made an important contribution to the resources and richness of Rajasthan. Their banks were, as in other parts of the world, the earliest cradles of civilisation. A survey of Banas and its tributaries, the Gambhiri, Berach and Wagen shows that man lived along the banks of these rivers at least 1,00,000 years ago.[13] Remains of the Harappan period have been discovered at Kālībangān on the southern bank of the Ghaggar. The Āhār civilisation flourished on the banks of Āhār and Gilund on the Banas around 2000 BC.[14] Sarasvatī-Dṛṣadvatī region is associated with the activities of the early Aryans. A study of the Luni basin has revealed traces of a man who lived in the stone age.[15] Half of the agricultural produce of Marwar is said to be the gift of the river Luni.

The mineral resources of Rajasthan were conducive to the growth of various industries. There are deposits of iron in Udaipur, Alwar and Jaipur, silver and zinc at Zawar (Udaipur), lead (sisā) near Ajmer, copper at Singhana near Khetri in Jaipur,[16] zinc and copper at Jalor and Sojat in Marwar,[17] and copper and iron at Dungarpur.[18] Bikaner and Jodhpur yield a considerable amount of gypsum.[19] The region has plenty of fine building stone, of which red sandstone from Bikaner and marble from Makrana in Nāgaur district of Jodhpur have been extensively used since ancient times. Large salt resources were available in Marwar, as noted above.

The people of Rajasthan made full utilisation of this mineral wealth. The ancient town of Bairat (Jaipur) is situated in the midst of a circular valley surrounded by low bare red-hills which have all along been famous for their copper mines. Abul-Fazl in his *Ain-i-Akbarī* mentions Virāṭanagara as possessing very profitable copper-mines.[20] The upper platform at Bījaka-Kī-Pahārī revealed a broad and thick iron slag, the remains presumably of a temporary smithy set up for the making of iron and copper objects for the use of the occupants of the monastery.[21] Besides the circular temple assignable to the Mauryan period were found large quantities of iron cramps, nails of different sizes, large size fish-plates with nails sticking in their broad ends, an iron chisel and a copper needle.[22] Masses of corroded iron found at Naliāsar (Jaipur) reveal that it was a blacksmith's workshop.[23] A large quantity of iron refuse found at Rairh (Jaipur) proves that it was a great metallurgical centre.[24] There are traces of the existence of numerous smithies where iron tools and implements of different types were made. A well-preserved smelting furnace with a large quantity of iron-slag has also been found at Noh (Bharatpur).[25]

The geographical location of Rajasthan ensured its participation in inter-regional trade. The routes connecting Delhi and Punjab with Gujarat passed through Rajasthan from ancient times. In the time of Pāṇini the Dvārāvatī-Kamboja route passed through Ānarta, Abu and touching Mādhyamikā and Āhār proceeded northwards towards Kambojas.[26] The route from Abu to the east passed through Pushkara, Naliāsar, Bairat, Rairh, Nagara etc. The route along the Ghaggar was the branch of the grand northern route. Archaeological and literary evidence indicates that this route passing through Rangmahal was active from second to the seventh century AD.[27] Last of all, one may remark that the isolated existence of the people in inaccessible hills and sands developed in them a love for individual independence which in a land where communication was difficult, could not but encourage feudal tendencies and establishment of numerous kingdoms.[28]

Political Background

The eighth and ninth centuries represent a significant epoch in the history of Rajasthan, marked by political unity and the emergence of powerful clans which made Rajasthan a power to be reckoned with. Rajasthan before the eighth century had lacked political unity and played a relatively insignificant role on the Indian political scene. During the Gupta period various republican tribes inhabiting it, the Mālavas, Yaudheyas and Arjunāyanas paid homage and tribute to Samudragupta.[29] Archaeological evidence of destruction of Buddhist monuments at Bairat (Jaipur) and shrines at Rangmahal (Bikaner), Baḍopal etc. and the Bhimchaunri inscription of Kota indicate that the area was later overrun by the Hūṇas.[30] Around VS 589, a governor of Yaśodharman of Malwa is known to have ruled the territories extending from the Pāriyātra mountains (pathār of Aravallis) to the river Narmada.[31] In the seventh century AD Rajasthan was divided into small kingdoms, the Cāpas ruling at Bhillamāla; Pratihāras descended from the king Hariśandra and his wife Bhadrā at Mandor; Guhillas ruling a part of Mewar and Mauryas at Chittor and parts of Kota.[32]

In the eighth century AD the Arabs who had conquered Syria, Egypt, north Africa, Spain, southern France and Persia turned their attention to India. In AD 712 they took Sindh. Al Bilādurī (died AD 892–3) records that expeditions sent by Junaid, the governor of Sindh under Khalif Hishām (AD 724–43) conquered Jurz or Gurjara and Bailamān or Vallamaṇḍala (Jaisalmer) and attacked Marmad or Marwar, Barus or Broach, Ujjain and Malwa (Māliba).[33] According to the Navsārī plates of Pulakeśirāja (Pulakeśin), the governor of Gujarat, he repulsed a formidable invasion of the Tājikas or Arabs who had defeated the Saindhavas, Kacchellas, Saurashtra, Cāvoṭaka (Cāpa), Mauryas and Gurjaras and penetrated as far south as Navasārī (Gujarat).[34]

Disunited as it was, it is evident that Rajasthan at first failed to check these invasions. But then as noted by the Gwalior praśasti of Bhoja, Nāgabhaṭa I appeared like Nārāyaṇa in response to the prayer of the oppressed people and crushed the large armies of the powerful *Mleccha* ruler, the destroyer of virtue.[35] The Arab raids changed the political map of Rajasthan. Of the older ruling dynasties, the Cāpa family was destroyed and the Maurya power weakened. In place of the small kingdoms existing in Rajasthan, the Pratihāra line of Nāgabhaṭa I, which had risen to prominence as the protector of Rajasthan against foreign aggression, carved a mighty empire and thenceforth played a dominant role in north Indian politics. In this task they were ably assisted by various Rājasthānī clans such as the Cāhamānas of Sambhar (Jaipur) and the Guhilas of Cāṭsu (Jaipur) which thereby gained considerable power and prestige and thenceforth played an important role in Rajasthan.

The Pratihāra kingdom continued to act as a bulwark against the Muslims under the successors of Nāgabhaṭa I. Nāgabhaṭa II is credited with the forceful seizure of the forts of the Turuṣkas,[36] who may be identified with the Arabs. According to the account of the Arab traveller, Sulaiman, dated AD 851, the king of Jurz, identified by scholars with Bhoja, was unfriendly to the Arabs and the greatest foe of the Mohammedan faith among the princes of India.[37] Under a succession of able monarchs, the Pratihāra empire grew steadily. Nāgabhaṭa I gained control over Lāṭa, parts of Rājpūtānā and Central India. Vatsarāja carried out extensive campaigns and succeeded in taking Kannauj. He defeated the Gauḍa ruler, though later he was himself defeated by the Rāṣṭrakūṭa ruler, Dhruva and was restricted to Rajasthan. Nāgabhaṭa II emulated the feats of his father and though defeated by Govinda III, the Rāṣṭrakūṭa ruler, reigned over the greater part of Rājpūtānā, Kathiawar,

U.P. and parts of Central India, his empire extending up to Gwalior and Kannauj. After a temporary setback due to the weak reign of Rāmabhadra, the empire expanded again under Bhoja (*c.* AD 836–92) and included Rajasthan, U.P., Central India, Saurashtra, south-eastern and western Punjab as well as parts of Bihar. His successor, Mahendrapāla maintained control over this vast extent of territory.[38] Thus the Pratihāras ruled over the most extensive and durable empire established in northern India after the Gupta empire. It was also efficiently administered, as was recognised even by its foes. Sulaiman, besides speaking of the prosperity of the empire of Jurz and its fine cavalry, observed that no country in India was more safe from robbers.[39] An inherent weakness of the empire was that it was based on the support of various feudatories, who revolted when the ruler was weak.[40]

Under the dynamic leadership of the Pratihāras various clans of Rajasthan ventured out and the prowess of their warriors was felt in distant lands. Amongst them were the valiant Cāhamānas who later were to launch on an imperial career of their own.[41] According to the *Pṛthvīrājavijaya*, Durlabharāja, of the Sapādalakṣa branch, said to be a feudatory of Vatsarāja, led his army to Bengal.[42] His son Gūvaka I achieved fame as a warrior at the court of Nāgabhaṭa II.[43] The Guhilas of Cāṭsū formed another important clan. According to the Cāṭsū inscription of Bālāditya, Śaṅkaragaṇa, probably a feudatory of Nāgabhaṭa II, defeated the Gauḍa ruler and made the land serve his overlord like a slave-girl captured in battle. His son Harṣa defeated the northern rulers and presented Bhoja with excellent horses. Guhila II, a feudatory either of Bhoja or Mahendrapāla, is said to have defeated the lord of Gauḍa and levied tribute from the eastern rulers.[44] Kakka of the Mandor Pratihāra family also gained renown at Mudgagiri (Munger, Bihar) in a battle with the Gauḍas.[45]

Prākrit Sources

The rule of the Pratihāras, as we have seen, gave Rajasthan political unity, peace and stability. This was not their only contribution. The time was conducive to the growth of literature, philosophy, culture and commerce. In spite of their military preoccupations they found time to patronise scholars. According to the *Prabhāvakacarita*, Nāgabhaṭa II was a great patron of letters, distributing equally his favours to orthodox Hindu and Jaina Scholars.[46] The learned Rājaśekhara was the preceptor of Mahendrapāla.[47] The Jaina *ācāryas* Haribhadra and Uddyotana flourished in Rajasthan during this period. The Prākrit works of Haribhadra, the *Samarāiccakahā* and *Dhūrtākhyāna*, are two important works of the period. An erudite scholar, Haribhadra was also a prolific writer, who had to his credit several works besides these two. Tradition ascribes to him the composition of 1,400 *prakaraṇas*. He was the author of Sanskrit commentaries on the *āgamas*, independent philosophical works and stories written for religious instruction. In his works like the *Anekāntajayapatākā* and *Anekāntavādapraveśa* he not merely expounded the Jaina philosophy of *anekānta* but reviewed critically other current philosophical systems. The popularity of the former is evident from the laudatory references to it in the Jaina literature and the pride eminent Jaina teachers took in studying and teaching it. The *Gaṇadharasārdhaśatakabṛhadvṛtti* (vs 1295) speaks of Jinavallabha's proficiency in the treatise. Jinapatisūri (died vs 1277) sent his students to study the book at the feet of Yaśobhadrācārya. Jinapati's rival Pradyumnasūri boasted of having read the work.[48] Of Haribhadra's other philosophical works, the *Yogabindu* and *Yogadṛṣṭisamuccaya* form a valuable synthesis of old Jaina and *Pātañjala* yogic systems.[49] Haribhadra's commentary of the *Nyāyapraveśa* of *Diṅnāga* introduced the Jainas to Buddhist logic. In his religious compositions like the *Dharmasaṃgrahaṇī, Kṣetrasamāsaṭīkā, Pañcavastu, Dharmabindu, Aṣṭaka, Ṣoḍaśaka, Pancāśaka* and *Saṃbodhaprakaraṇa*, he not merely expounded Jaina principles but sounded a clarion call for all-sided reform, doctrinal as well as social.[50] In his *Ṣaḍdarśana-Samuccaya* he gave a brilliant exposition of the different systems of philosophy of the day.

His works reveal his intimate knowledge of not only the Jaina doctrines, but of Brāhmaṇa and Buddhist doctrines as well. In his Sanskrit commentaries on canonical works he breaks new ground as the earlier commentaries were written in Prākrit.[51] Later references show that his birth place was Citrakūṭa or Chittor.[52] The *Prabhāvakacarita*, AD 1278, tells us that he was a *purohita* of King Jitāri in that town. He was so proud of his knowledge that he proclaimed that he would become the pupil of anyone whose proposition he could not understand. One day he heard an old nun reciting a *gāthā* which utterly baffled his understanding. When he asked her to explain its meaning she referred him to her guru, Jinabhaṭasūri. He was initiated and accepted the nun, Yākinī Mahattarā, as his spiritual mother.[53] The essential parts of this story are confirmed by Municandra *ṭīkā* of Haribhadra's Upadeśapadāni, AD 1118.[54] Haribhadra's *ṭīkā* of the *Āvaśyakasūtra* also tells us that he was the spiritual son of Yākinīmahattarā.[55] That Haribhadra was a brāhmaṇa by caste is stated in Sumatigaṇi's vṛtti of *Gaṇadharasārdhaśataka*, AD 1239 and is implicit in the story of *Prabhāvakacarita*.[56] His mastery over Sanskrit and comprehensive knowledge also indicate that he was a brāhmaṇa by caste.[57] The *Dhūrtākhyāna* which was narrated for the benefit of the residents of Chittor[58] shows that his association with the place continued even after initiation. As Uddyotana in the *Kuvalayamālā* mentions Haribhadra as his teacher in scriptures[59] and *yuktiśāstra* (logic)[60] and makes reference to his authorship of many books,[61] Muni Jinavijaya points out that he cannot be placed after AD 778, the date the *Kuvalayamālā* was composed.[62] He studies various references to earlier authors in the works of Haribhadra and shows that they belong to the seventh century AD. He notes that he does not quite quote Śaṅkara and accordingly places Haribhadra around AD 700–70.[63] Jacobi accepts this reasoning in his introduction to the *Samarāiccakahā* and places his literary activity about AD 750 onwards.[64]

Haribhadra was a great reformer and holds a special place amongst the Śvetāmbara Jaina *ācāryas*. Corrupt practices had crept into the monastic order. Jaina sādhus were living in *caityas* and *maṭhas*, putting to personal use the money collected in the name of Jina temples, wearing scented and coloured clothes and taking rich food. Haribhadra raised his powerful voice against all these malpractices and saved Jainism from further degeneration.[65] He wrote works like the *Samarāiccakahā* and *Dhūrtākhyāna* in simple conversational style for the edification of common laymen who may not study or understand intricate philosophical works. The above account of the life and works of Haribhadra amply shows that the writer of our Prākrit works, *Dhūrtākhyāna* and *Samarāiccakahā*, was an eminent Jaina *ācārya*, who was an authority on Jaina dogma and was well conversant with other tenets as well. As a brāhmaṇa by birth, he must have been well acquainted with popular customs and rituals. In consequence, his Prākrit works constitute a rich and valuable source of information on contemporary eighth-century social and cultural life.

The Prākrit work *Kuvalayamālā* is the only work of Uddyotana known to us so far. According to its *praśasti* it was composed by Uddyotana while he was staying at Jābālipura or Jalor in AD 778. The ruling king was Śrī Raṇahastin Vatsarāja, who crushed his enemies and was a source of joy to those who were friendly,[66] identified by scholars as Vatsarāja Pratihāra.[67] Coins bearing the legend 'Śrī Raṇahastin' have been discovered at Kannauj, U.P., Rajasthan and Saurashtra. The characters appear to be post-Gupta Brāhmī said to be not earlier than eighth century AD and their provenance suggests that they belong to Vatsarāja Pratihāra, who is qualified by the adjective Raṇahastin by Uddyotana.[68] The work was summarised into Sanskrit by Ratnaprabhasūri in the thirteenth century AD. Like his *guru* Haribhadra, Uddyotana shows a thorough knowledge of Jaina scriptures. A man of great learning, he quotes extensively from works of *aśvasāstra*,[69] *rāśiphala*,[70] *samudraśāstra*,[71] *nimitta*[72] etc. His characters are drawn from different layers of society so that his works reflect the entire society and not any isolated socio-religious sector. Though part of his description may be traditional, most of it is a faithful description of contemporary life. He imparts to his work a traditional format by setting the plot of the main story around Ayodhya, several hundred years ago, in imitation of the Jaina canonical works. In the course of his narration he describes what are purportedly various far-away cities such as Campā, Ayodhya, Kośala etc. but as tradition speaks of him wandering as a *yati* chiefly in Rajasthan and neighbouring parts of Gujarat and he mentions various contemporary features such as tantricism, feudalism etc. there is no doubt that his portrayal is actually based on his observation of contemporary Rājasthānī society, though he has thought it proper to include here and there conventional patterns of description current in Jaina Mahārāṣṭrī texts. To quote Uddyotana himself, references to practices such as *guggula dhāraṇa* (bearing the guggula) have been included in the *Kuvalayamālā*, primarily since false views were prevalent in contemporary society.[73] Comparisons drawn with various Brahmanical gods and goddesses, he tells us again, are to be justified on the ground that they were popular deities of those times, albeit non-Jaina.[74]

The *Karpūramañjarī*, the Prākrit play written by Rājaśekhara, which gives an insight into contemporary customs and practices is a valuable source of information for the ninth century AD. It is probably his first play since it is produced at the request of his wife and not a king, like the rest of his plays.[75] In the play he declares himself to be the teacher of Nirbhara or Nirbhaya, or Mahendrapāla,[76] whose known dates range from AD 893–907, while the earliest record of his successor Mahipāla belongs to AD 914. Thus the play is to be placed about AD 900. He was the author of three other plays, the *Viddhaśālabhañjikā*, the *Bālarāmāyaṇa* and the unfinished *Bālabhārata* which was represented before Mahipāla.[77] He also wrote a work on poetics, the *Kāvyamīmāṃsā*. His works tell us that he belonged to a Yāyāvara brāhmaṇa family, whose poetic skill was traditional. He married Avantisundarī of the Cāhamāna family and was apparently a Śaiva by faith.[78] Rājaśekhara was connected with the court of Kannauj and was not a Rājasthānī writer, but as the customs and practices described in the *Karpūramañjarī*, e.g., the *Vaṭasāvitrīvrata*, even now prevail in Rajasthan, they may be reasonably assumed to be the common heritage of U.P., which were after all neighbouring states forming part of a common empire.

The importance of our Jaina Prākrit sources is many sided. They represent some of the best Jaina narrative literature. They are composed by two of the most distinguished and learned śvetāmbara *ācāryas*, a feature that lends comprehensiveness to their works. They are original works and no mere abridgement or rewriting of earlier works or themes, which adds to their value as contemporary sources of information. It has been often charged that the brahmanical law books represent old dictums long after they have ceased to be operative. Our sources give us supplementary information which coupled with epigraphic evidence helps us to draw a correct picture of the time. Their value is heightened by the fact that they are the chief literary sources belonging to Rajasthan for the period that have come down to us so far.

Notes and References

1. The above account is based on the geographical account given by G.H. Ojha in his various volumes of the *Rājpūtāne kā Itihās,* Dasharatha Sharma in the *Rajasthan Through the Ages* and *Rajasthan—A Symposium* brought out by the Rajasthan government.
2. Uṣavadāta, the son-in-law of Nahapāna, led an expedition against the Mālavas and made numerous gifts after bathing at the Pushkara lake (Nasik Cave Inscription No. 10, *EI*, VIII, p. 78). Rudradāman while defeating the Yaudheyas spoke of their being untamable on account of their pride. (Junagarh inscription); The Sui Vihār inscription of Kanishka shows his occupation of the Bahawalpur and the region adjoining it (D.C. Sircar, *Select Inscriptions,* p. 135).
3. D. Sharma, *RTTA,* Chapters IV and V.
4. The statement of Rudradāman in the Junagarh inscription (see fn. 2 above) and legend *yaudheyānāṃ jayamantradharāṇāṃ* i.e., the seal of the Yaudheyas who possess the victory formula ensuring victory, indicated this. The Mālavas celebrated the *ekaṣaṣṭi* sacrifice to proclaim their victory over the Śakas. The Yaudheyas and Mālavas played a part in driving out the Kuṣāṇas in the third century (Altekar and Majumdar, ed. *Vākāṭaka Gupta Age,* pp. 27, 30, 34).

5. Tod, *Annals and Antiquities of Rajasthan,* p. 789.
6. G.H. Ojha, *Udaipur Rājya kā Itihās,* p. 10; Idem, *Dūṅgarpur Rājya kā Itihās,* p. 6.
7. D. Sharma, *RTTA,* p. 9.
8. R.S. Tripathi, *History of Kannauj,* p. 230.
9. D. Sharma, op. cit., p. 8.
10. *Jātaka,* Vol. I, pp. 98 f.; Motichandra, *Trade and Trade Routes in Ancient India,* pp. 58–60.
11. Tod, *Annals and Antiquities of Rajasthan,* pp. 1107–8.
12. Ibid., p. 1269.
13. H.D. Sankalia, 'Beginning of Civilisation in Rajasthan', in *Researcher,* I, p. 5.
14. Ibid., pp. 8–15.
15. Ibid., p. 6; D. Sharma, *RTTA,* p. 34.
16. G.H. Ojha, *Rājpūtāne kā Itihās,* Vol. I, p. 7.
17. G.H. Ojha, *Jodhpur Rājya kā Itihās,* p. 8.
18. G.H. Ojha, *Dūṅgarpur Rājya kā Itihās,* p. 6.
19. M.L. Sethi, 'Mines and Minerals', in *Rajasthan—A Symposium,* Govt. of Rajasthan, p. 66.
20. Cunningham, *AGI,* p. 342; B.C. Law, *J. Sircar Commemoration Volume,* p. 220.
21. D.R. Sahni, *Archaeological Remains and Excavations at Bairāṭ,* p. 25.
22. Ibid., p. 32.
23. D.R. Sahni, *Archaeological Remains and Excavations at Sambhar, Jaipur,* p. 33; K.C. Jain, *Ancient Cities and Towns of Rajasthan,* p. 112.
24. K.N. Puri, *Excavations at Rairh;* K.C. Jain, op. cit., p. 128.
25. Indian Archaeology—A Review, 1970–71, p. 62; K. Prasad, *Cities, Crafts and Commerce under the Kuṣāṇas,* p. 42.
26. AIOC, 22nd Session, 1965, Presidential Address, p. 13; K.C. Jain, *Ancient Cities and Towns of Rajasthan,* p. 513.
27. K.C. Jain, op. cit., pp. 513–14.
28. D. Sharma, *RTTA,* p. 9.
29. Allahabad Pillar Inscription, *CII,* III, pp. 6 f.; Sircar ed. *Select Inscriptions,* pp. 254 f.
30. D. Sharma, *RTTA,* p. 61.
31. Mandasore Inscription of Yaśodharman, AD 532, *CII,* III, pp. 152 ff.; Sircar, *Select Inscriptions,* pp. 386 f.
32. D. Sharma, *RTTA,* p. 101.
33. *ED,* I, p. 126.
34. Navsārī Inscription, AD 738; A.S. Altekar, *Rāṣṭrakūṭas and Their Times,* p. 32; R.C. Majumdar, *Classical Age,* pp. 172–3; D. Sharma, *RTTA,* pp. 106–7, 109.
35. *EI,* XVIII, p. 112.

36. Gwalior Praśasti of Bhoja, *EI*, XVIII, p. 112.
37. *ED*, I, p. 4.
38. D. Sharma, *RTTA*, pp. 123, 141, 158, 166; Idem, *Lectures on Rajput History and Culture*, pp. 11–12.
39. *ED*, I, p. 4.
40. Some of the *sāmantas* appear to have revolted in the time of Rāmabhadra. The Paramāras of Malwa tried to be independent in the time of Mahipāla, D. Sharma, *RTTA*, pp. 355–56.
41. Pṛthvīrāja III and Hammīra, who came in conflict with Mohammed Ghori and Alāuddin Khiljī respectively are well known.
42. D. Sharma, *ECD*, p. 28.
43. Harsa Inscription, *EI*, II, pp. 119 f.
44. *EI*, XII, p. 15.
45. *EI*, XVIII, p. 98.
46. D. Sharma, 'Imperial Pratihāras—A Revised Study', *Journal of Indian History*, XVII, p. 105.
47. *Karpūra.*, I. 5.
48. *Khartaragacchapaṭṭāvalī*, D. Sharma, Authors and Subjects studied in Rajasthan, *Rājendrasūri Commemoration Volume*, p. 844.
49. Ibid.
50. Ibid., p. 843., fn. 12.
51. Jacobi, *Introduction to the SK*, pp. xi–xii.
52. Ibid., p. vi.
53. Ibid., pp. viii–ix.
54. Ibid., pp. v, ix.
55. Ibid., p. iv.
56. Ibid., p. vii.
57. Ibid., p. viii.
58. *Dhū.*, vv. 123–5.
59. *KM*, p. 4.
60. Ibid., p. 282.
61. Ibid.
62. *Śrī Haribhadrasya samayanirṇayah*, AIOC, 1919.
63. Ibid.
64. Jacobi, op. cit., p. iii.
65. D. Sharma, *ECD*, p. 250.
66. *KM*, p. 283.
67. A.N. Upadhye, *KM*, pt. II; D. Sharma, Presidential Address, *IHC*, 1968.
68. D. Sharma, *JNSI*, XVIII, pp. 222–3; P. L. Gupta, *JNSI*, XX; A.N. Upadhye, *KM*, pt. II, pp. 105 f.
69. *KM*, pp. 23–4.
70. Ibid., pp. 19–20.
71. Ibid., pp. 129–31.

72. Ibid., pp. 268–9.
73. कीसं पइण्णं राया दढवम्मो कुणइ गुग्गुलाईयं। अज्ज वि मिच्छादिट्ठी जुज्जइ सव्वं पि भणिउं जें। *KM*, p. 281.
74. हरि-खंद-रुद्द-कुसुमाउहेसु उवमाण णागरी-वण्णे। कालम्मि तम्मि कत्ता उवमाणं किं असंतेहिं।। Ibid.
75. A.B. Keith, *Sanskrit Drama*, p. 232; Konow, *Karpūra.*, p. 184.
76. *Karpūra.*, I. 9.
77. A.B. Keith, *Sanskrit Drama*, pp. 232 f.
78. Konow, *Karpūra.*, pp. 178 f.

2

Social Structure

THE FOURFOLD DISTINCTION of caste has been an outstanding feature of Indian society since very early times. Broadly speaking these distinctions, with the duties and social standing of each class more or less well defined, were maintained throughout our period. But in certain respects, the centuries were unique. On the north-western horizon the Hūṇa threat had dwindled away, only to be replaced by the Arab menace. The period following the disappearance of the Gupta empire and Hūṇa incursions had seen an increasing concern for the enforcement of *varṇāśramadharma* on the part of various post-Gupta rulers, such as Yaśodharman,[1] Harivarman,[2] Ādityavarman Maukharī[3] and Prabhākaravardhana.[4] With the Arabs infiltrating as far into the Indian interior as Malwa, Broach and Marwar,[5] there was even more reason to enforce proper observance of caste rules so as to ensure that detrimental external influences did not undermine traditional social values.[6] The *Dharmaśāstra* writers averred that a country where *varṇāśramadharma* did not prevail was a *mlecchadeśa*.[7] At the same time a striking development took place. A perusal of the origins of the various clans of Rajasthan which rose into prominence during this period and in the later period came to be known as the Rajputs indicates that people from various sections of society, be they brāhmaṇas, kṣatriyas or descendants of foreign fighting tribes took up arms, presumably to defend their country from foreign aggression.[8] Writers like Medhātithi recognised that the office of kingship extended to anyone who ruled and had kingly qualities.[9] Feudal relationships also developed during the period and caste distinctions apparently did not figure in such ties.[10] Jainism became firmly entrenched in Rajasthan. It entertained a liberal attitude towards caste.[11] Tantricism which gathered increasing force during the period also did not recognise caste distinctions.[12] Under the circumstances while the concept of *jāti*, which determines the social status of a person on the basis of birth and heredity,[13] had a strong hold on the people, the ancient concept of *varṇa* which assigns to a person a social status in accordance with his character, culture and profession,[14] could be seen in operation time and again, so that the avenues for social mobility remained open.

The ancient theory of the origin of the four *varṇas* from the creator's body[15] finds place in the *Dhūrtākhyāna* which relates the legend regarding Brahmā's claim that the four *varṇas* emerged from his mouth, arms, thighs and feet respectively.[16] That Haribhadra seeks to expose its irrationality suggests that it had a strong hold on the popular mind. It may be noted that the legend is also recounted by Alberuni in later times.[17] It is a reflection of the fourfold classification of society that Uddyotana starts his work by drawing the main characters of his story from the brāhmaṇa, kṣatriya, vaiśya and śūdra families respectively.[18] The word *jāti*, was applied to these distinctions and we read of *vaiśyajāti* Gaṅgāditya[19] and *śūdrajātīya* Dhanadeva.[20] Sons are invariably described as adopting their father's profession.[21] Sharp lines of distinction, we learn, were drawn between Aryans and non-Aryans, and amongst the Aryans, between the higher and lower castes. 'Even when born as a human being', sermonizes the Jaina sage in the *Kuvalayamālā*, 'one rarely attains birth as an Aryan. Even amongst Aryans there are despised (*nindita*) and low (*adhama*) *jātis*.'[22] That these classes consisted of *caṇḍāla* and other *antyajas* is evident from other references.[23] The fourfold division of society is reflected in the passage of Medhātithi which requires the dead bodies of śūdras, vaiśyas, kṣatriyas and brāhmaṇas to be carried out of the city by the south, west, north and east gates respectively.[24] The hereditariness of professions was noticed by Sulaiman (AD 851) who states that the nobility was considered to form but one family, it was the same with learned men and physicians.[25]

The passage in the *Kuvalayamālā* where one of the advocates of caste expounds its theory in the court of Dṛḍhavarman throws interesting light on the nature of the caste system and the composition of the traditional second caste of society. 'The *rāja dharma*', it is said, 'is for the *rājā*, *brāhmaṇadharma* for the brāhmaṇa, *vaiśyadharma* for the vaiśya, and the prescribed religion for the śūdras.'[26] While *cāturvarṇya* clearly emerges as the basis of society it is significant that mention is not made of kṣatriyas as such but of *rājā* and *rājadharma*. This may be taken as a reflection of the actual situation where the second class came to be identified more and more with the ruling class, the members of which may or may not have been members of the kṣatriya class, a development which is sanctioned by Medhātithi[27] and evidenced by epigraphs. As we know from the Jodhpur inscription of Bauka, the Pratihāras were descendants of the brāhmaṇa Hariścandra.[28] A brāhmaṇa origin has been ascribed also to the Cāhamānas[29] and Paramāras[30] on the basis of available epigraphic evidence.

From the evidence of our works, it is evident that the caste system was not so rigid as to limit social contacts between the four castes and prevent intermarriages and inter-dining amongst them. The *Samarāiccakahā* speaks of the intimate friendship which existed between a brāhmaṇa and a vaiśya youth, both belonging to families of repute.[31] Elsewhere, we read how a prince and a vaiśya youth who had been childhood friends, maintained their friendship in later days with the prince taking food with the latter and staying with him.[32] In the *Kuvalayamālā* a śūdra trader freely participates in the activities of other *vaṇiks* and enjoys the hospitality of a *śreṣṭhin.*[33] Brāhmaṇas blessed his voyage and were feasted at his ship's departure ceremony.[34] The references to inter-caste marriages,[35] though few, leave no doubt about their prevalence, and must have added to the flexibility of the caste system. Medhātithi allows a brāhmaṇa to adopt a kṣatriya boy.[36] Of the later Smṛtis, Vedavyāsa expressly declares that all *dvijātis* who know each other's families may partake of food at each other's places.[37] Bṛhadyama, Vedavyāsa and Parāśara follow Manu and Yājñavalkya in permitting brāhmaṇas to take food from a śūdra who is a sharecropper, friend of the family, cowherd, slave and a barber.[38]

Caste considerations were subordinated to material ones in the materialistic environment of the cities and the real status of an individual was determined by his calling rather than caste. In the *Kuvalayamālā*, on observing the efficient salesmanship of a trader, a *seṭṭhi* offers his lovely daughter in marriage to him without caring to inquire about his family. 'By the characteristics of an individual,' says he to the prospective bridegroom, who would have supplied him with the necessary details, 'may be ascertained his family, by the family his character, his virtues, and by his virtues his potential. Your courteousness and your characteristics have sufficiently acquainted me with your character, virtues and potential, and I have accordingly made up my mind to give my daughter to you.'[39] That guilds at urban centres cut across narrow barriers of caste is suggested by the Pehoā record (AD 882) where we find a brāhmaṇa trader as member of the guild of horse dealers,[40] and also contemporary south Indian inscriptions.[41] Epigraphic evidence also shows that caste distinctions did not figure in the selection of urban residential sites. At Tattānandapura, the house site of a brāhmaṇa is mentioned as lying next to that of a *vaṇik* in the eastern market areas.[42]

However the attitude towards the lower classes and non-aryans was not so liberal. There is evidence that notions of untouchability were associated at least with certain sections of them. Caṇḍālas, as in earlier times, continued to live in separate settlements.[43] The *Samarāiccakahā* relates how a *purohita's* son felt disgust at the sight of a dancing party of washermen walking beside his own party on the occasion of the spring (madana) festival, and had their leader put into prison.[44] In the *Kuvalayamālā* prince Kuvalayacandra confronting the leader of the bhillas' raiding party addressed him thus: 'Being a thief you are despicable. Being a Bhilla you are not worthy even to be looked at by me.'[45] It is indeed unfortunate that such feelings of superiority were entertained by the higher castes towards the lower. Smṛtis such as Atri, Śātātapa and Bṛhaspati are liberal enough to ordain that there was no taint in touching an untouchable in a temple, religious processions, marriages, festivals, calamities and battles etc.,[46] but it must have been hard to actually set aside the discriminatory attitude normally entertained towards them, even on these occasions.

The association of untouchability with these classes has been traced to the unclean and cruel nature of their professions,[47] the cultural backwardness of the aboriginal tribes and their precarious living as hunters, fowlers and food gatherers, the gradual withdrawal of the upper varṇas from works of primary production leading to development of contempt for manual labour, combined with primitive ideas of taboo and impurity associated with certain materials such as corpses.[48] A study in the history of the untouchables reveals that while caṇḍālas had clearly emerged as untouchables by AD 200, the degradation of various occupational groups such as the *carmakāras* and *rajakas* to the category was a novel feature of the period AD 600–1200,[49] as also the listing of aboriginal groups of Bhillas, Kaivartas etc. among the *antyajas*. To regard the former development as principally the product of the material milieu characterised by a decline of trade and commerce, growing agrarian character of society, stagnant village economy and backward artisans[50] without taking into consideration the other social processes of the period would be incorrect, especially in the light of the evidence of flourishing urban economy and crafts from Rajasthan,[51] which is matched by epigraphic and archaeological evidence of flourishing urban centres and economic mobility from the Indo-Gangetic divide, upper Ganges basin and Malwa plateau.[52] The development may be linked with the extension of untouchability to temple (*devalaka*) brāhmaṇas and members of heterodox sects in the works like the *Mitākṣara*, Aparārka and the *Smṛticandrikā*[53] (twelfth century) besides persons who were sinners or subject to physical impurities, regarded as untouchables by Manu,[54] which serves as an indication of the growing spirit of exclusiveness and ceremonial purity advocated by the conservative sections of brāhmaṇas, also evident in the ban on interdining with śūdras by some contemporary Smṛti writers.[55] This must have also contributed to the association of untouchability with the aboriginal groups, greater contact with whom as a result of land grants and territorial expansion must have accentuated the backwardness of tribal cultures and aroused greater feeling of contempt for them.[56] Then again, the greater integration of tribals into the brahmanical set up may also have led to a greater measure of economic dependence and exploitation with their attendant ritual and social disabilities.[57] The theory of impurity of these classes served to justify their low position, keep them segregated and secure their exploitation.[58]

But it is to be noted to the credit of society that women abducted by non-Aryans were not abandoned as untouchables. Thus in the *Samarāiccakahā* we read of an old brāhmaṇa advising a merchant's son to get back his wife from her Śabara abductors by payment of ransom and the couple's subsequent happy union.[59] This liberal attitude had the authority of the Dharmaśāstras. Atri and Devala go so far as to provide for purification of women ravished by *mlecchas* and conceiving thereby.[60]

The *Kuvalayamālā* and *Samarāiccakahā*, being Jaina works, give us a deep insight into the Jaina views on caste. In keeping with the injunctions of the Jaina canons,[61] *jātimada* or false caste pride is severely condemned. In the *Kuvalayamālā* the preceptor, Dharmanandana, admonishes the king that the people who revile others out of caste pride are unaware that one such deed has to be paid for many times over and advises him to shun caste pride.[62] The same idea is stressed in the *Samarāiccakahā* where the son of a *purohita* is shown to have been reborn as a dog because of his false caste-pride.[63] High and low birth, the Jaina monks preached, depended on one's *karma* (action). Numerous instances are related where one's bad *karma* led to rebirth in low castes such as the caṇḍāla or in animal births,[64] while good *karma* acquired by adoption of the Jaina faith led to birth in higher castes or birth in heaven.[65] It followed that birth in low castes did not bar the way to salvation. Even a śūdra was eligible for initiation into the Jaina order[66] and could attain salvation in due course of time.[67] So too a Śabara who was inclined to adopt the Jaina faith.[68]

The humane attitude of the Jainas towards the caṇḍālas is especially noteworthy. While the Jainas recognise their position as the lowest of castes, they refrain from passing uncharitable and unmerited remarks about them. Rather the portrayal of Haribhadra emphasises that the caṇḍāla is occupied in a cruel profession like hanging because it is his traditional occupation. He is neither heartless nor ungrateful to his saviour. Asked to hang Dhana whose bearing showed him to be innocent, the caṇḍāla hangman (*vadhakacaṇḍāla*) first offered to fulfil the victim's last wish and then declared himself unable to strike, causing Dhana to reflect thus: 'Kind towards those in distress, benevolent and compassionate; he is not a caṇḍāla by *karma*, but a caṇḍāla by *jāti* alone. He is indeed a man of virtue.'[69] Another caṇḍāla hangman, on recognising a condemned victim to be his past saviour refused to kill him and prevailed upon him to escape by threatening to commit suicide otherwise, unmindful of the king's wrath that he incurred upon himself thereby.[70] Both Haribhadra and Uddyotana were great crusaders for righteousness and one may well assume that their enlightened views on caste were not without some impact on contemporary Rājasthānī society.

Brāhmaṇas

The brāhmaṇas enjoyed a highly honoured place in society. Regarded as symbols of auspiciousness they were invariably present at all important social and religious functions. Numerous brāhmaṇas could be heard chanting at a royal wedding ceremony.[71] Merchants venturing on distant sea voyages feasted the brāhmaṇas and their benedictions mingled together with the auspicious music played at the ship's departure.[72] Mahābrāhmaṇas uttering blessings were present at the outer audience-hall of the king Dṛḍhavarman of the *Kuvalayamālā*.[73] On the birth of the prince, we are told, the king invited the mahābrāhmaṇas, honoured them, and decided upon a suitable name in consultation with them.[74]

Feeding the brāhmaṇas was considered meritorious both for this world and the other. The *Samarāiccakahā* refers to the preparations for a brāhmaṇa feast made by a ruler engaged in the worship of the tutelary deity (*kuladevatā*) for the purpose of obtaining better game.[75] Elsewhere in the *Samarāiccakahā*, we read of a king who despatched one half of a Rohita fish to the brāhmaṇas for the *śrāddha* ceremony of his father and grandfather.[76] The *Kuvalayamālā* refers to the feeding of the brāhmaṇas on the occasion of the marriage of princess Kuvalayamālā.[77] The practice of feeding brāhmaṇas had been popularised by the Smṛtis[78] and Purāṇas.[79] While various Smṛtis such as Manu, Yājñavalkya, Atri, Bṛhatparāśara, Laghvāśvalāyana[80] declare that brāhmaṇas invited for *śrāddha* must possess learning and character, the *Skandapurāṇa* recommends that *śrāddha* should be offered straightforwardly without scrutiny.[81]

Study (*adhyayana*), teaching (*adhyāpana*), performing sacrifices (*yajana*), officiating at sacrifices (*yājana*), making gifts (*dāna*) and receiving gifts (*pratigraha*) are the traditional sixfold duties prescribed for the brāhmaṇas by Manu, Yājñavalkya as well as several later Smṛtis such as Atri, Laghuhārita, Śaṁkha and Gautama.[82] A large number of brāhmaṇas appear to have lived in conformity with this pattern of life and dedicated themselves to the affairs of religion and learning. In the *Kuvalayamālā's* description of the dusk, we read of the abodes of brāhmaṇas resounding with the sound of the *gāyatrīmantra* and the sound of the chanting of Vedas emanating from the establishments of the brāhmaṇas (*brāhmaṇaśālās*).[83] The epithets ascribed such as *caturveda*[84] (master of the four vedas), *śrotriya*[85] (versed in Śruti), *dharmaśāstrasaṃghātapāṭhaka*[86] (learned in various religious scriptures) indicate their mastery over the *Vedas* and other scriptures which included the lores of Manu, Vyāsa, Vālmīki, Mārkaṇḍeya, *Mahābhārata* and *Gītā*.[87] In the Jodhpur inscription of Bauka, the brāhmaṇa Haricandra, the founder of the Pratihāra family, is described as 'versed in the meaning of the Vedas and śāstras'.[88]

The priestly profession was a popular and respected means of livelihood. In the *Samarāiccakahā* we come across the *purohita* Yajñadatta, who possessed a deep knowledge of the Dharmaśāstras, was well versed in worldly behaviour and was held in high esteem by all.[89] The king placed the highest confidence in the *purohita* and did not hesitate to employ him in a private mission of confidence. The *Samarāiccakahā* describes how when king Guṇasena became aware that he had deeply offended an ascetic, he sent the *purohita* Somadeva to quietly find out how matters lay at the hermitage before himself proceeding to the spot.[90] The priest was believed to possess the capability of securing one's desired object by means of religious ceremonies. Thus in the *Samarāiccakahā* we find a *purohita* kindling the fire at the instance of a queen desirous of obtaining a charm.[91] Elsewhere we read of *purohitas* performing pacificatory rites (*śāntikarma*) with due oblations and *mantras* to relieve the severe headache of a monarch.[92] A priest in the service of the king was known as *nṛpapurohita.*[93] In the *Kuvalayamālā* we read of *mahāpurohitas* comparable to Śukra attending the king's court.[94] But the magico-mythical authority of the *purohita* had suffered a diminution on account of the cult of *yajña* losing its earlier importance.[95] He does not appear to have any role to play in administrative affairs: his sphere of activity remained confined to the task of minding the spiritual affairs of the ruler. He was the ruler's companion when he went to listen to a monk's sermon,[96] but he was not a party to the consultations held in the inner audience hall.[97]

The mention of the brāhmaṇa *saciva* (minister) Indraśarman 'who minded the affairs of the entire kingdom' in the *Samarāiccakahā*[98] shows that besides following the customary occupations of studying the Vedas and officiating at sacrifices some brāhmaṇas also took up state service. Although Manu had expressly declared *yajana, yājana, adhyayana, adhyāpana, dāna* and *pratigraha* to be the duties of a brāhmaṇa, he himself had paved the way for their entrance into government service when he advocated that brāhmaṇas should be appointed as judges[99] and prime ministers.[100] The Pāla epigraphs and the *Rājataraṅgiṇī* reveal that many brāhmaṇas served as ministers and councillors under the Pālas and rulers of Kashmir.[101]

The practice of making gifts of oxen, land and plough to brāhmaṇas, mentioned in the *Kuvalayamālā*,[102] could have been meaningful only if they practised agriculture, either directly, or indirectly, getting it cultivated by others. The Kāmān inscription from the Bharatpur state furnishes evidence of three plough measures of land which had been previously cultivated by the brāhmaṇas Sahulla, Jajja and others.[103] In the seventh century, Hieun Tsang had come across a brāhmaṇa cultivator in the Ṭakka region.[104] While the earlier Dharmaśāstras were divided regarding the propriety of a brāhmaṇa taking up agriculture,[105] the *Parāśara Smṛti* (*c.* AD 600–900),[106] *Vṛddha Hārita Smṛti*,[107] Lakṣmīdhara[108] (twelfth century) and *Śukranitisāra*[109] permitted the brāhmaṇa to adopt agriculture as a means of livelihood provided he meted out considerate treatment to the oxen and made over part of the produce to the king, gods and brāhmaṇas. This development was in keeping with the growing practice of land grants to them from the fourth-fifth century onwards.[110] Land grants of fourth to sixth century AD from Maharashtra and Gujarat which gave the recipient the right to cultivate the land or get it cultivated, indicate the existence of a considerable number of brāhmaṇa cultivators and landowners.[111] *Pañcalāṅgalakadāna* which included gifts of plough and oxen appears in the list of sixteen *mahādānas* in the Purāṇas from this period.[112]

Some brāhmaṇas, as in earlier times[113] fell back on professions assigned to other castes by the Smṛtis. The brāhmaṇa Kapiñjala, mentioned in the *Karpūramañjarī*, was a jester in the king's court.[114] The description of ten kinds of *vipras*, viz., *deva, muni, dvija, kṣatra, vaiśya, śūdra, niṣāda, paśu, mleccha* and *caṇḍāla* in the *Atri Smṛti*[115] shows that brāhmaṇas were following the most diverse professions. Hārita too, as quoted by Aparārka, speaks of brāhmaṇas engaged in non-brahmanical professions.[116] The Pehoā inscription mentions the three sons of a *bhaṭṭa* in the list of horse-dealers.[117] Poets, astronomers, philosophers, and diviners, according to Abu Zaid, belonged to this class.[118] The taking up of the vocations of kṣatriyas and vaiśyas in time of adversity has been sanctioned by various early Smṛtis such as *Manu*,[119] *Yājñavalkya*[120] and *Nārada*.[121] Lack of aptitude and inclination necessary for the pursuit of the spiritual pattern of life laid down by the Smṛtis,[122] the lure of material wealth, availability of varied means of subsistence in the wake of urbanisation,[123] and sheer economic necessity arising from slender means of subsistence[124] appear to have been some of the factors responsible for this practice.

Brāhmaṇas were considered to be the worthiest recipient of gifts. Gifts made to them were deemed to confer great merit on the donor. In the *Kuvalayamālā* a sinner is advised to gift away all his belongings, wealth, grain, clothes, utensils, beddings, seats, sticks and animals etc. to the brāhmaṇas as a part of expiation.[125] Making gifts to them was regarded as a commendable way of spending one's wealth.[126] The mention of an *agrahāra* of brāhmaṇas in the *Kuvalayamālā*[127] shows that gifts of land were also made to them. Historical instances of such land grants are recorded in the Barāh C.P. (AD 836) and Daulatpurā grant (AD 843) of Bhoja.[128] The Barton museum inscription, ascribed to the reign of Bhoja refers to a person as having gone to heaven after distributing untold wealth to the brāhmaṇas.[129] The Dholpur inscription of Caṇḍamahāsena (VS 898) tells us that he was extremely liberal to brāhmaṇas whom he rewarded in various ways.[130] Gifts to brāhmaṇas are highly eulogised in the Smṛtis[131] and Purāṇas.[132] According to the *Varāha* and *Matsya Purāṇa*, even a donor guilty of the most heinous crimes such as adultery or murder of a brāhmaṇa or father could get rid of his sins by making gifts.[133]

Reminiscent of the Buddhist notion of charity or *dāna*, from which it may have been derived,[134] the *dāna-puṇya* reciprocity has been viewed as an attempt to compensate the decline of the gift-exchange economy in large towns and its gradual replacement by an approximation of the impersonal market economy of commerce.[135] That the emergence of *dāna* as a means of acquiring merit and expiation of sin furnished the brāhmaṇas with an effective and substantial means of subsistence is evident from the above account. It considerably augmented their income which had suffered a decline due to the increasing popularity of purāṇic and heterodox sects.[136] Learned brāhmaṇas who secured grants of lands were able to devote themselves to learned pursuits, free from pecuniary anxieties[137] as they now possessed a dependable and enduring source of income. This must have also enhanced their social prestige.

In virtue of their wide learning, the brāhmaṇas enjoyed the position of the custodians of the sacred law. They elucidated the canon for the benefit of the masses and pronounced expiations for grave sins. The *Kuvalayamālā* visualises a situation where a penitent sinner, prevented from committing suicide by the people, appeals to the brāhmaṇas that he be allowed to put an end to his wretched life. The brāhmaṇas hastened to assure the sinner of the existence of an appropriate penance for him, each one suggesting a particular mode of expiation, citing Sanskrit quotations from the scriptures in his support. Eventually they declared that the best course open for him was to go on a pilgrimage and the sinner acted accordingly.[138] It may be observed that in the power to decree and grant expiation the brāhmaṇas had an effective source of social authority over the rural masses.

Learned brāhmaṇas were highly respected by rulers and their opinions carried great weight amongst the people. On proceeding to the king's court, the *Samarāiccakahā* tells us, the brāhmaṇa youth who had mastered the various scriptures received great honour and regard from the king and stayed on with him.[139] His irresponsible statement that the *parivrājaka* Yogātman had eloped with a young widow caused Yogātman to be excommunicated by his fellow-ascetics, notwithstanding the excellent reputation that he had to his credit.[140] In the *Karpūramañjarī*, Rājaśekhara proudly refers to his dignified status as the preceptor of Mahendrapāla.[141] The fact that brāhmaṇas were honoured by Indians as forming the most noble caste did not escape the notice of even the Arab traveller Al Masudi[142] (died AD 956).

The evidence of the *Karpūramañjarī* further suggests that society had come to accord a privileged status to the brāhmaṇas in general as well solely on the basis of their birth, often in complete disregard of their lack of qualifications. Thus the talented Vicakṣaṇā in the *Karpūra-mañjarī* addresses the illiterate brāhmaṇa Kapiñjala thus: 'There is no rivalling you, for you though unlettered as the iron beam of a goldsmith's balance are employed for weighing jewels, while though lettered I am like a common balance not employed in weighing gold.'[143] Kapiñjala on the other hand felt that putting the attendant Vicakṣaṇā on the same level as a brāhmaṇa was like putting wine and *pañcagavya*, the five cow products, viz., milk, curds, butter or ghee, urine and cowdung in the same vessel and using glass side by side with gems and ornaments.[144] 'Commend me to such a royal court', said he, 'when it is a devil's way off, a court where a slave girl sets up rivalry with a brāhmaṇa.'[145] Similar ideas about their greatness are to be found in the later Smṛtis. The *Vṛddha Gautama Smṛti* has declared that a brāhmaṇa whether well conducted or of bad conduct, whether vulgar or of polished intellect, should not be disrespected like fire covered with ashes.[146] Medhātithi also accords to the brāhmaṇas the privilege of receiving honour in spite of the lack of learning and character.[147]

While it has been seen that exaggerated claims were being put forward in favour of the brāhmaṇas and they were is an advantageous position as compared to other *varṇas*, it cannot be gainsaid that the society at the same time did expect a brāhmaṇa to live up to the expectations it had from him and tended to look down upon the brāhmaṇas who failed to do so. In a story in the *Kuvalayamālā*[148] the son of a brāhmaṇa realised this harsh reality of life when he found himself an orphan at a young age, uninitiated and a brāhmaṇa in name alone.[149] While he escaped a few beatings because of his high descent, he found himself to be an object of much derision[150] because of his unbrahmanical way of life. He was forced to migrate to another place, bereft as he was of *dharma, artha* and *kāma*, the principal objects (*puruṣārthas*) of mankind, and not even sure of securing a daily meal. Following Manu and Yājñavalkya,[151] the Laghvāśvalāyana[152] declares that learned brāhmaṇas are the most worthy of respect. Parāśara declares the brāhmaṇa who does not repeat the *gāyatrī mantra* to be more impure than a śūdra[153] and brāhmaṇas who did not offer oblations to sacred fires and were bereft of *saṃdhyā* adorations to be all śūdras.[154] The brāhmaṇa's pre-eminence, according to Viśvarūpa (AD 800–850), was based upon his function of religious instruction and as such was strictly dependent upon their Vedic learning.[155]

Further, the *Samarāiccakahā* shows that the brāhmaṇa was not above punishment, though he may have been exempt from the death penalty. He was not allowed to get away with crime, no matter how distinguished his parentage was. When the deceit of the royal priest's son, Yajñadeva, who stole the valuable goods of a merchant and falsely implicated his friend, was discovered by the king, he ordered Yajñadeva's tongue to be cut off and his eyes to be cut out.[156] Alberuni corroborates to a similar practice in later times when he states that though the brāhmaṇa was above the death sentence if he was found guilty of stealing a costly and precious article he was blinded and his right hand and left foot were cut off.[157] Exemption from capital and corporal punishment was an important privilege claimed by most ancient writers such as Gautama, Kauṭliya, Manu, Yājñavalkya, Nārada and Vṛddhahārita, who laid down banishment, shaving of the head, branding and parading on an ass to be the utmost punishment for a brāhmaṇa.[158] But even they do not appear to have countenanced theft by a brāhmaṇa and we find that in cases of theft Gautama and Manu prescribe heavier punishments for brāhmaṇas than for other castes.[159]

It is also evident that no matter how high the ritual status of a brāhmaṇa may have been the ups and downs of fortune affected him as much as the other sections of society and the economic position of many of them was far from enviable. Thus in the *Kuvalayamālā*, Svayaṃbhūdeva, the son of a rich brāhmaṇa, residing in an *agrahāra*, found himself in dire straits when his father passed away. The occurrence of a famine made matters worse and he was forced to seek his fortune in the outside world.[160] There are other instances to show that a section of brāhmaṇas lived in poverty. The *Kuvalayamālā* speaks of brāhmaṇas born in utter poverty.[161] Highly learned brāhmaṇas also belonged to this class. *Śrotriya* brāhmaṇa Yajñadatta, described in the *Kuvalayamālā* was so thin and emaciated that all his veins were visible.[162] The Smṛtis prescribed mainly three means of livelihood for the brāhmaṇas, officiating at sacrifices, teaching and acceptance of presents.[163] Of these, sacrifices were not so popular as in preceding ages. The ancient rules required that the teachers should not fix beforehand any fee for their teaching work, therefore teaching could not have brought much wealth either. With the Jaina sādhus and temples, śaiva tapasvins and śaiva temples, śākta temples and so on, all asking for charity in some form or the other, the share of gifts coming to the brāhmaṇas also must have been limited. The subsistence crisis faced by smārta brāhmaṇas due to the diminution of gifts caused by the growing popularity of Purāṇic and heterodox sects and corresponding unpopularity of sacrificial ritual is reflected in the *Purāṇas* which made strenuous efforts to induce people to make gifts to brāhmaṇas who were *śrotriya* (versed in *śruti*), *kulīna* (of high lineage), *sāgnika* (maintaining sacred fire in the house i.e., performing sacrifices), *vedapāraga* (vedic educated), *annārthin* (wanting food), *kuṭumbin* (burdened with families), *daridra* (poor) and so forth.[164]

Kṣatriyas

The references to the kṣatriya in our works are few and far between. A general idea of their professions and social position may however be gathered from these. The chief occupation of the kṣatriyas continued to be that of shouldering the burden of the empire and fighting. Protection of the people and the profession of arms were the exclusive duties ordained for kṣatriyas by the early Smṛtis such as Manu and Yājñavalkya,[165] which is reiterated by later works such as Atri[166] and Śaṃkha.[167] Uddyotana in the few places where he goes into details regarding the family of the rulers, identifies them as kṣatriyas.[168] Descendants of the Ikṣvāku kṣatriyas, Dṛḍhavarman and his brother, Ratnamukuṭa, ruled at Ayodhya and Ratnapurī respectively.[169] In the *Samarāiccakahā* where a king hands over his throne to his sister's son, it is specifically stated that he belonged to the kṣatriya line.[170] The *ṭhakkura* Kṣetrabhaṭa, mentioned in the *Kuvalayamālā* as a scion of the royal family, served as a warrior in the service of the king and so did his son and grandsons.[171] Two distinctive roles played by the kṣatriyas of those times can be distinguished from the above mentioned references, firstly as members of the ruling aristocracy and secondly as ordinary kṣatriyas forming the general military order. These two sections of the kṣatriyas appear to have been in the mind of Ibn Khurdadba (died in AD 912) when he spoke of the *sābkufrīa* and *katarīya*, the former comprising the highest caste from which kings were chosen, the latter those who could drink three cups of wine and whose daughters could be married by the brāhmaṇas.[172] The word *sābkufrīa* has been equated with the Sanskrit word *satkṣatriya* and the word *katarīya* with the Sanskrit kṣatriya.[173]

As regards the social position and privileges of a kṣatriya, that of the ruling class must have naturally been quite high. In the *Samarāiccakahā* we read how a prince made fun of the unfortunate misshaped son of the king's *purohita*, seating him on a donkey and leading him in mock parade through the streets daily.[174] Their high position in society led Ibn Khurdadba to place the *sābkufrīa* before the brāhmaṇas.[175] Some of the *rājaputras*[176] and *ṭhakkuras*[177] who received grants of lands as rewards for their military services may have emerged as a class of influential landholders if the assignments were substantial enough and became hereditary as in the case of Ṭhakkura Kṣetrabhaṭa.[178] The term *rāyautta or rājaputra* has been used in our works for the scions of a royal family[179] and the members of the warrior class,[180] a considerable number of whom must have been kṣatriyas.

The Smṛti works while declaring living by arms and protection of mankind to be the means of livelihood for kṣatriyas had recommended for them the following three activities: celebration of sacrifices, study and the making of gifts.[181] In the praśasti of the *Kuvalayamālā* Uddyotana traces his descent from a kṣatriya devoted to the three *karmas.*[182] In the *Kuvalayamālā* itself we read of Dṛḍhavarman offering sacrifices (*bali*) at the various crossroads.[183] Prince Kuvalayacandra went through a rigorous curriculum and mastered as many as 72 arts and sciences.[184] The king showered manifold gifts on his subjects on various occasions, such as the birth of a son,[185] marriage of the prince[186] and the time of initiation.[187] The kṣatriyas thus appear to have acted in accordance with the injunctions of the Smṛti. That their ritual status was quite high can be seen from the inclusion of Vedic studies in the prince's curriculum.[188] Alberuni remarked that the kṣatriyas read the Veda and learnt it, though they could not teach it.[189]

The kṣatriyas of this period traced their descent from the solar and lunar lines. The *Somavaṃśa*,[190] *Ādityavaṃśa* and the *Śaśivaṃśa*[191] find mention in the *Kuvalayamālā*. An illustrious lineage is ascribed to the prince Kuvalayacandra who is said to have belonged to the Ikṣvāku race, the history of which is described in detail. In accordance with the Jaina tradition, the origin of the race is ascribed to Ṛṣabha, who wished for the sugarcane (*ikṣu*) seen in the hands of Indra. From his two sons, Bharata, whose son was Ādityaśas, and Bāhubali, whose son was Somayaśas, started the *Ādityavaṃśa* and *Śaśivaṃśa* respectively. Kuvalayacandra belonged to the latter line.[192] Great importance was attached to these genealogies. Prince Mahendra on meeting Kuvalayacandra hailed him thus: Victory, O young offshoot (*bālāṃkura*) of the ikṣvāku race, the moon of the *soma* branch, the son of Dṛḍhavarman etc.[193] Elsewhere though asked but for the name of their *ācārya*, the group of monks instantly responds by furnishing the information that he belongs to the ikṣvāku *vaṃśa.*[194] The *Samarāiccakahā* speaks of birth in the ikṣvāku *vaṃśa* as birth in a good family (*kulajanma*).[195] Rājaśekhara in the *Karpūramañjarī* refers to the Pratihāra ruler Mahendrapāla as crest-jewel of the Raghu family (*Raghukulacūḍāmaṇi*).[196] To belong to the same *vaṃśa* was a great bond. Uddyotana relates how a Bhilla chief who was actually a *somavaṃśin* kṣatriya by birth fallen to evil days was delighted to know that Darpaparigraha belonged to the same race and appointed him successor.[197] Epigraphic evidence shows that the various ruling families of Rajasthan from the ninth century onwards started tracing their ancestry from these vaṃśas. In the Gwalior inscription of Bhoja the Pratihāras claim to have descended from Lakṣmaṇa, the brother of Rāma, hero of the solar race.[198] The origin of the Cāhamānas has also been traced to the sun and the moon.[199] A plausible explanation for the increasing importance attached to the genealogies and their fabrication during this period seems to have been the desire to ensure the continuity of the traditional relationship between the ruling and priestly class.[200] For this ruling families which were not kṣatriyas had to be given a ritual status and hence arose the need for the fabrication of pedigree. It may be noted that even foreign tribes like the Śakas, Yavanas etc. had been awarded a proper social status in our society, albeit as *vrātya* kṣatriyas.[201]

Vaiśyas

Though the word vaiśya is employed only once in the *Kuvalayamālā*,[202] innumerable references to traders such as *vaṇiks, śreṣṭhins*, and *sārthavāhas* (caravan leaders) who correspond to the traditional vaiśya order, are to be found in our works which reveal that the vaiśyas formed a wealthy, prosperous and respected community in Rajasthan. The *śreṣṭhin* Bandhudatta, the *Samarāiccakahā* tells us, averted his face not from supplicants but the wives of others; coveted the acquisition of dharma but not the wealth of others; was content with his wealth, but not with his charity; and was lacking in vices, not in riches. By him the city was graced as the Malaya forest by the Pārijāta, the spring by the blossoming of flowers, the rainy season by the clouds, and the winter season by moonlight.[203] Elsewhere in the *Samarāiccakahā* we read of the *sārthavāha* Vaiśramaṇa, highly esteemed by the king, kind to the poor, orphan and destitute, akin to the moon for the lotus-like relatives, and devoted to the pursuit of the *trivarga*, three objects of worldly existence, *dharma, artha* and *kāma.*[204] *Śreṣṭhins and mahāśreṣṭhins* with riches comparable to Dhanapati or Vaiśramaṇa, the god of wealth, find mention in the *Kuvalayamālā*.[205] Rich *vaṇiks* were to be found in the villages[206] as well as in towns.[207] Inscriptional evidence of the affluence of traders during the period comes from the Sakraī inscription (Jaipur) which records the construction of a temple porch of the goddess in vs 879 by the local *goṣṭhī* (managing committee) composed of 11 members, all of whom were *śreṣthins*.[208]

A good idea of the avocations pursued by the vaiśyas of those times can be had from the *Kuvalayamālā*. A *vaṇik* declares the honourable means of gaining wealth as *diśāgamana, mitrakaraṇa, naravarasevā,* proficiency in *māṇa* and *pramāṇa, dhātuvada, mantra, devatārādhana, sāgaratarana, rohanakhanana, vāṇijya* and *śilpa*.[209] Thus it would appear that the vaiśyas travelled far and wide, becoming friendly with other people; took up service under the king; cultivated skill in handling of weights and measures; practised the miraculous lores of *dhātuvāda, devatārādhana* and *rohanakhanana* (digging the mountain);[210] had recourse to *mantra*; crossed the seas and worked as artisans and traders to earn their livelihood. Further details can be added from the context in the *Kuvalayamālā* which takes up the account of two *vaṇikputras* who due to the early demise of their father were forced to try their hands at various professions to earn a living. They first turned to trade (*vaṇik-karma*) but could not sell their goods at a profit. They then took to agriculture, cattle rearing, service on a ship, digging (*khanana*), *dhātuvāda, olagā*,[211] and *mantra* by turn, changing their professions as bad luck dogged them everywhere.[212]

Of the occupations of the vaiśya mentioned above agriculture, cattle rearing and trade were their traditional vocations.[213] Among these again, the first preference appears to have gone to trade.[214] The *seṭṭhis* mentioned in our works appear to have been mainly associated with mercantile activities, as were the *vaṇiks*.[215] Agriculture and cattle-rearing, the accounts of Hieun Tsang[216] and Ibn Khurdadba[217] indicate, had passed largely into the hands of the śūdras.[218] The causes of this development appear to be varied. Vaiśyas who adopted Jainisṃ and Buddhism, no doubt found the practice of agriculture inconsistent with the principles of *ahiṃsā* laid down by these two religions. Haribhadra disapproved of *sphoṭikarma*, i.e. digging and hoeing for cultivation by Jaina laymen.[219] Even kṣatriyas in Rajasthan are known to have taken to trade and vegetarianism under the influence of Jainism.[220] The emergence of a new class of landholders as a result of the growing practice of land grants to brāhmaṇas and warriors[221] which disturbed the exclusive position of vaiśyas as peasant proprietors as well as large scale śūdra infiltration into the agricultural profession, must have provided another inducement to the vaiśyas to turn more and more to the mercantile profession. It has been suggested that the increasing denunciation of manual labour and depression of peasantry, as illustrated by the case of the *kīnāśa*,[222] who were degraded from vaiśya to śūdra status, must have made the vaiśyas turn to trade and commerce.[223] But this cannot be related to contemporary conditions in Rajasthan, where peasants were actually enjoying the benefits of an expansion of its agrarian economy.[224] Rather, the lucrative profits offered by flourishing trade which went on side by side may be held to be partly responsible for their predilection for trade.

The pursuit of miraculous lores was an obsession for all classes of society at this time and may not be taken as an activity in any way specially connected with the vaiśya class. Taking up of arms by vaiśyas in case of distress, indication of which is to be found in the *Kuvalayamālā* which describes how the *vaṇikputras* who went to render *olagā* were defeated in battle and taken prisoners,[225] was also permitted by the Smṛtis.[226] Historical references of vaiśyas usurping the functions of kṣatriyas, not only the bearing of arms, but also the functions of a ruler, are not lacking.[227]

In mentioning *śilpa* as an honourable occupation for the vaiśyas, the *Kuvalayamālā* assigns them a function associated with sūdras as far back as the time of Kauṭilya,[228] though it may be noted that nowhere in the *Kuvalayamālā* does Uddyotana represent a vaiśya as actually adopting the profession even in distress, suggesting that the occupation was not quite so popular amongst the vaiśyas of Rajasthan,[229] though regarded as quite respectable. That some vaiśyas did practise *śilpa* can be seen from the identification of vaiśyas (baisuras) as artificers by Ibn Khurdadba.[230] To attach undue importance to this feature, and regard it as an index of the waning popularity of trade amongst the vaiśyas[231] would not be correct, at least as far as Rajasthan is concerned.[232] It could perhaps be attributed to the betterment in the position of the artisans consequent to the specialisation achieved in various crafts and spread of urbanism.[233]

The testimony of our works indicates that the vaiśyas were adventurous traders who sailed far and wide from the ports of Vaijayantī, Tāmralipti and Sopārā.[234] Realistic descriptions of sea voyages are to be found in our works.[235] *Sārthavāhas* led mighty caravans to distant places, making way from north to south through the Vindhya forests.[236] Mention is made of traders visiting Kośala for elephants, Uttarāpatha for horses, eastern India for yak-tails, Dvārakā for conch-shells, and Barbarakūla for ivory in exchange for textiles.[237] Medhātithi clearly envisages long distance trade by the vaiśyas when he advises the vaiśyas to get themselves familiarised with the products, customs and languages of different countries. He also specifically refers to his importing useful goods from other states into the kingdom in which he lives.[238] From the inscription of Allaṭa we learn that Mewar was a prosperous market visited by merchants from Karṇāṭa, Lāṭa, Madhyadeśa and Ṭakka in VS 1010.[239] Traders had their own associations. The *Kuvalayamālā* mentions a *deśī-vaṇik-melī*,[240] a term which has been translated as 'guild of dealers'.[241] A *deśī* of dealers, assembled from outside, which granted donations to a number of temples, is mentioned in the Pehoā inscription (AD 882).[242] Medhātithi also speaks of *śreṇīs* of tradesmen.[243] These guilds must have added to the power and prestige of the merchant class.

According to Alberuni there was not much distinction between a vaiśya and a śūdra. They lived together in the same towns and villages and mixed together in the same houses and dwellings.[244] If a vaiśya or a śūdra recited the Veda, his tongue was cut off.[245] This has lent strength to the view that the vaiśya had approximated to the position of the śūdra.[246] We have however no evidence of such a development in Rajasthan during our period. Various virtues are associated with a *śreṣṭhiputra* in the *Kuvalayamālā*. 'He is charming, amiable, virtuous, captivating, modest, well spoken, kind and liberal,' we are told.[247] Such praise would hardly have been showered on him if he held a low position in society. The *Samarāiccakahā* too appears to regard the vaiśya as well born. Thus when a brāhmaṇa alleges existence of stolen property in the *sārthavāhaputra's* house, the king refuses to believe him, saying, 'This is impossible, he is of noble descent, why will he act in a contrary manner?'[248] The brāhmaṇa too has nothing to say against the vaiśya's family and merely responds: 'What does the family have to do with the blame? Are there not worms on fragrant flowers?'[249] No discrimination against the vaiśyas is to be discerned in matters of punishment. Even though stolen goods are found in the sārthavāha's house, the king convinced of his innocence, merely banishes him, while he later prescribes severe punishment for the brāhmaṇa actually guilty of the crime.[250] Kakkuka's entrusting the temple of Jina built by him to a body of *goṣṭhikas* (trustees) comprising of the Jaina ascetic Jāmbava, Āmraka and the merchant Bhākuṭa shows that the vaiśyas enjoyed the confidence of kings.[251] Vaiśyas acted as trustees of temples, managed their funds and gave them religious endowments,[252] besides erecting temples themselves,[253] which shows that their ritual status and respectability was quite high. Later Smṛtis such as Śaṃkha, Atri and Vasiṣṭha reiterate the earlier rules of Manu and Yājñavalkya prescribing *dāna* (gifts), *ijyā* (sacrifice) and *adhyayana* (study) for vaiśyas as well as kṣatriyas.[254]

In the light of the above evidence one may well conclude that there was no degeneration of the vaiśya class as a whole during this period.[255] As in the time of Manu,[256] the status of a vaiśya must have been determined largely by his wealth. A wealthy vaiśya, a *śreṣṭhin* or *sārthavāha*, enjoyed respect, though a poor vaiśya, who perforce had to fall back on low occupations, may have had a status not very much different from that of a śūdra. The depiction of many of the heroes of Jaina stories as vaiśyas indicates the popularity of Jainism amongst them and it is inconceivable that they held a low social status at a time when Jainism was at the height of its popularity in Rajasthan.

The vaiśyas received good education.[257] They also took delight in giving alms and extended patronage to actors etc. In the *Samarāiccakahā* we read of the *sārthavāhaputra* who having acquired great riches abroad made liberal presents to the needy, eliciting the admiration and envy of fellow merchants who wished to act likewise.[258] In the *Kuvalayamālā*, a *śreṣṭhiputra* makes a generous gift of one lakh to an actor in appreciation of his *subhāṣita* (apophthegm).[259] Reference has already been made above to epigraphic evidence of numerous religious benefactions made by them. The education and benevolence of the vaiśyas must have ensured them a position of respect in society.

From the *Samarāiccakahā* we further learn that enterprising traders, returning home after successful ventures abroad, were honoured by the king. The king, himself went to receive Dharaṇa when he arrived laden with wealth from distant lands and later offered him the command of certain areas.[260] This indicates that sometimes they wielded political influence as well. From the Vaillabhaṭasvāmin inscription dated VS 933 we learn that the *śreṣṭhin* Vavviyāka and *sārthavāha* Icchuvāka figured prominently in the board which managed the civic affairs of the town of Gwalior.[261] From the Shergarh inscription (Kota) (AD 1017) it appears that three merchants constituted the town committee which was in charge of market dues.[262]

Śūdras

The position of śūdras, whose only duty, according to the *Manu Smṛti*, was to serve meekly the other three castes,[263] had substantially improved by our period. The use of iron on an extensive scale, especially during the Gupta period, had facilitated the transformation of śūdra slaves, and agricultural labourers into peasants.[264] The *Amarakośa* includes amongst the śūdras agricultural labourers, agriculturists, various craftsmen such as the garland-makers, washermen, potters, bricklayers, leather-workers, blacksmiths, shell-cutters, goldsmiths and workers in copper.[265] Agriculture and all varieties of crafts thus passed largely into the hand of the śūdras. Hieun Tsang described them as an agricultural class engaged in ploughing and tillage.[266]

These changes in the position of the śūdras are reflected in our Prākrit works and later Smṛtis. In our works, the śūdra of the period continues to be ranked distinct from and lower than the brāhmaṇas, kṣatriyas and vaiśyas, but birth in the śūdra caste is not considered despicable. Sinners are reborn as *antyajas*, not as śūdras. The interesting episode of śūdra *sārthavāhaputra* Dhanadeva in the *Kuvalayamālā* indicates that certain sections of śūdras enjoyed high economic and religious status. They went in for trade in a big way, thus encroaching upon a traditional vaiśya preserve. Dhanadeva was the son of an affluent śūdra *sārthavāha*. Desirous of further increasing his family wealth, he approached his father and expressed before him his desire to embark on a trade venture to Dakṣiṇāpatha. Though the money was not at all needed, his father, after initial protests, allowed him to go because he considered his son's coveted pursuit to be a part of their *dharma*. His reasoning ran thus: 'His enthusiasm is befitting. This is his duty, this is appropriate, this is worthy of him. This is but our *dharma*.'[267] The evidence of the Dharmaśāstras indicates that there was nothing new in a śūdra's taking up trade. As early as the time of Yājñavalkya it had been conceded that if a śūdra could not maintain himself by service of the twice-born, he could become a trader.[268] The evidence of the *Bṛhaspati Smṛti, Mārkaṇḍeya Purāṇa* and *Viṣṇu Purāṇa* indicates that by the Gupta period trade came to be regarded as a normal function of the śūdras though generally they may have served as pedlars.[269] Later Smṛtis such as Uśanas and Devala corroborate that trade, crafts and industries were considered to be the ordinary and not the exceptional avocations of the śūdras.[270]

As the śūdras came to be permitted to pursue the occupations of the higher classes they tended to be economically much better off than before. The śūdra *sārthavāha* in the *Kuvalayamālā* is said to have accumulated such a large amount of wealth that it was deemed to be sufficient not only for the expenses of his own lifetime but that of his son and grandson.[271] The flourishing state of various industries[272] implies that towns provided numerous independent means of livelihood to the artisan members of the śūdra class. In the villages too, where the vaiśyas had largely withdrawn from agricultural operations, the class of śūdras which subsequently emerged as an independent çlass of cultivators must have been the main beneficiaries of the agricultural prosperity.[273] Medhātithi, evidently in recognition of the śūdra's improved economic status, declared that if a śūdra had property of his own and lived upon it, not supporting himself by depending on brāhmaṇas and others, he did nothing wrong.[274] Any further doubt about the existence of a prosperous class of śūdras is set at rest by referring to the provision of *pūrtadharma* for the śūdras by the Dharmaśāstras of this period.[275] A perusal of the list of activities put under *pūrta* will show that only a śūdra whose financial condition was sound could have financed these works of public utility and charity. The prosperity of śūdra artisans is reflected in the Kāmān stone inscription (AD 786–905) which refers to the guilds of potters, gardeners and artisans functioning like banks, receiving permanent deposits and in return paying a permanent cess whereby the maintenance of the temple of Kāmyakeśvara was provided for.[276] Outside Rajasthan, inscriptions record generous religious endowments made by artisans in Gwalior[277] and Sīyaḍoṇi.[278]

As agriculturists the śūdras had an important role to play in the rural economy, with the vaiśyas turning largely to trade. To their valuable contribution as artisans to the urban economy, they had added that of traders. This position as primary producer both in towns and villages and consequent material improvement was bound to bring a corresponding improvement in their social status. The accounts of the kali age[279] in various epics and purāṇic passages datable to the middle of the late third and early fourth century reflect the disturbances in the *cāturvarṇya* then caused by the rise of the śūdras and improvement in their economic status. The social distances between these wealthy śūdras and the upper classes came to be narrowed down. The śūdra *sārthavāha* in the *Kuvalayamālā* is described as residing in the house of a *śreṣṭhin* and freely mixing with the merchants (*vaṇiks*) of different regions, receiving from the latter an honoured welcome with offerings of essence, betel leaf and perfume.[280] Brāhmaṇas are said to have been fed and in turn showered blessings on him when he departed on a sea voyage along with a *śreṣṭhin*.[281] There is no evidence of the subjection of peasantry in our works. Jaina *ācāryas* who dilate on the manifold miseries of human life make no reference to any specific miseries of peasants or artisans. Various later Smṛtis such as Baijavāpa, Jātukarṇya, Auśanas and Laghuviṣṇu distinguish a pious śūdra (*sacchūdra*) from an ordinary one and extend to the former the privileges of *śrāddha*, *saṃskāras* and *pākayajñas*.[282] In the VS 744 metal image inscription from Rajasthan, the sculptor of the image, Śivanāga has been called Brahmā himself.[283] Medhātithi recognised that a śūdra could be a councillor or an officer for inflicting punishments, though he was not to pronounce judgements.[284] A section of śūdras appears to have been considerably well educated.[285]

The right to perform acts of charity was an important religious privilege extended to śūdras during our period.[286] In the list of praiseworthy channels of expending wealth for a śūdra, the *Kuvalayamālā* includes alms to the poor, gifts to brāhmaṇas, erection of temples (*devakulas*), excavation of tanks and wells, opening of alms-houses, establishment of hospitals and help to the distressed.[287] It is interesting to note that performance of Vedic rites finds no place in this enumeration. The later Smṛtis aver that a śūdra is entitled to the performance of *pūrtadharma* though not *iṣṭa*.[288] *Pūrtadharma* stood for building of wells, tanks, temples, parks and distribution of food and *iṣṭa* for vedic rites.[289] It may seem at first glance that the religious disability imposed upon a śūdra by denying him the performance of *iṣṭa* was a serious one. But in the light of the great importance attached by the Purāṇas to *pūrtadharma*[290] and the declining importance of *iṣṭa* it appears that the śūdra had nothing much to lose by being deprived of *iṣṭa*. The *Varāha Purāṇa* and some Smṛtis have gone so far as to declare that a man secures only heaven by *iṣṭa*, but he secures *mokṣa* by *pūrta*.[291] This again implies that in the performance of *pūrta* the śūdra had a religious privilege of considerable importance. It must have been accorded to them not only in recognition of their improved economic status but the influence of heterodox sects like Jainism which admitted the śūdras into the monastic order on a basis of equality.[292] Inscriptional evidence of various religious endowments made by artisans have already been mentioned above. The important role played by them in maintenance and upkeep of temples must have also contributed to a rise in his religious status.

But it is also pertinent to remark that mainly only those śūdras who etched out an independent and prosperous livelihood for themselves, such as the śūdra *sārthavāha* in the *Kuvalayamālā* must have been allowed to enjoy the privileges mentioned above. Others who continued to perform their traditional duty of serving the twice-born, and did not enter the fold of the heterodox sects, must have suffered discrimination, as in earlier periods. Of these classes, which may be identified as the *asacchūdras* of the Smṛtis, our works give no details.

Antyajas

Besides the four varṇas, our works refer to those classes, which though within the aryan fold, occupied a position in society that was distinctly inferior and totally unenviable. The *Samarāiccakahā* speaks of those who though born as aryans roamed around as *caṇḍālas, ḍombiliyas, rajakas* (washermen), *carmakāras* (leather-workers), *śākunikas* (fowlers) and *matsyabandhas* (fishermen), and did not have a *kulajanma* (birth in a good family).[293] The *Kuvalayamālā* mentions the *caṇḍālas, Bhillas, dombas, śaukarikas*, and *matsyabandhas* who were bereft of *dharma, artha* and *kāma* and were akin to *mlecchas.*[294] The *Dhūrtākhyāna* speaks of the work of a *rajaka* as a low profession.[295] The Smṛtis of our period placed them lowest in the social order and classified them as *antyajas*. The *carmakāras, rajakas, kaivartas* and *Bhillas* find mention in the list of *antyajas* in the Smṛtis of Yama, Aṅgiras and Atri.[296] Alberuni includes amongst the *antyajas* the fuller, fisherman, hunters of wild animals and birds,[297] who correspond to the *rajakas, matsyabandhas, śaukarikas* and *śākunikas* of our works, as well as *ḍombas* and *caṇḍālas*. A perusal of the occupations of these indicates that they were either unclean or cruel in nature by brahmanical standards and this is apparently an important factor that prompted their segregation from the rest of society[298] since early times.[299]

Caṇḍālas lived outside the city in separate settlements, which are referred to as Pāṇavāḍaya or Prāṇavāṭaka in our works,[300] under the authority of the caṇḍālamahattaras.[301] Criminals condemned to death were led there by the king's officials and handed over to the highly trusted caṇḍālas, who performed the task of execution by turn.[302] Reference has already been made above to the Jaina teacher's sympathetic attitude towards the caṇḍālas.[303] The caṇḍāla's feelings towards his abhorrent occupation have been highlighted in the story of the caṇḍāla Khangilaka. The greatest boon that he could think of asking for himself was that his people may not be employed as executioners thenceforth.[304] Exemption from the horrible duty of execution presented a more attractive proposition than all the riches of the world for the *vadhakacaṇḍāla* (executioner) whose family occupation was that of executing. So miserable indeed was the plight of a caṇḍāla that birth as a caṇḍāla is once and again shown to be the consequence of grave sin.[305] The caṇḍālas were assigned a low status since Vedic times.[306] The *Agni Purāṇa* also declares that the caṇḍālas shall be employed for execution of criminals, shall wear the clothes of the dead, while they live outside the village and must not touch others.[307] Even Medhātithi, who adopts a liberal attitudes towards śūdras, holds that wood and things as well as walls of houses are defiled by the touch of a caṇḍāla[308] and that vessels other than those of gold and silver in which caṇḍālas and *śvapākas* have eaten are to be thrown away.[309] The liberal attitude of some towards the caṇḍāla is reflected in his statement that the caṇḍāla's shadow does not pollute, which is in contravention of the dictates of Atri, Aṅgiras and Śātātapa which prescribed purification by bath for crossing the caṇḍāla's shadow.[310]

Music appears to have been an integral part of the life of the *ḍombas*, one of the other low classes enumerated above. So accustomed were the *ḍomba* children to the *paṭaha* drum, according to Uddyotana, that they were not in the least upset by its (loud) sound.[311] Kalhaṇa in his *Rājataraṅgiṇī* relates how king Cakravarman fell in love with a *ḍomba* musician's daughters, who were themselves clever musicians and dancers.[312] The *cāryapadas* tell us that their women were of low character and moved about singing and dancing.[313]

Some members of the *antyaja* class did not lack worldly wealth, but their status remained low. Thus in the *Dhūrtākhyāna* Khaṇḍapānā while relating that she was born in a prosperous family of *rajakas* endowed with much wealth mentioned in the same breath that she was low by profession.[314] That contact with *rajakas* was not welcome has been seen above.[315] However it cannot be gainsaid that the ignominy associated with birth as a caṇḍāla, their segregation from the rest of the society and their despicable profession of execution would place them lowest in society.

Mlecchas

The *mlecchas*, the *Kuvalayamālā* tell us, were non-aryans, by nature sinful, extremely fierce, cruel and merciless. The word *dharma* did not exist for them even in their dreams.[316] Included amongst them, according to Uddyotana, were the Śakas, Yavanas, Śabaras, Babbaras, Kākas, Muruṇḍas, Oḍras, Gonḍs, Kappaṇiya, Aravāga, Hūṇa, Romasa, Pārasa, Khasa, Khāsiya, Ḍombilika, Lakusa, Bokkasa, Bhillas, Pulindas, Āndhra, Kottha, Bharruya, Koñcas, Cañchuka, Mālava, Draviḍa, Kuḍakkha, Kikkaya, Kirāta, Hayamukha, Gajamukha, Kharamukha, Turagamukha, Meṇḍakamukha, Hayakarṇa and Gajakarṇa.[317] A shorter list occurring elsewhere in the *Kuvalayamālā* refers to the low birth of Śakas, Yavanas, Barbara, Kirāta, Khasa, Pārasa, Bhilla, Muruṇḍa,

Oḍḍa, Bokkasa, Śabara, Pulinda and Siṅghala.[318] It is obvious that various aboriginal and totemistic tribes as well as foreign tribes who did not prescribe to the brahmanical way of life were regarded as *mlecchas* and looked down upon. Nāgabhaṭa's victory over the Arabs is represented as 'the crushing of the armies of the powerful *mleccha* ruler, the destroyer of virtue' by Bālāditya, the writer of Bhoja's Gwalior *Praśasti*.[319] Manu had declared the *mleccha* country to be that which was beyond *āryāvarta*, the land fit for sacrifices.[320] Medhātithi states that they are the people who are known as lying beyond the pale of the four castes, and mentions amongst them the Medas, Āndhras, Śabaras and Pulindas.[321]

Of the numerous indigenous tribes who along with foreign immigrants were held to be *mlecchas*, the principal ones that the Jaina authors were acquainted with and considered to be representative of their culture were the Kirātas, Śabaras, Pulindas and Bhillas. Various references to their forest retreats are found in our works. Śabaras living in the Kādambarī forest[322] and Dantaratnikā forest[323] find mention in the *Samarāiccakahā.* The *Kuvalayamālā* speaks of the Śabaras, Pulindas and Kirātas who dwelt in the Vindhya forests[324] and Bhillas in the Sahya forests.[325] Similar settlements must have existed in the Aravallī mountains. Rajasthan is well known for its Bhillas who are believed to have given Bhillamāla its present name.

Uddyotana draws a vivid picture of a *mlecchapallī* in the Vindhyas, which though undoubtedly exaggerated for poetic effect, testifies to an entirely different life led by some of these tribes. They were not influenced by brahmanical culture. Amputation of hand and feet, hanging of people, impalement, blows of hand and feet, killing of brāhmaṇas, drinking of wine, theft and abuses were common incidents of life there.[326] Even observance of ordinary ethical rules such as refraining from giving false testimony, abduction of women or depriving a man of his entire possessions were considered virtues amongst them.[327] As the *Kuvalayamālā* poetically puts it, brāhmaṇas were killed (as freely) as one would kill wild horses, drinking wine was like partaking of sacrificial oblation (*puroḍāśa*), knowledge of the art of theft was like the knowledge of *oṃkāra*, abusing another person's sister was like reciting the *gāyatrī mantra*, and oaths to kill another person's mother, sister and husband as well as to drink another's blood were also quite common.[328] An idea of their dress and appearance can be had from the *Samarāiccakahā* which describes a group of young Śabaras, bearing the complexion of wild buffaloes and the clouds, their hair tied up with creepers, clad in *valkala*, a round bow in their hands and accompanied by a group of dogs.[329]

Bloody rituals involving human and animal sacrifices and occult practices were associated with these aboriginal tribes. Kālasena, the Śabara chief, swore to enter fire if his benefactor Dharaṇa was not found within five days and to immolate ten men before Bhagavatī if he was found.[330] Travellers were captured for the purpose, and the time fixed being over, the funeral pyre was prepared and Kālasena, bathed, draped in *valkala*, wearing a chaplet of *karṇavīra* flowers, proceeded to the bloodstained temple of the goddess to fulfil his terrible vow,[331] intent on sacrificing the promised men before the goddess even though his wish had not been granted.[332] Elsewhere in the *Samarāiccakahā* we come across a Śabara *vaidya* who cures diseases by means of magic rituals.[333] In the *Kuvalayamālā* we read of *Śābarī vidyā*, which is associated with occult practices.[334]

Living in the forests, these tribes must have subsisted mainly by hunting. This would explain the presence of heaps of maimed and killed buffaloes, cows, goats, parrots, peacocks, quails etc. in the *mleccha-pallī*.[335] In *Samarāiccakahā* a Śabara chief is described as involved in the killing of many animals, a terror to the wild boars, buffaloes and deer of the forest.[336] The Śabara chief is said to have hunted lions single-handed.[337] Large piles of ivory and yaktails at the *pallī*[338] suggest that they may have been used not merely for their personal beauty but also for their value in trade. The *Āvaśyaka Cūrṇi* refers to money being awarded to the Pulindas, who killed elephants and brought tusks.[339]

Firmly entrenched in the mountain fastness, many of these *mlecchas* took to roadside brigandry as a profitable pastime and constituted a terror to the travellers. Traders and merchants passing by were easy targets for these organised bands of robbers. The *Kuvalayamālā* recounts how when a caravan of traders camped near the *bhillapallīs* of the Sahya mountains, they apprehensively took several precautionary measures. They formed a circular array, moved the worthless goods to the outside, arranged for watchmen to keep vigil at night and kept their weapons in readiness. But at day break, as they were making arrangements for departure, the Bhillas swooped down with startling rapidity and swiftly overcoming all opposition took possession of all their goods.[340] Merchants crossing through the forest near Narmada would be terrified at the prospect of a possible meeting with the Pulindas.[341] The *Samarāiccakahā* mentions not only such attacks on caravans[342] but also capture of men for sacrifices.[343]

The pillaging activities of these tribes were not restricted to their mountain habitats but extended to neighbouring villages as well. The *Samarāiccakahā* speaks of a Śabara chief Vindhyaketu who wrought such destruction in a town that it looked like a veritable cemetery.[344] Certain people were also abducted, amongst whom was a *sārthavāhaputra's* wife. On enquiring, the *sārthavāhaputra* learnt that such incidents had occurred before in neighbouring areas and that the abducted people had been released on due payment of ransom without having suffered any blemish on their character or physical harm.[345] The activities of these Śabaras sometimes invited the punitive expeditions of neighbouring kingdoms.[346] When the rulers were powerful they, as in an instance in the *Samarāiccakahā*,[347] successfully subdued the tribals. The Dholpur inscription of Caṇḍamahāsena, AD 842, informs us that the lords of the *mlecchas* settled on both sides of the river Chambala paid him homage.[348] These *mlecchas* were probably Bhillas.[349] The Gwalior praśasti refers to Nāgabhaṭa's peaceful seizure of the hill-fort of the Kirāta.[350] The Ghaṭiyālā inscription credits Kakkuka with the resettlement of Rohiṃsakūpa which had been rendered uninhabitable by the Ābhiras and with destruction by fire of the Bhilla villages (*pallīs*) on the hills in the inaccessible Vaṭanānaka district.[351]

Not all of those who were dubbed *mlecchas* were cruel and fierce. There were amongst them simple forest folks, peaceful and amiable whom it was a pleasure to behold and converse with. The picturesque description of such a *patraśabara* couple in the *Kuvalayamālā* depicts the male wearing *valkala*, with his hair tied upward with a creeper, profusely adorned with flowers and a peacock-crest and the female wearing a garland of *guñjā* berries, adorned with pearls and a yaktail crest.[352] A king stranded helpless in the deep forest was befriended by a Śabara chief who fed him, tended his horse, and kept watch over him during the night.[353] Their habitations deep in the forest, many of these Śabaras had little to do with the outside world. The *Samarāiccakahā* describes the perplexity of the Śabara chief who on returning from the palace of the king where he had been lavishly entertained out of gratitude for the help rendered by the latter in the forest, realised that he was unable to describe the luxuries of the palace for the benefit of his listeners. He could have compared them only to the primitive things which his hearers were acquainted with and that was altogether insufficient to give them an idea of the actual splendour of the royal palace. For ornaments they had but *guñjās*, as food they had but red chalk (*gairika*).[354]

Some aboriginals ventured out of their forest precincts and rose to honourable positions in the courts of Aryan kings. The *Kuvalayamālā* refers to Śabara *senāpatiputra* Suṣeṇa who was not only entrusted with the important duty of commanding the operations against the Mālava king but also granted personal audience in the inner audience hall (*ābhyantaropasthānamaṇḍapa*) by his suzerain, who placed his right hand on his head to honour him and offered a seat.[355] The honour thus bestowed on Suṣeṇa suggests general acceptance of the aboriginal tribes in the society. Their value as soldiers had been realised as far back as the time of Kauṭilya who counted *mleccha* tribes like the Kirātas and *āṭavikas* or foresters amongst the most heroic recruits for the army[356] and this evidently facilitated their rise to important positions in the aryan hierarchy. The development of feudal ties in our period appear to have further contributed to a betterment in their position.[357]

Even as the process of assimilation went on the traditional discrimination against them appears to have persisted. A Pulinda *rājaputra* is said to have attended the royal assembly in the *Kuvalayamālā*.[358] But when he inadvertently occupied the place of a kṣatriya prince, he was uncremoniously struck down with a sword by the latter, in spite of his apologetic promise that the offence would not be repeated. The kṣatriya had felt that his life was not worth living after he had been insulted and his honour sullied by the Pulinda.[359] Smṛti writers like Vedavyāsa consider aboriginal tribes such as Bhillas as untouchables.[360] Such a sentiment finds expression in the *Kuvalayamālā* as well.[361] Atri says that if a *dvija* comes into contact with a *caṇḍāla, mleccha* etc. he should not take his meals (without first bathing) and if he comes into contact with them while taking his meals, he should stop, throw away his food and bathe.[362]

Slow assimilation of the *mlecchas* is however to be seen not only in the political, but social and religious spheres as well.[363] The proliferation of mixed castes to 61 in a late chapter of Manu and more than 100 in the *Brahmavaivarta Purāṇa* serves as an indication of the pace at which tribal peoples were converted into castes.[364] The mode of assimilation varied in accordance with the individual capability and occupation of the diverse disparate members who constituted the so called *mleccha* class. Considering their status separately we find that a special status was accorded to the *mleccha* warriors and *mleccha* tribal chiefs. These associates and followers belonging to the aboriginal tribes appear to have been treated honourably by the ruler as were *senāpatiputra* Suṣeṇa,[365] the Pulinda *rājaputra*,[366] and the Śabara chief[367] in the *Samarāiccakahā*. The Hūṇas were also regarded as *mlecchas*, but a Guhilla king of the Udaipur region is known to have proudly married the daughter of a Hūṇa king.[368] Later the Hūṇas are known to have found a place amongst the pure class of *rājaputras*.[369]

On the other hand, from the bracketing of Bhillas with *antyajas* in the *Kuvalayamālā*[370] and the inclusion of Bhillas amongst *antyajas* by later Smṛtis such as Yama, Aṅgiras and Atri,[371] it appears that a sizable section of the ordinary members of the aboriginal tribes were accorded the status of *antyajas*, in marked contrast to their absorption as kṣatriyas or vaiśyas in earlier times.[372] Medhātithi also spoke of assigning to the *mlecchas* a position similar to that of the caṇḍālas in *Āryavarta* when the *cāturvarṇya* system was introduced in a *mleccha* country.[373] A study of the social and political developments of Rajasthan during this period reveals the establishment of a territorial polity in place of an erstwhile tribal polity. The conquests of the Pratihāra and other Rajput monarchs[374] brought Aryan civilisation into proximity with backward civilisations as conquerors as well as bearers of superior technology and advanced urban civilisation. These developments, keeping in mind the growing disassociation of higher classes from manual labour, make the contemptuous treatment of tribals as *antyajas* understandable.

That the privilege of participation in religious rituals was extended to respectable members of the *mleccha* class can be seen from the *Samarāiccakahā* where the prince Sena unhesitatingly employs his friend, the Śabara chief, in bringing flowers etc. for the worship of the miraculous wishing tree, on which the fulfilment of his dearest wish depends, and succeeding in his purpose, sees off the latter with all honour.[375] The Jainas regard the Śabaras as of low birth but redeemable by adoption of the Jaina faith. Those who came into contact with Jaina monks, and fed and helped them, it is said, were blessed in turn and taught right conduct, by practice of which they gained wealth, heaven or birth in a royal family.[376] This liberal attitude entertained towards the *mlecchas* by the various reformist sects had facilitated the gradual assimilation of *mlecchas* into the cultural mainstream of India since early times.[377] In Hinduism itself, the cult of the terrific goddess, believed to be of non-aryan origin,[378] found universal acceptance during this period.

In conclusion, one may remark that birth in a particular varṇa, as in earlier times, assigned a general predetermined social status to a person and oriented him towards the adoption of a particular group of professions. The hunters, fowlers, fishermen, looters of caravans etc. who followed sinful occupations involving injury to living beings, the *Kuvalayamālā* tells us, did so because they considered it to be their family practice or livelihood ordained by the creator himself.[379] At the same time, the rules of society were not so rigid or immobile, as is evident from the composition of the ruling class and slow assimilation of the non-aryans into the aryan fold, also the actual degree of respect enjoyed by a person depended very much on his qualifications and economic status. Thus, as seen above, an illiterate brāhmaṇa would be scoffed at, while an industrious śūdra appears to have suffered no discrimination on account of his low caste, and enjoyed wealth as well as social prestige.

Brāhmaṇas besides pursuing the traditional occupations of study, teaching and sacrificing and taking up state service as ministers, as allowed to them by the Dharmaśāstras, appear to have been closely associated with agriculture, a development which is in keeping with the practice of land grants to them during the period. Non-brahmanical occupations, such as those of a jester, were also practised. The economic status of learned brāhmaṇas who were fortunate enough to gain the office of ministers and *purohitas* of rulers as well as those who proceeded to the royal court where they gained recognition for their learning and were honoured must have naturally been quite high as was that of the brāhmaṇas who were endowed with a land grant. The projection of *dāna* as a means of expiation and gaining religious merit, with the ambit of *dāna* extending to śūdras as well, provided the brāhmaṇas in general with an effective and substantial means of subsistence, the grant of land in particular providing them with an enduring source of income. Officiating at ceremonies such as names-giving, marriages and ceremonies performed on the occasion of a ship's departure also must have augmented their earnings, while feasts on occasions of *śrāddha* (funeral repasts), marriage and other ceremonial occasions ensured them a recurring supply of good food.

As regards the politico-legal status of the brāhmaṇa and the extent of his authority over the masses, brāhmaṇas who served as ministers of rulers and 'minded the affairs of the entire kingdom' evidently wielded considerable political power. In virtue of their learning, the opinion of learned brāhmaṇas, though not serving in an administrative capacity, also carried great weight with the rulers. But the magico-mythical authority of the *purohita* suffered a diminution inasmuch as his sphere of activity remained confined to minding the spiritual affairs of the king and did not extend to administrative affairs. A brāhmaṇa did not enjoy special legal privileges and if found guilty of a crime was punished, irrespective of his high family connections, and the lower vaiśya varṇa of the affected party. This reflects the nullifying of special brahmanical privileges in an urban milieu where the urban middle class had emerged as a respectable class, not to be discriminated against. In the power of brāhmaṇas to pronounce expiations for sins, on the other hand, one may discern an effective source of social authority over the rural masses.

A high social status was naturally assured for those brāhmaṇas who were endowed with learning, political influence and high economic status. Besides, illiterate brāhmaṇas following non-brahmanical occupations also made a claim to a privileged social status, a claim that was in consonance with the high social status accorded to the brāhmaṇas in general by the Smṛtis. The society nevertheless accorded a high degree of respect only to brāhmaṇas leading a traditional idealistic way of life and land grants were given only to such brāhmaṇas.

Performance of the functions of rulers and warriors remained the chief vocations of a kṣatriya. As military services came to be rewarded with grants of land, concomitant with the growing feudal tendencies, members of the warrior class known as *rājapūtras* and *ṭhakkuras* emerged as members of the landed aristocracy. But the professions of ruler and warriors were no longer restricted to their caste. Other castes, including vaiśyas and tribals were also gaining a place in the order of warriors and the composition of the ruling class was also miscellaneous. The high political and economic status of kṣatriyas as members of the ruling class and landed aristocracy, the performance of the vital function of a warrior, as well as their qualities of bravery, valour, and protection of the distressed ensured them a privileged social status. The comprehensive education of princes and their liberality must have further enhanced their social prestige. The inclusion of Vedic studies in their curriculum indicates that their ritual status was high. Kṣatriyas attached great importance to their high ancestry and took pride in tracing their descent from solar and lunar lines.

Trade was the chief vocation practised by vaiśyas distinguished by the designations of *vaṇik, śreṣṭhi* and *sārthavāha*, though other conventional means of livelihood such as agriculture and cattle-rearing were also practised by them. The profession of *śilpa* or crafts was considered to be a respectable occupation for them but was not usually adopted.

Pressure of economic circumstances sometimes impelled them to take up the profession of arms. Enterprising traders served the invaluable function of exchange of goods between different and distant cities and countries. The inconsistency of agriculture with the principle of non-violence advocated vigorously by Jainism, lucrative profits offered by trade, the emergence of warriors and brāhmaṇas as landlords as well as śūdras as agriculturists whereby erstwhile vaiśya preserves were encroached upon, in Rajasthan where trade and Jainism both flourished, may be held to be factors responsible for the vaiśya's preference for trade.

Śreṣṭhins and *sārthavāhas* possessed considerable wealth which they further invested in trade to earn greater profits. They were well educated, performed a useful social function by giving alms to the needy as well as by extending patronage to actors and enjoyed a high social status commensurate with their high economic status. But all the other members of the vaiśya caste were not so well off economically, especially so presumably because brāhmaṇas and śūdras had taken to their traditional means of livelihood, thereby narrowing down the opening for vaiśyas. The social status of this poor vaiśya must have been correspondingly lower than that of the wealthy members of his class. The legal status of vaiśyas was high and there was no discrimination against him by the ruler in matters of punishment for crimes, as contrasted with the punishments meted out to a member of the brāhmaṇa caste, which reflects the high civic status of the vaiśya in an urban set-up. Rich *sārthavāhas* who returned home with wealth were honoured by the ruler and made members of the ruling aristocracy by bestowal of the command of certain areas.

While śūdras of the earlier period had been mainly pedlars, an enterprising section of śūdras now engaged themselves in long-distance commercial transactions and amassed considerable wealth. As they came to play an important part in economy through promotion of trade in addition to their contribution as peasants and artisans in the flourishing rural and urban economy respectively, leading to a substantial improvement in their material condition, there was a corresponding improvement in their social and religious status, which may be partly ascribed also to the liberal attitude of heterodox sects like tantricism and Jainism towards śūdras, with Jainism offering them initiation in the Jaina monastic order on an equal status. They mixed freely with vaiśya traders while brāhmaṇas were fed and blessed them at ceremonies associated with their commercial ventures. They gained the important religious right to *pūrtadharma*, the right to confer alms to the poor and make gifts to the brāhmaṇas, erect temples, excavate tanks and wells, open alms-houses, establish hospitals and extend help to the distressed, philanthropic works which must have brought them social prestige, besides providing the brāhmaṇas with an additional means of subsistence. But in the countryside the emergent influential landed aristocracy consisting of brāhmaṇas and kṣatriyas held superior land rights than ordinary śūdra peasants though there is no evidence of peasant subjection.

The class of *antyajas* comprising caṇḍālas, leather-workers, washermen, fishermen, fowlers, Bhillas and ḍombas was socially despised and notions of untouchability were entertained towards sections of washermen, Bhillas and caṇḍālas. Caṇḍālas who lived in segregated settlements and were assigned the task of executioners appear to have been the most degraded amongst them. Jaina saints tried to inculcate a feeling of sympathy towards them amongst their followers by emphasizing that caṇḍāla executioners were not cruel at heart but merely performing their duty. Some washermen were economically well off but their social status also remained low.

The *mlecchas* included various indigenous and foreign tribes who did not subscribe to the brahmanical way of life. The practices of amputation of limbs, hanging, killing, theft, and abusing characterised the residents of a *mleccha* settlement. Some of the aboriginals lived by hunting and trading in ivory. Others subsisted by roadside brigandry, pillaging of villages and kidnapping for ransom. Consequently powerful rulers carried out retributive expeditions against them and subdued them. They performed bloody rituals involving human and animal sacrifices and cultivated occult practices. Some tribals living in the remote forest remained unacquainted with the outside world.

The gradual expansion of territorial polity entailed close interaction with tribals at various levels and slow assimilation of the so-called *mlecchas*. The socio-political status accorded to them varied in accordance with the occupations they followed and their tribal standing. Good warriors became military commanders. Tribal princes gained a place in the royal court. With development of feudal ties, tribal chiefs who were co-vassals came to be regarded as brothers. But tribals at large appear to have been given the status of *antyajas* due to their backwardness, lack of advanced technology and cultural lag. The absorption of various non-aryan elements in the Śakti cult indicates religious integration of tribals through absorption of their religious practices. Jainas regarded them as worthy of redemption and admitted them into the sect without discrimination. Members of the class who had embraced Jainism were treated as equals by followers of Jainism.

Notes and References

1. *CII,* Vol. III, no. 35.
2. *CII,* Vol. III, p. 222.
3. Harāha inscription, *EI,* XIV, pp. 110 f.
4. Bānskherā plate of Harṣa, *EI,* IV, p. 210.
5. Al Bilāduri, *ED,* I, p. 126. see Chapter 1, p. 6.
6. U.N. Ghoshal observes that on the advent of Islam Hindu society adopted a more restrictive attitude and practically closed its doors against admission from outside (*Age of Imperial Kannauj*, p. 498). B.N.S. Yadava also observes that under the conditions of foreign invasions and political disorders a great need was felt to reinforce caste duties (*Society and Culture in Northern India*, p. 4). He notes that the earlier formulation of the classic theory of caste by Manu took place in circumstances of Yavana and Śaka Pahlava invasions (Idem, p. 3).
7. चातुर्वर्ण व्यवस्थानं यस्मिन् देशे न विद्यते । स म्लेच्छदेशो विज्ञेय आर्य्यावर्तस्ततः परः । *Vṛddha Viṣṇu Smṛti,* Chapter 84.
8. D. Sharma, *Lectures on Rajput History*, p. 10; Idem. *RTTA,* p. 105. Suvira Jaiswal notes that in times of crisis class differentiation begins to cut across as well within caste formations and the process of fusion and fission of castes gets accelerated ('Studies in Early Indian Social History' in R.S. Sharma ed. *Survey of Research in Economic and Social History of India*, p. 57).
9. *On Manu,* IV.84.
10. See feudalism.
11. See below, pp. 19–20.
12. See tantricism.
13. Kane, *HD,* Vol. II, pt. 1, pp. 54–5.
14. Ibid.
15. *Ṛgveda*, X, 90. 12; *Manu,* I. 31; *Mbh. Śānti.* 72, 4–5.
16. कत्ता अहं ति बंभा भणइ जओ वयण-बाह-ऊरूहिं ।
    पाएसु अ णिक्खंतं चाउव्वण्णं जगमिणं ति ।। *Dhū.*, II. 46.
17. Sachau, I, pp. 100–1.
18. *KM,* pp. 45, 50, 56, 65.
19. Ibid., p. 56.

20. Ibid., p. 65; The connotation of the term 'jāti' is a matter of controversy. Suvira Jaiswal postulates that the two terms 'varṇa' and 'jāti' have been used interchangeably and indiscriminately in Sanskrit literature ('Studies in Early Indian Social History', in *Survey of Research in Economic and Social History of India,* ed. R.S. Sharma, p. 47).
21. *KM*, pp. 50, 57, 65 etc.
22. मनुयत्तणे वि लद्धे अंतर-दीवेसु णेय-रूवेसु।
    अच्छंति भमंत च्चिय आरिय-खेत्तं ण पावेंति।।
    आरिय-खेत्तमि पुणो णिंदिय-अहमासु होंति जाईसु।। Ibid., p. 88.
23. *SK*, p. 286; *KM*, p. 40; see antyajas.
24. *On Manu,* V. 91.
25. *ED*, I, p. 6.
26. राईण रायधम्मो बंभण-धम्मो य बंभणाणं तु।
    वेसाण वेस-धम्मो णियओ धम्मो य सुद्दाण।। *KM*, p. 205.
27. *On Manu,* IV. 84, see above, p. 15.
28. *EI*, XVIII, pp. 87 f.
29. D. Sharma, *ECD*, pp. 9–10.
30. P. Bhatia, *The Paramāras*, p. 19; Instances of the occupation of the kṣatriyas being usurped by other castes are known also during the earlier period. Hieun Tsang refers the brāhmaṇa kings of Ujjayinī, Chi-ki-to and Maheśvarapura, vaiśya kings of Kannauj and Pariyātra and śūdra kings of Matipura and Sindh. Beal, I, pp. 179, 190, 209; II, pp. 271–2.
31. *SK*, pp. 88–9.
32. Ibid., p. 328.
33. *KM*, p. 65.
34. Ibid., p. 67.
35. See marriages, p. 73.
36. *On Manu,* IX. 168.
37. *Vedavyāsa,* III. 56.
38. *Bṛhadyama,* III. 10; *Vedavyāsa,* III. 49; *Parāśara,* XI. 20; *Manu,* IV. 253; *Yājñavalkya,* I. 168.
39. रूवेण णज्जइ कुलं कुलेणं सीलं तहा य सीलेण। णज्जंति गुणा तेहि मि णज्जइ सत्तं पि पुरिसाण।। तहा तुह विणय-रूवेहिं चेय सिट्ठो अम्ह सील-सत्तादि-गुण-वित्थारो। सव्वहा एसा तुज्झं मए समप्पिय त्ति। *KM*, p. 105.
40. *EI*, I, pp. 184 f.; B.D. Chattopadhyaya, 'Trade and Urban Centres in Early Medieval North India', *IHR,* Vol. I, No. 2, p. 211.
41. B.D. Chattopadhyaya, op. cit.
42. Āhār inscription no. 4, *EI,* XIX, pp. 52 f.; Chattopadhyaya, op. cit., p. 209.
43. *SK*, pp. 213, 264, 430, 705.
44. जाइकुलाइगव्विएणं 'कहं नीयचच्चरी अम्हाण चच्चरीए समासन्नं परिव्वयइ' त्ति कयत्थिया वत्थसोहगा। Ibid., p. 42.
45. चोरो त्ति णिंदणिज्जो भिल्लो त्ति ण दंसणे वि मह जोग्गो। *KM*, p. 136.
46. *Atri,* verse 249; *Śātātapa* quoted by *Smṛticandrikā,* I, p. 119; *Bṛhaspati*, qd. Kane, *HD*, II (i), p. 175.

47. Kane, op. cit., pp. 169 f.
48. R.S. Sharma, *Śūdras in Ancient India,* p. 146; S. Jaiswal, Presidential Address, *IHC,* 1977, p. 38.
49. V. Jha, 'Stages in History of Untouchables', *IHR,* II, no. 1, p. 30.
50. V. Jha, op. cit., p. 30; Idem. 'Leather Workers in Ancient and Medieval India', *IHC,* 1979, p. 104.
51. See urban and rural life.
52. B.D. Chattopadhyaya, 'Trade and Urban Centres in Early Medieval North India', *IHR,* I, no. 2, pp. 203–19.
53. *Mitākṣara on Yājña.,* III. 30; *Aparārka,* pp. 922–3; *Smṛticandrikā,* I, p. 118; qd. Kane, *HD,* II (i), p. 169.
54. *Manu,* V. 85; IX. 235–9.
55. *Śaṃkha,* 14.4; *Aṅgiras,* 55, 57.
56. See *mlecchas,* pp. 41, 43.
57. B.N.S. Yadava, 'Note on History of Untouchables', *IHR,* II (ii), p. 515.
58. S. Jaiswal, Presidential Address, *IHC,* 1977, p. 29; R.N. Nandi, 'Client, Ritual and Conflict in Early Brahmanical Order', *IHR,* VI, nos. 1–2, p. 73.
59. *SK,* pp. 98 f.
60. *Atri,* 197–8, *Devala,* 48–9.
61. The *Sūtrakṛtāṅga* had stated that when a man drunk with caste pride etc. slighted, blamed, abused, reviled, despised somebody else and extolled himself, 'he is my inferior, I am of better caste or family etc.', he went forth from womb to womb, birth to birth, from death to death, from hell to hell. *Sūtrakṛtāṅga,* II, 2.17; Cf. also *Uttarādhyayana*, Chapter XII; *Ratnakaraṇḍaka,* I.28.
62. णिय-जाइ-मओमत्तो णिंदसि रे सेसयं जणं जइया।
    तइया मूढ ण-याणसि एकस्स कए बहुं चुक्को। *KM,* p. 37.
    मा कुणह जाइ-गव्वं। Ibid., p. 43.
63. *SK,* p. 42.
64. Ibid., pp. 43–4, 605, 679.
65. *KM,* pp. 92, 119; *SK,* pp. 160, 654, 679.
66. Ibid., p. 72.
67. Ibid., p. 272.
68. *SK,* pp. 657–8, 679–80.
69. दीणसत्तवच्छलो परोवयारनिरओ अणुयम्पारई न एस कम्मचण्डालो, किं तु जाइचण्डालो। सज्जणो खु एसो। *SK,* p. 214.
70. *SK,* pp. 431–2.
71. पढति बंभण-संघाइं। *KM,* p. 171.
72. भुंजाविज्जंति बंभणे . . . पढंति बंभण-कुलाइं आसीसा। Ibid., p. 67.
73. सत्थिकारेंति चउवयण-समा महाबंभणा। Ibid., p. 16.
74. *KM,* p. 21.
75. *SK,* p. 260.
76. एयस्स रोहियमच्छस्स पुच्छभायं तायं अज्जियं च उद्दसिऊण माहणाणं रन्धावेहि। Ibid., p. 258.

77. *KM*, p. 170.
78. *Manu*, III. 128 f.
79. *Vāyu Purāṇa*, 75. 13–14, 80.55.
80. *Manu*, III.128 f., 184; *Yājña*, I. 219–21; *Atri*, 352–4; *Bṛhatparāśara*, V. 15 f.; *Laghvāśvalāyana*, *śrāddhaprayogīprakaraṇa*, 15, 20.
81. Qd. by Aparārka, p. 455; Kane, *HD*, II, pt. 1, p. 117.
82. *Manu*, I. 88; X. 75; *Yājña*, I. 118; *Atri*, 13; *Laghuhārita*, I. 18; *Śaṃkha*, I.2; *Gautama*, X.
83. गायत्ती-जव-वावडइं बंभण-घरइं . . . गंभीर-वेय-पढण-रवइं बंभण-सालिसु। *KM*, p. 82.
84. Ibid., p. 258.
85. Ibid., pp. 48, 117.
86. *SK*, p. 7.
87. *KM*, p. 48.
88. वेदशास्त्रार्थपारग:। *EI*, XVIII, pp. 87 f.
89. धम्मसत्थसंघायपाढओ लोगववहारनीइकुसलो अप्पारम्भपरिग्गहो जन्नदत्तो नाम पुरोहिओ त्ति। *SK*, p. 7.
90. ता गच्छ, भो सोमदेवपुरोहिय, ममाविन्नायपरियणभावो चेव, गवेसिऊण तस्स महातवस्सिस्स वुत्तन्तं। Ibid., p. 30.
91. पारद्धं पुरोहिएणं रायमहिसीए सव्वविग्घविघाययं चरुकम्मं। Ibid., p. 494.
92. पत्थुयं पुरोहिएहिं मन्तगब्भिणाहुइप्पयाणसारं सन्तिकम्मं। Ibid., p. 17. Lakṣmīdhara (twelfth century) devotes a full chapter to the ceremonies to be performed by the *purohita* to ward off calamities in a kingdom. Rājadharma, p. 176.
93. Ibid., p. 88.
94. सुक्क-सरिसा महापुरोहिया। *KM*, p. 16.
95. The *purohita* ceased to be a member of the ministry from AD 200. Altekar, *State and Government in Ancient India*, p. 169.
96. *KM*, p. 209.
97. Ibid., p. 9.
98. सयलरज्जचिन्तओ अत्ताणनिव्विसेसो इन्दसम्मो नाम माहणसचिवो। *SK*, p. 133.
99. *Manu*, VIII. 9.
100. *Manu*, VII. 58. In the *Kādambarī* (seventh century), Kumārapālita and Śukanāsa, the ministers of Śūdraka and Candrapīḍa respectively are described as brāhmaṇas. *Kādambarī*, pp. 13, 56.
101. *EI*, II, p. 161; *RT*, IV. 137, 496; VI. 168, 19 and 224.
102. गो-भूमि-धण्ण-दाणं हलप्पयाणं य बंभण-जणस्स जं कीरई सो धम्मो। *KM*, p. 205. बंभणाणं अग्गाहारं। Ibid., p. 258.
103. *EI*, XXIV, pp. 29 f.
104. Beal, II, p. 73.
105. Kane, *HD*, II (i), pp. 125–6.
106. II. 2–4, 7, 14.
107. VII. 179 and 182.
108. *Gṛhastha*, pp. 194–5.
109. IV. 3.19.

110. R.S. Sharma, *Śūdras in Ancient India,* p. 339.
111. R.S. Sharma, *Political Ideas and Institutions,* p. 223; Idem, *Indian Feudalism,* p. 47.
112. *Matsya,* 283. It is included amongst the 16 mahādānas also by the *Agni Purāṇa,* Chapter 210 and *Liṅga Purāṇa,* Chapter 28 f.
113. The *Daśabrāhmaṇa Jātaka* mentions ten classes of brāhmaṇas viz. physician, messenger, tax collector, woodcutter, tradesmen, cultivator, shepherd, butcher, military guard and hunter (N.K. Dutt, *Origin and Growth of Caste,* Vol. I, p. 218). In the Gupta period too some brāhmaṇas were traders, other architects, some government servants and others like the Vākāṭakas, Kadambas, and Matṛviṣṇu, the Gupta feudatory in central India had taken up the professions of arms (A.S. Altekar, *Vākāṭaka Gupta Age,* p. 344).
114. *Karpūra.,* I. 20.
115. *Atri,* vv. 273 f.
116. Aparārka's commentary on *Yājñavalkya,* p. 937; qd. Kane, op. cit., p. 126.
117. *EI,* I, pp. 184 f.
118. *ED,* I, p. 10.
119. *Manu,* X. 80–94.
120. *Yājña,* III.35.
121. *Nārada,* Ṛṇadāna, 56.
122. Kane, *HD,* II (i), p. 118. An apposite instance of this was Bhadraśarman nicknamed Caṇḍasoma because of his cruel and unbecoming behaviour, *KM,* p. 45.
123. Jaimal Rai, *The Rural-Urban Economy and Social Changes in India,* pp. 273 f.; R.N. Nandi, 'Client, Ritual and Conflict in Early Brahmanical Order', *IHR,* VI, nos. 1–2, pp. 68–9.
124. Kane, op. cit., p. 118; R.N. Nandi, op. cit., pp. 70, 113; Jaimal Rai, op. cit., p. 355. See below for subsistence crisis. p. 54, 55.
125. सयलं घर-सव्वस्सं धण-धण्ण-वत्थ-पत्त-सयणासण-डंड-भंड-दुपय-चउप्पयाइयं बंभणाणं दाऊण। *KM,* p. 48.
126. दक्खेसु बंभणे। *KM,* p. 65.
127. सरलपुरं णाम बंभणाणं अग्गाहारं। *KM,* p. 258.
128. *EI,* XIX, p. 15; *EI,* V, p. 208.
129. *EI,* XIX, pp. 174 f.
130. *ZDMG,* XL, pp. 38 f.; qd. D. Sharma, *ECD,* p. 19.
131. Cf. G.S. Ghurye, *Caste and Race in India,* p. 88; दानमेकं कलौ युगे। *Manu* I. 87; तेभ्यो दत्तमनन्तं हि इत्याह भगवान्यम। *Bṛhadyama,* verse 55.
132. Cf. *Varāha,* 100, 12–13; *Matsya,* 206, 16; 90, 11; *Viṣṇudharmottara,* II, 32, 26–33.
133. *Varāha,* 100, 12–13; *Matsya,* 206, 16; 90, 11.
134. Romila Thapar, *Ancient Indian Social History,* p. 116.
135. Ibid., p. 117.
136. Infra, pp. 54–6.

137. *KM,* p. 258.
138. *KM,* p. 48.
139. समुप्पन्नो ते विज्जाहिमाणो। ठिओ गज्जणयसामिणो वीरसेणस्स समीवे, संपूइओ तेण, विइणं जीवणं, बहुमन्नए राया। *SK,* p. 227.
140. *SK,* p. 228.
141. रहुउलचूडामणिणो महिन्दवालस्स को अ गुरू। *Karpūra.,* I.5. बालकवि कईराओ णिब्भरराअस्स तह उवज्झाओ . . . माहप्पारूढं। Ibid., I. 9.
142. *ED,* I, p. 19.
143. का तुम्हेहि समं पाडिसिद्धी। जदो तुमं णाराओ विय णिरक्खरो वि रदणतुलाए णिउंजीअसि। अहं उण तुला विअ लद्धक्खरा वि ण सुवणतुलणे णिउंजीआमि। *Karpūra,* I. 20[12-14].
144. चेटिओ बम्हणेण समसीसिआए दीसदि मइरा पंचगव्वं च एक्कस्सिं भण्डए करीअदि कच्चं माणिक्कं च समं आहरणे पउंजीअदि। Ibid., I. 20[26].
145. इदिसं राअउलं दूरे वन्दीअदि जहिं दासी बम्हणेण समं पाडिसिद्धिं करेदि। Ibid., I. 20[33].
146. Chapter III, 512–13 and 518, Jiv. qd. Kane, *HD,* II (i), p. 117.
147. Qd. U.N. Ghoshal, *History of Indian Political Ideas,* p. 433. Such views had been expressed as early as the time of Manu who emphatically declared that a brāhmaṇa, whether learned or not, was a great deity, like the fire which is not contaminated even in a cremation-ground; a brāhmaṇa employed in the meanest occupations must be honoured as a great deity (*Manu,* IX. 317–19).
148. *KM,* pp. 117–18.
149. अकय-बंभणक्कारो अबद्ध-मुंज-मेहलो। Ibid., p. 117.
150. लोएण उवहसिज्जइ किर एसो बंभणो आसि। Ibid., p. 118.
151. *Manu,* I. 97; *Yājña,* I. 199.
152. सर्वेषां चापि वै मान्यो वेदविद् द्विज एव हि। *Laghvāśvalāyana,* XXII, 2.
153. गायत्रीरहितो विप्रः शूद्रादप्यशुर्चिभवेत्। *Parāśara,* VIII. 31.
154. अग्निकार्य्यात् परिभ्रष्टाः संध्योपासनवर्जिताः। वेदंचैवानधीयानाः सर्वे ते वृषलाः स्मृता। *Parāśara,* XII. 29.
155. On Yājña, I. 199.
156. एयस्स जिब्भं छिन्दिऊण उप्पाडेह लोयणाइं। *SK,* p. 95.
157. Sachau, II. p. 162.
158. *Gautama,* XII.43; *Kauṭilya,* IV.8; *Manu,* VIII.125, 380–1; *Yājña.,* II.270; *Nārada* (sāhasa, 9–10); *Vṛddhahārita,* VII, 191.
159. *Gautama,* 12. 12–14; *Manu,* VIII. 337–8.
160. *KM,* pp. 258–9.
161. जम्म दलिद्दो (दरिद्दो)। Ibid., pp. 45, 117.
162. जण्णयत्तो णाम सोत्तिय-बंभणो। सो य केरिसो। अवि य। कसिणो दुब्बल-देहो खर-फरुसो रुक्ख-पंडर-सरीरो। दीसन्त धमणि-जालो जम्म-दरिद्दो तहिं वसइ। Ibid., p. 117.
163. त्रीणि कर्माणि जीविका। याजनाध्यापने चैव विशुद्धाच्च प्रतिग्रहः प्रतिग्रहोऽध्यापनश्च याजनं चेति वृत्तयः। *Atri,* 13.
164. R.C. Hazra, *Studies in the Purāṇic Records on Hindu Rites and Customs,* p. 253; R.N. Nandi, 'Client, Ritual and Conflict in Early Brahmanical Order', *IHR,* VI, nos. 1–2, pp. 112–13.
165. *Manu,* I. 89; X. 79–80; *Yājña,* I. 119.

166. क्षत्रियस्यापि . . . शस्त्रोपजीवनं भूतरक्षणं चेति वृत्तय: । *Atri,* 14.
167. क्षत्रिस्यविशेषेण प्रजानां परिपालनम् । *Śaṃkha,* I. 4.
168. *KM,* pp. 137, 147, 155, 215.
169. Ibid., p. 140.
170. ठाविओ रज्जंमि नियभाइणेओ पसत्थजोएण उचिओ खत्तियवंसस्स मुणिचन्दकुमारो त्ति । *SK,* p. 769.
171. *KM,* p. 50.
172. *ED,* I, p. 16.
173. A.S. Altekar, *Rāṣṭrakūṭas and Their Times,* p. 319.
174. *SK,* p. 8.
175. *ED,* I, p. 16.
176. *SK,* p. 635.
177. *KM,* p. 50.
178. See Chapter 3.
179. *KM,* pp. 73 f.
180. *SK,* p. 635.
181. *Manu,* X. 79; *Atri,* 14; *Vasiṣṭha,* II. 21–2.
182. तिकम्माभिरओ महादुवारम्मि खत्तिओ पयडो । *KM,* p. 282.
183. Ibid., p. 14.
184. Ibid., p. 22.
185. Ibid., p. 18.
186. *SK,* p. 22.
187. Ibid., pp. 401, 596, 803.
188. *KM,* p. 22.
189. Sachau, II. 136.
190. *KM,* pp. 146, 155.
191. Ibid.
192. Ibid.
193. इक्खागुवंस-बालंकुर सोम-साहा-णहयल-मियंक । *KM,* p. 155.
194. इक्खागु-वंस-जाओ . . . दप्पप्फलिहो त्ति आयरिओ । Ibid., p. 215.
195. *SK,* p. 286.
196. *Karpūra.,* I. 5.
197. किं तु सोमवंस-संभवस्स रयणमउडस्स पुत्तो । दे सुन्दरं जायं, एक्को अम्हाण वंसो । तुमं एत्थ रज्जे होसु संपयं । *KM,* p. 146.
198. *EI,* XVIII, p. 110.
199. D. Sharma, *ECD,* p. 5.
200. Romila Thapar, *Ancient Indian Social History,* pp. 131 f.
201. *Manu,* X. 43–5.
202. *KM,* p. 56.
203. सो य परन्मुहो परकलत्ते न अब्भत्थणाए, अलुद्धो परविभवे न धम्मोवज्जणे, असंतुट्ठो परोवयारे न धणागमे, अहिगओ पीईए न मच्छरेणं, दरिद्दो दोसेहिं न विहवेणं । तेण सा नयरी मलयवणं पिव परिजाएण वसन्तो विय कुसमुग्गमेण पाउससिरी विय मेहावलीए सरयकालो विय चन्दमण्डलेण अहियं विभूसिय त्ति । *SK,* p. 406.
204. *SK,* p. 191.

205. *KM*, p. 103.
206. Ibid., p. 57.
207. Ibid., p. 190.
208. *PRAS, WC*, 1909–10, p. 56.
209. अत्थस्स पुण उवाया दिसि-गमणं होइ मित्त-करणं च।
णरवर सेवा कुसलत्तणं च माणप्पमाणेसुं।
धाउव्वाओ मंतं च देवयाराहणं च केसिं च।
सायर-तरणं तह रोहणम्मि खणणं वणिज्जं च।।
णाणाविहं च कम्मं विज्जा-सिप्पाइं णेय-रूवाइं।
अत्थस्स साहयाइं अणिंदियाइं च एयाइं।। *KM*, p. 57.
210. See chapters on education and tantricism for reference to these lores.
211. See below and sāmantas for connotation of the term *olagā*.
212. *KM*, p. 191.
213. These were the conventional means of livelihood recommended for them by the Smṛtis and Purāṇas. *Manu*, I. 90; IX. 326–33; *Yājña*, I. 119; *Hārita*, II. 6; *Viṣṇu*, 3/8/30; *Vāyu*, 8/165/*Brahmāṇḍa*, 2/7/162 Purāṇas.
214. *KM*, pp. 57, 191.
215. Ibid., pp. 65 f., 74; *SK*, p. 105.
216. Hieun Tsang in his account had described vaiśyas as the merchant class that engaged in commercial exchange and profit at home and abroad. Beal, I. 82.
217. *ED*, I. p. 16.
218. Cf. R.S. Sharma, *Śūdras in Ancient India*, p. 260; B.N.S. Yadava, *Society and Culture in Northern India*, pp. 13, 40.
219. नो खलु समायरइ इमे अइयारे। तं जहा . . . फोडियकम्मं। *SK*, p. 50.
220. D. Sharma, *RTTA*, p. 438.
221. See feudalism.
222. B.N.S. Yadava, *Society and Culture in Northern India*, p. 41.
223. S. Jaiswal, 'Studies in Early Indian Social History', *IHR*, VI, 1–2, p. 39.
224. B.D. Chattopadhyaya, 'Origin of Rajputs', *IHR*, III, no. 1, pp. 62–4.
225. *KM*, p. 191.
226. The taking up of arms by vaiśyas is allowed by Manu in case of danger to religion and by Vasiṣṭha in the case of danger to one's life as well. *Manu*, VIII.348; *Vasiṣṭha*, III.26.
227. Cf. Beal, I. 179; 209.
228. Kauṭilya listed the practice of arts and crafts (*Kārukuśīlvakarma)* amongst the distinctive functions of the śūdras. *Arthaśāstra*, I. 3.8.
229. The idea of a vaiśya taking up mechanical arts was abhorrent to the author of the *Viṣṇu Purāṇa* which denounced it as a practice of the kali age. *Viṣṇu*, VI.1.36, qd. R.C. Hazra, *Studies in Purāṇic Records on Hindu Rites and Customs*, p. 209.
230. *ED*, I, p. 16.
231. B.N.S. Yadava, *Society and Culture in Northern India*, pp. 11 f., 273.

232. See below, and rural and urban life.
233. See rural and urban life.
234. *SK,* pp. 204–5, 327–8, 443, 585. See Chapter 9.
235. Ibid., p. 202; *KM,* p. 67.
236. *KM,* pp. 75, 134–5.
237. *KM,* pp. 65–6. See Chapter 9.
238. *On Manu,* I.90.31; IX. 331–2.
239. *IA,* Vol. 58, pp. 161–2.
240. *KM,* p. 65.
241. D. Sharma, *RTTA,* p. 496.
242. *EI,* I, pp. 184 f.
243. *On Manu,* VII. 41.
244. Sachau, I. 101.
245. Sachau, I, 125; II, 136.
246. Altekar, *Rāṣṭrakūṭas and Their Times,* pp. 332–3; G.S. Ghurye, *Caste and Race in India,* pp. 85, 93, 101.
247. सो य सोम्मो सुहओ सयणो सुमणोहरो वाई कुसलो विणीओ पियंवओ दयालू दक्खिणो। *KM,* p. 224.
248. असंभावणिज्जमेयं, कुलप्पसुओ खु एसो ता कहं इमं अच्चन्तविरूद्धं करिस्सइ। *SK,* p. 90.
249. को य दोसो कुलस्य। किं न हवन्ति सुरभिकुसुमेसु किमिओ। Ibid., p. 91.
250. *SK,* pp. 93–5.
251. Ghaṭiyālā inscription no. 2, *JRAS,* 1895, pp. 513–21. The donation of a field measuring 200 by 225 cubits by the town of Sīyaḍoṇī (U.P.) to Śrīnārāyaṇabhaṭṭāraka, set up by a merchant, indicates that the townsfolk had no scruples about donating land to a deity established by a vaiśya. Sīyaḍoṇī inscription, *EI,* I, l.1–4, pp. 162 f.
252. Supra, p. 64.
253. The Sāmolī inscription (vs 703) tells of the building of a temple of Araṇyavāsini by Jēntaka, the chief of the mahājanas, *EI,* XX, pp. 97 f.
254. *Śaṃkha,* I. 3; *Atri,* 14–15; *Vasiṣṭha,* II, 21–2; *Manu,* X. 79.
255. It has been pointed that even in later times the great Smṛti commentator Lakṣmīdhara permits the vaiśya to study the Vedas and by laying down that a vaiśya should not trade in certain articles such as salt, wine, curds, milk, lac, hides, flesh etc. assigns him a status much different from that of the śūdra. Garhasthyakāṇḍa, p. 258; qd. D. Sharma, *RTTA,* p. 437.
256. ज्यैष्ठ्यं . . . वैश्यानां धान्यधनतः। *Manu,* II. 55.
257. *SK,* pp. 105, 407.
258. सत्थवाहपुत्तो ति। देसन्तराओ बहुयं दविणजायं विढविऊण महाकत्तिगीएं दीणाणाहमणिवारियं महादाणं देन्तो त्ति। Ibid., p. 195.
259. *KM,* p. 104.
260. कयमुद्‌दङ्‌गसासणावणनिमित्तं पुणो वि धरणसमीव समागओ राया। *SK,* p. 463.
261. *EI,* I, pp. 159 f.
262. *EI,* XXIII, pp. 137 f.

263. *Manu,* I. 91. The practice of handicrafts was allowed to them only if they failed to find service with the twice-born and were threatened with the loss of their sons and wives. Ibid., X.99.
264. R.S. Sharma, *Śūdras in Ancient India,* pp. 252–61.
265. Śūdravarga.
266. Beal, I. 82.
267. सुन्दरो चेय एस उच्छाहो। कायव्वमिणं, जुत्तमिणं, सरिसमिणं धम्मो चेय अम्हाणं, जं अउव्वं अत्थागमणं कीरइ त्ति। *KM*, p. 65.
268. *Yājña,* I. 120.
269. *Bṛhaspati Smṛti,* v. 530; *Mārkaṇḍeya Purāṇa,* 28. 3–8; *Viṣṇu Purāṇa,* III. 8. 32–3, R.S. Sharma, *Śūdras in Ancient India,* p. 267.
270. *Uśnas* qd. in *Smṛticandrikā,* I, p. 171; Devala in *Mitākṣara on Yājña,* I. 120.
271. अत्थि तुहं महं पि पुत्त-पवोत्ताणं पि विउलो अत्थ-सारो। *KM,* p. 65.
272. See urban and rural life.
273. See urban and rural life.
274. *On Manu,* VIII, 415. The old view upheld by Manu ordained that a śūdra, though able to accumulate wealth, should not do so. *Manu,* X. 129.
275. See below (p. 36).
276. *EI,* XXIV, pp. 329 f.
277. Perpetual religious endowments made by rich oil-millers and gardeners, ensuring supply of one *palikā* of oil per mill every month and 50 garlands daily, are recorded in the Vaillabhaṭasvāmin inscription of Gwalior. *EI,* I, pp. 154 f.
278. The Sīyaḍoṇī inscription records gifts of guilds of betel-sellers, oil-makers and stone-cutters to Viṣṇu Bhaṭṭāraka. *EI,* I, pp. 162 f.
279. R.S. Sharma, 'The Kali Age: A Period of Social Crisis' in D.N. Jha ed. *Feudal Social Formation in Early India,* pp. 45 f.; D.N. Jha, Presidential Address, *IHC,* 1979, pp. 20–1; B.N.S. Yadava, 'The Accounts of the Kali Age and the Social Transition from Antiquity to the Middle Ages', *IHR,* Vol. V, nos. 1–2, pp. 31 f.
280. *KM,* p. 65.
281. *KM,* p. 67.
282. *Baijavāpa,* qd. *Vīramitrodaya,* Paribhāṣā, p. 135; *Jātukarṇya,* v. 50; *Laghuviṣṇu,* v. 105.
283. Line 4, Nahar, Jaina Lekha Saṃgraha, pt. II, p. 170.
284. *On Manu,* III. 67.
285. See education.
286. The Gupta period had seen the acquisition of various religious rights by the śūdra including the right to perform the *Pañcamahāyajñas,* penances, various birth ceremonies, *śrāddha* rites, *pūjā, vrata,* right to make and worship images and the right to make gifts; R.S. Sharma, *Śūdras in Ancient India*, pp. 296 f.
287. देसु किवणाणं, विभयसु वमीणयाणं। दक्खेसु बंभणे, कारावेसु देवउले, खाणेसु तलाय-बंधे, बंधावेसु वावीओ, पालेसु सत्तायारे, पयत्तेसु आरोग्ग-सालाओ, उद्धरेसु दीण-विहले त्ति। *KM*, p. 65.

288. *Atri,* 46; *Likhita,* v. 46; *Laghuśaṃkha,* v.46.
289. Ibid., p. 844.
290. Kane, *HD,* V, pt. ii, pp. 947 f.
291. *Varāha,* 172.33; *Yama,* 68; *Atri,* 45; qd. Kane, *HD,* Vol. V, pt. ii, p. 949.
292. *KM,* p. 72.
293. आरियदेसजम्मं। तत्थ विय चण्डालडोम्बिलयरययचम्मयरसाउणियमच्छबंधाइएसु आहिण्डिऊण इक्खागाइसु कुलजम्मं। *SK,* p. 286.
294. धम्मत्थ-काम रहिया ते वि मेच्छ व्व। *KM,* p. 40.
295. *Dhū.,* V. 41.
296. *Yama,* 54; *Aṅgiras,* 3; *Atri,* 197.
297. Sachau, I, 101.
298. Cf. Kane, *HD,* Vol. II, pt. 1, pp. 169 f. Also see above, p. 17.
299. Cf. *Vasiṣṭha Dharmasūtra,* XIV, *Āpastamba Dharmasūtra,* I. 5.16–18 (N.K. Dutt, *Origin and Growth of Caste in India,* Vol. I, p. 151); *Sutta vibhanga, Pacittiya,* II.2.1 (Fick, *Social Organisation in North-Eastern India during Times of Buddha,* pp. 326–7); Beal, I.74.
300. *SK,* pp. 213, 264, 430, 705.
301. Ibid., p. 430.
302. Ibid.
303. See p. 20.
304. ता करेउ देवो पसायं, अलं अम्हाणं इमीए बुहजणगरहिणज्जाए उभयलोविरूद्धाए जीविगाए त्ति। पडिहारेण भणियं। अरे दव्वजायं पत्थेहि, किं इमेणं। खंगिलेण भणियं। अओ वि अवरं दव्वजायं ति। *SK,* p. 218.
305. *SK,* pp. 43–4, 264, 705.
306. Cf. Kane, *HD,* II, pt. 1, pp. 44, 81. According to Fahien they lived apart and on entering the city would strike on a piece of wood so that people could avoid them (Fo-kwo-ki, p. 38).
307. *Agni Purāṇa,* 151–10 f.
308. *On Manu,* V.12.
309. *On Manu,* X.51.
310. *Atri,* 288–9; *Aṅgiras* quoted by Vijñāneśvara on *Yājña.,* III.30; *Śātātapa* qd. by Aparārka on Yājña, III.292.
311. किं होइ डोंब-डिंभो पडहय-सद्दस्स उत्तसइ। *KM,* p. 38.
312. Ghurye, *Caste and Race in India,* p. 313.
313. *Bauddha gan o doha;* 19, 32 qd. R.C. Majumdar, *History of Bengal,* p. 593.
314. रायउलरययस्स विक्खाया . . . बहुधणधन्नसमिद्धं अम्ह धरं रायरिद्धिसमसरिसं।
णामेण दड्ढिआ हं णीआ गोएहिं कम्मेहिं।। *Dhū.,* V. 40–1.
315. See p. 18.
316. पावा पयंड-चंडा अणारिया णिग्घिणा निरासंसा।
धम्मो त्ति अक्खराइं णवि ते सुविणे वि जाणंति। *KM,* p. 40.
317. *KM,* p. 40.
318. Ibid., p. 2.

319. *EI*, XVIII. pp. 107 f.
320. *Manu*, II. 23.
321. *On Manu*, II. 23.
322. *SK*, p. 420.
323. Ibid., p. 537.
324. *KM*, p. 28.
325. Ibid., p. 135.
326. पत्त-साड-समइं हत्थ-पाय-छेज्जइं, अंदोलय-हेला-सरिसइं उब्बंधणइं, सीहासण-सुहइं सूलारोवणइं, अंगवालिया-करइं करि-चलण-चमढणइं। Ibid., p. 112.
327. ण भणंति कूड-सक्खेजं, ण लुंपंति अप्प-धण्णं पुरिसं, ण मुसंति महिलियं। *KM*, p. 146.
328. दुट्टु-घोट्ट-जइसउं बंभणु-मारियव्वउ . . . पुरोडासु-जइसओ सुरा-पाणु, ओंकारो जइसओ चोर-विण्णाणु। गायत्ति-जइसओ बहिणि-गालि। जहिं च सवहइं माइं से भहिणिं से पइं मारेमि तओ लोहिउं पियमि त्ति। Ibid., p. 112.
329. गवलजलयवणा वेल्लिबद्धुद्धकेसहारा वक्कलद्धनिवसणा कणियकोडण्डवावडग्गहत्था सुणयवन्द्रसंगया . . . सबरजुवाणय। *SK*, p. 415. Similar descriptions of their settlements and habits are to be found in other literary works. See *Niśītha Cūrṇi*, 15, p. 1110; *Kādambarī*, p. 32; *Harṣacarita*, pp. 231–2; Trans. Cowell, pp. 230–2.
330. *SK*, p. 423.
331. Ibid., p. 435.
332. Ibid.
333. Ibid., p. 480.
334. *KM*, pp. 132–3.
335. Ibid., p. 112.
336. *SK*, p. 654.
337. Ibid., pp. 415 f.
338. कलधोय-धोय-सिहर-सरिसाइं वण-करि-महादंत-संचयइं . . . तण-मह-क्खल-समइं च दिट्ठाइं चारु-चमरी-पुच्छ-पब्भारइं। *KM*, p. 112.
339. *Āvaśyaka Cūrṇi*, II, p. 296; J.C. Jain, *Life in Ancient India as Depicted in the Jaina Canons*, p. 100.
340. *KM*, p. 135.
341. Ibid., p. 61.
342. *SK*, pp. 420, 537.
343. Ibid., pp. 420, 535.
344. Ibid., p. 98.
345. सवरेहिं अवणीओ जणो आसि। सो निरवसेसो अखण्डियचरित्तसव्वस्सो महया दविणजाएण मुक्को। *SK*, p. 98.
346. Ibid., p. 547.
347. *SK*, pp. 547 f.
348. Hultzch, *ZDMG*, XL, pp. 38 f., qd. D. Sharma, *ECD*, p. 19.
349. Ibid.
350. *EI*, XVIII, pp. 107 f.

351. *JRAS*, 1895, pp. 513 f.
352. *KM*, p. 133.
353. *SK*, p. 797.
354. सो साहिउं न सक्कइ उवमारहियंमि तत्थ रणंमि। ते दिन्ति तत्थ उवमा पत्थरगुहरुक्खमालेसु। *SK*, p. 801.
355. सबर-सेणावइ-पुत्तो सुसेणो णाम।... मालव-णरिंद-विजयत्थं गओ।... राइणा वि 'आसणं आसणं' ति आइसमाणेण पसारिय-दीहर-दाहिण-भुया-दंड-कोमल-करयलेणं उत्तिमंगे छिविऊण संमाणिओ। *KM*, p. 9.
356. *Arthaśāstra*, VII. 14. According to the *Hitopadeśa* and *Kāmandakīya Nītiśāstra*, the forces of the *āṭavikas* or foresters were cruel, rapacious and hardy, and therefore best suited to lead an attack. *Hitopadeśa* III. 96; VIII. 23.
357. See feudalism.
358. पुलिंद-रायउत्तं उवविट्ठं। *KM*, p. 50.
359. अहो, इमिणा मह पुलिंदेण परिहओ कओ। ताव जीवियं जाव इमाणं परिभवं सहिज्जइ त्ति। *KM*, p. 51.
360. I. 12–13, 440.
361. *KM*, p. 136, see above, p. 18.
362. *Atri*, 267–9.
363. According to R.S. Sharma (*Śūdras in Ancient India*, pp. 339–40), large-scale land grants to brāhmaṇas during the fourth-seventh centuries in peripheral, backward areas played a significant part in the assimilation of tribals into the social order.
364. R.S. Sharma, *Perspectives in Social and Economic History of Early India*, p. 32; Idem, *Śūdras in Ancient India*, Appendix I & II.
365. *KM*, p. 9, see above.
366. Ibid., p. 50, see above.
367. *SK*, pp. 654 f., see below.
368. Āṭpur inscription of Śaktikumāra, *IA*, XXXIX, 191f.
369. *Kānhaḍade Prabandha;* qd. D. Sharma, *RTTA*, p. 440.
370. *KM*, p. 40.
371. *Yama*, 54; *Aṅgiras*, 3; *Atri*, 197.
372. R.S. Sharma, *Śūdras in Ancient India*, p. 338.
373. *On Manu*, II.23.
374. Kakkuka took Rohiṃsakūpa from the Ābhiras; Nāgabhaṭa defeated the Kirātas. See above, p. 41.
375. *SK*, pp. 564, 566.
376. Ibid., pp. 654 f., 679.
377. Cf. Romila Thapar, 'Image of the Barbarian', in *Ancient Indian Social History*, pp. 176–8. The Yavana Heliodorous was a Bhāgvata (D.C. Sircar, ed., *Select Inscriptions*, I, pp. 90–1). The Junagarh inscription represents Rudradāman as a Sanskrit scholar and protector of varṇas (D.C. Sircar, ed., *Select Inscriptions*, I, pp. 172–4). Nahapāna's son-in-law Uṣavadāta

bathed at Pushkara and made liberal donations (Nasik Cave inscription, *EI*, VIII, p. 178). Mihirakula was a Śaiva. Verse 6, Mandasore inscription of Yaśodharman (*Select Inscriptions*, op. cit., p. 394).

378. See religion.

379. जे होंति णिरणुकंपा वाहा तह कूर-कम्मा-वाउरिया ।
केवट्टा सोणहिया . . . गाम-महाणयर-सत्थ घाया य ।
एए करेंति कम्मं मह कुल-णीइ त्ति णिच्छिय-मईया ।
अवरे भणंति वित्ती अम्हाण कया पयावइणा ।। *KM*, pp. 35–6.

3

Sāmantas and Development of Feudal Ties in Society

SĀMANTA, A TERM which in the *Arthaśāstra* of Kauṭilya[1] was used in the sense of 'independent neighbour', had come to be used in the sense of a vassal from the fifth century onwards.[2] Numerous vassals served the Vardhana empire in the seventh century.[3] The *sāmanta* system was widely prevalent in the eighth century AD, with Pratihāras, Pālas and Rāṣṭrakūṭas, the three important dynasties of India, having well organised feudal polities.[4] For the Pratihāra rulers of Rajasthan, who must have well realised the difficulties involved in exerting direct administrative control over distant regions situated far and wide amidst the inhospitable deserts of Rajasthan, ruling through the help of feudatory rulers must have held even greater appeal than for others.

Prākrit sources faithfully reflect contemporary conditions when the lord-vassal nexus was firmly established and the *sāmantas* had emerged as an influential section of society. *Sāmanta-nivaha-nata-caraṇa*,[5] *sāmanta-praṇata-caraṇa*[6] and *aneka-sāmanta-praṇipatita-caraṇa-yugala*,[7] one at whose feet bowed numerous *sāmantas*, are the normal epithets they apply to a prosperous ruler, which clearly indicates the importance attached to the class of vassals. Various grades of vassals appear to have existed. Thus our works mention not only *sāmantas* but *mahāsāmantas*,[8] and *pradhānasāmantas*,[9] who were obviously feudatories of a higher rank than the *sāmantas*. The *Kuvalayamālā* refers to feudatory rulers called *narendras*, who recognised king Dṛḍhavarman as their *svāmin* (lord).[10] Attending the court of the same ruler, we read in another context, were *mahānarendras*,[11] whose comparison with Karṇa, the legendary hero of the *Mahābhārata*, who received the kingdom of Aṅga from Duryodhana, strongly suggests that they too were subordinate rulers. That *sāmantas* formed an integral part of contemporary polity is evident also from inscriptions. The foremost ruling dynasty of Rajasthan, the Imperial Pratihāras, had under them several feudatories such as the Guhilas of Cāṭsū (Jaipur state), Cālukyas of Saurashtra, the Cāhamānas of Śakambharī (Jaipur) and the Pratihāras of Mandor.[12] Bālāditya's Cāṭsū inscription (*c.* tenth century) describes Guhila II, a feudatory of either Bhoja or Mahendrapāla I, as a devoted follower of his *svāmin* or master.[13]

Attendance of *sāmantas* at the king's court was a regular feature.[14] Mention is made of their participation in the various social and religious activities of the ruler. They accompanied him when he went to pay his respects to Jaina saints,[15] when he went on a riding excursion through the city,[16] and when he went for initiation into the Jaina order of monks.[17] In time of war, they are said to have accompanied the overlord in his military expedition against his enemy.[18] The inscriptions of the period record several historical instances where military service was rendered to the sovereign by his feudatories. Thus the Cāṭsū inscription of Bālāditya,[19] Jodhpur inscription of Bauka (AD 837)[20] and Ūnā (Kathiawar) grant of Avanivarman (AD 899),[21] show that their ancestors, viz., Śaṅkaragaṇa, Kakka and Vāhukadhavala respectively, played an important part in the wars of their feudal overlord Nāgabhaṭa II against Dharmapāla of Bengal.[22] The Cāṭsū inscription states that Śaṅkaragaṇa defeated the Gauḍa, in spite of the latter's strong elephant force, and made the land serve his overlord like a slave girl captured in battle.[23]

As regards the position of the *sāmantas* vis-a-vis the king, Uddyotana's simile between the bending low of trees full of flowers and the bowing of *sāmantas*[24] clearly underlines their subordinate status. Haribhadra refers to them as dependents of the king, albeit the foremost among them.[25] That they were under obligation to render homage, court attendance and military service to the overlord may be inferred from the account already given above. But it may also be remarked that notwithstanding the position of subordination held by them, the very nature of the services they were made to render to the sovereign appears to have helped them to gain a position of importance in the administration, especially so when the centre was weak. Being present right at the court, they were able to influence court decisions and play a vital role in matters like succession. As the military success of the sovereign depended on them to a large extent, their pride and power increased considerably. Sufficient evidence of this increasing power is to be found in our works. The *Samarāiccakahā* gives the *sāmantamaṇḍala* (the body of *sāmantas*) the credit for putting prince Jaya on the throne after the death of his father.[26] In the same work we read of the powerful *sāmanta* Durmati, who, proud of his military strength and possessions, rose in rebellion against his overlord.[27] It is significant that Haribhadra describes a prosperous kingdom as one in which the *sāmantamaṇḍala* is devoted to the ruler[28] and that such a kingdom is further described as free from all sources of nuisance.[29] Obviously the *sāmantas* could prove to be a source of vexation if disaffected. How necessary their coopera-tion was considered to be can be seen also from the fact that disregard of the *sāmantas* is enumerated amongst the signs that forebode the loss of one's kingdom in the *Samarāiccakahā*.[30] The high titles held by cer-tain Pratihāra feudatories reflect their high status. Bhartṛvaḍḍha II of Broach was a *Paramamāheśvara samadhigatapañcamahāśabda-mahāsāmantādhipati*,[31] Undabhaṭa of Sīyaḍoṇī was a *Mahāpratihāra-samadhigataśeṣamahāśabda-mahāsāmantādhipati*.[32] Epigraphic evi-dence reveals that while some feudatories made grants with the sanctions of the king, others did so on their own initiative.[33]

As long as the *sāmantas* fulfilled their obligations towards him, the king treated them with regard and took every step to ensure their conti-nuing goodwill and cooperation. The *Kuvalayamālā* speaks of gifts of chariots being made to the *mahāsāmantas* on the occasion of the birth of prince Kuvalayacandra.[34] In the *Samarāiccakahā* when the marriage of a prince is fixed, the *sāmantas* along with the towns-people are instantly informed of the happy event, on the advice of the ministers.[35] Later, mention is made of the *sāmantas* being honoured when the *pāṇi-grahaṇa* ceremony is performed.[36] We read of the king honouring his *sāmantas* also when he goes for initiation, putting his successor on the throne.[37] They were assigned an important role in the *rājyābhiṣeka* and *yauvarājyābhiṣeka* ceremonies. Led by the king, the *Kuvalayamālā* tells us, they would pour scented water from golden pitchers on the heir-apparent, shouting 'Victory to the Yuvarāja', as part of the coronation ceremony of the heir-apparent.[38] A similar besprinkling ceremony by the *sāmantas*, we learn from the *Samarāiccakahā*, marked the corona-tion ceremony of a new ruler, with the erstwhile monarch expressly calling upon the assembled *sāmantas* to recognise his successor as king thenceforth.[39] By intimately associating them with the coronation ceremonies, the king must have sought to gain their cooperation and thereby secure a peaceful succession. Even *sāmantas*, who chose to rebel against the overlord, the *Samarāiccakahā* tells us, if repentant when vanquished, were graciously forgiven and shown great respect.[40] The ties between the overlord and *sāmantas* were at times further strengthened by matrimonial alliances. Thus in the *Samarāiccakahā* we read of the marriage of the prince being arranged with the daughter of his maternal uncle, the *mahāsāmanta* Lakṣmīkānta.[41] Epigraphic evidence reveals that Bhartṛvaḍḍha II of Broach,[42] feudatory of Nāgabhaṭa I, as well as Undabhaṭa of Sīyaḍoṇī[43] and Balavarman of Saurashtra,[44] feudatories of Mahendrapāla I, had been rewarded by their suzerains with the privilege of *pañcamahāśabda*, which denoted the use of the five musical instruments, *śṛṅga, śaṃkha, bherī, jayaghaṇṭā* and *tammaṭa*.[45] According to the *Pṛthvīrājavijaya*, Gūvaka II, Cāhamāna of Śakambharī, gave his sister Kalāvatī in marriage to the 'paramount' sovereign of Kānyakubja, identifiable with Bhoja.[46]

Through their close association and mutual dependence there grew a special bond between the king and *sāmanta*, leading them to regard each other as *sambhandins* or kinsmen, even though unrelated by ties of kinship or marriage. Thus in the *Samarāiccakahā* we find that when the frontier chief Vigraha rebels the prince marches against him but restrains his followers from taking stringent measures, saying, 'This Vigraha is an insignificant chief. But he has been paying tribute to my father and therefore is our kinsman. Therefore no precipitate military action is to be taken against him.'[47] And when the defeated Vigraha offers to serve the prince, we see the latter addressing him thus 'Do not say so, as the *bhṛtya* (liegeman) of my father, you are my elder brother. So if you like, go and see my father.'[48] How strong the bond created by allegiance was can be seen further from the fact that the overlord appears to have felt it obligatory to render help to the vassal when he was in trouble, even if the cause of the latter was not quite justifiable. Thus in the *Samarāiccakahā*[49] when the Śabara chief who had accepted the overlordship of prince Kumārasena was attacked by soldiers who came to punish him for his previous misdeeds, the prince helped his vassal saying, 'He has become my liegeman. Hence, even though he has been doing reprehensible things, I cannot be indifferent when he engages in fight.'

This feeling of feudal kinship appears to have permeated also the relationship between vassals owing allegiance to the same overlord. Thus a Śabara chief who just a moment ago had been plundering the caravan of the vaiśya Sānudeva, after having been defeated by the prince who accompanied the caravan and accepted the latter's overlordship, addresses the same vaiśya thus: O noble one, we did not know that this great man accompanied you. We have been vanquished by him and recognise him as our overlord. Hence you are our kinsman (*sambhandin*) and we cannot loot your property.[50] Sānudeva too at once recognised the new relationship saying, 'with the *āryaputra* (the prince) as my *svāmin* and you as my kinsman, what is there that I do not have.'[51] That a vaiśya could acknowledge an aboriginal Śabara chief, whose social status was far inferior to his, as a kinsman without hesitation just because they both had a common overlord shows that the bonds of feudal kinship were so strong that they set the ground for a new set of social relationships which had no place for caste prejudices. It may however be noted that these bonds must have taken root and flourished only where the control of the central authority was strong. Had it been otherwise, no *sāmanta* would have ever rebelled.

On the basis of the evidence of our Prākrit sources, the growth of feudal relationships during our period may be traced to the practice of converting vanquished princes into tributary vassals and the practice of assigning land grants in lieu of military service. Thus the *Kuvalaya-mālā* speaks of *karapālaśikhā-nirjita-sāmantas* or *sāmantas* vanquished by the might of the sword, who offered homage at the feet of the king Dṛḍhavarman.[52] This evidence may be set beside the account of the ninth century Arab traveller Sulaiman who writes: 'When a king subdues a neighbouring state he places over it a man belonging to the family of the fallen prince, who carries on the government in the name of the conqueror.'[53] Medhātithi recommends installation of a scion of the fallen royal family if it continued to command the loyalty of the people on condition that he shared his income with his sovereign, consulting the latter in all matters as well as helping him with treasury and force.[54]

The practice of granting land in return of military service may be inferred from the story of Kṣetrabhaṭa in the *Kuvalayamālā*. Kṣetrabhaṭa was an old *ṭhakkura* who having fallen on evil days began the *avalagā* of the ruler of Ujjayainī. In return for his services the king bestowed on him the prosperous village of Kūpavrinda where he resided. As times passed, the old *ṭhakkura*, with his limbs bearing the marks of wounds inflicted by the swords of opposing warriors in hundreds of battles, and his age telling on his body, lost the strength to render active service. He thereupon put his son, Vīrabhaṭa in the king's service, and himself sat at home. In due course Śaktibhaṭa, the son of Vīrabhaṭa, continued the service, attending the king's court, where a special seat was reserved for him. This Śaktibhaṭa is described as quick to draw his sword,[55] which may be said to be an act of feudal vanity. It would appear from the above account that the *avalagā* or *olagā* rendered by the *ṭhakkura* was some kind of personal and military service which was rewardable by a grant of land. It may be taken to be hereditary since the son and grandson of the *ṭhakkura* are said to have continued the service after him.[56] The use of *olagā* in the sense of military service can be seen in yet another context in the *Kuvalayamālā* where we read of two *vaṇikputras* who tried to gain a livelihood through *olagā*, but being ill-fated were captured in war.[57] A Jaina saint who appeared in the vicinity later, advised them to render *olagā* to *Sarvajña* (the omniscient, i.e., Jina) and battle with the *indriya* (sense-organs) foes wielding the sword of *tapa* (austerity).[58] In the *Samarāiccakahā*, where the rebel named Vigraha, on being vanquished by the prince offers to render *olagā* to him,[59] we may discern the sense of feudal service. As these are the earliest instances of the use of the word *olagā* in Rajasthan, which occurs in the present sense of personal and military feudal service in various later Rājasthānī texts and Rājasthānī folk songs,[60] they represent an important stage in the development of feudal relations. In the *Samarāiccakahā* too, we come across *ṭhakkuras*, who engage in battle with a Śabara chief and capture him at the orders of their ruler.[61] It also speaks of *grāmas* (villages), *ākaras* (mines) and *maṇḍabas* (towns) being distributed among the *rājaputras* who successfully secured the territory (*viṣaya*) belonging to the rebel ruler Vigraha.[62] The Kāhlā (U.P.) plates refer to the grant of land in Gorakhpur by Bhoja to a Kalacuri chief called Gunaṃbodhideva who had taken away by force the royal fortune of Gauḍa.[63] From Bihar, we have the earliest available epigraphic evidence of the use of the word 'avalagna' in the Dūdhpāni inscription, assignable again to the eighth century AD,[64] the same as the Prākrit works.

The instance of the two *vaṇikputras*, who took up *olagā* when they failed to earn a living by other means of livelihood, mentioned in the *Kuvalayamālā*, as referred to above,[65] further indicates that sometimes people entered into feudal ties due to personal compulsions, in this case economic, rendering service in exchange for subsistence. The Dūdhapāni inscription which records that the people of three villages made the merchant Udayamāna their chief (*rājā*) with the king's consent, as he had at their request rendered *avalagna* to the king on their behalf,[66] also suggests the evidence of commendation of some sorts.

It is evident from the above that the *sāmantas* formed an integral part of contemporary polity. This is indicated by constant references to rulers surrounded by subordinate *sāmantas* and existence of various ranks of *sāmantas* including *mahāsāmantas* and *pradhānasāmantas* constituting an influential section of society. They rendered military service to the sovereign, paid tribute, attended court and took part in the socio-religious activities of the ruler. Their position was theoretically one of subordination, but as powerful *sāmantas* amassed considerable territory, some became proud and intractable and even strove to overthrow the control of the central authority. They played a decisive role in obtaining a secure succession for rulers and their cooperation was considered to be imperative for the stability of the kingdom.

Rulers honoured them and presented them gifts on occasions of royal festivities at the time of birth and marriage. They had a conspicuous part to play in coronation ceremonies and their friendship with the ruler was sometimes cemented with matrimonial alliances. As the idea of feudal kinship developed the overlord and vassal on one hand and co-vassals on the other hand started regarding themselves as relatives of each other. The class of *sāmantas* comprised defeated rulers as well as *ṭhakkuras* and *rājaputras* who were granted land by the sovereign in return of military service. *Olagā* was a new term standing for a kind of feudal military service which was rewarded by a grant of land and sometimes entered upon by some because of economic compulsion, indicating an important stage in the development of feudal relations. Diverse classes such as kṣatriyas, vaiśyas and ṭribals were drawn within the vortex of feudal relations, so that a privileged class drawn from various sections of society came into being.

Notes and References

1. *Arthaśāstra,* I. 6.
2. R.S. Sharma, *Indian Feudalism,* pp. 24 f.
3. Bāṇa in the *Harṣacarita* refers to *sāmantas, mahāsāmantas, pradhānasāmantas, āptasāmantas, pratisāmantas and śatrumahāsāmantas.* V.S. Agrawala, *Harṣacarita Ek Sāṃskritika Adhyayana,* pp. 217–18.
4. R.S. Sharma, op. cit., Chapter II.
5. *KM,* p. 9.
6. Ibid., p. 73.
7. *SK,* pp. 11, 61.
8. *KM,* pp. 18, 24, 200; *SK,* pp. 63, 400, 789.
9. *SK,* pp. 397, 692, 769, 803.
10. *KM,* p. 209.

11. उवविट्ठा कण्ण-णरिंदस्स व महाणरिंदा। Ibid., p. 16.
12. See below.
13. *EI*, XII, p. 15, svāminiṣṭaḥ.
14. *KM*, pp. 9, 27, 188, 200; *SK*, pp. 243, 799.
15. *SK*, p. 789.
16. *KM*, p. 24.
17. *KM*, pp. 209, 211; *SK*, pp. 685, 692, 769.
18. सामन्तेहि समेओ। *SK*, p. 573.
19. *EI*, XII, pp. 10–17.
20. *EI*, XVIII, pp. 95 f.
21. *EI*, IX, pp. 6–10.
22. D. Sharma, *RTTA*, p. 141.
23. *EI*, XII, pp. 10–17.
24. सामन्ता इव पणया रुक्खा बहु-कुसुम-भारेण। *KM*, p. 51.
25. सामन्तप्पमुहाणमणुजीवीणं। *SK*, p. 243.
26. अहिसित्तो रज्जंमि सामन्तमण्डलेण जयकुमारो। Ibid., p. 396.
27. दुम्मई नाम सामन्तराया दुग्गभूमिबलगव्विओ वित्थक्को सीहरायस्स। Ibid., p. 121.
28. अणुरत्तसामन्तमण्डलो। Ibid., pp. 116, 689.
29. रहियं कण्टएहिं। Ibid., p. 689.
30. . . . अवमाणिया सामन्ता। *SK*, p. 569.
31. Hānsoṭ plates, AD 756, *EI*, XII, p. 202.
32. Sīyaḍoṇi Inscription, Grant of AD 907, *EI*, I, pp. 169, 173.
33. *EI*, IX, no. I, R.S. Sharma, *Indian Feudalism*, p. 90.
34. उवणिज्जंति महासामंताणं गुरु-चक्क-णेमी-घणघणाराव-बहिरिय-दिसिवहाओ हारि-रहवर-णियर-पत्थारीओ। *KM*, p. 18.
35. . . . पयासियं सामन्तनायराणं। *SK*, p. 518.
36. निवत्तो हत्थग्गहो। सम्माणिया सामन्ता। *SK*, p. 520.
37. Ibid., pp. 596, 768.
38. *KM*, p. 200.
39. *SK*, p. 397.
40. अभय दाऊण बहुमाणिओ राइणा, कओ से अहिययरसक्कारो। Ibid., p. 124.
41. Ibid., pp. 63 f.
42. Hānsoṭ plates, AD 756, *EI*, XII, p. 202.
43. Sīyaḍoṇi Inscription grant of AD 907, *EI*, I, pp. 162 f.
44. Ūnā Inscription of AD 893, *EI*, IX, pp. 1 f.
45. A.S. Altekar, *Rāṣṭrakūṭas and Their Times*, p. 263. He gives the explanation on the basis of the work of Jaina writer, Revakopayachara.
46. D. Sharma, *ECD*, p. 30.
47. अप्पो य एसो विग्गहो भुत्तो य ताएणं ठिओ संबन्धिपक्खे। ता न जुत्तमेयंमि एगपए पोरुसं दंसेउं। *SK*, p. 635; D. Sharma, *RTTA*, p. 340.
48. मा एवं भण, तायभिच्चो तुमं मम जेट्ठभाउगो। ता जइ भवओ वि बहुमयं, ता तायसयासं चेव गच्छसु त्ति। *SK*, p. 639; D. Sharma, op. cit.
49. पडिवन्नभिच्चभावो य एसो। ता जइवि अजुत्तयारी, तहावि न जुतमेयंमि पयट्टे उयासीणयं भाविउं त्ति। Ibid., p. 547; D. Sharma, op. cit., p. 339.

50. अज्ज, न विन्नायं अम्हेहिं, जहा एसो महापुरिसो इह गच्छइ त्ति। विणिज्जिया य णेण अम्हे। महाणुभावयाए पडिवन्नो य एस अम्मेहिं सामी। अओ संबन्धिओ तुमं ति। *SK*, p. 539; D. Sharma, op. cit., p. 339.
51. भद्द, सामिसालंमि अज्जउत्ते तुमंमि य संबन्धिए किं मम नत्थि त्ति। Ibid., p. 540; D. Sharma, op. cit.
52. करवाल-सिहा-णिज्जिय-महंत-सामंत-णिवह-णय-चलणो। *KM*, p. 9.
53. *ED*, I, p. 7.
54. *On Manu*, VII, 201–2.
55. *KM*, p. 50.
56. Ibid.
57. . . . लग्गा ओलग्गिउं इमे दो वि। तत्थ वि एसो जाओ संगामो पाडिया बद्धा। Ibid.. p. 191.
58. ओल्लगह सव्वण्णु इंदिय-रिउ-डामरेहिं जुज्झसु य। तव-कड्ढिय-करवाला जइ कज्जं सिद्धि-णयरीए। *KM*, p. 193.
59. करेउ देवा पसायं मम ओलग्गाए। *SK*, p. 639.
60. *Bharateśvara-Bāhubali-rāsa*, twelfth century; *Kāṇhaḍadeprabandha* AD 1385; *Payāḍā Nihāl-de-sultan; Dhola mārūrā Dūhā*, etc.; D. Sharma, 'The Feudal term "Avalagā" or "olagā" ', *Journal of the Ganganatha Jha Kendriya Sanskrit Vidyapitha*, XXVIII, pt. 1–2, pp. 608–10.
61. *SK*, p. 548.
62. विइणाइं गामागरमडम्बाइ रायपुत्ताण। Ibid., p. 635.
63. *Bhojadevāptabhūmiḥ-EI*, VII, pp. 85 f.
64. *EI*, II, pp. 345 ff.
65. *KM*, p. 191; See vaiśyas above.
66. *EI*, II, pp. 345 ff.

4

Family, Marriage and Position of Women

As IN EARLIER centuries, the joint family system and patriarchal organisation of society continued to be the characteristic features of our times. The *Kuvalayamālā* shows that the importance of the son was many-sided and the birth of a son was very much desired. Popular sayings like *aputrasya gatir nāsti*, a sonless person has no refuge, are quoted therein.[1] Even a good dynasty, towering high above others like a mighty tree atop the lofty peaks of the mount Meru, it is said, was liable to be uprooted by enemies who attacked it with the fury of the destruction time (*pralaya*) winds, for the want of a son, who would have strengthened, at it were, its very roots.[2] His birth, we learn, was a religious necessity, as he alone was considered to be entitled to the offering of water and funeral cakes to the ancestors.[3] The man endowed with valour, learning, and riches, but bereft of a son, was considered to be akin to a tree famed for its flowers but fruitless.[4] Such an attitude is hardly surprising as the son had been assigned a special position since early times.[5] The water and funeral cakes (*piṇḍa*) offered by him to the ancestors were deemed to be so efficacious that the *Viṣṇu Dharmaśāstra, Mahābhārata* and *Matsyapurāṇa* say that one should desire many sons in the hope that one of them may repair to the Ganga.[6]

Great reverence was shown to the father as well as other elders in the family. The son would offer salutations at the feet of his father,[7] mother,[8] elder brother,[9] and sister.[10] For him his mother was like Sāvitrī, Sarasvatī, Ganga and Prithvī (earth).[11] The newly anointed prince Jaya, whose mother came to plead for the life of his younger brother Vijaya, who had been taken into custody to prevent his making trouble, immediately called for his brother and installed him as ruler in his own place.[12] His mother thereupon declaring that she was now as apprehensive about his safety as she had been before for Vijaya's life, he resolved to become a monk, and both mother and son entered the order together.[13] When the mother of another ruler, who was a believer in *ahiṃsā* (non-violence), insisted that he immolate a number of animals to ward off evil consequences, he sacrificed a cock made of paste to please her,[14] though in principle he was against such an act too.

A married son usually continued to live with his father, mother, brothers and sisters.[15] In the absence of his father, he would be expected to shoulder the responsibilities of the household, behave like a father towards his unwed sister and arrange for her marriage.[16] There are instances of cordial relationship between the different members of the family, between the wife and her husband's people, and brothers and sisters. In the *Samarāiccakahā*, we read how a widowed sister was well looked after by her brothers after the death of their parents. They permitted her to spend large sums on the building of a temple, despite the grumbling of their wives.[17] An affectionate mother-in-law addressed her daughter-in-law as *putrī*.[18] On perceiving that her daughter-in-law wished to accompany her husband on his journey she sympathised with her and prevailed upon her son to take his wife along.[19] But the mention of *sāsuvikatthana*, i.e. ironical remarks of a mother-in-law amongst the five causes of a woman's anger[20] shows that dissensions between the two were not unknown. Sometimes brothers could not get on together, as the *Samarāiccakahā* shows, in this case the younger brother feeling jealous of the elder one, as he was the heir-apparent, and this would lead to separation of the two.[21]

Marriage was regarded as an important institution of family life which enabled one to fulfil his worldly duty by obtaining offspring and perpetuating the family-line.[22] The main factors taken into consideration by the bride's father before arranging a marriage were, according to our works, the age, family, learning, wealth, looks, virtues, and nature of the bridegroom.[23] Marriage with families of equal status was preferred.[24] These qualifications are the same as recommended for scrutiny by various later Smṛtis.[25]

The *Samarāiccakahā* further mentions the desirability of marriage between co-religionists. Bandhudeva asked for the hand of Sarvāṅgasundarī. Her father approved of him but would not agree to the wedding as he was not a co-religionist (*sadhārmika*). Bandhudeva therefore allowed himself to be converted and feigned great zeal for the new faith, whereupon he gained consent for marriage.[26] In Jineśvara's *Kathākośa*-

prakaraṇa also we read of a marriage proposal being considered unsuitable because while the boy's father was a Jaina, the bride's father happened to be a Buddhist.[27]

Marriages were generally arranged between members of the same caste.[28] But *anuloma* marriages, i.e., marriages of males of higher castes with females of lower ones were not unknown. In the *Kuvalayamālā* we read of a king's marriage with a merchant's daughter.[29] Avantisundarī, the wife of the brāhmaṇa poet Rājaśekhara, was a kṣatriya, as we learn from the *Karpūramañjarī* which refers to her as the crest-garland of the Cāhamāna family.[30] The Jodhpur inscription of Bauka (AD 837) states that one of the wives of Haricandra, the brāhmaṇa founder of the family, was a kṣatriya.[31] According to Ibn Khurdadba (died AD 912) the brāhmaṇas could take the daughters of kṣatriyas, though they did not give their daughters to kṣatriyas.[32] The evidence of the Dharmaśāstras indicates how while some *anuloma* marriages continued to take place, intercaste marriages were gradually going out of vogue.[33] The commentary of Medhātithi suggests that marriages of brāhmaṇas with kṣatriya and vaiśya girls took place rarely in his days, but not with śūdra women.[34] While Manu had ordained that sons begotten by twice-born men on wives of the next lower order belonged to their father's caste,[35] the view that the progeny of *anuloma* marriages is of the mother's *varṇa* presented by Medhātithi[36] reflects the unfavourable attitude adopted towards these marriages.

Another restriction imposed by the Smṛti writers was on *sapiṇḍa* marriages, i.e., marriage between those who were related to each other within seven generations on the father's side and five generations on the mother's side.[37] But that marriages amongst maternal cousins were not unknown is evident from the *Samarāiccakahā* which contains instances of marriage with a maternal uncle's daughter.[38] Such references are also to be found in the *Upamitibhavaprapañcākathā*, a tenth century work from Rajasthan.[39] The prevalence of such a custom is noted by the *Baudhāyana Dharmasūtra*[40] and Medhātithi,[41] which however choose to condemn it, the former classifying it as a South Indian practice. Recognised as a Rajput custom,[42] it has been regarded as a result of the impact and subsequent absorption of the northern people with some southern people, among whom cross-cousin marriages were prevalent.[43]

Arranged marriages were the order of the day. Contemporary literature is no doubt replete with instances of heroes and heroines falling in love with each other but the couples do not contemplate marriage without their father's consent. Their marriages take place only when the initiative in the matter is taken by the parents from either side sometimes after perceiving the attachment of their children,[44] and sometimes perchance.[45] The importance attached to the approval of parents and sacramental marriage is well brought out in the *Kuvalayamālā* where prince Kuvalayacandra though madly in love with princess Kuvalayamālā, keeps his distance from her, even though he has won her hand in open *svayaṃavara*, as the nuptial ceremonies have yet to be performed. 'A maiden with whom the *pāṇigrahaṇa* (holding the hand) ceremony has not been performed in the presence of the elders, Gods and the brāhmaṇas', he told his friend, 'I do regard as a dreadful blazing pyre', and the latter commended his statement as one befitting his noble descent.[46] Devala lays down that even in *gāndharva* marriages the ritual should be performed after the union.[47] Medhātithi disfavours *gāndharva* marriages because they lack a sacramental character and stresses the necessity of performance of rites.[48]

The reference to *Svayaṃvarapariṇītā bhāryā* (wife married in *svayaṃvara*) of Dṛḍhavarman[49] and the description of the *svayaṃvara* of Kuvalayamālā by Uddyotana[50] shows that the ancient practice of *svayaṃvara* was still prevalent in royal families. The *svayaṃvara* of Kuvalayamālā was in the form of a contest of poetic skill, in which the princes exhibited in public an incomplete verse which the suitor was to complete. The correct solution was kept in the treasury for verification.[51] The *Pṛthvīrājavijaya* speaks of the sister of Gūvaka II, Kalāvatī, who had twelve suitors for her hand, besides the ruler of Kannauj, probably Bhoja I (vs 893–950), to whom she was eventually married.[52] According to the *Dvayāśrayamahākāvya*, the two sisters of Mahendra of Nāḍol (*c*. eleventh century) chose their husbands in a *svayaṃvara*.[53]

Polygamy seems to be quite the accepted practice amongst the affluent sections of society. In the *Samarāiccakahā*, Mahārāja Khadgasena sends two of his daughters to be married to prince Samarāditya.[54] In the *Kuvalayamālā* a queen perceives her husband falling in love with another girl at first sight. She herself summons the girl's father and arranges her marriage with the king. Some days later the king sees the portrait of another girl and proceeds to secure her hand as well.[55] Elsewhere *śreṣṭhiputra* Sāgaradatta is said to have married two girls in the course of his voyages abroad while he already has a wife at home.[56] In the *Karpūramañjarī*, the queen of king Caṇḍapāla arranges for the second marriage of her husband led by the belief that he would thereby become an emperor, even though she is a jealous wife.[57] The Jodhpur inscription of Bauka speaks of the two marriages of Haricandra, the brāhmaṇa founder of the Pratihāra line of Mandor.[58] Devala says that a śūdra may have only one wife, the vaiśya two, a kṣatriya three and a brāhmaṇa four but a king may have as many as he desires.[59] The great spiritual importance of sons, early marriages and consequent illiteracy of women appear to have encouraged the practice.[60] It was also a luxury which only the richer sections of society could afford. The poorer sections of society could not possibly maintain a large family. This accounts for the higher incidence of polygamy among the rich and the royalty.

The majority of girls and boys from aristocratic and wealthy families were married at a mature age. 'She attained puberty (*prāptā yauvanam*) and was married' is the standard description pertaining to girls from these families in the *Samarāiccakahā*.[61] The instances of love marriages and *svayaṃvaras*[62] confirm that girls were grown up brides at the time of marriage. But early marriages were also prevalent. The *Samarāiccakahā* speaks of Vīramatī, the daughter of Vinītaseṭṭhi, who was a child widow.[63] The *Karpūramañjarī* speaks of *bālaraṇḍās* (child-widows) who beguiled themselves with the sweetmeats of wishes.[64] The prevalence of pre-puberty marriages among brāhmaṇas is attested to by the *Kuvalayamālā* which relates how a brāhmaṇa boy and girl, after marriage, gradually attained puberty, the girl thereupon attracting the eyes of the village youth.[65] The later Smṛtis and Medhātithi unanimously support pre-puberty marriages.[66] The ramifications of the caste system which limited the scope of finding a bridegroom, prevalence of *satī* which raised the possibility of the girl losing both her parents at one stroke, and the joint family system which made it unnecessary for the husband to be an earning member at the time of marriage have been regarded as some of the factors which encouraged the parents to see their daughters well settled early in life.[67] Attention has also been drawn to the religious insistence on the necessity of progeny, the insistence on and desire to ensure pre-marriage chastity and the girl's position as an economic liability for her parents which may also have encouraged this custom.[68] In the case of the warrior class, it has been pointed out, life was uncertain, and therefore the father was less anxious to marry his daughter early and run the risk of her being a child-widow.[69]

Remarriage of women, generally condemned by the Smṛtis,[70] was not in vogue. Society did not permit second marriage to a woman under any circumstances. The *Kuvalayamālā* has the story of the daughter of a *mahāseṭṭhi*, Suvarṇadevī, whose husband left for trade in Lankāpurī and was not heard of for twelve years. Her youthful passions surged beyond control and feeling despondent that the love of a husband was not in her fate she decided to commit suicide.[71] Being the daughter of a rich merchant, she could have easily got another husband, had it been permitted by the customs of the time. Equally tragic was the fate of Guṇaśrī, a *sārthavāha's* daughter, the untimely death of whose husband left her a virgin widow and she spent the rest of her life in renunciation.[72] The episode of Vīramatī, the daughter of a *seṭṭhi*, a child-widow who later eloped with a gardener[73] shows that the prohibition extended even to child-widows. This is supported by the evidence of the *Karpūra-mañjarī*.[74]

The lot of the widow was unenviable. From the reference to unwidowed women performing the wedding rites in the *Kuvalayamālā* it is apparent that they had no place in the auspicious ceremonies. A widow in the *Kuvalayamālā* laments her fate thus: 'To live as a widow is to live a life afflicted with misery and stigma of ill-fate, treated with contempt by one's own relatives.'[75] In the *Samarāiccakahā* when Śikhin goes to meet his mother, he finds her so much reduced in appearance since the death of her husband that he does not recognise her at first.[76] 'A widow', says Vṛddhahārita 'should give up adorning her hair, chewing betel-nut, wearing perfumes, flowers, ornaments, and dyed clothes, taking food from a vessel of bronze, taking two meals a day and applying colly-rium to her eyes.'[77]

Not unoften childless widows lived on at their father's home which provided them with a hospitable shelter.[78] Religion was another refuge for these unfortunate women and they entered the religious orders[79] or staying at home performed austerities, devoting themselves to the worship of God.[80] Widowed queen mothers had an important position, especially if their sons were minors. The *Samarāiccakahā* relates the story of a queen who fearing that she would lose her influence if her husband became a monk, deliberately killed him, so that she may retain the same as a guardian of the young king.[81]

The practice of *anumaraṇa* or *satī*, which had gained currency in society much before our times,[82] enjoyed considerable popularity during this period. Thus in the *Kuvalayamālā* a vidyādhara declares it to be the duty of a woman to put an end to her life on the death of her husband.[83] Elsewhere Uddyotana compares *saṃdhyā*, or evening, to a girl of a good family who on the death of her husband, the sun, puts on *kusumbha* red clothes and follows him into the sea.[84] In the *Samarāic-*

cakahā we read of a queen mounting the funeral pyre of her husband so that she may be united with him in her next existence.[85] Elsewhere princess Ratnāvalī resolves to enter the flames to join her husband in heaven on hearing the rumours of her husband's death even though positive proof of it is wanting.[86] Of actual instances of *satī* in Rajasthan, the Dholpur inscription of Caṇḍamahāsena (AD 842) records that his wife Kaṇahullā became a *satī*.[87] The Ghaṭiyālā inscription of Rāṇuka (AD 890) records that his wife Sāṃvaladevī was a *satī*.[88] Various Smṛtis of the period extol the *satī* system. For Aṅgiras *satī* was the only course which religion prescribed for a widow.[89] The *Dakṣa Smṛti*[90] and *Parāśara Smṛti*[91] promised eternal bliss in heaven to a *satī* who died on the funeral pyre of her husband.

The Jaina view regarding widowhood represented in the *Samarāic-cakahā* is that since continuous suffering is an integral part of worldly existence, solace should be sought with the teachings of Jina and the situation of widowhood be faced with equanimity.[92] Medhātithi also did not approve of the practice of *satī* and pointed out that it was opposed to the express Vedic text that prohibited suicide to all.[93] It is evident that the rational view upheld by Bāṇa who condemned *anumaraṇa* as a foolish and fruitless practice[94] continued to have its exponents during the eighth century though the practice was steadily gaining ground. The *tantras* also pointed out that the woman was the embodiment of the supreme goddess, and boldly declared that if a person burnt her with her husband he would be condemned to eternal hell.[95] That *satī* was not considered incumbent upon a widow is evident from the observation of Sulaiman that wives of kings sometime burnt themselves with their husbands but it was for them to decide whether they would do so or not.[96] But the prohibition of widow remarriage and the unalluring prospect of the miserable life of a widow as against the hope of joining the husband in the other world must have encouraged the practice.

Position of Women

The theory of perpetual tutelage advocated by Manu[97] continued to hold ground. Thus in the *Kuvalayamālā* a woman separated from her lover, giving birth to twins, addresses her new-born infant thus: 'My son, thou art the lord, the refuge, and kinsman of this woman who has been deserted by her husband, and separated from her parents. In childhood a woman is protected by her father, in youth by her husband, and in old age by her son. A woman is never without a lord.'[98] The inferior status accorded to a woman is also evident from the observation that a man who was inconstant, crafty, deceitful and untrustworthy would be born as a woman in the next birth.[99] Medhātithi observes that women should have no freedom of action regarding the great objects of human existence (*dharma, artha* and *kāma*), but should obtain permission of their husbands or male relations before spending money on such acts.[100] Arguing that a woman's mind is not under her control, and she lacks the requisite strength, he concludes that she shall be guarded by male relations at all times.[101]

Even for a childless couple, yearning for progeny, the prospect of having a daughter was not quite attractive, as we learn from the *Kuvalayamālā*.[102] The description of birth festivities as 'surpassing those associated with a boy' when the girl was eventually born to them also suggests that normally they were held at a lower key when the issue was a girl.[103] But once born the daughter does not appear to have been discriminated against and was brought up with utmost love and care.[104] She is spoken of as the beloved of her parents, moving about the house without restrictions.[105] Girls were not so welcome in Hindu society since they were not eligible for oblations to the manes.[106] The problem of selecting a proper bridegroom for the girl, the absence of widow-remarriage, and prevalence of *satī* made her a constant source of anxiety and grief for her parents.[107]

The wife occupied a position of honour in the household. In the *Kuvalayamālā* she is called *gṛhalakṣmī*, the goddess of prosperity.[108] A king addresses his wife as 'Devī'.[109] Her anger was a matter of grave concern and all possible means were employed to pacify her.[110] Decisions to renounce the world were taken in consultation with her.[111] The husband made every effort to provide for her needs.[112] Loving husbands hastened to make new ornaments for their wives if they lost their old ones[113] and to pay ransom to their wive's abductors.[114] The story of Rudradeva, who sought the hand of another girl when his wife became averse to worldly pleasures due to religious instruction, and on receiving a refusal from the girl's father, sought to obtain her by killing his wife[115] indicates that society did not consider supersession of the wife quite respectable. Exhibiting a liberal attitude towards the wife, Medhātithi declares that the husband has no dominion (*prabhutva*) over his wife and she shall attend on him if he behaves in the right manner.[116] A harassed wife is given the right to appeal to the king.[117] He does not sanction the abandonment of a faithful wife even if she is of harsh speech[118] and holds that a wife should be maintained even if she hates her husband.[119]

But there is no doubt that the husband occupied a position superior to the wife. For her he was a veritable deity. Utterances like *bhartṛ devatā nāryaḥ* (husbands are the gods of women),[120] and *pati śaraṇā mahilā* (husband is the refuge of a woman)[121] occur frequently in the *Kuvalayamālā*. The queen is shown falling at the feet of her husband when she has a request to make or wishes to express gratitude towards him.[122] Kuvalayamālā, a princess, having chosen Kuvalayacandra as her husband, anxiously awaits an indication that he would have her as a slave (*dāsī*).[123]

Women belonging to royal families received liberal education and training in fine arts. A princess in the *Kuvalayamālā* is represented as having instructed a parrot in the knowledge of letters, *viśākhila śāstra*, and the science dealing with the characteristics of men and animals.[124] The pastimes of another princess included painting (*ālekhya*), dancing (*nartana*), singing (*gīta*), grammar (*vyākaraṇa*), writing (*lekhana*), reading books (*pustakapāṭhana*) and playing the *vīṇa*.[125] The princess Kuvalayamālā preferred to divert herself with intellectual pursuits rather than fruitless talk and showed interest in various types of riddles of words and completion of unfinished verses.[126] She was an expert in the art of *patracchedya*, the art of cutting designs on leaves, and sent to prince Kuvalayacandra a *patracchedya* female swan cut on a *bhūrja* leaf.[127] The *dvipadī* verse inscribed beneath the swan testifies to her skill as a poetess.[128] In the *Samarāiccakahā* princess Ratnāvalī produces an exact copy of the prince's portrait, much to the admiration of her mother.[129] The heroine of the *Karpūramañjarī* is also depicted as composing couplets.[130] Coming to historical references, we have the instance of Rudrāṇī, the wife of Candana of Śākambharī (vs 950–75), who was known as Ātmaprabha on account of her yogic powers.[131] Gūvaka II's sister, Kalāvatī is described as proficient in 64 *kalās*.[132]

Besides princesses, other women living in royal courts were also highly accomplished. In the *Samarāiccakahā*, the companion of the princess, a daughter of her nurse, adds a *dvipadī* stanza to the painting of her mistress.[133] The female attendant of the queen in the *Karpūramañjarī* is said to have been so proficient in the art of poetry that she won tributes from the king himself.[134] The personnel of the queen's apartment included women who were *subhāṣitapāṭhakas* or reciters of witty sayings.[135] Outside the court circle, we hear of the female cheat,

Khaṇḍapānā, in the *Dhūrtākhyāna*, who is represented as the authoress of a treatise on the *Arthaśāstra*,[136] well versed in scriptures such as the *Mahābhārata, Rāmāyaṇa* and the *Purāṇas*.[137] With her superior wit and wisdom, she outwitted her male accomplices who openly confessed that women by birth were wiser than men.[138] In the *Kuvalayamālā* the towns-women, who gather to see prince Kuvalayacandra, sing and play on the *vīṇā, muraja* and other musical instruments to attract his attention.[139] In actual life, we have the instance of Avantisundarī, the wife of the poet Rājaśekhara, who took an active interest in the staging of the play *Karpūramañjarī*.[140] She was also a good poetess and her opinions on poetic subjects are quoted by Rājaśekhara himself in his *Kāvyamīmāṃsā*.[141] Rājaśekhara also testifies to the existence of princesses, daughters of *mahāmātras*, courtesans and wives of actors, who were well versed in sciences and poetesses.[142]

But not all women were equally educated. Observing that his wife still cherished the memory of her dead lover, Purandara reflected thus: Oh! her foolishness, her love, or else, ignorant of the scriptures (*śāstras*), these women are verily like this.[143] Medhātithi speaks of the general ignorance of the Sanskrit language amongst them.[144] Asahāya, the commentator on Nārada in the eighth century AD, justifies the theory of tutelage on the ground that their intellect was not quite well developed like that of men on account of their not having the benefit of proper training and education.[145] However as noted above in well-to-do families they appear to have received good educational facilities. That even ordinary women were not totally bereft of education during our period is evident from Medhātithi[146] who in consonance with the dictates of Manu,[147] Yājñavalkya[148] and the *Kāmasūtra*[149] expects her to be sufficiently educated to keep the accounts of the household.

Women took up various careers. Some were trained in the use of arms. The *Kuvalayamālā* speaks of a woman *pratihārī* (doorkeeper) armed with a sword (*maṇḍalāgra*), a part of whose duty was to announce and usher visitors to the king's inner audience-hall.[150] Among the queen's attendants mentioned in the *Karpūramañjarī* were chowry-holders, bath-keepers, betel-box bearers, ladies-in-waiting and reciters of *subhāṣitas*.[151] They too were not without military training and are depicted as bearing swords, bows, arrows, lances and staffs.[152] Some women were employed as nurses for princes and princesses.[153] Others served as household slaves.[154] Some worked as maid servants, fetching water etc.[155] The Gwalior inscription refers to Bhoja having subdued the demons (*asuras*) with the help of a band of women.[156] Medhātithi refers to women taking up diverse occupations such as spinning, lace-making and fan-making as a means of subsistence.[157]

Courtesans had a special place in society. No occasion of any importance was complete without them. In the *Kuvalayamālā*, *vāravilāsinīs* could be seen busily performing their tasks in the king's court.[158] In the *Samarāiccakahā* a king overwrought with happiness at the birth of a son is said to have gone amidst the towns-folk accompanied by dancing *vāravilayās*.[159] Dancing *vāravilayās*[160] and *veśyāvilayās*[161] formed part of the bridal procession of the prince. In the king's palace, *vilāsinīs* attended upon honoured guests, massaging them with oil, applying various scents and perfumes, and serving food and betel leaves to them.[162] The *Samarāiccakahā* refers to the *veśyās* and their love for money.[163] They were probably inferior to the *vāravilāsinīs*. The reference to song and dances by *vilāsinīs* at the temple[164] points to the institution of *devadāsīs* at temples. Māgha, a resident of Bhīnmal, speaks of courtesans accompanying the armies on their marches.[165] Dancing girls at temples were noticed by Abu Zaid.[166] The Vasantgarh inscription of Varmalāta (AD 624) speaks of a courtesan Būṭā who was attached to the temple of Śrimātā.[167] Reference to this class is also found in the Bayānā inscription of VS 1012.[168] According to Alberuni the Indian rulers encouraged the institution because of its financial benefits.[169] From the *Dharmabindu* we learn that Haribhadra raised his voice against it, comparing a *veśyā* to the washing stone of a washerman and the potsherd in which a dog had its meal.[170]

Some women renounced the world and took up the monastic vows. Women ascetics who joined the brahmanical order of *tāpasīs* and Jaina order of *sādhvīs* are referred to in our works. Age appears to have been no consideration for admittance into the order of *tāpasīs* and even young women were initiated by the *kulapati*.[171] They dwelt in hermitages, wore *valkala*, and practised severe austerities. Accordingly they received all respect even from princes.[172] Jaina *sādhvīs* also enjoyed a position of honour. Jainism not only admitted them into the monastic fold, but also considered them to be entitled to the highest knowledge, *kevala jñāna*.[173] Tradition recounts that Yākinī mahattarā, a Jaina nun, was responsible for the conversion of Haribhadra Sūri to Jainism, when he could not interpret a *gāthā* recited by her and consequently acknowledged her as his spiritual mother.[174]

Perfidious women are vehemently censured in the Prākrit works. The crafty nature of such women is thus bewailed: 'She is the abode of all vice, the origin of deceit, the repository of falsehood, the gateway to the path of misery, the stairway to hell and the bar preventing entry to the happy land.'[175] Again, 'Oh! this poisonous creeper named woman, a veritable meteor sans fire, cholera, an unforeboded pestilence, a noose sans rope, a prison without fetters, a death without cause' etc.[176] An absolutely chaste behaviour was expected of the wife even if her husband was not to be heard of.[177] The practice of cutting the lips, ears and nose of unchaste women is referred to in the *Kuvalayamālā*.[178] From the *Samarāiccakahā* we learn that sometimes a husband would bid his wife to leave his house at the slightest suspicion of her unfaithfulness.[179] The Smṛtis also prescribe various penances and punishments for adulteress women.[180] Vṛddha-Hārita prescribes that in the case of a woman who is a confirmed adulteress, or who destroys her foetus, her husband should have her ears, nose and lips cut off and then she should be banished.[181] Medhātithi would have the adulteress pair put to death.[182]

But there is no doubt that women in general in many ways enjoyed a position of honour and dignity in society. As shown above, she was revered as a mother, adored as a wife and loved as a daughter. The attitude of society towards women, excepting the widow, was fair and chivalrous. In the *Kuvalayamālā* king Purandaradatta deems it to be his duty to escort a woman hastening to meet her lover at the dead of night lest evil befall her.[183] Women were exempted from capital punishment. In the *Samarāiccakahā* a woman who made repeated attempts to kill her husband was merely banished from the kingdom because women were considered exempt from death (*avadhyā*).[184] Elsewhere too we find that on the wife and a male associate of a merchant being found guilty of strangling the latter and leaving him for dead, the male criminal was condemned to death while the woman was only exiled.[185]

The Jaina attitude towards women was on the whole fair and balanced. While men were advised to eschew the company of women since all worldly pleasures were considered ephermal,[186] women are not depicted as otherwise consciously acting as an impediment in the way of a husband desirous of salvation. Rather once enlightened they encouraged their husbands to tread upon the right path and entered the order along with them.[187] In the *Samarāiccakahā* even the newly wed brides of prince Samarāditya resolve to renounce worldly pleasures and strive after beatitude in deference to their husband's wishes.[188]

On the other hand the evils of polygamy, denial of widow remarriage, insistence on the custom of *satī* and lowering of marriage age represent a deterioration in the position of women. Quarrels amongst co-wives and lack of love from the husband's side are listed as two of the commonest causes that made women unhappy.[189]

To sum up, the joint family system was prevalent. It served a useful purpose by providing socio-economic security to its vulnerable members. Thus the eldest son bore the responsibility of the household in his father's absence and arranged for the marriage of his younger sister. A widowed sister resided with her brothers and was well provided for. The son was considered to be a family necessity as he served to perpetuate the line and a religious necessity because he alone had the right to make offerings to the ancestors.

Marriage was considered an important institution, the main objective of which was to obtain offspring and perpetuate the family line. The age, family, learning, wealth, looks and virtues of the bridegroom were carefully considered before settling a marriage. Marriages were generally arranged within the same caste. But caste rules being not very rigid *anuloma* marriages between brāhmaṇas and kṣatriyas as well as kṣatriyas and vaiśyas took place. In the urban centres, the virtues and potential of a prospective bridegroom rather than caste were at times the decisive factors for settling a marriage. Marriage between maternal cousins was in vogue. Great importance was attached to approval of parents and a sacramental marriage. *Svayaṃvara* marriage in which the maiden exercised her choice in the selection of a life-partner was prevalent in royal families. Polygamy was prevalent in the affluent sections of merchants and the ruling class. Instances of love marriages and *svayaṃvaras* indicate that late marriages continued to be in vogue in kṣatriya and vaiśya families. But pre-puberty marriages amongst brāhmaṇas and vaiśyas were also prevalent. Remarriage was not permitted. Widows were considered inauspicious and led a miserable existence, an important exception being the widowed queen mother who held an important position in polity, especially if she had minor sons. Some childless widows continued to reside with their parents. Others devoted themselves to religion. *Satī* system had become a popular practice though not universal.

The theory of perpetual tutelage of women held ground. The birth of a daughter was not quite desired, but she was brought up with love. The wife had a position of honour, but subsidiary to her husband. Women of royal families received good education. They were in some cases at least highly learned, composed poems and delighted in intellectual pastimes like solving riddles on words, and completion of unfinished verses. Women serving in royal courts were also literate and skilled in fine arts. Outside the court circle also there appear to have been some women scholars, well versed in scriptures and the *arthaśāstra*, as also women who were not so well educated. Some women were employed as doorkeepers in the royal court, attendants of the queen, nurses, household slaves and maid servants, with those who served in the court possessing military training. Some served as courtesans and were on attendance in the king's court, also forming part of the king's retinue when he went out on festive occasions. Others renounced the world, joined the brahmanical ascetic order or Jaina ascetic order and were highly respected. An important privilege held by women was exemption from capital punishment.

Notes and References

1. *KM*, p. 13.
2. Ibid.
3. सव्वाइं किर कज्जाइं पिइ-पिंड-पाणिय-पयाणाईणि विणा पुत्तेण ण संपडंति पुरिसाणं। Ibid.
4. Ibid.
5. *Manu*, IX, 138; *Mbh.*, Ādiparva, 74.27; *Rāmāyaṇa*, ii, 107–12.
6. *Viṣṇu Dharmaśūtra*, 85.70; *Vanaparva*, 84.97; *Matsya*, 207.39.
7. *KM*, pp. 21, 199.
8. Ibid., pp. 22, 263.
9. Ibid., p. 263.
10. Ibid.
11. तं धरणी सावित्ती सरस्सई तं भगीरही पुहई। Ibid., p. 263.
12. *SK*, pp. 396–7.
13. Ibid., p. 400.
14. Ibid., pp. 245 f.
15. *KM*, pp. 45–7.
16. Ibid.
17. *SK*, pp. 503 f.
18. *KM*, pp. 54–5.
19. *SK*, p. 197.
20. महिलाणं पंचहिं कारणेहिं कोवो संजायइ। तं जहा . . . सासु-वियत्थणेणं त्ति। *KM*, p. 11.
21. *SK*, p. 395 f.; Rules regarding separation of property to meet the eventuality of a split in the family had been laid down much earlier by the *Manu Smṛti*: *Manu*, IX, 104 f.
22. कायव्वा कुसलसंतती . . . अणुयत्तियव्वो कुलक्कमो। *SK*, p. 732.
23. *KM*, p. 105.
24. Ibid.

25. Yama says that one should seek for seven qualities in a bridegroom, viz. good family, good character, bodily appearance, fame, learning, wealth and support. Yama in *Smṛticandrikā*, I, p. 78. Vyāsa states that marriages should be arranged with one of equal age, learning and family. *Vyāsa*, II.5.
26. जोग्गो तुमं, किं तु न साहम्मिओ त्ति। *SK*, p. 507.
27. *Kathākośaprakaraṇa*, p. 97, line 25, qd. D. Sharma, *RTTA*, p. 452.
28. *KM*, pp. 45, 103; *SK*, pp. 83, 144, 151, 194, 408.
29. *KM*, pp. 252–3.
30. *Karpūra.*, I, 11.
31. *EI*, XVIII, p. 95.
32. *ED*, I, p. 16.
33. *Manu*, III. 12–13; *Yājñavalkya*, I. 56; *Vyāsa*, II, 11.
34. *On Manu*, III.14.
35. *Manu*, X. 6.
36. *On Manu*, X. 6.
37. *Yājña*, I. 52–3.
38. *SK*, pp. 63, 658–9, 731.
39. *Upamiti*, pp. 253, 481.
40. 1. 19–26 qd. Kane, *HD*, II, i, p. 458.
41. *On Manu*, II. 18; However medieval texts such as the *Smṛticandrikā* and *Parāśarīya Mādhava* support the practice and quote Vedic passages and Smṛti authority allowing such marriages. *Smṛticandrikā*, I. pp. 70–4, *Parāśaramādhavīya*, I.2., pp. 63–8; Kane, op. cit., pp. 460–2.
42. Irawati Karve, 'The Indian Social Organisation: An Anthropological Study' in *Cultural Heritage of India*, II, p. 539; *Kinship Organisation in India*, p. 170.
43. Irawati Karve, *Kinship Organisation in India*, p. 170.
44. *SK*, pp. 193, 627.
45. Ibid., p. 69.
46. *KM*, p. 168.
47. Devala quoted by Kullūka, *On Manu*, VIII. 226.
48. *On Manu*, VIII. 366.
49. *KM*, p. 9.
50. Ibid., p. 150.
51. Ibid.
52. *Pṛthvīrājavijaya*, V. 31; D. Sharma, op. cit., pp. 30, 288.
53. *Dvayāśrayamahākāvya*, VIII; D. Sharma, op. cit., pp. 143, 288.
54. *SK*, p. 731.
55. *KM*, pp. 233–4.
56. Ibid., p. 109.
57. *Karpūra.*, IV. 18.
58. *EI*, XVIII, pp. 87 f.; From the Vaillabhaṭasvāmin inscription, AD 875, we learn that Alla had five wives. *EI*, I, pp. 154 f.
59. Qd. In Gṛhastharatnākara, p. 85; Kane, *HD*, II, i, p. 552.

60. Kane, op. cit., p. 553; A.S. Altekar, *Position of Women in Ancient India,* pp. 105–7.
61. *SK,* pp. 83, 107, 151, 408, 658–9.
62. See above.
63. विणीयसेट्ठिस्स धूया बालविहवा वीरमई नाम। *SK,* p. 227.
64. बालरण्डा विरहिदो अ माणुसो मणोरधमोदएहिं अत्ताणअं विडम्बेदि। *Karpūra.,* III. 8.
65. *KM,* p. 45.
66. Yama qd. in Smṛtimūktāphala, p. 136; Saṃvarta, V. 67, qd. Smṛticandrikā, p. 79; Kane, *HD,* II, i, p. 443; Parāśara, VII. 6–9; *On Manu,* IX, 4; IX. 88.
67. A.S. Altekar, *Position of Women in Ancient India,* pp. 59–60.
68. A.L. Basham, *The Wonder that was India,* p. 168.
69. A.S. Altekar, op. cit., p. 58.
70. Cf. *Manu,* V. 157, 162; *On Manu,* V. 157; VIII. 28.
71. *KM,* p. 74.
72. *SK,* p. 501.
73. विणीयसेट्ठिस्स धूयाबालविहवा वीरमई नाम। Ibid., p. 227.
74. बालरण्डा . . . । *Karpūra.,* III. 8.
75. सयणो-परिभूयाओ दोहग्ग-कलंक-दुक्ख-तवियाओ। *KM,* p. 54.
76. *SK,* p. 186.
77. XI, 205–10.
78. *SK,* pp. 50, 227; *KM,* p. 74.
79. *SK,* p. 340.
80. रया तवविहाणंमि। Ibid., pp. 501 f.
81. *SK,* p. 251.
82. It is noticed by Vātsyāyana, Bhāsa, Kālidāsa and Śūdraka. Historical instances of *satī* are recorded in the Eran inscription of AD 510 and Bāṇa's *Harṣacarita.* cf. Altekar, *Position of Women in Ancient India,* p. 123.
83. महिलाण एस धम्मो मयम्मि दइए मरंति ता वस्सं। *KM,* p. 240.
84. सूर-णरिंदत्थवणे कुसंभ-रत्तंबराणुमग्गेण। कुल-बालिय व्व संझा अणुमरइ समुद्द-मज्झम्मि। Ibid., p. 82.
85. राया समरमियङ्को उप्पन्नो नवर जत्थ ठाणंमि। तत्थेव मंदभग्गा जाएज्ज अहं पि नियमेण। तो हुयवहं पविट्ठा। *SK,* p. 660.
86. पविसामि जलणं . . . पावेमि लहुं सुरलोयसंठियं अज्जउत्तं। Ibid., p. 665.
87. *ZDMG,* XL, p. 39; D. Sharma, *ECD,* p. 290.
88. Inscriptions of Northern India, no. 107; D. Sharma, *ECD,* p. 289.
89. Qd. by Aparārka on Yājñavalkya, I. 87; A.S. Altekar, *Position of Women in Ancient India,* p. 126.
90. *Dakṣa,* IV. 19.
91. *Parāśara,* IV, 27.
92. *SK,* pp. 668–9.
93. *On Manu,* V. 157.
94. *Kādambarī,* p. 173.
95. *Mahānirvāṇatantra,* X. 79–80.
96. *ED,* I, p. 6.

97. *Manu*, IX. 3; *Manu,* V. 147.
98. पुत्त तुमं मह णाहो तं सरणं तं गइं तुमं बंधू। दइएण विमुक्काए माया-पिइ-विप्पउत्ताए।। होइ कुमारीए पिया णाहो तह जोव्वणम्मि भत्तारो। थेरत्तणम्मि पुत्तो णत्थि अणाहा फुडं महिला। *KM,* p. 76.
99. जो चवलो सढ-भावो माया-कवडेहिं वंचए सुयणं।
 ण य कस्सइ वीसत्थो सो पुरिसो महिलिया होइ। Ibid., p. 231.
100. *On Manu,* IX. 2.
101. *On Manu,* IX. 3.
102. जं होउ तं होउ। *KM,* p. 162.
103. तओ तीए पुत्त-जम्माओ वि अहियं कयाइं वद्धावणयाइं। Ibid., p. 162.
104. Ibid., pp. 74, 107, 164; *SK,* pp. 64 ff., 517, 605.
105. वल्लहा य जणणि-जणयाणं। *KM,* p. 74; अहं दुहिया अच्चंत-दइया घरे अणिवारियप्पसरा परिब्भमामि। Ibid., p. 107.
106. Cf. *Aitereya Brāhmaṇa,* 33.1; 159.11; Kane, *HD,* II, i, pp. 509–10.
107. A.S. Altekar, *Position of Women in Ancient India,* pp. 4–5.
108. *KM,* p. 264.
109. Ibid., pp. 12, 214.
110. Ibid., pp. 12, 53.
111. Ibid., p. 214.
112. *SK,* pp. 425–6.
113. Ibid., p. 108.
114. Ibid., p. 98.
115. Ibid., pp. 84–5.
116. *On Manu,* qd. U.N. Ghoshal in *Age of Imperial Kannauj*, p. 377.
117. *On Manu,* IX. 1.
118. *On Manu,* IX. 95.
119. *On Manu,* qd. U.N. Ghoshal, op. cit.
120. *KM,* pp. 54, 240, 265.
121. Ibid., p. 181.
122. Ibid., pp. 12, 16.
123. Ibid., p. 164.
124. पाढिउं पयत्ता। थोयेणं वि कालेणं जाणियाइं अक्खराइं गहियं णट्ट-लक्खणं, जाणियं विसाहिलं, गहियाइं गय-गवय-मय-कुक्कुड-आस-पुरिस-महिला-लक्खणाइं। *KM,* p. 123. A.N. Upadhye suggests that Viśākhila is derived from Viśākha, which is another name for Kārttikeya and therefore may refer to some aspect of warfare, *Kuvalayamālā*, Part II, p. *130.
125. *KM,* p. 235.
126. अज्जउत्त अलं इमिणा बुहयण-परिणिंदिएण इयर-बहुमएण अत्तणो पयंसा-वयण-वित्थरेण, ता अण्णेण केण वि वियड्ढ-बुद्धि-परिकप्पिएण विनोएण अच्छामो। *KM,* p. 174.
127. Ibid., p. 160.
128. Ibid.
129. *SK,* pp. 623–4.
130. *Kārpūra.,* II. 7.
131. *Pṛthvirājavijaya,* V. 31; D. Sharma, *ECD,* p. 31.

132. *Pṛthvirājavijaya,* V. 38; D. Sharma, *ECD* p. 287.
133. *SK,* p. 72.
134. सच्चं विअक्खणा चतुरत्तणेण उत्तीणं विचित्तदाए रीदीणं। ता किं अणं कइचूडामणित्तणे ठिदा एसा। *Karpūra,* I. 20.
135. सुहासिदपाढिआओ। Ibid., IV. 9.
136. भणइ खंडवाणा विहसंती अत्यसत्थणिम्माया। *Dhū,* V. 1.
137. Ibid., IV. 14 f.
138. Ibid., V. 108–10.
139. *KM,* p. 26.
140. *Karpūra.,* I. 11.
141. *Kāvyamīmāṃsā,* G.O.S, pp. 20, 46, 57.
142. Ibid., p. 53.
143. अहो से मूढया, अहो अणुराओ। अहवा अणहीयसत्यो ईइसो चेव इत्थियायणो होइ। *SK,* p. 756.
144. *On Manu,* II. 33, 49.
145. On Nārada, X. 30.
146. *On Manu,* X. 11.
147. *Manu,* V. 150.
148. *Yājña,* I.83.
149. *Kāmasūtra,* Sūtras 32–3; H.C. Chakladar, *Social Life in Ancient India,* p. 175.
150. *KM,* p. 9.
151. चामर धारिणीओ . . . सेरन्धीओ . . . तम्बोलकरङ्कवाहिणीओ . . . मज्जणपालीओ सुहासिदपाढिआओ। *Karpūra.,* IV. 9.
152. Ibid., IV. 10.
153. *KM,* pp. 21, 161.
154. *Gṛhadāsīs, SK,* pp. 97, 144.
155. *EI,* XVIII, pp. 107 f.
156. Gwalior Praśasti, verse 22, EI, XVIII, pp. 99 f.
157. *On Manu,* IX. 75.
158. णिय-कम्म-वावडाओ अवहसिय-सुर-सुंदरी-वंद्र-लायण्णाओ वारविलासिणीओ। *KM,* p. 16.
159. *SK,* p. 602.
160. Ibid., p. 630.
161. Ibid., p. 519.
162. *KM,* pp. 157–8, 169.
163. वेसित्थिहियाहियय पिव अत्थवल्लहं। *SK,* p. 123.
164. *KM,* p. 50.
165. *Śiśupālavadha,* V. 27.
166. *ED,* I, p. 11.
167. *EI,* IX, p. 191.
168. *EI,* XXII, pp. 120 f.
169. Sachau, II. 157.
170. *Dharmabindu,* p. 15; D. Sharma, *RTTA,* p. 462.
171. *SK,* pp. 340, 343.
172. Ibid., pp. 337–8.

173. Ibid., p. 499.
174. *Prabhāvakacarita*, IX, pp. 4–47; Jacobi, Introduction to the *SK*, pp. viii–ix.
175. *SK*, p. 207.
176. Ibid., p. 242.
177. *KM*, p. 74.
178. दुस्सीलत्तण-चिंधं पाव-फलं कुसुम-पल्लवुब्भेयं। णासाहर-कण्णाणं छेयं तह भेयणं सहियं।। Ibid., p. 41.
179. *SK*, pp. 504–5.
180. In the penal law of Manu, such women were liable for capital punishment. *Manu*, VIII. 371; *Yājñavalkya* prescribed the cutting of ear and the like for adultery with men of lower castes. *Yājñavalkya*, II, 289.
181. *Vṛddha Hārita*, VII, 192.
182. *On Manu*, VIII, 359.
183. *KM*, p. 86.
184. 'अवज्झा इत्थिय' त्ति धाडिया णेण सरज्जाओ। *SK*, p. 298.
185. *SK*, p. 460.
186. *KM*, pp. 80, 89, 253.
187. Ibid., p. 214; *SK*, p. 149.
188. *SK*, pp. 744–5.
189. पणय-खलणेणं . . . पडिवक्ख-कलहेणं। *KM*, p. 11.

5

Religion

RELIGION PLAYED A very important part in the lives of the people. Great emphasis is laid upon the practice of *dharma* by the Jaina writers of the period. Of the three objects of human pursuit, *Dharma, Artha* and *Kāma* (righteous conduct, wealth and enjoyment of sensual pleasures), Uddyotana attaches the greatest importance to *dharma*. According to him, *dharma* was highest (*uttama*), *artha* was middling (*madhyama*), and *kāma* was lowest (*adhama*). *Artha*, he elaborates, is subject to various calamities, natural or otherwise. Given to the wicked, it may lead to sin. In the hands of a worthy recipient, it may yield some *kāma* and some *dharma* and therefore it was termed *madhyama*.[1] *Kāma* led neither to *dharma*, nor *artha* nor *mokṣa* (liberation) and therefore was deemed to be *adhama*.[2] Through *dharma*, on the other hand, one could achieve all the other ends, including *mokṣa*, therefore, the practice of *dharma* was most desirable.[3] Haribhadra extols the virtue of *dharma* in several laudatory verses. It was through *dharma*, according to him, one gained divinity, wealth and much fame; it was the sovereign remedy for all sorrows: it was strength, a shelter and a refuge. In short, whatever was found to be delightful to the heart and senses in the mundane existence of man, was all the consequence of *dharma*. At the time of one's death, when one was forced to relinquish all that one had preserved with great care, e.g., wealth, the body and relatives, it was *dharma* alone that proved to be a true companion and led one on to the heavens, freedom from miseries, eternal happiness and salvation.[4] By *dharma*, the Jaina *ācāryas* quite understandably meant the way of life prescribed by the Jaina *dharma* and Uddyotana appropriately concludes his observations on *dharma* with the declaration that the *dharma* preached by Jinendra is the best.[5]

Dharma, as Uddyotana tells us, was variously represented by different deities and teachers such as Govinda, Skanda, Rudra, Aravinda, Gajendra, Nāgendra, Candra, Kapila, Kaṇāda and Jina.[6] The supreme deity was indeed worshipped in diverse forms. Thus sailors caught in a gale in the high seas would call upon Nārāyaṇa, Caṇḍikā, Hara, Ravi, Vinayāka, Skanda, Yakṣa, Revanta and Buddha for soccour in their hour of distress.[7] Included in a long list of various gods and godlings in the *Kuvalayamālā* whom the credulous are said to have propitiated for worldly gains, are the names of Govinda, Skanda, Rudra, Vyantaras, Gaṇādhipa, Durgā, Yakṣa, Rākṣasa, Bhūta, Piśāca, Kinnara, Kiṃpuruṣa, Gandharva, Mahoraga, Candra, Tāraka, Uḍu, Graha, Āditya, Nāga, Udadhi, Suparṇa, Agni, Vidyuta and Indra.[8] The picture thus presented is one of a baffling multiplicity of gods and goddesses which is confirmed by the evidence of epigraphs[9] and foreign travellers. According to Ibn Khurdadba, there were forty-two sects in Hind, part of them believing in a Creator and Prophet, part denying the mission of a prophet, and a part atheist.[10]

But there was no narrow sectarianism. Rather there is evidence of the realisation of the essential unity of the supreme godhead, tolerance and harmony between the various religious sects. Thus a devotee would offer similar reverence to gods of different sects and even worship them all together. In the *Kuvalayamālā* we have the instance of king Dṛḍhavarman who propitiated diverse deities such as Skanda, Rudra, Govinda, Candra, Tridaśendra, Gajendra, Nāgendra, Aravinda as also Yakṣas, Rākṣasas, Bhūtas, Piśācas, Kinnaras, Kiṃpuruṣas and Mahoragas at the same time, without there being any apparent contradiction in his religious beliefs.[11] The *Kuvalayamālā's* description of the dusk is a testimony to the peaceful co-existence of the various religious sects. Establishments of various religious followings would simultaneously resound with the worship of the devout. One could hear the crackling sound of sessamum, ghee and fuel burning in the pavilion for recitation of mantras (*mantrajāpamaṇḍapa*); *Veda* recitation in abodes of brāhmaṇas (*brāhmaṇaśālās*); singing of hymns in temples of Rudra (*Rudrabhavanas*); sound of bell (*ghaṇṭā*) and drum (*ḍamaru*) from habitations of *Kāpālikas* (*Kāpālikagṛhas*); full-throated singing from *Dhārmikamaṭhas*, literally, the monastery of the religious; sound of the *toḍahiā* musical instruments from Śiva temples at crossings (*catvaraśivas*); recitation of *Bhagvadgītā* from abodes of ascetics (*āvasathas*); laudatory hymns (*stuti-stotras*) from Jaina temples; exhortation on compassion (*karuṇā*) in Buddhist *vihāras*; clanging of mighty bells in shrines of Durgā (*Kottajā gṛhas*); crowing of cocks and chirping of birds from temples of Kārttikeya and music and song from lofty temples (*Devagṛhas*) mingling together harmoniously.[12] Epigraphic records testify to the catholicity of the Imperial Pratihāras who changed their tutelary deity (*iṣṭadevatā*) from generation to generation.[13] The cultural unity of the period expressed itself in the images of Harihara, in which one face depicted Hari and other Hara or Śiva; Hari-Hara-Pitāmaha, in which Brahmā's face was also represented along with Śiva and Viṣṇu, and *Ardhanārīśvara*, in which the right half of the image represented Śiva and the other half Pārvatī, as well as *pañcāyatana* type of temples, in which one god occupied the central place of worship and the other the shrines in the four quarters, the east, west, north and south.[14]

Religious competition was not lacking. Nor did the followers of different religious persuasions forbear from claims to religious superiority. Uddyotana explicitly declares Jainism to be the best religion[15] and the Jaina gods to be superior to other Gods.[16] What was absent was a display of unnecessary religious acrimony, not only among the followers of different brahmanical sects, but even among the followers of orthodox and heterodox religions. Thus Uddyotana himself recognises the status of the various Purāṇic deities as gods of long standing fame,[17] their ability to confer worldly wealth[18] and speaks of them as *vidyāsiddhas*.[19] Haribhadra's satirisation of Purāṇic legends in the *Dhūrtākhyāna* is also that of a rationalist and not of a religious bigot. Siddharṣi Sūri also declares the essential unity underlying all faiths and systems of philosophy.[20]

Viṣṇu

One of the principal deities was Viṣṇu[21] known by his various names such as Nārāyaṇa,[22] Kṛṣṇa,[23] Keśava,[24] Cakrī,[25] Govinda[26] and Madhumatha.[27] Various legends current in those days glorifying him as the supreme god are noted in the *Dhūrtākhyāna*. Thus the myth regarding the birth of Brahmā from Viṣṇu's navel when he, the creator of the universe, was performing austerities on the bed of the ocean, at the time of the universal deluge, in a world that was devoid of all existence, the sun, moon, sky and earth, has been duly narrated.[28] Mention is made of the claim of Keśava that the earth and sky formed the cavity, the mountains his jaw and ocean his tongue.[29] Lakṣmī is mentioned as the consort of Madhumatha[30] and allusion is made to his residence in the milky ocean (*Kṣīrasāgara*) and bearing the *Kaustubha* jewel.[31] That his vehicle was Garuḍa can be seen from the reference to the immense speed at which Cakrī, seated on the Garuḍa, travelled.[32] In the form of Nārāyaṇa, he was described as dark-complexioned as the wild buffalo and collyrium.[33] Epigraphic[34] and archaeological evidence also testify to the popularity of Viṣṇu worship under the Pratihāras. The Jodhpur inscription of Bauka (VS 894),[35] begins with salutations to Viṣṇu, *Om Namo Viṣṇave*. *Śeṣaśāyī* images assignable to the period have been discovered near Kota and Harṣanātha.[36] The Yoga-Nārāyaṇa image from Didwana[37] and three Harihara temples at Osia[38] have been assigned to the eighth century AD. Early development of Vaiṣṇavism in Rajasthan is to be traced back to the worship of Saṃkarṣaṇa and Vāsudeva recorded in the Ghosuṇḍī (Chittor) inscription of *c.* 200 BC[39] and erection of Viṣṇu temple in the Gaṅgadhār (Jhalawad) inscription (AD 423).[40]

Reference to the Vāmana, Varāha and Vāsudeva-Kṛṣṇa incarnations in our works indicates their popularity during the period. The legend of Viṣṇu, who in the guise of a brāhmaṇa (*Dvija*) begged of Bali only three steps of ground and then deprived him of the entire earth, recounted in the *Dhūrtākhyāna*,[41] shows that the Vamanāvatāra was well known. It is also related how in his incarnation of Varāha, Madhumatha lifted the earth along with its mountains, forests etc.[42] The position of Kṛṣṇa as an *avatāra* was also well established as is evident from the complete identification of Kṛṣṇa and Keśava with Viṣṇu in the *Dhūrtākhyāna*,[43] where the same events are associated with both. The *Kuvalayamālā* also identifies Gopāla Kṛṣṇa with Nārāyaṇa and refers to the association of Nārāyaṇa with cows and cowherdesses in his childhood.[44] Kṛṣṇa was considered to be all pervàsive, present even in the minutest of objects.[45] The universe is said to have existed in him, though he dwelt in Devakī's womb.[46] Myths connected with him such as the placing of additional weight in the form of elephants, mountains etc. on the bow of Drupada, to frustrate the attempt of Śiśupāla to string it,[47] and the lifting of the Govardhana mountain,[48] were well known. From Harṣanātha (Sikar) we have a three-faced Viṣṇu in which the side faces represent Varāha and Nṛsiṃha; from Āhār (Udaipur) two reliefs representing the Matsya and Kacchapa incarnations; and from Bagherā (Ajmer division) a door jamb showing five incarnations of Viṣṇu, belonging to the Pratihāra period.[49] The temples at Osia (Jodhpur) depict various *Kṛṣṇa-līlā* scenes such as Vāsudeva taking the baby Kṛṣṇa on his head; Kṛṣṇa and Yaśodā; upturning the cart (*Śakaṭabhaṅga*); fight with horse and bull demons; *Govardhana-dhāraṇa* etc.[50] A fragmentary inscription of the early Pratihāra period from Mandor refers to Kṛṣṇa's play with Rādhā and the Gopīs at Gokula etc.[51] The bas-relief from Kāmān (Bharatpur) depicting the Matsya, Kūrma, Varāha, Nṛsiṃha and Vāmanāvatāras[52] and the reliefs from Mandor (near Jodhpur) depicting scenes from the life of Kṛṣṇa[53] indicate that the popularity of incarnations in Rajasthan dates back to earlier times.

The *avatāra* conception, which engendered a hopeful belief in the coming of a saviour, or *avatāra*, who would incarnate himself for the protection of the virtuous and destruction of the wicked,[54] offering strength and courage to its adherents in times of distress, and encouraging them to tread the path of virtue, added to the appeal of Vaiṣṇavism and served a useful social purpose. Its origins have been traced back to later Vedic times and various varying lists of *avatāras* are to be found in the *Nārāyaṇīya* section of the *Mahābhārata, Matsya Purāṇa, Vāyu Purāṇa, Agni Purāṇa* and *Varāha Purāṇa.*[55] By fusion of the cults of tribals, it facilitated their assimilation into the brahmanical mould.[56] It is significant in this context that the Gopāla Kṛṣṇa cult gained considerable popularity in Rajasthan, where the Ābhīras, who are associated with the popularisation of the marvellous deeds of the boy-god Kṛṣṇa and his dalliance with the cowherdesses[57] are known to have been a powerful tribe in the neighbourhood of Ghaṭiyālā up to the ninth century.[58]

Śiva

Śiva, referred to as Hara,[59] Śaṅkara,[60] Trinayana,[61] Rudra,[62] Umāpati,[63] and Paśupati[64] was another popular deity of those times, worshipped both in anthropomorphic and *liṅga* forms. His legendary exploits, such as the bearing of the Ganges on his head on her descent from the heavens[65] and the burning of Tripura with his flaming arrows,[66] which have been narrated in the Vedic literature[67] and the epics,[68] find mention in our works. Of particular interest is the legend cited in the *Dhūrtākhyāna* which obviously designed to indicate the superiority of Śiva over Viṣṇu and Brahmā relates how the latter ran up and down for a thousand years but failed to discover the end of the *Śivaliṅga.*[69] The same theme is represented by the *liṅgodbhava* image from the Harṣanātha temple, now in the Rājpūtānā museum, Ajmer, in which the long slender column on which Śiva's figure is depicted has the figures of Brahmā and Viṣṇu depicted on its sides in the act of soaring and coming downwards respectively; Brahmā and Viṣṇu are again shown as respectful attendants of Śiva.[70] Another such image found at 'Lāmbā' at Marwar has also been assigned to the Pratihāra period.[71] An early image of this type comes from the Daśāvatāra temple at Ellorā (Maharashtra).[72] The legend was known to the *Vāyu Purāṇa* which relates how when Viṣṇu and Brahmā were arguing over their respective contributions to the creation of the universe, the Śiva Liṅga, enveloped in flames, appeared before them, and they failed in their attempt to trace its upper and lower extremities.[73]

Śiva had a dual aspect, terrific as well as benign and propitious. In the *Dhūrtākhyāna* he is portrayed in his wrathful form, as a god who inspired terror, the bearer of the trident, who wearing a garland of human skulls, club with skull at top (*khaṭvāṅga*) in hand, delighted himself in the cemeteries.[74] As in the case of the Vedic *Rudra*, *bali* was offered to him at the cross roads.[75] *Śivamaṇḍapas* were also established and worship was offered at the crossings.[76] Gruesome rites were associated with his worship. In the *Kuvalayamālā* we read of a king contemplating cutting off slices of flesh from his body and offering them as oblations to Śiva in order to obtain a boon from him,[77] a hazardous venture, as pointed out by his ministers.[78] In his pacific form, the deity was known as Umāpati, the husband of Umā,[79] Hara, the consort of Gaurī,[80] and Śaṅkara, who had his beloved seated on his left side.[81] The left side of Hara is said to be female.[82] The epithet *Śaśiśekharasvāmi*[83] indicates that he bore a crescent on his head. He is known to ride the bull vehicle or *vṛṣabha.*[84] The sight of bulls in a caravan, we find, brings to the mind of Uddyotana the abode of Śiva teeming with bulls and resounding with their bellows.[85] Epigraphic[86] and archaeological[87] evidence testify to the popularity of Śaivism in Rajasthan from early times. Śiluka of the Pratihāra line of Mandor built a temple of Siddheśvara Mahādeva.[88] From Ābānerī (Jaipur) we have an excellent *ardhanārīśvara* image, Śiva holding a trident and accompanied by his mount, Nandī, a sublime product of early Pratihāra art, as also are the contemporary reliefs of this type from Osia, Menal etc.[89] From Harṣanātha (Sikar) come the images of Lakulīśa, Tāṇḍavanṛtya Śiva and Śiva-Pārvatī, assignable to the ninth-tenth centuries.[90] *Harihara* images are found in the Osia and Buckalā (Jodhpur) temples of the Pratihāra period.[91] The association of Śiva with the mother goddess must have added to his popularity by making it more attractive to the masses and acceptable to the worshippers of Śakti.

The temple of Mahākāla at Ujjayinī, described by Kālidāsa in his *Meghadūta*[92] and *Raghuvaṃśa*[93] and referred to in Bāṇa's *Kādambarī*,[94] continued to be a celebrated site of worship, the fame of which had spread as far as Rajasthan.[95] The reference to the crowd of those who had obtained superhuman faculties and those proficient in *tantra* and *mantra* at Mahākāla[96] indicates that the temple had come to be associated with tantric practices during this period. Bhadreśvara, Lalita, Someśvara, known as *Jyotirliṅgas* in later times had also gained fame as holy places visited by pilgrims for destruction of sins.[97]

Of the various Śaiva sects, the *Kāpālikas* and *Kāruṇikas* find mention in our works. Weird practices were associated with the *Kāpālikas*. In the *Kuvalayamālā* the conduct of a disconsolate woman, who placing the skeletal remains of her husband's body on her shoulders roamed about the cremation ground, clad in tattered clothes, her body besmeared with dust and dirty in appearance, and begging food is likened to that of a follower of the *Mahābhairavavrata* and again to that of a *Kāpālika* girl (*Kāpālikabālā*).[98] Elsewhere human flesh (*Mahāmāṃsa*) is said to be the food of *Kāpālikas* (*Kāpālika āhāra*).[99] Reference is also made to abodes of *Kāpālikas* resounding with the sound of bells and drums.[100] The *Caṇḍakauśika* (tenth century) also pictures *Kāpālikas* as armed with a club, carrying about a skull in hand, decorated with ashes and human bones.[101] In the *Prabodhacandrodaya* (twelfth century) the *Kāpālika* doctrine is identified with *Mahābhairavānuśāsana* and declared to consist of the worship of the Mahābhairava form of Śiva. The *Kāpālika* has been described as wearing a garland of human bones, living on cremation grounds and using a skull as a dish.[102] Noticed by Varāhamihira[103] in the Gupta period, the sect had gained prominence by the seventh century AD.[104] The ascetics dwelling in the temple of Kapāleśvara are called *Mahāvratins* in the Igātpurī grant (seventh century)[105] and in view of the evidence of the *Prabodhacandrodaya* noted above, the followers of the *Mahābhairavavrata* may also be taken to signify the *Kāpālikas*.[106]

Notwithstanding their reputation for following an outlandish way of life, the *Kāpālikas* appear to have enjoyed a position of great respectability. In the *Kuvalayamālā* we find the observance of the *Kāpālika* vow being prescribed as a means of expiation for the most heinous of crimes by certain village elders (*grāmamahattaras*).[107] The *Samarāiccakahā* has the story of a penitent gambler who desirous of respect, fame, good company and acts of benevolence reflected that in view of his lack of wealth and the ephermal nature of life the best course open for him was to adopt the religion that bestowed happiness in both the worlds and joined the *Kāpālika* order.[108] Elsewhere we find reference to Jaina occult *vidyās* to be practised in the guise of *Kāpālikas*.[109]

Miraculous powers were attributed to the members of this sect and the gambler is later represented as having attained the *Garuḍa mantra*, a most powerful mystic formula which acted as an instant antidote to snake-bites on recitation.[110] Bhavabhūti in his *Mālatīmādhava* (eighth century) attributes the power of speedy movement, attained by the practice of *yoga*, to them.[111] In the *Caṇḍakauśika* (tenth century), Dharma, in the guise of a *Kāpālika* declares that he is about to attain various magical powers, control over a goblin who has entered a corpse, possession of a thunderbolt, magic pills, and paints, union with a demoness, knowledge of alchemy and elixir of life.[112] From the *Ṣaḍdarśanasamuccaya* of Haribhadra it appears that the *Kāpālikas* did not care for the caste system while admitting people into their ascetic orders.[113] These features must have brought Śaivism closer to the people by catering to the religious needs and aspirations of the lower sections of society as well.

The school of thought referred to as *Karuṇāpara dharma* which believed in the destroying of moths and insects as an act of compassion[114] evidently represents the *Kāruṇika* sect of the Śaivas, referred to as Kāruṇikasiddhāntins by Vācaspatimiśra in his commentary on the *Brahmasūtrabhāṣya* of Śaṅkara[115] (ninth century).

Śakti Worship

The worship of Śakti, in her infinite forms, was extremely popular in Rajasthan. For her devotees she was a goddess par excellence, a manifestation of supreme power. In the *Kuvalayamālā*, Bhagavatī Rājyaśrī or Rājyalakṣmī is represented as the tutelary deity (*kuladevatā*) of the Ikṣvāku family.[116] In her anthropomorphic form she is visualised as playfully swaying the necklace on the breast of Viṣṇu (Madhumatha); enveloped in the bright rays of the *kaustubha* jewel; clothed in white amidst the waves of the milky ocean; wearing a tinkling girdle and jingling anklets; with masses of bees hovering around the lotus held in her hand; exceedingly beautiful and seated amidst a lotus,[117] from which we may identify her as Lakṣmī, as connoted by her name. But it is evident that for king Dṛḍhavarman, she was no mere goddess of prosperity, but the supreme deity, and it was her whom he saw manifest in various forms. Thus he invoked her by the different names of Kamalā, Lakṣmī, Śrī, Hrī (modesty), Kīrti (fame), Riddhi (prosperity), Nirvāṇī (giver of liberation), Jayā, Vijayā, Jayantī, Aparājitā (attributes of the goddess of victory), Kumārī (maiden), Bālā (daughter), Ambā and Ambālā (mother),[118] i.e., the goddess of fame, fortune, victory and the divine mother who could bestow even liberation. Duly propitiated by the king who sat in prayer entreating her to either grant him audience within three days or accept his head, the goddess is said to have appeared before him and granted the desired boon of a son.[119] Later, on a further request of the king for guidance regarding the religion worthy of practice, she is represented as having set forth the cardinal percepts of the *kuladharma* (family religion) for his enlightenment.[120]

The context reveals that the worship of the female principle as the personification of manifold energy had made considerable headway in Rajasthan. During the Gupta period Lakṣmī was conceived as the consort of Viṣṇu,[121] bearing the name Śrī and abstract qualities, Hrī (modesty), Medhā (talent), Dhṛti (patience), Puṣṭi (sustenance or growth), Kṣānti (forgiveness), Lajjā (bashfulness), Kīrti (fame), Bhūti (prosperity) etc.[122] The *Kuvalayamālā* assigns to her not only some of these traditional epithets but appellations attributed to Durgā in the *Mahābhārata*,[123] *Harivaṃśa*,[124] *Mārkaṇḍeya Purāṇa*,[125] and *Devī Purāṇa*,[126] which also mention Lakṣmī as one of the manifestations of the goddess.[127] Śakti worship is known to have come into greater prominence in Vaiṣṇavism from the eighth century onwards with the new conception of the female principle in the Vaiṣṇava *saṃhitās*.[128] In the *Pañcarātra* theology she came to be personified as the instrumental and material cause (*kriyāśakti and bhūtaśakti*, i.e., power of acting and becoming) at the root of creation.[129] In the *Lakṣmītantra*, a *pañcarātra* text compiled sometime between the ninth and twelfth centuries, Lakṣmī is conceived as inherent in the supreme being, possessing the powers of delusion, creation, sustenance, dissolution and grace.[130] The development indicates the growing popularity of the Śākta-tantric tradition.

In her fierce forms as Caṇḍikā, Cāmuṇḍā and Kātyāyanī the goddess was widely worshipped by both Aryans and non-Aryans. Blood rites involving head-offering, and sacrifices, human as well as animal, played an important part in the cult. In the *Kuvalayamālā* sailors in peril are seen making propitiative promises of an animal sacrifice to Caṇḍikā.[131] King Dṛḍhavarman, we read, was willing to cut off his head and present it to Kātyāyanī, in his anxiety to procure a son.[132] Kātyāyanī's representation in her *Mahiṣāsuramardinī* form, her foot placed on Mahiṣāsura whom she had felled with a trident (*triśūla*)[133] shows her identification with Durgā. The *Samarāiccakahā* refers to animal sacrifice before the tutelary goddess to ward off the evil effects of a bad omen.[134] In the *Karpūramañjarī*, the queen has a sanctuary of Cāmuṇḍā built at the foot of the banyan tree that stands in the middle of the pleasure-garden. Known also as Kālī, the dissolution of the universe was said to be her pleasure-house, the blood of the demons her fiery draught which she quaffed in the presence of Kāla, from a goblet made of the skull of *Parameṣṭhin* (Brahmā).[135]

From the *Samarāiccakahā* we learn that Caṇḍikā was the presiding deity of certain towns (*nagaradevatā*). Prayers were offered to her for the well being of one's relatives, with the worshipper fasting and thereafter residing at her sanctuary at night.[136] *Aṣṭamī*, *Navamī* and *Caturdaśī* were the days considered suitable for her propitiation.[137] The Caṇḍī aspect of the goddess had become popularised amongst the brahmanised people by the time of the composition of the *Caṇḍīmāhātmya* or *Devīmāhātmya* section of the *Mārkaṇḍeya Purāṇa*,[138] which comes from the sixth century at the latest.[139] The work recommends *bali* and offerings of animals to the goddess.[140] It also mentions the eighth, ninth and fourteenth days of the lunar fortnight as especially holy,[141] thus confirming the evidence of the Prākrit works.

Amongst the most ardent devotees of Caṇḍikā were the people of the wild forest tribes, who worshipped her with grim and terrifying blood rituals. The *Samarāiccakahā* gives a graphic description of the blood-stained shrine of Caṇḍikā who also known as Kātyāyanī, received worship from the Śabaras as their tutelary goddess. Its very precincts were gloomy and forbidding, marked by a decadent old tree, piles of worm eaten wood and an enormous snake-infested anthill. To the branches of the tree were attached pieces of cloth, heads, hooves, horns and necks of buffaloes and rams. With flocks of crows and vultures hovering around, obscuring the rays of the sun, the place, bestrewed with skeletons, bore the appearance of a veritable cemetery. Offerings of blood saturated the entire ground, presenting a sight gladdening to the ghouls. Human corpses formed the lofty wall (*prākāra*) around the shrine, and headless trunks made up its portals (*toraṇa*), to which was tied a garland of human skulls. Frightful lion-heads formed the spires (*śikharas*) of the wall while the skin of a leopard attached to a long bamboo served as a flag. Inside the sanctum was covered with freshly removed skin. Its ivory walls had tridents engraved on them. Skulls filled with human fat were lighted as lamps. Burning *bilva* and *guggula* provided the incense. The image of Kātyāyanī represented her in the terrific form (*ghorarūpā*), holding in her hands the *kodaṇḍa* (bow), *khadga* (sword), *ghaṇṭā* (bell) and the tail of *Mahiṣāsura*.[142] Human sacrifices were offered to her by the Śabaras anxious to secure their desired object by pleasing her.[143]

The popularity of the mother goddess among the tribals is very ancient and various non-Aryan elements have been distinguished in the evolution of the cult of the Devī or Durgā.[144] The lengthy hymn of 52 couplets addressed to Vindhyavāsinī, also called Caṇḍī, Śabarī, and Nārāyaṇī, which occurs in the *Gauḍavaho* of Vakpati, composed in AD 725, also pictures the gruesome temple of the goddess who was offered daily human sacrifice by the Śabaras.[145] By the eighth century, as we have seen above, these tribal cults had been gradually absorbed into the brahmanical religion, as cultural assimilation went apace with social and political assimilation.[146] It was presumably because of this aboriginal element in the formation of her character that the Purāṇic Devī became a terrible goddess who had to be appeased by human and animal sacrifices.[147]

By the appellation of Durgā too the deity was well known[148] amongst the Aryans. As Āryā or Ajjā she was propitiated with offerings of slices of human flesh.[149] Koṭṭajjā or Koṭṭāryā appears to have been another form of the goddess, who was worshipped with the ringing of bells.[150] Upadhye and V.S. Agrawala identify her as Korravai or Koṭṭavai, the goddess of the Tamil land, whose worship spread towards many centres in north India up to the Himalayas where at Koṭṭal Garh in Almora district there was a shrine dedicated to her.[151] As Gaurī, she formed the left half of Śiva's *Ardhanārīśvara* form.[152] On the fourth day of the *Hindolaka* or swing festival, women would pay homage to her as Bhagvatī Gaurī, the beloved of Hara,[153] with flowers and put up a swing in front of her image.[154] In the form of Lakṣmī or Śrī, she was represented as seated on the divine lotus, flanked by mighty elephants.[155] The *ardhanārīśvara* concept of Śiva reflects the greater influence of Śaktism on Śaivism that may be attributed to the growing importance of the mother goddess cult which postulated that Gods were ineffective without their Śaktis. The Gajalakṣmī form of the goddess and Gaurī aspect in which she was worshipped with flowers indicate the worship of her benign forms.

The mother goddess acquired an outstanding position amongst the votaries of Jaina faith as well. In the *Kuvalayamālā* Bhagvatī Rājyaśrī is shown to be instrumental in the instruction of King Dṛḍhavarman into the Jaina faith.[156] Kuvalayacandra, an adherent of the Jaina faith, himself recommends the worship of the goddess for this purpose.[157] The conception of Lakṣmī in Jainism is very old as the goddess is mentioned in the Kalpasūtra as one of the objects of Triśalā's dream.[158] The *śāsanadevīs* of the tīrthaṅkaras became objects of independent cult worship[159] which reveal śākta-tantric currents in Jainism. Other goddesses also assumed an important place in the Jaina pantheon. According to Uddyotana, he was able to compose one hundred verses in *anustubh* metre (*granthas*) within three hours (a *prahara*) due to the benign favour of Hrīdevī, who dwelt in his heart.[160] She is known to be a deity of the *Mahāpadmahrada* in Jaina mythology, who plays a significant role in Jaina rituals and *tantra*.[161] As believers in *ahiṃsā*, the Jainas looked down upon immolation of living beings to Caṇḍikā with disfavour and favoured her worship with flowers, incense etc.[162]

Archaeological and epigraphic evidence testify to the popularity of both the pacific (*saumya*) and fierce (*ugra*) aspects of Śakti worship in Rajasthan from early times.[163] Traces of Śākta ideas are found also in the literature of the Bauddhas during this period.[164] From epigraphs we learn that Nāgabhaṭa II, Bhoja and Mahendrapāla I were devotees of Bhagvatī.[165] The Daulatpurā inscription from Didwana (AD 843) bears a four-armed standing figure of the goddess with a lion placed on either side beside her feet.[166] From Narhaḍ we have an image of *Mahiṣāsuramardinī* assignable to the eighth century AD.[167] The slab from Mātā jī kī Sāla, Ghaṭiyālā (Marwar), bearing Kakkuka's inscription of VS 918 has the figure of a goddess seated on a lion, who is identified as the Jaina goddess Ambikā.[168] Beautiful representation of Gajalakṣmī come from Ābānerī (Jaipur, eighth century), Āmjhara (dist. Dungarpur, *c.* eighth-ninth centuries AD) and Sirohi (ninth century AD).[169]

Sun

The sun-god was also worshipped by many in Rajasthan. The *Kuvalayamālā* speaks of his widespread worship as Ravi[170] and Āditya.[171] Outside Rajasthan, Multan was a flourishing centre of the solar cult,[172] which must have been visited by quite a few pilgrims from Rajasthan as well. The *Kuvalayamālā* refers to the current belief that a visit to the Bhaṭṭāraka of Mūlasthāna could cure leprosy.[173] This Bhaṭṭāraka appears to be no other than the sun-god of Multan as we have also the story of Sāmba in the *Sāmba Purāṇa, Bhaviṣya Purāṇa, Varāha Purāṇa*, and *Skanda Purāṇa* which relates that Sāmba, cured of leprosy by worshipping Sūrya, built the temple of Mūlasthāna or Multāna in his honour.[174]

The Dholpur inscription of Cāhamāna Caṇḍamahāsena, AD 842, records the construction of a temple of the sun-god by him.[175] Osia, Mandor, Bhīnmāl and Sirohi were all important centres of sun-worship.[176]

Brahmā

The popularity of Brahmā had diminished considerably. Though regarded as the creator of the universe, he was not only surpassed by the other members of the Hindu triad but also ceased to figure amongst the principal cult deities of the period. The *Kuvalayamālā* which lists the names of various divinities, major as well as minor,[177] fails to mention Brahmā. Certain legends recorded in the *Dhūrtākhyāna* belittle him. Brahmā, we are told, once claimed to be the creator, as the four *varṇas* had emerged from his body. At this Keśava laughed ridiculingly and retorted that Brahmā was as good as his servant. The whole universe, he pointed out, existed within him, and since Brahmā himself had been born from his navel, it did not behove him to talk thus.[178]

Yet another legend in the *Dhūrtākhyāna* purportedly quoted from the *Mahābhārata* relates how Brahmā while practising severe austerities was distracted by the nymph Tilottamā, sent on purpose by Indra, and developed five faces to gaze at her, one of which was plucked by Śiva. Svedakuṇḍalin, a person born from the perspiration of Brahmā thereupon overthrew Śiva but his battle against Ratnakuṇḍalin, a being created from the blood of Viṣṇu, was declared drawn by the gods.[179] Brahmā, whose austerities had been destroyed, was unable to secure victory. The story of Śiva's cutting off one of the heads of the polycephalous Brahmā is related by various texts, such as the *Matsya,*[180] *Brahmāṇḍa*[181] and *Skanda*[182] *Purāṇas*. The *Liṅgodbhava mūrti*, referred to above, shows Brahmā as a respectful attendant of Śiva.

But that Brahmā was still worshipped in some localities can be seen in the *Samarāiccakahā* where painters refer to his skilful creation of the beautiful universe,[183] and the fulfilment of one's desires is attributed to the grace of Prajāpati.[184] The temple at Vasantgarh (Sirohi), built probably in the seventh century, has a two-armed and three-faced Brahmā image.[185] The Brahmā temple at Pushkara is also very ancient. Many Brahmā images have been discovered at Sevāḍī (Marwar), Basāḍ (Pratāpgarh), Sirod (Kota), Osia (Jodhpur) etc.[186]

Minor Gods

Among minor gods popularly worshipped in those days special mention may be made of Gaṇeśa, Skanda and Kāmadeva. The cult of Gaṇapati that rose to importance about the sixth century[187] had become well established in Rajasthan by our period. In the *Kuvalayamālā* the name of Gaṇādhipa is mentioned amongst popular non-Jaina deities,[188] while sailors in distress call upon Vināyaka for help.[189] The legend regarding the birth of Gaṇādhipati from the limbs of Pārvatī is mentioned in the *Dhūrtākhyāna.*[190] The Ghaṭiyālā inscription of Pratihāra Kakkuka (AD 862) opens with an obeisance to Vināyaka and is engraved on a column which has four images of Ganeśa facing the four quarters as its capital piece.[191] A beautiful Gaṇapati-Gajalakṣmī-Kubera relief (eighth-ninth century) comes from Ābānerī (Jaipur).[192] Among earlier representations of Gaṇeśa are the Tanesar (Udaipur) Gaṇapati image (fifth-sixth century AD) and Gaṇapati in the company of the Saptamātṛkas and Śiva at Mandor (seventh century AD).[193]

Skanda was well known by his various names such as Mahāsena,[194] Svāmī,[195] Svāmīkumāra[196] and Ṣaṇmukha.[197] The *Kuvalayamālā* includes the name of Skanda in its list of popular deities.[198] That he enjoyed considerable importance is evident from the reference to shrines dedicated to Skanda, known as *Ṣaṇmukhālayas*,[199] and *Svāmigṛhas.*[200] Peacocks (*śikhins*) and cocks (*kukkuṭas*) are the well known emblems of Skanda, associated with him since early times,[201] and the *Kuvalayamālā* significantly describes his temples as 'resounding with the cries of peacocks and cocks'.[202] From Choṭī Khāṭū (Nagaur) we have a beautiful six-armed and six-faced image of Skanda, assignable to the eighth century AD.[203] Earlier representations of Skanda come from Aghāpur (near Bharatpur), most probably of the Kuṣāṇa period; Mālavanagara (near Tonk), of the Gupta period, and Tanesar (Udaipur), belonging to the sixth century AD.[204]

Spring was the time for *Madanamahotsava*, when people visited the temple of Madana,[205] took out various *carcarīs* (song and dance groups) and made merry.[206] Kāmadeva was a popular god from ancient times and a beautiful plaque depicting the god has been discovered at Nagara (Jaipur), assignable to the early centuries before Christ.[207]

Tantricism

Tantricism enjoyed considerable popularity during this period. In contrast to earlier Purāṇas which chose to denounce the Tantras as deluding scriptures (*mohanaśāstras*),[208] the Purāṇas belonging to about the end of the eighth century or beginning of the ninth century began to recognise the tantras as one of the authorities on religious matters.[209] Hinduism, Jainism, Buddhism, all developed tantric aspects. The use of mystic practices, *mantra* (formulae) and *maṇḍala* (magic circles), it came to be increasingly believed, led one to the attainment of various supernatural powers (*siddhis*). A growing belief in the occult and the conception of power personified as a goddess characterised these tantric cults. The composition of various tantric texts, including Vaiṣṇavite *Pañcarātra Saṃhitās, Śaiva āgamas,* Buddhist *Tathāgata Guhyaka* and Śākta *Kubjikāmata Tantras*, is assigned to the seventh and eighth centuries.[210]

Among the Brahmanical tantric sects the *Kāpālikas* and *Kaulas* figure prominently in contemporary works. The weird practices of the former and miraculous powers associated with them have already been referred to in the account of the Śaivite sects. The latter finds mention in the *Karpūramañjarī* of Rājaśekhara. Bhairavānanda, an adherent of the *Kaula* way claims that he can bring the moon down, stop the sun and fetch the wives of *Yakṣas*, gods or *siddhas*.[211] As a proof of his miraculous powers, he transports Karpūramañjarī to the king's presence from afar,[212] makes *ketakī* flowers bloom out of season,[213] and is accepted as preceptor by no less a personage than the queen herself.[214] He declares the *Kaula* religion to be highly commendable as it led one to salvation through the use of meat, wine and women while others prescribed meditation (*dhyāna*), study of *Vedas*, sacrifices etc.[215] Drunk though he is, not a word against him is uttered in the entire play, which indicates the wide acceptance of such practices in those days.

The religious school which held that there was no difference between non-forbidden (*bhakṣya*) and forbidden (*abhakṣya*) food, prohibited and non-prohibited in sex relations (*agamya* and *gamya*) in the *Kuvalayamālā*[216] was also evidently representing the *Kaula* school as the same theory is presented by the *Kulārṇava tantra* which expects the *sādhaka* (aspirant) to go beyond dualities of all kinds.[217] The view was strongly criticised by the Jainas on the ground that it went against the principle of *Indriya nigraha* (control over the senses).[218]

Worship with the *pañcatattvas, matsya* (fish), *māṃsa* (flesh), *madya* (wine), *mudrā* (fried or parched grain) and *maithuna* (coition) was a distinctive feature of the tantric cults. It was difficult to restrict the use of these to religious purpose alone[219] and it is apparent from the *Karpūramañjarī* that various excesses had come to be committed under cover of *pañcatattva* worship. The *Yaśastilaka* of Somadeva also refers to the *Kulācāryas* who believed that salvation resulted from unhesitating indulgence in all kinds of food and drink, forbidden or otherwise.[220] These developments, it may be noted in all fairness to the exponents of the tantric religion, were not in keeping with the true spirit of tantricism. The author of the *Kulārṇava* strongly states: It is not to be supposed that religion consists in a mere enjoyment of these things, for then drunkards and meat-eaters would be regarded as highly religious personages.[221] Further these reprehensible features appear to have been current only amongst extremist sects such as the *Kaulas*. The popular practice of tantricism was restricted merely to use of mystic formulae and diagrams, as will be seen below.

While tantricism had gained popularity amongst almost every section of society, its closest association was with the forest tribes, amongst whom it is believed to have been prevalent since ancient times.[222] Reference has already been made to the bloody rites and human sacrifices that accompanied their worship of Caṇḍikā, an elaborate description of which is to be found in the *Samarāiccakahā*. In the *Samarāiccakahā* again we read of a god who appears in the guise of a Śabara physician, draws a magic circle, places inside it the patient Arhadatta, applies medicines consecrated with magic formulae and drives away the disease by means of his magic *vidyā*.[223] In the *Kuvalayamālā* an occult *vidyā* practised by vidyādharas is called *Śābarī vidyā* and its initiates don the apparel of patra-śabaras.[224] That other such *vidyās* were to be practised in the guise of Mātaṅgas, and Pulindas, in forests and mountains reveal strong aboriginal associations with these practices.[225] The reference to *Kāpālikabālā*[226] indicates that women also practised tantric *sādhanā*. Tantric texts such as the *Gautamīya Tantra*[227] and *Mahānirvāṇatantra*[228] confirm that tantric initiation was open to members of all castes and women.

In desperate circumstances, people from all walks of life resorted to tantric practices. The *Kuvalayamālā* relates how a queen had recourse to various modes of *mantra, maṇḍala* and *tantra* in order to obtain a much desired issue.[229] Elsewhere in the work we read that king Dṛḍhavarman, in his anxiety to procure a son, contemplated cutting off the flesh of his arms to please Śiva, presenting his head to *Mahiṣāsuramardinī*, selling human flesh (*mahāmāṃsa*) to the goblins (*vetālas*), burning *guggula* on his bare head and appeasing the mothers (*matṛkas*) with bloody rites.[230] In another story, the prince sells his flesh to the goblins to procure vital information.[231] Burning of *guggula*, which is specifically mentioned as a contemporary practice by Uddyotana,[232] was as the *Kuvalayamālā* tells us, extremely torturous as the entire head got scorched in the process.[233] Reference to the sale of human flesh and the burning of *guggula* occurs also in the earlier work of Bāṇa in his description of the rites performed for the recovery of Prabhākaravardhana,[234] indicating the origin of these practices in a period much earlier than ours.

The *Kuvalayamālā* refers to various *siddhis* or mystic powers cultivated in those days, such as the *Añjanasiddhi*,[235] which enabled one to perceive hidden treasures, *Mantrasiddhi*,[236] accomplished by means of *mudrā* and *maṇḍala, Tantrasiddhi*,[237] *Yakṣiṇīsiddhi* (control over a *yakṣiṇī*)[238] *Rākṣasasiddhi* (control over a demon),[239] *Paiśācīsiddhi* (control over a she-demon),[240] *Bilapraveśa*[241] (entry into a hole), *Asuravivarapraveśa*[242] (entry into the demon's cavern) and *Dhātuvāda*[243] (changing base metal into gold). An idea of the potency of these occult powers and rituals connected with them can be had from the *Samarāiccakahā*, in which we read of a *siddhaputra* known as Siddhasena because of his mystic powers. Asked by his friend for a display of his powers, he declared a *maṇḍala* (magic circle) to be necessary for the purpose. Accordingly white mustard and other necessary equipment was gathered and both he and his friend repaired to the cemetery at the dead of night. There the *Siddhaputra* drew a *maṇḍala*, lighted the fire, handed his friend a sword counselling him to remain vigilant, and started the recitation of the mantra (*mantrajāpa*). After a short while there appeared a yakṣa maiden (*yakṣakanyā*) of exquisite beauty, who presented the friend with a magic shawl that rendered the wearer invisible.[244] Reference to the pursuit of the accomplishments of *nidhivāda*, finding of hidden treasure, *dhātuvāda, asuravivarapraveśa, yakṣakanyākāmitva*, i.e., marriage with a *yakṣa's* daughter, *antardhāna*, i.e., getting invisible, and *siddhañjana* in the Harṣacarita and Kādambarī[245] testify to the cultivation of such *siddhis* in the earlier time of Bāṇa as well.

Uttarasādhakas and *uttarasādhikās* (male and female assistants) were considered necessary for the attainment of *vidyās* or spells. In the *Samarāiccakahā*, king Vijayadharma's wife is carried off by a *mantrasiddha* (adept in *mantras*) who wanted to make use of her for the attainment of some spell (*mantra-vidhāna*). The despondent king was assured by the magician that the queen would return safely after six months, physically unharmed and her virtue untouched.[246] The context is significant as it shows that the involvement of women in magical rites did not necessarily imply setting aside of rules of morality, as in the case of Bhairavānanda. Elsewhere we read how the want of an *uttarasādhaka* makes Sanatkumāra suffer anxious moments and despair over his ever securing the spell though he knows how to attain it.[247] Taking into account the aboriginal background of the tantric mother goddesses, the composition of tantric texts chiefly in outlying areas, the situation of the earliest *śaktapīṭhas* outside mid-India and the association of certain tantric texts with particular tribes, which suggest that tantricism originated in the tribal circle, the growth of tantricism in the early medieval period has been linked with the practice of land grants in tribal areas, which necessitated assignation of a high ritual status to tribals who had been recruited as śūdras and their women who enjoyed a higher status in tribal belts, that was accomplished by providing them with tantric initiation.[248] Whatever may be the origin of these practices, it cannot be gainsaid that the large-scale prevalence of tantric practices facilitated the gradual amalgamation of non-aryan races by minimising the cultural gulf that existed between them.

Jainism

Jainism, which was in existence in Rajasthan in the second century BC,[249] was in a flourishing state. Great Jaina saints such as Haribhadra Sūri came forward to raise their powerful voice against the growing malpractices of the Jaina sect and re-establish its ancient ascetic ideals, thus infusing Śvetāmbara Jainism with a new life. As noted above,[250] he wrote not only abstruse philosophical works but also popular tales for the edification of the masses. His work was ably carried on by his pupil Uddyotana, the author of the *Kuvalayamālā* and Siddharṣi Sūri, who completed the *Upamitibhavaprapañcākathā* at Bhillamāla in AD 905.

From the *praśasti* of Uddyotana in the *Kuvalayamālā* we learn that Jābālipura or Jalor was in his times a city rich in Jaina temples and abounding with Jaina laymen.[251] The *Kuvalayamālā* itself was composed by Uddyotana in a lofty temple dedicated to Ṛsabha-Jinendra, which was constructed at the instance of Vīrabhadra,[252] probably the same *ācārya* Vīrabhadra whom he names as his scriptural preceptor (*siddhānta guru*).[253] Uddyotana's teacher-ancestor Śivacandragaṇi, removed from him by four generations, is said to have moved from Pavaiyyā to Bhillamāla or Bhīnmāla with the express purpose of paying respects to Jina temples. His (Śivacandra's) pupil was Yakṣadatta bearing the title of *kṣamāśramaṇa*, of great glory and far spreading fame. This Yakṣadatta had many pupils endowed with penance, spiritual ability and miraculous gift (in their words) and they rendered the Gurjara country beautiful by Jina temples.[254] Jainism was thus deeply entrenched in Rajasthan in the time of Uddyotana. The ruling king of Jalor in the time of Uddyotana was Vatsarāja,[255] identified with the Pratihāra ruler of the same name.

Epigraphic, literary and numismatic evidence corroborates that Jainism enjoyed extensive patronage under the Imperial Pratihāras and other ruling families in Rajasthan. According to the *Purātanaprabandha-saṃgraha*, Nāgabhaṭa I extended his patronage to a Jaina scholar named Yakṣadeva who can be identified with *Kṣamāśramaṇa* Yakṣadatta of the *Kuvalayamālā*.[256] The Jaina temple of Osia, Jodhpur, refers to Vatsarāja of the Pratihāra dynasty, in whose reign the temple either existed or was built.[257] According to the *Prabhāvakacarita*, Nāga-bhaṭa II spent much money on setting of Jaina images acting under the advice of the Jaina *ācārya* Bappabhaṭṭi Sūri.[258] Kakkuka, the Pratihāra ruler of Mandor, though himself a brahmanical Hindu, built a temple of Jina at Rohiṃsakūpa.[259] Caves and ruined Digambara Jaina temples in Kota state are assignable to the period between the eighth and tenth centuries.[260] This attests that Jainism, which is known to have enjoyed some popularity in the seventh-century Rajasthan from the discovery of the beautiful metal images from Piṇḍavāḍā-Sirohi,[261] had acquired a strong hold in Rajasthan during the Pratihāra period.

Several factors appear to have been responsible for this development. Firstly, Rajasthan was the centre of the remarkable activity of various Jaina *ācāryas* as noted above, who endowed with deep learning, led an exemplary austere life and made sincere efforts to promote Jainism by means of religious narratives into which they introduced several jocular and amorous contexts to hold the attention of the masses, besides philosophical works for the edification of the learned. Secondly, if the Jaina tradition be believed, Jainism received the patronage of the Pratihāra rulers, Vatsarāja, Nāgabhaṭa I and Bhoja.[262] Thirdly, it received, as the evidence of the Prākrit works indicates, the support of the mercantile class, to whom Jainism appeared attractive as it gave them a high status in society, commensurate with their high economic status, and advocated *ahiṃsā* which was conducive to peace that promoted trade and production.[263] Lastly, Jainism also gained support of the lower classes because of its liberal attitude towards them.[264]

Jaina System of Worship

The Jaina system of worship consisted mainly of the worship of the tīrthaṅkaras. The introductory *maṅgala* (auspicious introduction) of the

Kuvalayamālā opens with appropriate salutations to Ṛṣabha, the first tīrthaṅkara, secondly to Mahāvīra and then the rest of the Jinas.[265] Under the influence of the brahmanical religion, the practice of image worship, which from the discovery of the Mauryan torso of a Jina figure at Lohānipur near Patna is to be traced at least to the Mauryan period,[266] became extremely popular. A set ritual of idol worship evolved. First came the *abhiṣeka* ceremony, the ceremonial bathing of the image with water collected in pitchers. Next the idol was anointed with fragrant pastes, decorated with flowers and incense was burnt before it. The worshipper would address verses of adoration to the Jina and prostrate himself before the image.[267] *Aṣṭamī* and *Caturdaśī* (eighth and fourteenth day) were the special days for such worship.[268] The devout started their day with *suprabhātastotras*, morning hymns addressed to the Jina and five exalted beings.[269]

The evidence of the *Kuvalayamālā* indicating the existence of numerous temples has already noted. Jaina laymen are said to have bathed, purified themselves and offered worship at these temples,[270] some of which were established in private houses.[271] The *Samarāiccakahā's* description of Ṛṣabha's temple, the *caitya* Śakrāvatāra, which was visited by the monk Samarāditya along with his pupils to pay homage, as standing amidst an immense garden, effulgent as the white lotus, milk, winter clouds, jasmine and moon; resplendent with manifold banners; the seat of the deity made of emerald slabs; its pavement paved with jewels; adorned with *śālabhañjikā* figurines, pearl festoons and jewel lamps; laden with the fragrance of incense; the image of Ṛṣabha to be approached by a jewelled staircase,[272] indicates the magnificence of temples built by rich devotees. The *Kuvalayamālā* also refers to a temple of Jina (*jinagṛha*) in heaven adorned with manifold images made of precious stones.[273]

The phrase *lāñchana-lāṃchita* (marked by a cognizance) used in connection with an image of Ṛṣabha[274] indicates the existence of distinctive signs of the tīrthaṅkaras. The practice of marking out a Jina figure with a distinctive sign did not exist in the Kuṣāṇa period[275] and their first appearance in art is known from the depiction of a conch symbol with the sculpture of Neminātha on the Vaibhāra hill, Rājgir (Bihar), having an inscription in Gupta characters, referring to Candragupta II.[276] The reference to Jina images of different colours, some dark-complexioned, some fashioned out of crystal, others out of sapphire, ruby, chrysoberyl and emerald[277] suggests that the practice of associating particular complexions with different tīrthaṅkaras was in existence. Details regarding their complexions including white, golden, red, black or dark-blue as well as cognizances are given in the *Tiloya-pannati, Pratiṣṭhāsāroddhāra* and the *Abhidhānacintāmaṇi* of Haribhadra.[278] Mention is also made of a colossal image of tīrthaṅkara Ṛṣabha, made of white marble.[279] This is significant as it shows the use of white marble for making tīrthaṅkara images during the eighth century, a practice later continued throughout the medieval period.[280] There is reference also to a huge yakṣa image with the miniature white marble figure of Jina as a crest.[281] An excellently worked image of Yakṣarāja Kubera, of the eighth century AD, depicting the miniature figures of a Jina both in the crown and head of the deity has been discovered at Bānsī (near Chittor).[282] The Vasantagarh (Sirohi) bronze image of Ṛṣabhanātha, dated AD 687, is the earliest Jina image discovered in Rajasthan so far.[283] Excellent stone images bearing perfect design and execution, graceful poses and facial expressions were made during the period between eighth and thirteenth century AD.[284] Two images of Neminātha of the eighth or ninth century AD have been discovered at Narhaḍ.[285]

The popularity of image worship, its elaborate rituals and the variety of icons indicate the large-scale infiltration of non-Jaina elements in Jainism which in early times had no place for them. As fervent hymns began to be addressed to Jina as the sole refuge, relative, mother and father,[286] *Bhakti* or devotion came to the forefront and Jainism no longer remained a dry ascetic religion which only a few could follow but was transformed into a vibrant religion with mass appeal. The change was in some ways for the worse, the works of Haribhadra would indicate, as some monks took to living in *caityas* and *maṭhas*, putting to personal use the money collected for religious purposes and even selling images.[287]

Along with idol worship, mental adoration of the Jina and the five *parameṣṭhins* collectively also formed an integral part of Jina worship. Mental worship of the Jina consisted of meditation on Jina as seated in the *samavasaraṇa* (preaching hall) and repetition of the *Jina-namaskāra-cauvīsī* (salutations to the 24 Jinas).[288] *Samavasaraṇa* literally means assemblage and refers to the preaching hall of a Jina, constructed by gods, where gods, men and animals assemble and take their apportioned seats to hear the sermon which the *tīrthaṅkara* delivers immediately after enlightenment.[289] The ceiling in the *Vimala vasahī* (Ābu), built in VS 1088 has a representation of the *samavasaraṇa* amongst its reliefs showing the life of Śāntinātha.[290]

The uttering of the *pañcanamaskāra* or salutations to the five *parameṣṭhins* or exalted beings, viz., the *Arhat, Siddha, Ācārya, Upādhyāya* and *Sādhus* was believed to have great efficacy in view of its religious sanctity, spiritual powers and miraculous force.[291] It was believed to lead not only human beings[292] but even animals[293] to divinity. Elaborate invocations to these five exalted beings occur in the *Kuvalayamālā*[294] which gives us quite a few details about them. The *Arhats* include the *Tīrthaṅkaras* of all times and a salutation to them is said to lead to emancipation.[295] The *Siddha* is one who has achieved destruction of all *karmas*.[296] The *Ācāryas* include the *Gaṇadharas* who are responsible for incorporating in *sūtras* the words of Jina which thereby have come down to us.[297] The *Upādhyāya* is one who propounds the contents of the *Aṅgas* and *Upāṅgas* (Jaina canonical works) for the benefit of the pupils.[298] The *Sādhu* is one who has attained *samyaktva* or right faith and leads a life regulated by the various Jaina vows.[299] Worship of the *pañcaparameṣṭhins* is very old. The *pañcaparameṣṭhi-mantra* is obtained in the beginning of the *Bhagvatī-sūtra* and the *Kalpa-sūtra*.[300] Khāravela's record (second century BC) opens with adoration to the *Arhats* and *Siddhas*.[301]

The fruit of worship of these deities and the ultimate aim behind their adoration was liberation. The Jaina deities, according to Uddyotana, are radically different in nature from other worldly (*laukika*) deities such as Skanda, Rudra etc. The latter are *sarāga* gods, subject to attachment, who like earthly rulers, bestow wealth and welfare when pleased and withdraw their favours the instant they are displeased. In reality, in giving fruits in response to devotion, worship etc. these gods are only *sahabhāvī*, coincidental with the results of one's own *karma* (action). The Jaina gods are *nirāga*, indifferent to praise and blame, who show the path to liberation when respected, and those who worship them get the happiness of *mokṣa* or liberation in due course.[302] Sins disappear at the sight of Jina just as mercury splits into pieces and flies in different directions.[303] The prayers to these deities recorded in the *Kuvalayamālā* are not prayers for help or worldly gains but essentially a meditation on the virtues of the divinity and expression of veneration and gratitude for their having shown the right faith, so that the worshipper may also attain liberation.[304] This is in keeping with the spirit of the canonical work, *Uttarādhyayana Sūtra*, which declared that by adoration of the twenty-four Jinas the soul arrived at purity of faith and promised no material advantages.[305]

The *Samarāiccakahā* draws an analogy between the Jina and the wishing stone, *mantras* etc. which are worshipped and without deriving any benefit from being worshipped still reward the worshipper.[306] The means of worship, Haribhadra elaborates, consists of the observance of right conduct, whereby one attains birth as a god, beautiful form, perception etc. and reaches final beatitude.[307] Thus though ritual worship found a place in Jainism in Rajasthan, leading Jaina saints appear to have impressed upon the laity the necessity to free oneself from the shackles of *karma* and strive for the goal of liberation rather than worship gods in the hope of mundane rewards.

Notwithstanding these high ideals enunciated by Jaina saints who envisaged only spiritual benefits for the worshipper however, the ascription of various beneficial results to uttering the name of Jina and devotion to him was bound to encourage the common people to worship the Jina in the hope of temporal gain. Parables such as those of Yajñasoma related by the *ācāryas* themselves must have further promoted this trend. Yajñasoma, we read, seeing an image of Ādinātha felt great respect for him and full of devotion (*bhakti*) surrendered himself to the Jina. Though unacquainted with the identity of the Jina or his teachings, he remained there, worshipping the image with flowers. In course of time, he died of colic and as he breathed his last with his eyes devotedly intent on the face of Ṛṣabha, he was born as a yakṣa, and explained to this people how he got the fruit of salutation (*namaskāra*) to Jina.[308] The *Varāṅgacarita*, a seventh-century work from Karnataka, goes so far as to enumerate concrete benefits accruing from the performance of Jina worship with eightfold objects. The offering of unbroken rice led to long life and that of curd to accomplishment of desired work.[309] The projecting of Jina worship as a rewarding undertaking for the common man who cared less for salvation than for worldly benefit enabled Jainism to compete with other faiths which held out similar promises and thereby served to popularise the faith.

Jaina Philosophy

True to their nature as *dharmakathās*, tales inducive to the adoption of liberation, the *Samarāiccakahā* and *Kuvalayamālā* give a detailed exposition of the Jaina religion, its practice and objective.[310] In consonance with the tenets propounded in the Jaina canonical works, the dogmatical details indicate that the ancient rigorous religious and mental discipline was sought to be inculcated by Haribhadra and Uddyotana. They also give a succinct summary of the salient features of Jainism as propounded by the preceptors. The *dharma* preached by the Jinendra, we are told, consists of charity (*dāna*), good conduct (*śīla*), austerity (*tapas*) and religious reflections (*bhāvanā*).[311] Charity is of three kinds, the gift of knowledge, of security and of things needful for religious life. Good conduct comprises the observance of the five vows; *tapas* of austerities, external and internal; and *bhāvanā* of religious reflections on renunciation, right faith, the law expounded by the tīrthaṅkaras, loneliness and helplessness etc.[312] Due to want of necessary wealth, moral rectitude and physical strength, Uddyotana observes, the first three are not practicable by all, therefore, *bhāvanā* should be cultivated,[313] as it paves the way for liberation. The works thus primarily laid stress on the development of moral and philanthropic virtues as was enunciated by the principles of *śīla* and *dāna* as well as on ascetic values and renunciation as was set down by the principles of *tapa* and *bhāvanā*.

Dharma (principle of motion), *adharma* (principle of rest), *ākāśa* (space), *jīva* (soul), and *pudgala* (matter or atom) are the five fundamentals that make up this world and as the last two, soul and matter interact there are nine principles, viz., *jīva* (animate objects), *ajīva* (inanimate objects), *āśrava* (influx of *karma*), *bandha* (bondage of *karma*), *puṇya* (merit), *pāpa* (demerit), *saṃvara* (prevention of *āśrava*), *nirjarā* (annihilation of *karma*) and *mokṣa* (liberation),[314] which illustrates how *karma* binds the soul and the ways and means of becoming free from it. Each one is responsible for his *karmas*, past and present. Either one has to experience their fruits or exhaust them through penances. The favour and frown of the Almighty and priestly *prāyaścittas* have no value at all.[315] *Karmas* are all powerful, their consequences certain and inescapable.[316] The grades of existence, physical disabilities, intellectual gifts, possessions and other worldly environments depend on one's *karmas*.[317] The eight kinds of *karma* that bind the soul are which obstruct right knowledge (*jñānāvaraṇīya*), which obstruct right faith (*darśanāvaraṇīya*), which lead to experiencing pain and pleasure (*vedanīya*), which lead to delusion (*mohanīya*), which prevent one's entrance on the path that leads to eternal bliss (*antarāya*), which determine the length of life (*āyuḥ*), which determine the name or individuality of the soul (*nāma*) and which determine his social status, *gotra*.[318] The karmic bondage is caused by *mithyatva* or false belief, *avirati* or lack of self-control, *kaṣāya* or four-fold passions, viz. anger, pride, greed and delusion, *pramāda* or negligence and *yoga* or activities of mind, speech and body.[319] Of these the *Kuvalayamālā* lays greatest stress on the need to control the *kaṣāyas*. If in operation, it says, the *kaṣāyas* should be rendered ineffective, for it is under their sway that the soul wanders in the world.[320] The righteous action of the body, speech and mind lead to *puṇya* and evil actions to *pāpa*.[321] The destruction of *karma* already acquired, *nirjarā* is achieved by austerities which are twofold, external and internal. The external austerities comprise fasting (*anaśana*), restricting oneself to little food (*ūnodaritā*), laying various types of restrictions on food, regarding time, place etc. (*vrittisaṃkṣepa*), abstention from dainty food (*rasaparityāga*), mortification of one's flesh (*kāyākleśa*) and withdrawing from one's surroundings (*saṃlīnatā*). Internal austerities include expiation (*prāyaścitta*), politeness (*vinaya*), service to the guru etc. (*vaiyāvritya*), meditation (*samādhi* or *dhyāna*), study (*svādhyāya*) and non-attachment to body (*vyutsarga*).[322] With the exhaustion of all *karma*, the soul attains omniscience and as all activities of mind, speech and body cease, finally the bliss of liberation.[323] Liberation is freedom from old age, disease and the cycle of birth and death, a state of eternal bliss.[324] A liberated soul is described as essentially pure being, possessing no known attribute whatsoever, the abode of infinite delight.[325]

Right faith (*samyak darśana*), right knowledge (*samyak jñāna*) and right conduct (*samyak cāritra*) together led to salvation.[326] Of these *samyak darśana* or *samyaktva* is of prime importance, as it is the basis on which the other two rest. In the *Kuvalayamālā* it has been glorified as a shelter and safety to the soul in the world. It is likened to a 'plank in the sea', 'a caravan in the forest', 'a track in the thicket' and 'a supporting branch on a precipice' etc.[327] One in possession of right faith was characterised by his unwavering devotion to Jainism, a deep conviction in its excellence as compared to other heretic faiths and qualities such as tranquility (*upaśama*), longing for liberation (*saṃvega*), disregard of worldly objects (*nirveda*), compassion (*anukaṃpā*) and friendship towards all (*maitrī*).[328] Right faith leads to right knowledge and adoption of right conduct.

Two courses were open to those desirous of adopting the Jaina way of life—that of the layman (*gṛhidharma*) and that of an ascetic (*yatidharma*).[329] The difference between the two is explained by Haribhadra by the apologue of the two roads. The road of monkhood is said to be a straight one, but narrow and hard to tread, though in all other respects quite safe. The road of the laity, which at the end runs into the direct road, is not quite straight, it is much easier to travel but abounds in danger. But if one is free from hate, love, anger, pride, deceit, greed, desire, the pleasure of the senses, is unperturbed by the twenty-two afflictions (*parisahas*), limits one's food and drink, and practices study (*svādhyāya*), he finally reaches the direct road.[330] *Gṛhidharma* consists of the practise of twelve vows, viz., the five *anuvratas*, three *guṇavratas* and four *śikṣāvratas*. On adopting these the householder was expected to abstain from the obvious (*sthūla*) transgressions of the vows of non-violence (*ahiṃsā*), truth (*satya*), non-stealing (*asteya*), non-possession (*aparigraha*) and chastity (*brahmacarya*). He would further limit his movements to a certain direction (*diśāparimāṇa*), and certain area, abstain from sinful actions (*anarthadaṇḍa*), devote himself to contemplation (*sāmāyika)*, fast on the eighth and fourteenth day of every fortnight (*poṣadhopavāsa*), limit his enjoyments and eat food only after giving food, drink and clothes to the monks.[331] Far more difficult to practise, but essential for liberation was the practise of *yatidharma*[332] which required the cultivation of the virtues of patience (*kṣānti*), humility (*mārdava*), straightforwardness (*ārjava*), freedom from greed (*mukti*), austerity (*tapa*), self-control (*saṃyama*), truthfulness (*satya*), purity (*śauca*) and poverty (*akiñcanatva*).[333] The five vows of *ahiṃsa, satya, asteya, aparigraha* and *brahmacarya* were observed by the monk in their strictest form as *mahāvratas* (great vows). Besides, the monk was expected to adhere to manifold regulations of conduct such as to endure the twenty-two hardships of hunger, thirst, heat etc., pull out the hair, sleep on the ground, not take a bath and abstain from taking food at night.[334]

Great stress was laid on *ahiṃsā* or non-violence in speech, mind and deed. Keeping others in captivity, flogging, mutilation, overloading, and unreasonably withholding food and drink from them were counted as transgressions of the vow.[335] In the *Samarāiccakahā*, a king who sacrifices a cock made out of paste and partakes of the 'flesh' of the artificial cock after it has been roasted acquires bad *karma* of long endurance.[336] In another instance a bitter exchange between mother and son, the son inquiring whether she had been impaled and the mother retorting by asking whether his hands had been cut off, results in the impalement of one and losing of the hands of the other in the next birth.[337]

Jaina Monastic Life

A zealous monk would constantly strive for perfection and his schedule was a busy one. According to the *Kuvalayamālā* his morning hours were devoted to *svādhyāya* or study of the sacred texts.[338] Paying a visit to the preceptor Dharmanandana, the king found the multitude of monks accompanying him immersed in the study of the various canonical texts (*aṅgas*), some of them extremely emaciated due to the practice of severe penance and some meditating on the words of Jina, seated in various postures of meditation such as the *padmāsana* (lotus posture), *Vīrāsana* (hero posture), *Utkuṭukāsana* and *godohāsana* (as if milking a cow).[339] Late at night, the monks remained occupied with various religious routine, i.e., self-study, teaching, reflecting, resolving doubts, exposition by those who had grasped the meaning, listening to the texts after reciting them, composing new hymns (*stotras*), practising meditation, and attending to the service of teachers, learning of the rules of *vinaya*, observation of the three jewels (*triratna*) in the form of *darśana, jñāna* and *cāritra*, extolling knowledge of the tīrthaṅkaras and gaṇadharas, interrogating about points of doubts about their scriptures, practising the art of disputation, developing points of controversies in matters relating to *dharma* and *adharma*, deliberating about bondage and salvation to souls, pursuing the highest form of meditation known as *śukladhyāna* and *dharmadhyāna*, condemning the evils of egoism, pride, anger, greed and speaking against the suffering of the world.[340] Thereafter they retired for sleep for but a short while and were up again in the third quarter of the night.[341] From the *Samarāiccakahā* we gather that the third quarter of the day was assigned to begging.[342] In the last quarter of the day we find the monk immersed in meditation in the *kāyotsarga* posture (standing with arms stiff with the body).[343] The routine is largely in keeping with the *Uttarādhyayana.*[344] The performance of the various *āsanas* came under *kāyākleśa* (self mortification) and the *āsanas* referred to by Haribhadra find mention in the *Sthānāṅga*,[345] *Uttarādhyayana*,[346] *Aupapātika sūtra*[347] and *Daśavaikālika*.[348] *Vīrāsana* is the adoption of the posture in which one sits on a throne with one's feet placed on the ground, in the absence of a throne.[349]

In keeping with the injunctions of the canons[350] the monks led a life of constant travelling,[351] except in the rainy season,[352] when they had a fixed abode. In the *Samarāiccakahā* we read of monks who stayed at places for very short durations, i.e., five nights in the town and one night in the village.[353] Haribhadra is reputed to have raised his voice against the practice of Jaina *sādhus* living a life of ease in *caityas* and *maṭhas*.[354] In the *Samarāiccakahā* too we find him comparing beautiful trees casting a deep shade to objectionable lodgings[355] which shows that he held high the values of ascetic abnegation. As such the life of a monk was extremely arduous and not easy for everyone to follow and initiation was bestowed by the preceptor only after he had made sure that the follower had understood its full implications.[356] The *Kuvalayamālā* relates that to an initiate lacking in necessary devotion the restrictions placed in every sphere including food and constant insistence on politeness, confession and atonement in case of transgression could prove extremely irksome.[357] The monks were initiated by and lived under the supervision of *ācāryas*, Jaina saints who had attained considerable spiritual progress, often possessed either superhuman knowledge (*avadhijñāna*) or omniscience, had gained control over their passions and their five senses, were free from seven types of fear, were compassionate to all living beings, practised the tenfold *dharma* and twelve austerities, were learned in the twelve aṅgas and with their body emaciated with penance preached the *dharma* for the benefit for the masses.[358]

Nuns had their own distinctive position in the Jaina monastic order. Like the monks they too were itinerant,[359] went begging for their food,[360] and performed severe penances that emaciated the body.[361] There is no evidence that the Jaina nun was considered in any way inferior to the Jaina monk. In the *Samarāiccakahā* a nun (*sādhvī*) is represented as having attained omniscience, and when the news spreads, even the king hastens to pay his respects and falls at her feet. Gods are said to appear in the sky as a rain of flowers showers down and jubilation manifests itself everywhere in the city.[362] Women were initiated into the Jaina order by a superior nun, the *Pravartini*, who also exercised general supervision over them.[363] The *Samarāiccakahā* shows that a new initiate sought her counsel in all matters and obtained her permission before going to deliver daily religious instruction at a layman's place.[364] An even higher position was evidently held by the *gaṇinī* who is represented in the *Samarāiccakahā* as a highly respected personage, in control of an order of nuns, who delivered extensive sermons on the Jaina law and acted as a spiritual guide to both men and women, including members of royal families.[365] Mention has been made elsewhere of Yākinī Mahattarā, who became the spiritual mother of Haribhadra Sūri.[366]

Initiation Ritual

The Jaina *dīkṣā* or initiation ritual was a solemn affair. The preceptor, when approached by an aspirant for ordination into monkhood, first assured himself of the sincerity of the initiate by enlarging upon the hardships in a monk's life, before he gave his assent to the latter's request.[367] Young age apparently did not figure as a disqualification. Rather, verses in praise of *bālamunis* (child ascetics) in the *Kuvalaya-mālā* indicate that renunciation during boyhood was actually lauded in Uddyotana's time.[368] The eight years old prince Mahāratha is said to have been initiated into the order by Lord Mahāvīra[369] with the words 'Why delay'. Turning to the Jaina canonical texts, we find that the *Sthānāṅga* excludes those who are too young from entering the monastic order,[370] but there are exceptional cases, like that of Aimutta Kumāra.[371]

The aspirant to monkhood would prepare for *dīkṣā* only after he had obtained the permission of his parents.[372] If he was a king, the acquiescence of his ministers was also secured.[373] An auspicious time for initiation was chosen astrologically.[374] Members of well-to-do families had various gifts distributed and prayers offered at various temples.[375] On the day of initiation, the *Kuvalayamālā* tells us, king Dṛḍhavarman having bathed, perfumed and ornamented himself profusely, travelled in a palanquin to the place of initiation, paid his respects to the preceptor, and formally declared his intention to be initiated. The preceptor finding the initiate to be sincere and the occasion auspicious, had the Jaina temple decorated and Jina image bathed and worshipped with flowers. The king then took off all his ornaments and costly clothes, donned the apparel of a monk and sat before the Jina, received the *Rayoharaṇa* (hand-broom), pulled out three fistfuls of his hair and repeated the *sāmāyika* thrice. The preceptor delivered a religious discourse on the occasion.[376] A similar description of the initiation of prince Śikhin is to be found in the *Samarāiccakahā*[377] which also speaks of the offering of the *sāmāyika, stava, kāyotsarga* and respectful address to the preceptor (*vandanā*). The part of the procedure adopted at the *dīkṣā* ceremony including plucking off the hair and acceptance of the ascetic's equipment is very ancient and is described in the *Nāyā-dhammakahā*.[378] The *sāmāyika*, a short vow to be brought to one's mind promising to shun for life all that is blamable in thoughts, words, deeds, etc., *Cauvisitthava*, a hymnical prayer to the 24 tīrthaṅkaras, *Vandaṇaga*, respectful address to the superior and *kāyotsarga* are mentioned amongst the 73 practices constituting the exertion in righteousness by the *Uttarādhyayana*[379] and declared to be necessary or indispensable (*āvaśyaka*) in the later *Āvaśyakaniryukti*[380] and dealt with in detail. A new monk, the *Kuvalayamālā* tells us, could be distinguished by his white garments, the bunch of feathers in his hand and lately pulled out hair.[381] The bunch of feathers evidently served as a *rayoharaṇa*. The expression *pañca-muṭṭhiya-loya* being a favourite of Uddyotana,[382] it appears that five handfuls of hair were usually pulled out at the time of initiation. The *Ācārāṅgasūtra* also speaks of Mahāvīra plucking out his hair in five handfuls.[383] The *Kuvalayamālā* refers to nine equipments of the Jaina monk, but mentions only three specifically, the *rayoharaṇa*,[384] face-cloth (*mukhapottiyā*)[385] and the begging bowl[386] (*paḍigraha* or *pātra*).

Sallekhanā

Another popular Jaina ritual was *sallekhanā* or voluntary fasting unto death, a ritual which was open to both laymen as well as monks (*śrāvaka* and *śramaṇa*),[387] to men as well as women. It involved not merely renunciation of food but an exercise in rigorous spiritual discipline. Thus on adopting *sallekhanā*, the devotee abandoned all violations (in thought, word or act, and all that is committed, commissioned and consented to) of the sixfold vows (five *mahāvratas* and *rātribhojanaviramana*, giving up food at night), all notions of mineness in the context of possessions, relations and attachments, and all passions (*kaṣāyas*), all activities, through words or deeds, which could cause even remote pain to others.[388] He forgave all, apologised to all and wanted all to forgive him.[389] Offering due confession and repentance for various omissions and transgressions, the devotee dedicated the remainder of his days to religious reflection and adoration of the five *parameṣṭhins* and willingly embraced death.[390] *Sallekhanā*, if properly observed, thus, required fasting, and physical as well as mental discipline, as was emphasised by Jaina *ācāryas* time and again. Forgiveness of offences committed against oneself, repentance for all sins, complete observance of the five vows, casting aside the feelings of love, hatred, companionship, sorrow, fear, dejection etc., progressive renunciation of food and drink, and *pañcanamasakāra* are duly recommended in the *Ratnakaraṇḍaka* of Samantabhadra, a preceptor who lived in an early century.[391] *Sallekhanā*, declared Pūjyapāda-Devanandi, assigned to the fifth to seventh century, is to 'emaciate' both body and passions.[392] The *Bhagvatī Ārādhanā* of Śivārya also declares *sallekhanā* to be twofold, internal dealing with anger and other passions and external, dealing with the body.[393]

The rite of *sallekhanā*, going by the instances of the *Kuvalayamālā* was performed by the Jaina devotee when he knew his end to be near.[394] But fasting unto death was allowed also in dire extremities. The

Samarāiccakahā gives the instance of an innocent man who is impaled as punishment for a crime, and a woman whose hands were cut off by a robber to extract her bangles, seeking permission to starve themselves to death from a Jaina monk who had elucidated the fatal consequences of their sins in the past birth. The monk remarking that it befitted the circumstances advised them to give up attachments, cultivate friendship towards all beings, repent for former sins, and to have belief in right knowledge, conduct and faith taught by the tīrthaṅkaras.[395] Turning to the canonical works we find that while the *Tattvārthasūtra* recommended the adoption of *sallekhanā* when death was near,[396] the *Ratnakaraṇḍaka* declared that *sallekhanā* was giving up the body in times of unavoidable calamity, famines, old age and incurable disease with a view to obtain religious merit.[397]

The observance of *sallekhanā* was considered to be a highly meritorious act and Uddyotana describes it as *paṇḍitamaraṇa* or the wise man's death, which enabled one to get rid of the world, achieve liberation and attain the status of the *siddhas*, the exhaustion of *karmas* thereby ensuring that one died but once.[398] All other kinds of death, according to him, represented *bālamaraṇa*, or the fool's death, which only served to perpetuate one's stay in the world.[399] Early texts like the *Sthānāṅga*[400] and *Uttarādhyayana*[401] also distinguished between *bāla* and *paṇḍitamaraṇa* and lauded the practice of the latter. Death with ones's will, declared the *Uttarādhyayana*, is that of wise men, and at best happens but once.[402]

Uddyotana speaks approvingly of three kinds of *paṇḍitamaraṇa*, viz., *pādapamaraṇa, iṅginīmaraṇa* and *lagaṇḍamaraṇa*.[403] The *Samarāiccakahā* refers to various monks giving up their life by *pādapogamana*,[404] which evidently is the same as *pādapamaraṇa*. There is also a solitary reference to *lagaṇḍamaraṇa*.[405] The characteristics of three types of *sallekhanā, bhaktapratyākhyāna, iṅgitamaraṇa* and *pādapogamana* have been set forth in the *Ācārāṅga Sūtra*.[406] Of these the first involved suicide by rejecting food, in which the devotee spread a bed of straw and sat motionless. *Iṅgitamaraṇa* required the devotee to lie on the bare ground, but permitted him to move his limbs. *Pādapogamana* required the devotee to stand motionless (as a felled tree). The *Bhagavatī Ārādhanā* declared the above three types of *maraṇa* to be *paṇḍitamaraṇa*, adopted by a monk who acted in accordance with the prescribed conduct.[407] *Lagaṇḍaśāyī* is mentioned among the *kāyākleśa* postures by the canonical texts,[408] meaning lying like a curved piece of wood, with hollow back and this posture seems to have been adopted for performance of *sallekhanā*. The adherence to strict rules of begging, incessant touring and solemn rites of *sallekhanā* indicates that dedicated monks continued to live up to the ancient ascetic ideals and pursue a life of self-abnegation.

Jaina Tantricism

Jainism did not remain unaffected by tantric influences. While the grosser tantric practices such as *pañcatattva* worship made little headway in Jainism, a pre-eminently ascetic religion, there was a growing belief in the miraculous potency of occult practices. Mystic practices and mantras acquired great significance. The practice of magic spells and charms was not new to Jainism. The *Sūtrakṛtāṅga* mentions various occult sciences which people acquired for attaining success such as the art to make one happy or miserable, incantations, conjuring, art of casting people to sleep, of opening doors etc.,[409] but condemns them as evil. But the *Niryukti* (*c.* fourth century AD) and *Cūrṇi* literature (*c.* seventh century AD) speak of Jaina monks who got alms by conjuring, employing incantations, tricks, and distributing roots and bulbs to cure various diseases.[410] The *Joṇipāhuḍa* was an important work on magic.[411] The *Bṛhatkalpabhāṣya* and *Niśītha Cūrṇi* speak of the accomplishment of *vidyās* by magical practices.[412] The widespread popularity of tantricism made these tantric elements stronger.

From the *Kuvalayamālā* it appears that in the eighth century the shrine of Ṛṣabhanātha, the first *tīrthaṅkara*, had become a *siddhikṣetra*, a centre for the performance and perfection of occult practices. So popular were these mystic cults that their origin was associated with the *tīrthaṅkaras* themselves. Thus in the *Kuvalayamālā*, we read of a vidyādhara couple, who in the guise of patra-śabaras, were under the auspices of the image of Ṛṣabha, pursuing the cultivation of the *śābarī vidyā*, one of the *vidyās* said to be bestowed by Dharanendra on Nami and Vinami, pleased by their worship of Ṛṣabha.[413] Dharanendra is the yakṣa of tīrthaṅkara Pārśvanātha and the association of both Ṛṣabha and him with the *śābarī vidyā* is significant. Initiation into the *śābarī vidyā* involved elaborate worship of the image of Ṛṣabha, occult practices like muttering of *mantras* and uttering of the *vidyā* into the ears of the initiate (*sādhaka*), donning of the Śabara apparel and adoption of the vow of silence (*maunavrata*) and continence (*brahmacarya*) by the *sādhaka*.[414] The *Samarāiccakahā* also reveals that the vidyādharas, semi-divine beings with the power to fly through the air,[415] who occupied an important place in Jainism, were associated with the practice of occult vidyās. It describes how the vidyādhara Cakrasena acquired a mighty spell (*mahāvidyā*). The preparatory operations (*pūrvasevā*) alone took twelve months. When he started the main operation (*pradhānasevā*) he promised security to all living beings within 48 *yojanas* for seven days, gave strict orders to the vidyādharas to prevent killing of any creatures and entered a cave to recite the *mantra* seven lakh times.[416] He taught Sanatkumara the spell Ajitabalā and the way to practise it.[417] Another vidyādhara possessed the *mahākālī vidyā*.[418] In the *Kuvalayamālā*, we read of the vidyādhara maidens summoning the *Prajñapti vidyā*, which was personified as well as deified and helped them to gain knowledge of things at a distance, in this case the whereabouts of the prince Kamagajendra.[419] *Prajñapti* and *Mahākālī* figure in the list of *vidyādevīs*,[420] who form a group of tantric goddesses in the Jaina pantheon.[421] The story of Dharaṇa bestowing 48,000 *vidyās* on Nami and Vinami among which were *mahārohinī, prajñapti (paṇṇatti), gauri* (gori), *vidyutmukhī (vijjumukhi), mahājalā* etc. is related by the *Kalpa ṭīkā* and *Vasudevahiṇḍī*.[422] A valuable set of sixteen mahāvidyās is preserved in the dome of the beautiful *sabhāmaṇḍapa* of the Vimala Vasahī, Mt. Abu, built in *c.* AD 1147.[423]

The yakṣiṇīs, attendant spirits of the tīrthaṅkaras, came to be looked upon as bestower of occult powers during this period and tantric rites were associated with their worship. The *Samarāiccakahā* gives a detailed account of the propitiation of goddess Ajitabalā for the acquisition of a spell. Ajitabalā is the *śāsanadevī* or attendant spirit of tīrthaṅkara Ajitanātha. To acquire the spell, the *sādhaka* had first to enlist the services of an assistant or *uttarasādhaka*. The initial preparation or *pūrvasevā* lasted for six months, during which the worshipper observed the vow of silence, subsisted on limited fruit diet and led the life of a celibate (*brahmacārī*). Then started the *pradhānasevā* or main part of the *sādhanā*. The *uttarasādhaka* was appointed *dikpāla*, the guardian of the quarters. The *sādhaka* himself adopted the *padmāsana* posture, performed the *mudrās* or special positions of fingers and movement of hands, drew the magic circle (*maṇḍala*) and then started the recitation of the *mantra* for one lakh times. Suddenly the atmosphere grew sinister. It seemed the sky gods laughed loudly, the unseasonal clouds thundered, the ocean roared and the earth shook. Terrifying apparitions materialised before the worshipper such as an elephant in rut, and a wicked demoness (*piśācī*), frightfully dark with eyes flashing like lightening, wearing human skin dripping with blood and a garland of severed hand and feet, quaffing blood off a skull and running towards him shouting 'kill, kill'. But as he sat unperturbed and persisted in his *sādhanā* the apparitions simply faded away and the goddess Ajitabalā herself appeared before him. The *sādhaka* wisely did not leave off the recitation of the mantra nor did he salute Ajitabalā until his recitation of the mantra was complete. Thus did he acquire the spell Ajitabalā and was crowned king of the vidyādharas by the order of the goddess.[424] *Mantra, maṇḍala* and *mudrā*, it is evident from the above account, had come to occupy a significant place in Jainism. Representations of the yakṣī Ambikā, exhibiting both her awe-inspiring aspect, riding a lion, and propitious, in the accompaniment of a child and mangoes come from ninth and tenth century Rajasthan.[425] Evidence from South India also reveals the development of yakṣiṇīs into tantric cult goddesses by the close of the ninth century.[426] In Tamilnadu, the worship of yakṣiṇī appears to have superseded and overshadowed even that of Jina himself.[427] It would appear that the yakṣiṇī cult was developed in order to combat the influence of the popular female deities of other competing faiths.[428] Gradually with the desire to attract the common man by appealing to popular forms of worship, they were associated with occult practices and superhuman powers, as the tīrthaṅkaras being projected as idealised human beings could not serve as agents of the occult.[429]

Great mystic value was attached to the *pañca-namaskāra* which is glorified by Uddyotana in various ways.[430] Even one bereft of right conduct (*cāritra*) and knowledge (*jñāna*) could attain divine birth by recourse to it.[431] *Ṇamo Arhantāṇam Ṇamo Savvasiddhāṇam* is the mantra that Kuvalayacandra bestowed on the alchemists who entreated him to disclose the *mantra* whereby he successfully converted base metal into gold while they failed repeatedly.[432] Somadeva also eloquently praises the *pañcaparameṣṭhimantra*[433] and regards it as 'the eternal foundation of all branches of knowledge'.[434]

A perfect tantric atmosphere is created in the *Kuvalayamālā* where a prince goes to the cemetery to propitiate the ghouls (*vetālas*) by the sale of his flesh so that he may obtain knowledge of the whereabouts of an elusive robber. A *vetāla* appears, demands and eats his freshly cut and roasted bony flesh, drinks his blood offered in the prince's severed head.[435] This raises an inquiry from one of the listeners of the narrative as eating of flesh by *vetālas, piśācas* and *rākṣasas* who belong to *devayoṇi* is against Jaina dogmas. Uddyotana's explanation of the episode is that *vetālas* as *vyantara* class of devas did not eat the flesh but threw it away. They were sportive like children and simply sought to test the courage of the prince.[436] This justification is hardly satisfactory and the inclusion of such a context in a work like the *Kuvalayamālā* suggests that the Jainas had come to look upon even such uncanny practices with toleration and sometimes may even have taken recourse to them. The *vetālas* are represented as being quite pleased with the above mode of propitiation and rewarded the prince by imparting the necessary information. Monks learned in the *tantra* and *mantra* find mention elsewhere in the *Kuvalayamālā*.[437] Jaina tantricism however remained strikingly different from tantricism of other sects, with its provision for the vow of silence, celibacy and absence of an *uttarasādhikā* in the practice of occult rites, as noted above.

Other Religious Sects

Various schools of religious and philosophical thought were in existence, besides the principal religious systems already referred to above. Of these we can have some idea from an interesting context in the *Kuvalayamālā* in which exponents of as many as thirty-two different religious beliefs come forward to present their views before king Dṛḍhavarman.[438]

First of all came the sect which advocated the doctrine that the souls (*jīvas*) had momentary existence, the trees had no consciousness, the world was impermanent and *nirvāṇa* signified non-existence.[439] This corresponds to the well-known Buddhistic view. Though the *Kuvalayamālā* makes passing references to Buddha worship[440] and Buddhist monks[441] elsewhere, Buddhism does not appear to have been in a flourishing state in Rajasthan except in areas like Kota where the Shergarh inscription (AD 790) records the construction of a Buddhist temple and monastery by a Nāga chief Devadatta.[442] Though Buddhism was popular in Rajasthan in the early period[443] it was in a state of decline by the time of Hieun Tsang.[444] The process must have been hastened by the activities of Haribhadra Sūri, who is traditionally known as a great enemy of the Buddhists.[445]

Next came the *tridaṇḍins*, who believed that the soul was all-pervasive and could be released from *prakṛti* by means of *dhyāna* and *yoga*. They also laid stress on achieving cleanliness through use of water and earth.[446] Yājñavalkya had laid down that an ascetic (*yati*) should be a *tridaṇḍi*,[447] the reference here being to the three staffs or *daṇḍas* that he carried. But a real *tridaṇḍin* according to Manu[448] and Dakṣa[449] was one who had restraint over his mind, speech and body.

Another view stated anonymously held that the soul was all-pervasive, but was inactive and held down by *prakṛti*. It could however be liberated by the practice of *Yoga*.[450] This view appears to be based on the *sāṅkhya-yoga* philosophy. Others saw the supreme soul as eternal, imperishable and abiding in all things. The king criticised the view saying that if the soul were but one, when one being experienced sorrow, so would others.[451] The view represented seems to belong to the *advaita* sect.

Some believed in the efficacy of sacrifices. One advocated animal sacrifices; another the *vaiśvadeva* sacrifices and offering of food as an oblation to the fire. Sacrifices which were in vogue in third and fourth century Rajasthan,[452] thus continued, though considering the paucity of inscriptional evidence hereafter, they suffered a decline due to the growing popularity of the Purāṇic and Jaina religion. There was also *ṛṣidharma* which consisted of shedding all attachments and retiring to the forest, wearing *valkala* and subsisting on roots, fruits and flowers.[453] Another *dharma* advocated was the *gṛhasthadharma* (dharma of the householder) which included giving of gifts to the brāhmaṇas and *śramaṇas*, the poor and distressed, and worship of the preceptor.[454] Another sect represented an *advaitavāda* (unduality) of an unconventional type, which made no distinction between *bhakṣyā* and *abhakṣya*, what should be eaten or what should not be eaten, *gamya* and *agamya*, prohibited and non-prohibited women.[455] Such an *advaitavāda* could perhaps be recognised only by the *tañtrikas*.[456]

The followers of another sect went so far as to give up even their wives and body for the sake of religion, a case of the cult of devotion carried to the extremities.[457] Others believed in suicide, regarding it as an act of courage and a means of reaching a better world.[458] Some again were in favour of specific suicidal practices such as falling off the precipice[459] or bearing the *guggula*.[460]

The undertaking of public works, such as the excavation of wells and ponds, and establishment of places where water was distributed free to travellers was espoused by the followers of one sect, who may be identified as the *pūrtadharmins*.[461] The popular belief that one's sins could be washed away by bathing in the Ganga, and other rivers, seas and *tīrthas* was presented by others.[462] Some simply believed in *varṇāśrama dharma*.[463] Building temples with the money one earned and arranging for the worship of the deities was the *dharma* commended by others.[464] Some believed that one's sins could be washed away by the chanting of *mantras*.[465] Others favoured meditation, which according to them led to emancipation, perception of the Supreme soul and heaven.[466] Respect paid to parents, elders, gods and men was the *dharma* prescribed by some.[467] The atheist (*nāstika*) view was presented by a sectarian who believed in eating, drinking and making merry, saying that there was neither soul, nor another world, nor any objective of life excepting enjoyment.[468] There were also sectarians who believed in gifts of land, cows, wealth and ploughs to brāhmaṇas.[469]

The killing of tigers, lions, snakes, thieves, and other wicked beings was represented as *dharma* by others.[470] The *pāṇḍurabhikṣu* abstained from the use of all dairy products such as milk, curd, ghee and beef.[471] There were also certain fatalists. One said, 'He who has made the peacocks multicoloured and the swans white he alone should think of our *dharma* and *adharma*, why should we worry?'[472] Another said, 'He who is piously inclined, remains that way and the same is the case of those inclined towards sin.'[473] Certain sectarians believed that *Īśvara* (god) was the guiding force responsible for the bad and good actions of men.[474] The influence of the *sāṅkhya* philosophy can be traced in the view that one who knew the *puruṣa* and the 25 *tattvas*, could not be tainted by sin even if he committed the *brahmahatyā* (murder of a brāhmaṇa).[475] Last of all came the Jaina doctrine which preached abstinence from violence, untruth, stealing etc. and adored *Arhat* as the deity.[476]

The *Samarāiccakahā* gives a detailed exposition of the current philosophy of *nāstikavāda*,[477] which held that the soul was the product of the five elements which by their combination constituted the body and when they reverted to their original form, death is said to have occurred. In reality, it asserted, no soul left the body and departed to the other world, therefore there was no reason to give up pleasures for its sake. Further, human birth depended on the composition of the elements, and not one's merit or demerit. Various interesting arguments to support his case were brought forward by the *nāstikavādin* Piṅgakeśa. His grandfather, he said, was wicked and therefore ought to be in hell but he had not come to warn him, as he would have, as a loving relative. His father on the other hand was a good man and should be in heaven but did not come to instruct him. This proved that there was no soul. Again, a robber put in an iron vessel hermetically sealed died, but no soul was observed to issue from the vessel. Another dead robber was dissected into minute particles, but among them too no soul was found. The materialist philosophy known as *Cārvāka* or *Lokāyata* which finds mention in various earlier works such as the *Arthaśāstra* of Kauṭliya,[478] *Rāmāyaṇa*,[479] and Bāṇa's *Harṣacarita*,[480] is described by Haribhadra in his *Ṣaḍdarśanasamuccaya* as well. Rājaśekhara in his *Kāvyamīmāṃsā* refers to their belief that consciousness in living beings arises out of a combination of the elements, in the same way as a few ingredients produce wine.[481]

The *Samarāiccakahā* also refers to the *Pāṇḍuribhikṣus* as does the *Kuvalayamālā* and their practice of abstaining from milk etc.[482] They are mentioned in the *Harṣacarita*.[483] According to the *Niśītha Cūrṇi*, the disciples of Gosāla, the Ājīvakas were called *Pāṇḍuribhikṣus*.[484] Accordingly V.S. Agrawala identifies them with the *Ājīvakas*.[485]

Brahmanical Ascetics

In our works we also read of Brahmanical ascetics, who dwelt in *tapovanas* or hermitages situated amidst the sylvan forest surroundings, leading a life of rigorous self-discipline.[486] Their food consisted only of roots and fruits.[487] We have in the *Samarāiccakahā* a vivid picture of the *kulapati* or head of the ascetics (*tāpasas*) wearing *valkala* and bearing matted heir, a *tripuṇḍra* mark (consisting of three lines of ashes) on his forehead and an ascetic's water-pot (*kamaṇḍalu*) by his side, peacefully seated on a seat of *kuśa* grass in the midst of a plantain arbour, immersed in deep meditation, turning around a necklace of rosary beads (*rudrākṣamālā*) with his right hand, his throat and lips moving slightly as he chanted *mantras*, his eyes concentrated on his nose and completely withdrawn from all other activities.[488] Elsewhere there is the description of a *tāpasī*, a middle aged female ascetic, with a *puṇḍraka* mark of ashes on her forehead, her matted hair tied above, bearing a putrañjīvaka necklace in her right hand and a *kamaṇḍalu* in her left hand, her body emaciated by long and severe penance.[489] Sulaiman also noted that in India there were persons who in accordance with their profession, wandered in woods and mountains, rarely communicated with the rest of mankind, sometimes having nothing to eat but herbs and fruits of the forest.[490] The references to female ascetics[491] in the *Samarāiccakahā* indicate that notwithstanding the injunctions of the Smṛtis like *Atri* and *Yama* against women's adoption of an ascetic's life,[492] women did adopt it.

The ascetics were expected to lead a life of severe self-restraint, to have their eyes touched with heated iron rods rather than cast glances at the female form, to consume poison rather than succumb to sensual pleasures, to have their tongues cut off rather than speak an untruth.[493] We read of an ascetic who took the terrible vow of eating but once a month, never entering more than one house for getting his meals, regardless whether he got one or not.[494] As a consequence of his austerities, we are told elsewhere, a superior came to be endowed with superhuman knowledge (*divyajñāna*) whereby he could read one's past and foresee the future.[495] On becoming an ascetic, one forgot all earlier enmities. Even the person whose cruel behaviour had driven one to renounce the world in dire despair was now regarded as the *kalyāṇamitra* or benefactor for having led one to the adoption of *dharma.*[496] Worldly wealth held no fascination for an ascetic for he placed gold and pearls at par with straw.[497] Of the activities of *tāpasīs*, besides performance of austerities, the *Samarāiccakahā* mentions culling of flowers, paying obeisance to the fire, listening to Purāṇic stories and entertaining guests.[498] The members of the ascetic order were held in high regard even by the rulers.[499] Thus when two *tāpasakumāras* called upon the king and proffered their blessings, he accorded them due honour by rising and offering them a seat.[500] Later the king visited the hermitage and paid his respects to the superior, inviting him and his disciples to take food at his place.[501]

To conclude, the multiplicity of deities was coincidental with a realisation of the essential unity of the godhead which actuated individuals to propitiate multifarious deities simultaneously. Toleration, peaceful co-existence and mutual respect of deities marked the relationship between the different sects, orthodox as well as heterodox, even as refutation of the religious views of other religious schools continued and the superiority of one's own religion was upheld.

The Purāṇic deities enjoyed a dominant position in the brahmanical pantheon, completely overshadowing older Vedic deities. Amidst the Purāṇic trinity itself, Śiva and Viṣṇu occupied a position of pre-eminence as the central figures of two flourishing theistic sects, while the worship of Brahmā was relegated to the background. Viṣṇu was worshipped variously as Nārāyaṇa, Keśava, Madhumatha, the consort of Lakṣmī and in his incarnatory forms as Varāha, Vāmana and Kṛṣṇa. The incarnation concept contributed to the popularity of Vaiṣṇavism because of the fusion of tribal cults and projection of Viṣṇu as a redeemer who offered succour to the distressed in the world. The assimilation of the powerful Ābhīra tribe of Rajasthan which was closely associated with the popularisation of the Kṛṣna cult must have been facilitated by the acceptance of Kṛṣṇa as an *avatāra.*

Śiva, worshipped both in anthropomorphic and *liṅga* forms, had a dual aspect, benign as well as terrific. His pacific form *ardhanārīśvara* indicates the synthesis of Śaivism and Śaktism. The legend describing the inability of Viṣṇu and Brahmā to locate the extremities of the

Śivaliṅga was obviously designed to establish his superiority. Tantric practices were associated with the Śiva temple at Mahākāla. They also manifested themselves in the Śaiva Kāpālika sect, adherents of which roamed in cemeteries, consumed human flesh and were credited with acquisition of miraculous powers. The prescription of the Kāpālika way of life as a means of expiation and practise of Jaina occult *vidyās* in the guise of Kāpālikas indicates the high respectability of the sect. Another sect of the Śaivas was the Kāruṇika which believed in destroying lower forms of life as an act of compassion.

The mother goddess, representing the dynamic female principle or śakti, conceived in her various aspects as mother, daughter, the goddess of prosperity, goddess of victory and as the destroyer of demons as Caṇḍikā and Kātyāyanī, was widely worshipped and given the honoured place of guardian deity of cities. Blood rites involving human sacrifices characterised her worship as Caṇḍikā by non-Aryans while the rites of head offering and animal sacrifices to the goddess were current amongst the Aryanised people. That her cult had absorbed within itself various aboriginal mother goddess cults in the course of its evolution is indicated by the bloody rites performed to please her and her association with the wild forest tribes, features which were earlier associated with non-aryan goddesses. As Lakṣmī and Gaurī, she gained an important place in Vaiṣṇavism and Śaivism and added to the popularity of these religions. Jainism, in which the importance of Lakṣmī, Hrī and the yakṣiṇīs reveals the inroad of śākta tantric currents, favoured the worship of the goddess with flowers and incense in lieu of flesh offerings.

While the Kāpālikas and Kaulas were the two prominent brahmanical tantric sects, both deemed to lead to acquisition of supernatural powers, the latter representing an extremist sect associated with the use of flesh, wine and women, various tantric features including mystic practices, *mantra* and magic circles had found universal acceptance and were practised by both men and women. The rites of head offering, sale of human flesh to goblins and burning of the incense on the head had made headway in contemporary religious practices. Various occult powers were cultivated by tantric means, with the aid of female as well male assistants, the involvement of the former being in general free from any immorality, the case of the Kaulas being an exception. The offering of an instant antidote for incurable afflictions like snake bites and the attainment of supernatural powers within a short span of time makes the appeal of tantricism understandable. Further it was practised by all sections of society, including women and appeared to provide an easy alternative to the cumbersome discipline imposed by other religions. The close association of tantric vidyās and practices with tribals suggests that the growth of tantric religious practices was largely the result of a fusion between the brahmanical and tribal cults consequent to the increased contact between the two due to the colonisation of tribal areas by rulers.

Śvetāmbara Jainism was a living faith in Rajasthan under the guidance of dedicated *ācāryas* like Haribhadra and Uddyotana, enjoying extensive patronage from royal families and the mercantile class. Numerous temples dedicated to tīrthaṅkaras, whose images were distinguished from each other by distinctive signs, were in existence and a set ritual of idol worship involving an elaborate bathing ceremony had evolved. The adoption of the popular mode of brahmanical mode of idol worship gave the religion an impetus by providing its followers with a definite object for meditation and adoration. Mental adoration of the Jina and worship of the five *parameṣthins* also formed an integral part of Jaina worship, the aim and fruit envisaged being liberation and not worldly gains, but here also the ascription of various beneficial results to *bhakti* or devotion to the Jina as an immediate effect was bound to tempt the common people to worship Jina for temporal gains and must have served to further popularise the faith. The uncompromising Jaina *karma* theory with its insistence that one was responsible for one's words, acts and thoughts and no divine intervention could undo the effect of one's *karma* was a forceful incentive to the individual to act better, which was put across to the people in an attractive manner through stories. The ancient canonical injunctions requiring rigorous self-discipline, *ahiṃsā* and an itinerant monastic life were upheld by Haribhadra and Uddyotana. A dynamic religion, Jainism drew followers from all castes. Haribhadra was a brāhmaṇa, Uddyotana was a kṣatriya. Śūdras and caṇḍālas were also welcomed into the fold, while a large number of vaiśyas appear to have embraced the religion. Women initiates were highly respected, considered worthy of attaining omniscience and acted as spiritual guides for men as well as women. Two important Jaina rituals were the monk's initiation ritual, which was an elaborate affair and the *sallekhanā* ritual, which involved giving up of life by renunciation of food by a Jaina devotee willingly in his old age or sometimes in dire extremities while immersed in religious reflection in an equanimous state of mind.

Jaina monks became learned in *tantra* and *mantra*. Cultivation of occult *vidyās* by means of *mantra* found place in Jainism. The conception of *yakṣiṇīs*, the attendant spirits of tīrthaṅkaras, as bestowers of occult powers and their worship by tantric rites attracted the common man by appealing to popular forms of worship while Jaina tantricism remained distinct and free from the worst features of tantricism by its vow of silence, celibacy and absence of female assistants.

NOTES AND REFERENCES

1. *KM*, p. 2.
2. Ibid.
3. Ibid.
4. *SK*, pp. 4–5.
5. सव्व धम्माणं उवरिं रेहइ जिणयंद-भासिओ धम्मो त्ति। *KM*, p. 3.
6. गोविंद-खंद-रुंदारविंदणाह-गइंद-णाइंद-चंद-कविल-कणाद। Ibid., p. 2.
7. Ibid., p. 68.
8. *KM*, p. 256.
9. Pratihāra records, see below.
10. *ED*, I, p. 17.
11. *KM*, p. 14.
12. Ibid., pp. 82–3.
13. According to the Pratāpgarh inscription of Mahendrapāla II (AD 946), Devaśakti, Vatsarāja, Nāgabhaṭa II and Rāmabhadra were the devotees of Viṣṇu, Maheśvara, Bhagavatī and Āditya respectively. *EI*, XIV, pp. 176 f. The Barāh C.P. of Bhoja confirms this, *EI*, XIX, pp. 18 f. The Sāgartāl (Gwalior) inscription shows that Bhoja I, though himself a worshipper of Bhagavatī, erected within his seraglio a temple dedicated to Narakadviṣ (Viṣṇu). *EI*, XVIII, pp. 99 f.
14. D. Sharma, *Lectures on Rajput History and Culture*, pp. 95–6.
15. *KM*, p. 3.
16. Ibid., pp. 257–8, see below, p. 111.
17. णामाइं सुणिज्जंति वि सासय-रूवेसु सव्वेसु। *KM*, p. 281.
18. एयाण पूयणं अच्चणं च जो कुणइ परम-भत्तीए।
राय व्व तस्स तुट्ठा देंति धणादी य कल्लाणे। Ibid., p. 257.
19. रुद्दा खंदा य पुणो अइबहुए विज्ज-सिद्ध त्ति। Ibid., p. 281.
20. दर्शनं व्यापकत्वेन न विवादोऽस्ति तैः सह। Upamiti, VIII. vv. 895–900.
21. *Dhū.*, I. 39; I. 54; III. 90; IV. 80.
22. *KM*, pp. 26, 68.
23. *Dhū.*, II. 56; V. 112.

24. Ibid., I. 79; II. 41, 45, 58; V. 59.
25. *KM*, p. 27.
26. Ibid., pp. 2, 14, 256.
27. Ibid., pp. 9, 14.
28. विण्हू जगस्स कत्ता सो किर एगण्णवम्मि लोगम्मि . . . तप्पइ तवं अणंतो . . . बंभो णाहीइ पउमगब्भाओ । *Dhū.*, I. 54–6.
29. अब्भा-भूमि कउट्ठे पव्वयदाढे समुद्दजीहाले ।
पविसेहि मज्झ उअरे जा पिच्छ सविब्भमं पुहइं । Ibid., II. 48.
30. महुमहस्स लच्छी । *KM*, p. 9.
31. Ibid., p. 14.
32. पट्ठि णिवेसिय-चक्की गरुलो इव तक्खणं तुरओ । Ibid., p. 27.
33. णारायणो त्ति जइ गवल-कज्जल-सवण्णो । Ibid., p. 26.
34. Gwalior Praśasti of Bhoja, *EI*, XVIII, pp. 99 f., Sīyaḍoṇi inscription, tenth century. *EI*, I, pp. 167 ff.
35. *EI*, XVIII, pp. 87 f.
36. D. Sharma, *RTTA*, p. 369.
37. R.C. Agrawala, 'Ancient Sculptures and Terracottas from Rajasthan', *Researcher*, I, pp. 18–19.
38. Percy Brown, *Indian Architecture*, p. 135.
39. *Select Inscriptions*, Vol. I, ed. D.C. Sircar, pp. 91–2.
40. *Select Inscriptions*, Vol. I, pp. 379–85.
41. जण्णे बलिस्स विण्हू दिआइवेसेण । तिण्णि कमे जाइत्ता हरइ ससेलं वसुमइं सो । *Dhū.*, III. 90–1.
42. . . . मेइणी महुमहेणं । काउं वराहरूवं ससेलवणकाणणा धरिया । Ibid., III. 96.
43. *Dhū.* I. 39 and V.59 speak of the attempts of Viṣṇu and Kṛṣṇa respectively to measure the *linga*. *Dhū.* I. 56 and II. 49 refer to Brahmā's coming out of the navel of Viṣṇu and Keśava respectively. Kṛṣṇa is referred to as Keśava in *Dhū.*, 56–8.
44. *KM*, p. 149.
45. कण्हो सव्वबीअमज्झगओ । सुहुमेसु बायरेसु अ तिलतुसमित्तेसु दव्वेसु । । *Dhū.*, V. 112.
46. Ibid., II. 41.
47. Ibid., vv. 56–7.
48. सत्ताहवद्दलम्मी धरिओ गोवद्धणो महुमहेणं । Ibid., IV. 88.
49. D. Sharma, *Lectures on Rajput History and Culture*, p. 98.
50. R.C. Agrawala's, 'Kṛṣṇa and Balarāma in Rajasthan Sculptures and Epigraphs', *IHQ*, XXX, no. 4, p. 346.
51. Ibid., p. 341.
52. *PRAS*, WC, 1919, pp. 64–5.
53. R.C. Agrawala's article, op. cit., p. 341.
54. *Bhagvadgītā*, IV. 8.
55. D.C. Sircar, 'Early History of Vaiṣṇavism', in *Cultural Heritage of India*, Vol. IV, pp. 132–4; *Classical Age*, pp. 415–16.
56. S. Jaiswal, *The Origin and Development of Vaiṣṇavism*, p. 214.
57. R.G. Bhandarkar, *Vaiṣṇavism, Śaivism and Minor Religious Systems*,

pp. 52, 143; H.C. Raychaudhuri, *Materials for the Study of the Early History of the Vaiṣṇava Sect,* p. 45; D.C. Sircar in *Cultural Heritage of India,* Vol. IV, pp. 123–4.

58. *Ābhīrajanadārunaḥ*—Ghatiyālā ins. no. 1 of Kakkuka, vs 918.
59. *KM*, pp. 9, 26, 68; *Dhū.*, I. 52, 63; III. 59; IV. 28.
60. *KM*, p. 9; *Dhū.*, I. 75.
61. *KM*, p. 13.
62. *KM*, pp. 2, 14; *Dhū.*, I. 77, 79; III. 69, 72.
63. *Dhū.*, III. 60.
64. Ibid., I. 60, 91.
65. वाससहस्सं गंगा जडासु वामोहिआ जइ हरेणं। Ibid., I. 52.
    गंगा . . . पडिया धरिया सीसेण पसुवइणा। Ibid., I. 90–2.
66. तिणयण-जइसय सर-मोक्खग्गि-णिडड्ढ-तिउर-महाणयर व। *KM*, p. 112; तिउरंतयरं। *Dhū.*, III. 70.
67. Cf. *Taittirīya Saṃhitā,* VI. 2.3. for Rudra's destruction of Tripura.
68. Cf. *Rāma,* I. 40/4ff. and *Mbh.* Vana. 109 for bearing of Ganga and *Rāmā.* VI. 73/35 and *Mbh.* Karṇa, Chapters 33 and 34, Anuśāsana 160. 25–31 for Tripura.
69. अण्णं च बंभ-विण्हू उड्ढंच अहो अ वेवि धावंता।
    अंतं जस्स ण पत्ता वाससहस्सेण दिव्वेण।।
    लिंगं महप्पमाणं। *Dhū.*, I. 39–40.
70. J.I.S.O.A., Vol. IX, pl. X.
71. R.C. Agrawala, 'Rajasthan kī Prācīna Mūrtikalā me Liṅgodbhava', *Maru Bhārati*, XVIII, 2, p. 85.
72. T.A.G. Rao, *Elements of Hindu Iconography*, qd. J.N. Banerjee, *Development of Hindu Iconography*, p. 463; Mahadevan, *Classical Age,* p. 434.
73. *Vāyupurāṇa*, Chapter 55, p. 62.
74. णरसिरकवालमालाउलस्स खट्टंगवग्गहत्थस्स। जस्स रई पेअवने को तस्स जणो समल्लिअइ।। *Dhū.*, III. 60–4.
75. असेस-तिय-चउक्क-चच्चर-सिंघाडग-सिवाणं . . . बलिं दाऊण। *KM*, p. 14.
76. णयर-चच्चर-सिव-मंडवे। Ibid., p. 99.
77. णिसियासि-छेय-धारा-गलंत-रुहिर-लव-छिमिछिमायंत।
    तिणयण-पुरओ हुणिऊण णियय-मंसे भुय-प्फलिहा।। Ibid., p. 13.
78. सहिसेहर-सामि . . . समाहरण-प्पमुहा पाण-संसय-कारिणो उवाया। Ibid.
79. *Dhū.*, III. 60.
80. हरस्स व गौरी। *KM*, p. 9.
81. पिय-पणइणी-सणाह-वाम-पासस्स संकरस्स। Ibid.
82. हरेण समाणो जइ जुवई-घडिय-हीण-वामद्धो। Ibid., p. 26.
83. Ibid., p. 13.
84. उद्दाम-संचरंत-तिनयन-वसभ-ढेंक्कंता। Ibid., p. 71.
85. हर-णिवासु जइसओ ढेंक्कतं-दरिय-वसह-सोहिओ। Ibid., p. 134, संकर-जइसय-भूई-परिभोग-ढेक्कंत-दरिय-वसहेक्क-वियावड। Ibid., p. 149.
86. The śivaliṅgas and terracotta reliefs from the Kuṣāṇa period; handle of

earthern pot depicting descent of Ganges from the locks of Śiva from the Gupta period, and Śiva images of the sixth and seventh centuries indicate the wide prevalence of Śiva worship in pre-Pratihāra Rajasthan. Cf. R.C. Agrawala, 'Rajasthan ke Prācīna Deva Bhavana', *Varadā,* VI, i, pp. 5 f.; Satya Prakash, *Researcher,* I, p. 43; D. Sharma, *RTTA,* p. 64.

87. The Sādaḍī inscription from Udaipur district (AD 490), Khaṇḍelā inscription from Śekhāvāṭī (AD 644) and Karkoṭanagara inscription from Jaipur (AD 684) testify to the early popularity of the *ardhanārīśvara* form. Cf. भूयोऽपिसा जयति या शशिशेखरस्य देहार्द्धमुद्वहति भक्ततया हरस्य . . . गौरिरूद्धार्द्धदेहोप्यविषयमनसां। *EI*, XXX, p. 120; *ASIR*, 1934–5, pp. 73–4; *Bhārata Kaumudī,* I, 1945, p. 273.
88. सिद्धेश्वरो महोदव: कारितस्तुङ्गमंदिर: । Jodhpur inscription of Bauka, *EI,* XVIII. pp. 87 f.
89. R.C. Agrawala, 'Ancient Sculptures and Terracottas from Rajasthan', *Researcher,* I, p. 17; Idem, 'Rajasthan kī Prācīna Mūrtikalā me Ardhanāriśvara Bhāva kī Abhivyakti', *Maru Bhāratī,* VI. 2.
90. R.C. Agrawala, 'Sīkar Saṃgrahālaya kī Mahatvapūrṇa Prastara Pratimāyen', *Varadā,* I, 1–2.
91. R.C. Agrawala, 'Pratihārayugīn Kuch Mahatvapūrṇa Mandira va Pratimāyen', *Varadā,* VI, i, pp. 16 f.
92. *Meghadūta,* vv. 34 f.
93. *Raghuvaṃśa,* VI. 34.
94. *Kādambarī,* p. 53.
95. *KM,* pp. 12, 55.
96. जोय-जोयणी-सिद्ध-तंत-मंत-सेवियस्स महाकालस्स। *KM,* p. 12.
97. See pilgrimages.
98. खंधारोविय-कंकाला जर-चीर-णियंसणा धूलि-पंडर-सरीरा उद्ध-केसा मलिण-वेसा महा-भइरव-वयं पिव चरंती भिक्खं भमिऊण . . . एवं च जं किंचि भुंजिऊण दियहे दियहे कयाहारा कावालिय-बालिय व्व रक्खसी वा पिसाइ व तस्सेय रक्खण-वावडा अच्छिउं पयत्ता तम्मि महा-मसाण-मज्झम्मि। *KM,* p. 225.
99. इमे महामंसं अण्णं वा कावलियं आहारं आहारेंति। *KM,* p. 248.
100. घंटा-डमरुय-सद्दइं कावालिय-घरेसु। Ibid., p. 82.
101. *Caṇḍakauśika,* Act IV.
102. Qd. Handiqui, op. cit., pp. 356–7.
103. LXXXVI. 22; qd. A.M. Shastri, *India as seen in the Bṛhatsaṃhitā of Varāhamihira,* p. 138.
104. This is indicated by the worship of Śiva as *Kapāleśvara* mentioned in the Nirmand (Kangra district) and Igātpurī (Nasik, Maharashtra) copper plate inscriptions, and the *Mattavilāsaprahasana,* attributed to Mahendravarman Pallava (AD 600–30), which depicts the drunken revelry of a Śaiva mendicant, bearing a human skull in lieu of an alms-bowl and accordingly calling himself a *kapālin.* cf. J.N. Banerjee, *Paurāṇic and Tantric Religion,* pp. 96–7; Bhandarkar, *Vaiṣṇavism, Śaivism and Minor Religious Systems,* p. 168; S.K. De, *History of Sanskrit Literature,* Vol. I, p. 254.

105. See fn. 104.
106. In the twelfth century the temple of Nityapramoditadeva at Dhoḍ (Udaipur) is known to have given shelter to Kāpālikas. Dhoḍ Inscription, AD 1172.
107. कउं प्रावु मित्तस्स वंचण कावालिय-व्रत-धरणे। *KM*, p. 63.
108. दरिदस्स हि न वित्थिरइ जसो। न वियम्भए कित्ती, न सज्जणेण संगमो न परोवयारसंपायणं ति . . . अङ्गीकरोमि भयवन्तं उभयलोयसुहावहं धम्मं। *SK*, p. 201.
109. See Jaina tantricism.
110. पढियमेत्तसिद्धं तक्खयाहिदट्ठस्स वि पाणधारयं भयवया विणयाणन्दणेण पणीयं गारुडमन्तं ति। *SK*, pp. 209, 217.
111. *Mālatīmādhava*, Act V.
112. *Caṇḍakauśika*, Act IV.
113. Qd. D. Sharma, *ECD*, p. 262.
114. दुक्खिय-कीड-पयंगा मोएऊणं कुजाइ-जम्माइं। अण्णत्थ होंति सुहिया एसो करुणापरो धम्मो। *KM*, p. 206.
115. D. Sharma, *RTTA*, p. 412; B.N. Sharma, *Social Life in Northern India*, p. 220.
116. *KM*, pp. 13, 201.
117. जय महुमह-वच्छत्थल-हारंदोलिर-ललंत-दुल्ललिए। जय कोत्थुह-रयण-विसट्टमाण-फुड-किरण-विच्छुरिए।। जय खीरोय-महोवहि-तरंग-रंगंत-धवल-तणु-वसणे। जय कमलायर-महुयर-रणंत-भमरउले . . . कमलम्मि पेसियच्छिं लच्छी अह पेच्छइ णरिंदो। *KM*, p. 14.
118. देवी णिसुणेसु वयणं कमला लच्छी सिरी हिरी कित्ती। तं चिय रिद्धी णेव्वाणी। Ibid., p. 14. जय विजय जयंति जए जयाहि अवराइए जय कुमारि। जय अंबे अंबाले जय तं पिए लच्छी।। Ibid., p. 201.
119. Ibid., pp. 14–15.
120. Ibid., p. 201.
121. Junagarh inscription of Skandagupta describes Viṣṇu as the perpetual abode of Lakṣmī, *Select Inscriptions*, I, pp. 299 f., *Raghuvaṃśa*, canto X, describes Viṣṇu as lying on the great serpent in the ocean with Lakṣmī rubbing his feet.
122. H.D. Bhattacharya, in *Classical Age*, p. 447; N.N. Bhattacharya, *Indian Mother Goddess*, p. 127.
123. Jayā, Vijayā, Kumārī, Hrī, Kīrtī, Śrī, IV, 6; Jayā, Vijayā, Kumārī, VI, 23.
124. Aryastava, *Harivaṃśa*, qd. J.N. Banerjee, *Paurāṇic and Tantric Religion*, pp. 119–20.
125. Śri, Hrī, I. 60; Kaumārī, IX. 14; Mātrī, V. 31; Ambā, XI. 5, XIII. 6. Jananī parā, I.55; Svargamuktipradāyinī, XI, 6. Svargapavargadā, XI. 7 *Devīmāhātmya*.
126. Jayā, Vijayā, Aparājitā, Jayantī, II–XX, qd. N.N. Bhattacharya, op. cit.
127. Aryastava, *Harivaṃśa*, Devīmāhātmya, V. 9, 26; XI.21; XII. 36.
128. N.N. Bhattacharya, op. cit., p. 215.
129. J.N. Banerjee, *Paurāṇic and Tantric Religion*, pp. 43, 59, 118.
130. N.N. Bhattacharya, op. cit., pp. 216–17.
131. को वि चंडियाए पसुं भणइ। *KM*, p. 68.
132. कच्चाइणीए पुरओ सीसेण बलिं पि दाऊण। Ibid., p. 13.

133. तिसूल-णिवडिय-महिसोवरि-णिमिय-चारु-चलणाए कच्चाइणीए। *KM*, p. 13.
134. *SK*, p. 249.
135. कप्पन्तकेलिभवणे कालस्स पुरोऽसुराण रुहिरसुरं।।
जअइ पिअन्ती काली परमेट्ठिकवालचसएण।। *Karpūra.*, IV. 19.
136. अपटुसरीरे तुमंमि उवाइयं भयवईए नयरिदेवयाए, जहा किण्हपक्खट्ठमीए गहिओववासवयाए आययणवासो कायव्वो। *SK*, p. 292.
137. न अज्ज अट्ठमी न नवमी न चउद्दसी। तं कि पुण से निवासकारणं। *SK*, p. 295.
138. She is conceived as a terrible war goddess, a saviour and slayer of numerous demons, including Mahiṣāsura, who was also manifest as Cāmuṇḍā, Kālī, Durgā and Pārvatī.
139. Farquhar, *An Outline of Religious Literature of India*, p. 150.
140. *Devīmāhātmya*, XII. 9–10; 19.
141. Ibid., XII. 3.
142. *SK*, pp. 435–7.
143. Ibid., pp. 423, 437.
144. Cf. Ārya-stava, *Harivaṃśa; Mbh.* IV. 6; J.N. Banerjee, *Development of Hindu Iconography*, pp. 491–2; Idem. *Paurāṇic and Tantric Religion*, pp. 119–20; R.C. Hazra, *Studies in the Upapurāṇas*, pp. 16–22. The *Kādambarī* of Bāṇa also describes the bloodstained temple of Cāṇḍikā, the goddess of Śabaras, who was appeased by animal and human sacrifices. *Kādambarī*, pūrvabhāga, pp. 224-28.
145. vv. 285–347.
146. See *mlecchas*.
147. Bhandarkar, *Vaiṣṇavism, Śaiyism and Minor Religious Systems*, p. 223.
148. *KM*, p. 256 names Durgā in the list of important deities.
149. पयंड-भुय-सिहर-वच्छ-णिच्छल्लणा-रुहिर-पकं। अज्जं चिय अज्जाए देमि बलिं मंस-खंडेहिं।। *KM*, p. 104.
150. Ibid., p. 83.
151. V.S. Agrawala, *KM*, pt. II, p. 121; Upadhye, Ibid., p. *139.
152. अद्धणारीसरस्स वामद्धे अकधिदा वि गोरी मुणीअदि। *Karpūra.*, I. 28.
153. हिन्दोलअप्पभंजणीए चदुत्थीए हरवल्लहा देवी देवीए अच्चिदा। Ibid., II. 6.
154. देवीए पुरदो कप्पूरमंजरी हिन्दोलए आरोविदव्वा। Ibid., II. 29.
155. सिरि-जइसिया, महागइंद-सणाहा दिव्व-पउमासणव्व। *KM*, p. 27.
156. Ibid., pp. 201–2.
157. Ibid., p. 201.
158. *Kalpa*, 4. 66–87.
159. See Jaina tantricism.
160. दियहस्स पहर-मेत्ते गंथ-सयं कुणइ भणसु को पुरिसो। हियय-गया हिरि-देवी जइ मे लिहंतस्स णो होइ। *KM*, p. 281.
161. Upadhye, *KM*, pt. II, 158.
162. *SK*, p. 441.
163. Cf. K.N. Puri, *Excavations of Rairh*, pp. 26 f.; Gangadhar inscription, AD 423, *Select Inscriptions*, Vol. I, pp. 379–85; Choṭī Sādaḍī inscription, AD 490, *EI*, XXX, p. 120; Sāmoli inscription, AD 646, *EI*, XX, pp. 97 f.

164. Farquhar, *An Outline of Religious Literature of India,* Chapter V.
165. Daulatpurā Grant of Bhoja, *EI,* V, pp. 208 f.; Pratāpgarh Inscription of Mahendrapāla II, *EI,* XIV, pp. 176 f.
166. *EI,* V, pp. 208 f.
167. D. Sharma, *Lectures on Rajput History and Culture,* p. 100.
168. *PRAS, WC,* 1907, p. 34; R.C. Agrawala, 'Some Interesting Sculptures of the Goddess Ambikā from Marwar', *IHQ,* XXXII, iv, pp. 434–5.
169. R.C. Agrawala, 'A Rare Image of Gajalakṣmī from Rajasthan', *JBRS,* XXXV, pt. 1–4, pp. 184–7; Idem, 'Rajasthan kī Mūrtikalā me Gajalakṣmī evaṃ Sarasvatī', *Varadā,* VIII, iii, pp. 1–5.
170. *KM,* p. 68.
171. *KM,* p. 256.
172. It is noted by Hieun Tsang, Beal, II, 274.
173. *KM,* p. 55.
174. Cited. D. Sharma, *RTTA,* p. 384.
175. *ZDMG,* XL, pp. 38 ff.; qd. D. Sharma, *ECD,* p. 19.
176. L.P. Pandey, *Sun Worship in Ancient India,* pp. 231 f.
177. *KM,* pp. 2, 24, 68, 256.
178. *Dhū.,* II. 45–9.
179. Ibid., I. 58–80.
180. *Matsya Purāṇa,* 183. 81–3.
181. *Brahmāṇḍa,* 4/40/50–6.
182. *Skanda Purāṇa,* Avantikhaṇḍa, Chapter 2.
183. अइसयनिउणत्तं पुण एत्थ सुण भयवओ पयावइणो। जेण सुन्दरमिणं लडहं रूवं विणिम्मवियं। *SK,* p. 609.
184. परितुट्ठो य भयवं पयावई, जेण। Ibid., p. 628.
185. ASIR, 1906–7, p. 173.
186. R.C. Agrawala, 'Rajasthan ke Prācīna Brahmā Mandir tathā Brahmā Mūrtiyān', *Maru Bhāratī,* II, iii, p. 86.
187. Bhandarkar, *Vaiṣṇavism, Śaivism and Minor Religious Systems,* pp. 212, 214.
188. *KM,* p. 256.
189. Ibid., p. 68.
190. *Dhū.,* V. 114.
191. Ghaṭiyālā Inscription, *EI,* IX, p. 279.
192. R.C. Agrawala, 'Rajasthan kī Prācīna Mūrtikalā me Gaṇapati', *Maru Bhāratī,* XV, iii, p. 50.
193. Ibid.
194. *Dhū.,* I.29; III, 53, 82, 85.
195. Ibid., I. 18, 28.
196. *KM,* p. 26.
197. Ibid., p. 83; *Dhū.,* V. 115.
198. *KM,* pp. 2, 14, 68, 256.
199. Ibid., p. 83.

200. *Dhū.*, I. 18, 28.
201. J.N. Banerjee, *Development of Hindu Iconography,* pp. 106, 366.
202. *KM,* p. 83.
203. R.C. Agrawala, 'Rājasthanī Śilpa kī kucha Mahatvapūrṇa Upalabdhiyān', *Varadā*, XIV, iii, p. 2.
204. Ibid.
205. *KM*, p. 17.
206. *SK*, pp. 522–3, 719–20.
207. R.C. Agrawala, 'Ancient Sculptures and Terracottas from Rajasthan', *Researcher,* I.
208. Hazra, *Purāṇic Records on Hindu Rites and Customs,* pp. 225–6, 260.
209. *Devībhāġvata,* VII. 39, 28–31; *Varāha,* 66. 10–11b; *Bhaviṣya,* II, 11, 1.
210. Farquhar, *An Outline of the Religious Literature of India,* pp. 182, 194, 199, 210.
211. *Karpūra.*, I. 25.
212. Ibid., I. 25.
213. Ibid., II. 6.
214. Ibid., IV. 18.
215. रण्डा चण्डा दिक्खिआ धम्मदारा मज्जं मंसं पिज्जाए खज्जए अ। . . . कोलो धम्मो कस्स णो भाइ रम्मो। Ibid., I. 22–4.
216. भक्खाभक्खाण समं गम्मागम्माण अंतरं णत्थि। *KM*, p. 204.
217. अपेयमपि पेयं स्यादभक्ष्यं भक्ष्यमेव च। अगम्यमपिगम्यं स्यात् कौलिकानां कुलेश्वरि।। Chapter IX.
218. एयं लोय-विरूद्धं परलोय-विरुद्धयं पि पच्चक्खं। धम्मो उण इंदिय-णिग्गहेण। *KM*, p. 204.
219. Chintaharan Chakravarti, *Tantras—Studies on their Religion and Literature,* pp. 35–6, 43–4.
220. Handiqui, *Yaśastilaka and Indian Culture,* p. 204.
221. *Kulārṇava,* II. 117–18, qd. C. Chakravarti, article 'Ideals of Tantra Rites', *IHQ,* Vol. X, p. 489.
222. Chintaharan Chakravarti, *Tantras—Studies on their Religion and Literature,* p. 45.
223. ठाविओ मण्डलंमि अरहदत्तो, सव्वजणसमक्खमेव अहिमन्तिऊण पउत्ताइं ओसहाइं। *SK*, p. 482.
224. *KM*, pp. 131–3.
225. अण्णा गिरिवरेसु . . . अण्णा मातंग-वेस-धारीहिं . . . अण्णा पुलिंद-रूवेणं ति। Ibid., p. 132.
226. See Kāpālikas.
227. The *Gautamīya Tantra* declares that people of all castes, whether men or women, may receive its mantras. Chapter I, qd. Avalon, *Principles of Tantra,* Vol. I, Introduction.
228. The *Mahānirvāṇatantra,* a later tantric work, says that the low kaula who refuses to initiate a yavana into the *Kaula-dharma,* considering him to be inferior, or a woman, out of disrespect for her, goes the downward way. *Mahānirvāṇa,* XIV, v. 187 and 184.
229. कत्थ मंताइं, कत्थ वा मंडलाइं . . . लिहिज्जंति मंडलाइं . . . मेलिज्जंति तंताइं। *KM*, p. 162.
230. Ibid., p. 13.

231. Ibid., pp. 247–8, See Jaina tantricism.
232. Ibid., p. 28.
233. डज्झंत-बहल-परिमल-फुरंत-सिर-सयल-मिसिमिसायंतं। धरिऊण गुग्गुलं . . . । Ibid., p. 13.
234. *Harṣacarita,* Chapter V; V.S. Agrawala, *Harṣacarita, Ek Sāṃskritika Adhyayana,* p. 89.
235. *KM,* pp. 191, 193, 197.
236. Ibid.
237. Ibid., p. 196.
238. Ibid., pp. 191, 193, 196.
239. Ibid., p. 196.
240. Ibid.
241. Ibid., p. 191.
242. Ibid.
243. Ibid., pp. 191, 193, 196.
244. *SK,* pp. 329–30.
245. *Harṣacarita,* p. 103; *Kādambarī,* pp. 226–7; V.S. Agrawala, *Harṣacarita, Ek Sāṃskritika Adhyayana,* p. 58.
246. मन्तसिद्धो . . . मन्तविहाणनिमित्तं नणु जाया तुह मए नीया।।
 . . . न य तीए सीलभेओ जायइ देहस्स पीडा वा।। *SK,* pp. 642–3.
247. कहं पुण विणा उत्तरसाहएण एयं पसाहेमि त्ति। Ibid., p. 366.
248. R.S. Sharma, 'Material Milieu of Tantricism', in R.S. Sharma (ed.), *Indian Society: Historical Probings,* pp. 175 f.
249. K.C. Jain, *Ancient Cities and Towns of Rajasthan,* pp. 529–30.
250. See introduction.
251. तुंगमलंघं जिण-भवण-मणहरं सावयाउलं विसमं। जावालिउंर अट्ठावयं व। *KM,* p. 282. Jalor is situated about 75 miles south of Jodhpur.
252. तुंगं धवलं मणहारि-रयण-पसरंत-धयवडाडोयं। उसभं जिणिंदाययणं करावियं वीरभद्देण।। तत्थ ठिएण . . . । *KM,* p. 282.
253. Ibid.
254. Ibid. According to Uddyotana Pavaiyyā was on the river Chandrabhāga, identified with modern Chenab. Bhinmal is about 169 kms. south-west of Jodhpur.
255. सिरि-वच्छराय-णामो रण-हत्थी पत्थिवो जइया।। *KM,* p. 283.
256. D. Sharma, *RTTA,* p. 121; Idem, 'The Original Capital of the Imperial Pratihāras', *Bhāratīya Vidyā,* XVIII, pp. 76–7. The *Purātanaprabandha-saṃgraha* is based on a manuscript copied in vs 1528. Some portions of it however are compiled as early as vs 129, Muni Jinavijaya in introduction to the work in Singhī Jaina Granthamālā.
257. Archaeological Survey of India Report, 1908–9, p. 108.
258. *Bappabhaṭṭiprabandha* 127–41; D. Sharma, *RTTA,* p. 143.
259. Ghaṭiyālā Inscription no. 2, *Journal of the Royal Asiatic Society,* 1895, pp. 513–21.
260. K.C. Jain, *Jainism in Rajasthan,* pp. 114–15.
261. U.P. Shah, *Lalitkalā,* I.

262. See above; A.D. Pusalkar in R.C. Majumdar (ed.), *Age of Imperial Kannauj,* p. 289; K.C. Jain, *Jainism in Rajasthan,* p. 19.
263. D.D. Kosambi, *An Introduction to the Study of Indian History,* p. 158.
264. See caste system.
265. *KM,* p. 1.
266. U.P. Shah, *Studies in Jaina Art,* pp. 5–6; Idem, 'Jaina Iconography—A Brief Survey' in *Bhāratīya Purātattva,* pp. 184–6.
267. *KM,* pp. 95, 115, 116, 128, 132–3; *SK,* p. 502.
268. अट्ठमी-चउद्दसीए सव्व-परियण-परियरिएण इहागंतव्वं भगवओ पूया-णिमित्तं। *KM,* p. 120.
269. सुप्रभातं जिनेन्द्राणां धर्मबोधिविधायिनाम्। Ibid., p. 198.
    नमस्ते भोग-निर्मुक्त नमस्ते द्वेष-वर्जित। Ibid., p. 214.
    The bathing ritual of the Jinas which had been detailed in a work as early as the *Paumacariya,* had developed into a complex ceremony by the time of the *Varāṅgacarita* (seventh century) which described it as a daylong public festival. R.B.P. Singh, *Jainism in Early Medieval Karnataka,* p. 24. R.N. Nandi, *Religious Institutions and Cults in the Deccan,* pp. 34–6.
270. *KM,* pp. 32, 198.
271. कारावियं जिणहरं, कारावियाओ पडिमाओ। *SK,* p. 503.
272. Ibid., pp. 770–1.
273. *KM,* p. 95. Temple worship was glorified by many Jaina works in the seventh century. The *Padmapurāṇa* of Raviṣena exhorts people to perform Jaina worship and erect Jaina images for attainment of temporal as well as eternal blessings. *Padmapurāṇa,* pt. I, Chapter 14, vv. 92–3, p. 313, cited by R.B.P. Singh, *Jainism in Early Medieval Karnataka,* p. 24; The *Varāṅgacarita* states that the construction of temples entitles a person engrossed in worldly affairs to attain heaven. *Varāṅgacarita,* Chapter XXII, v. 57, cited by R.N. Nandi, *Religious Institutions and Cults in the Deccan,* p. 13.
274. *KM,* p. 128.
275. B.C. Bhattacharya, *Jaina Iconography,* p. 28; U.P. Shah, *Studies in Jaina Art,* p. 11.
276. Ramprasad Chinda, *ASIR,* 1925–6; U.P. Shah, op. cit., p. 14.
277. अण्णोण्ण-वण्ण-घडिए... फलिय-मणि-णिम्मलयरा केवि। *KM,* p. 95.
278. U.P. Shah, 'Jaina Iconography—A Brief Survey' in *Bharātiya Purātattva,* pp. 189–90.
279. मुत्ता-सेल-विणिम्मिया। *KM,* p. 119.
280. V.S. Agrawala, *KM,* pt. II, p. 123.
281. महंतं दिव्व-जक्ख-पडिमं ... भगवओ अरहओ मउडम्मि पडिमा मुत्ता-सेल-विणिम्मविया। *KM,* p. 115; णिवेसिओ मउलीए भगवं जिणयंदो। Ibid., p. 120.
282. R.C. Agrawala, 'Ancient Sculptures and Terracottas from Rajasthan', *Researcher,* I, p. 18; D. Sharma, *RTTA,* p. 396.
283. U.P. Shah, *Studies in Jaina Art,* p. 16; *Lalit Kalā,* I.
284. K.C. Jain, *Jainism in Rajasthan,* p. 131.

285. K.C. Jain, op. cit., p. 132.
286. णाह तुमं चिय सरणं तं चिय बंधू पिया य माया य। *KM*, p. 115.
287. D. Sharma, *ECD*, p. 250.
288. झाइओ एक्कं खणंतरं समवसरणत्थो भगवं। जविया य जिण-णमोक्कार-चउव्वीसिया। *KM*, pp. 139, 183.
289. U.P. Shah, *Studies in Jaina Art*, p. 84.
290. Ibid., p. 94.
291. *KM*, p. 279, para §425.
292. Ibid., pp. 94, 96, 120.
293. Ibid., pp. 111–12.
294. Ibid., pp. 95, 198, 277–9.
295. मोक्खं जेण पावेमि। Ibid., p. 277.
296. . . . भव-सय-सहस्स-बद्धं धंतं कम्मिंधणं जेहिं।। *KM*, p. 277.
297. . . . गणहराणं जिण-वयणं जेहिं सुत्त-बंधेणं। Ibid., p. 278.
298. . . . संगोवंगं सुयं धरेताणं। Ibid.
299. . . . विलुत्त-मिच्छत्त-पत्त-सम्मत्ते . . . वय-गुणेहिं संजुत्ते। Ibid., p. 279.
300. U.P. Shah, *Studies in Jaina Art*, p. 97.
301. *Select Inscriptions*, Vol. I, pp. 206 f.
302. *KM*, pp. 256–7.
303. जय य रसिंदो अथंभिओ अग्गि-मज्झ-पक्खित्तो। फुडिऊण तक्खणं चिय दिसो-दिसं वच्चइ अदिट्ठो। तह जिण-दंसण जलणेण तावियो पाव-पारय-रसोहो। Ibid., p. 258.
304. Ibid., pp. 115, 116, 198, 214, 277–9 etc.
305. *Uttarādhyayana sūtra*, XXIX, 9.
306. *SK*, p. 781.
307. *SK*, pp. 780–1.
308. *KM*, pp. 119–20.
309. *Varāṅgacarita*, Chapter 23, v. 19–20; cited by R.B.P. Singh, *Jainism in Early Medieval Karnataka*, pp. 29–30.
310. *SK*, pp. 45 f., 154 f.; *KM*, pp. 35 f., 88 f., 97 f., 142 f., 177 f., 185 f., 197 f., 217 f., 227 f., 242 f., 269 f.
311. *KM*, p. 3; *SK*, p. 154. धम्मो त्ति। सो उण चउव्विहो। तं जहा। दाणमइओ, सीलमइओ, तवोमइओ, भावणामइओ त्ति। *KM*, p. 3.
312. *KM*, p. 3; *SK*, pp. 154–60.
313. *KM*, p. 3.
314. Ibid., pp. 142, 217.
315. *KM*, p. 49; *KM*, pt. II, p. 135.
316. *KM*, p. 212.
317. Ibid., p. 230.
318. *SK*, p. 46.
319. Ibid.; *KM*, p. 143.
320. *KM*, pp. 81–2.
321. Ibid., p. 143.
322. Ibid., p. 144; *SK*, p. 159.
323. *KM*, p. 144.

324. Ibid., pp. 64, 80, 144, 190, 222, 232; *SK*, p. 46.
जत्थ ण जरा ण मच्चू ण वाहिणो णेय सव्व-दुक्खाइं।
सासय-सिव-सुह-सोक्खं अइरा मोक्खं पि पाविहिसि।। *KM*, p. 64.
325. *SK*, p. 801.
326. *KM*, pp. 201, 217, 232.
327. Ibid., pp. 177–8.
328. Ibid., p. 218.
329. *SK*, pp. 45, 116; *KM*, pp. 95–6, 222 f.
330. *SK*, pp. 391–5.
331. *KM*, p. 222.
332. उज्जुयपन्थो साहुधम्मो . . . न य भावओ अपडिवन्नसाहुधम्मा।
संसाराडविं लङ्घेन्ति। *SK*, p. 394.
333. *KM*, p. 96; *SK*, pp. 46, 115.
334. *SK*, p. 162.
335. बंध-वहच्छवि-छेदो अइभारारोवणं चउत्थं तु। पाणण्ण-निरोधो। *KM*, p. 222.
336. *SK*, pp. 249 f.
337. Ibid., pp. 583–4.
338. सज्झाय-रए तवस्सिणो धीरे। *KM*, p. 34.
339. Ibid.
340. *KM*, p. 87; V.S. Agrawala, *Kuvalayamālā*, part II, p. 121.
341. साहुणो भंगवते कय-सज्झाय-वावारे कयावस्सय-करणे य खणंतरं णिद्दं सेविऊण विबुद्धे वेरत्तियं कालं काउमाढत्ता। *KM*, p. 91.
342. भयवं कल्ले तइयपोरिसीए भिक्खानिमित्तं इह पविट्ठो। *SK*, p. 296.
343. ओगाढा चरिमा, ठिओ भगवं काउस्सग्गेणं। Ibid., p. 291.
344. It divided the day of the monk into four parts, of which the first and last were devoted to study, second part to *dhyāna* or meditation, and third to *bikṣā* or begging. It lays down that after study, in the last quarter of the fourth part the monk was to go through *Kāyotsarga*. In the four quarters of the night he was to study, meditate, leave off sleep and study again respectively. *Uttarādhyayana*, XXVI, 11–12, 18, 39, 44.
345. *Sthānāṅga* mentions utkuṭukāsana and vīrāsana; *Sthānāṅga*, VII.49; V.42.
346. *Uttarādhyayana*, XXX, 27.
347. *Aupapātika śūtra*, 19 mentions utkuṭukāsana and vīrāsana.
348. *Daśavaikālika*, VII.
349. Nathmal's commentary on Ṭhānāṅga, p. 618.
350. *Acārāṅga*, II. 3.1; *Uttarādhyayana*, VI. 16.
351. *SK*, pp. 53, 183, 290, 401, 490, 597.
352. Ibid., p. 38; *KM*, p. 147.
353. गामे एगरायं नगरे पंचरायविहारेणं। Ibid., pp. 290, 490, 597.
354. *Saṃbodhaprakaraṇa*; D. Sharma, *ECD*, p. 250.
355. *SK*, p. 394.
356. Ibid., pp. 61, 466.
357. *KM*, p. 100.

358. *SK*, pp. 36, 82, 136, 236, 301, 465; *KM*, pp. 34 f., 215.
359. *SK*, pp. 83, 510, 511.
360. Ibid., pp. 511, 660, 662; *KM*, p. 99.
361. विविहतवखवियदेहा। *SK*, p. 83.
362. *SK*, p. 498.
363. *KM*, pp. 100, 216; *SK*, pp. 510 f.
364. *SK*, pp. 511 f.
365. Ibid., pp. 83–4, 498 f., 661–3, 667 f., 685.
366. See women.
367. *SK*, pp. 161–2, 466 f.
368. धण्णा हु बाल-मुणिणो बालत्तणयम्मि गहिय-सामण्णा . . . । *KM*, p. 213.
369. *KM*, p. 269.
370. *Sthānāṅga*, 165a.
371. *Viyāhapannatti*, 219a.
372. *SK*, pp. 181, 287, 399, 489; *KM*, pp. 261–3.
373. *SK*, p. 595; *KM*, p. 209.
374. *SK*, pp. 181, 401, 596; *KM*, p. 209.
375. *KM*, p. 208; *SK*, pp. 181, 290, 401, 596, 803.
376. *KM*, pp. 208–9.
377. कओ णेण काउस्सग्गो, चिन्तिओ थओ . . . तिणि वाराओ कड्ढियं सामाइयं . . . वन्दिऊण गुरुं . . . । *SK*, pp. 182–3.
378. *Nāyā*, pp. 24–34; cited by J.C. Jain, op. cit., p. 195.
379. *Uttarādhyayana*, Chapter XXIX.
380. Schubring, op. cit., pp. 119, 269.
381. लोय-कय-उत्तिमंगो सिय-वसणो पिच्छएण हत्थम्मि। *KM*, p. 184.
382. Ibid., pp. 142, 194, 216, 229.
383. *Ācārāṅga*, II, 15.23; *SBE*, XXII, pt. I, p. 199, ed. Jacobi.
384. *KM*, pp. 141, 194, 209.
385. Ibid., p. 194.
386. Ibid.
387. समणो व सावओ वा मरणं संलेहणा-पुव्वं। *KM*, p. 222.
388. Ibid., p. 271.
389. खामेमि सव्व-जीवे सव्वे जीवा खमन्तु मे। मेत्ती मे सव्व-भूएसु वेरं मज्झ न केणइ।। Ibid., p. 272.
390. Ibid., pp. 269–79.
391. *Ratnakaraṇḍaka*, V. 3–7.
392. सम्यक्कायकषायलेखना सल्लेखना। *Sarvārthasiddhi*, 7–22.
393. सल्लेखना य दुविहा अब्भंतरिया य बहिरा चेव।
    अब्भंतरा कसायेसु बहिरा होदि हु सरीरे।। gāthā 208, *Bhagvatī Ārādhanā*.
394. तुज्झ थोव आउयं त्ति जाणिऊण जहासुहं संलेहणा-कम्मं। *KM*, p. 269.
    णिय-आउक्खयं जाणिऊण कय-संलेहणाइ-कप्पो। Ibid., p. 270.
395. छड्डेह सव्वभावेसु दुक्खमूलं ममत्तं, भावेह निरवसेसेसु जीवेस परमपयकारणं मेत्तिं, दुगुंच्छेह सुद्धभावेणं पुव्वदुक्कडाइं, बहुमन्नेह तित्थयरपणीए नाणदंसणचरित्ते। *SK*, p. 591.
396. मारणान्तिकीं सल्लेखना जोषिता। *Tattvārthasūtra*, VII. 22.

397. उपसर्गे दुर्भिक्षे जरसि रुजायां च निःप्रतीकारे।
धर्माय तनु-विमोचनमाहुः सल्लेखनामार्याः।। *Ratnakaraṇḍaka,* VI. 1.
398. *KM,* pp. 273, 276–7.
399. बालं संसार-फलं पंडिय-मरणं च णेव्वाणं etc. । *KM,* p. 273.
400. *Sthānāṅga,* 93b; cited by Schubring, *The Doctrine of the Jainas,* p. 288.
401. *Uttarādhyayana,* V.
402. Ibid.
403. *KM,* p. 276.
404. *SK,* pp. 54, 495, 701.
405. Ibid., p. 599.
406. *Ācārāṅga,* I.7.8.1–25.
407. पायोपगमणमरणं भत्तपइण्णा य इंगिणि चेव।
तिविहं पंडितमरणं साहुस्स जहुत्तचारिस्स।। *Bhagavatī Ārādhanā,* 28.
408. *Sthānāṅga,* VIII. 4.9; *Aupapātikasūtra,* 19.
409. *Sūtrakṛtāṅga,* 2.215.
410. *Piṇḍa niryukti,* 497 f.; *Āvaśyaka Cūrṇi,* p. 554.
411. J.C. Jain, op. cit., p. 227.
412. *Niśītha Cūrṇi,* p. 748; *Bṛhatakalpabhāṣya,* I, 1235.
413. *KM,* pp. 131–3.
414. असिहारएण बंभ-चरिया-विहाणेण एत्थ वियरइ . . . पडिवण्णं मूणव्वयं ति । *KM,* pp. 132–3.
415. Ibid., p. 132.
416. Ibid., p. 363.
417. Ibid., p. 366.
418. Ibid., p. 375.
419. आहूया भगवई पण्णत्ती णाम विज्जा . . . । *KM,* p. 236.
420. B.C. Bhattacharya, *Jaina Iconography,* Chapter VI.
421. U.P. Shah, 'Jaina Iconography—A Brief Survey', *Bhāratīya Purātattva,* p. 210.
422. *Kalpaṭīkā,* p. 203; *Vasudevaḥiṇḍī,* p. 164.
423. U.P. Shah, 'Jaina Iconography—A Brief Survey', *Bhāratīya Purātattva,* p. 211.
424. *SK,* pp. 369–71.
425. R.C. Agrawala, 'Some Interesting Sculptures of the Jaina Goddess Ambikā from Marwar', *IHQ,* XXII, (iv), pp. 434–5.
426. They were worshipped with the aid of mystic diagrams, syllabic incantations, gestures of fingers etc., a detailed account of which is to be found in the tantric treatises *Jvālinī Kalpa* compiled at Mānyakheṭa in AD 939 and *Bhairavapadmāvatīkalpa,* AD 1047, of Mallisena, belonging to Karnataka. cf. R.N. Nandi, *Religious Institutions and Cults in the Deccan,* Chapters IX, X, p. 173; R.B.P. Singh, *Jainism in Early Medieval Karnataka,* pp. 51 f.
427. P.B. Desai, *Jainism in South India and Some Jaina Epigraphs,* p. 72.
428. Ibid., p. 73.
429. R.N. Nandi, op. cit., p. 147.

430. See above, p. 111.
431. चारित्तं पि ण वट्टइ णाणं णो जस्स परिणयं किंचि। पंच-णमोक्कार-फलं अवस्स देवत्तणं तस्स। *KM,* p. 279.
432. Ibid., p. 197.
433. Handiqui, *Yaśastilaka and Indian Culture,* p. 272.
434. Ibid., p. 280.
435. *KM,* pp. 247–8.
436. भगवं किं पिसाया रक्खसा वा देव-जोणिया इमे महामंसं अण्णं वा कावलियं आहारं आहारेंति . . . पयईए इमे वंतरा केलीगिल-सहावा बाल व्व होंति। तेण पुरिसेहि सह खेलंति, सत्तवंतं च दट्ठूण परितोसं वच्चंति . . . तेण पक्खित्तं तं मासं . . . । *KM,* p. 248.
437. Ibid., p. 34.
438. Ibid., pp. 203–7.
439. जीवो खण-भंगिल्लो तरुवरा जगमणिच्चं। णिव्वाणो वि अभावो धम्मो . . . । *KM,* p. 203.
440. को वि बुद्धस्स। Ibid., p. 68.
441. सक्क-तावसाईणं। Ibid., p. 14.
442. *IA,* XIV, pp. 45–6.
443. Cf. Dayaram Sahni, *Archaeological Remains and Excavations at Bairāṭ,* p. 28; R.C. Agrawala, 'Lālsoṭ Buddhist Pillars', *Lalit Kalā,* XI.
444. Beal, I, p. 179; II, p. 270.
445. *Prabhāvakacarita,* qd. Jacobi, Introduction to the *SK,* pp. xv, xvi, xvii.
446. सव्व गओ अह जीवो मुच्चइ पयईए झाण-जोएहिं। पुहइ-जल-सोय-सुद्धो एस तिंडडीण धम्मवरो।। *KM,* p. 203.
447. *Yājña,* III. 58.
448. *Manu,* XII. 10.
449. *Dakṣa,* VII. 30.
450. *KM,* p. 203.
451. Ibid.
452. Cf. Ghosuṇḍī inscription (Udaipur), *EI,* XVI, p. 27; Nāndsā (Udaipur) inscription, *Indian Antiquary,* LVIII, p. 53; *EI,* XXVI, pp. 118 f.; *EI,* XXIII, p. 52; *CII,* III, pp. 74 f., 253; G.H. Ojha, *Udaipur Rājya kā Itihāsa,* p. 55; D. Sharma, *RTTA*, pp. 58, 66.
453. *KM,* p. 204.
454. दिज्जइ बंभण-समणे विहले दीणे य दुक्खिए किंचि। गुरु-पूयणं पि कीरइ सारो धम्माण गिहि-धम्मो। Ibid.
455. Ibid.
456. See tantricism.
457. *KM,* p. 204.
458. Ibid.
459. See superstitious beliefs.
460. See tantricism.
461. खाणे कूव-तलाए बंधइ वावीओ देइ य पवाओ। *KM,* p. 205.
462. Ibid.
463. Ibid.
464. Ibid.

465. Ibid.
466. Ibid.
467. Ibid.
468. Ibid.
469. Ibid.
470. Ibid., p. 206.
471. Ibid.
472. Ibid.
473. Ibid.
474. Ibid.
475. Ibid.
476. Ibid.
477. *SK*, pp. 170–4.
478. *Arthaśāstra*, 1.2.10.
479. *Rāmāyaṇa*, II, 114/30.
480. *Harṣacarita*, p. 236.
481. भूतभ्यश्चैतन्यं मदशक्तिवत् । *Kāvyamīmāṃsā*, p. 37.
482. पण्डर-भिक्खू . . . साहिओ से गोरसपडिवज्जणाइओ निययकिरियाकलावो । *SK*, pp. 552–3.
483. *Harṣcarita*, p. 236.
484. *Niśītha Cūrni*, p. 865.
485. V.S. Agrawala, *Harṣcarita, Ek Sāṃskritika Adhyayana*, p. 224.
486. *SK*, pp. 9 f., 337 f., 543 f.
487. Ibid., p. 348.
488. Ibid., p. 9.
489. *SK*, p. 337.
490. *ED*, I, p. 6.
491. *SK*, pp. 335–7.
492. *Atri*, (136–7); Yama quoted in *Smṛticandrikā* (on vyavahāra, p. 254).
493. *SK*, p. 543.
494. *SK*, pp. 11 f.
495. Ibid., pp. 341, 343.
496. Ibid., p. 14.
497. समतणमणिमुत्तकञ्चणाणं . . . । Ibid., p. 31.
498. Ibid., p. 344.
499. Ibid., pp. 13, 338.
500. Ibid., p. 13.
501. Ibid.

6

Popular Religious Practices and Socio-religious Rites

THE VARIOUS INDIAN religious systems differed radically in many respects but there were certain features appertaining to the practical aspect of religion which were common to all. They all believed in performance of charity, penance and pilgrimage to be a most effective means of securing religious merit. The importance of these practices cannot be underestimated as they not only served as an outlet to the religious feelings of the people, but also helped smoothen sectarian differences by making all part of a common culture. The performance of socio-religious rites at the time of birth, marriage and death was also universal and the ceremonies more or less similar, contributing to the cultural unity of the period.

Charity

One way in which Hindu charity expressed itself was *pūrtadharma* which included building of temples, wells, tanks, parks, distribution of food and gifts on occasions such as eclipses and some other *tithis* (lunar days).[1] Mention had already been made above of the importance attached by the Purāṇas to the practice, which as our sources also testify,[2] was open not merely to members of the upper classes but śūdras as well, the latter being entitled to distribute gifts to brāhmaṇas and charity to the poor, to build temples, tanks and wells, and open alms-houses and hospitals.[3] By conferring upon the lower classes a means of accruing high religious merit, it increased the appeal of the Hindu faith along with the allied practice of *tīrthayātrā* and strengthened its base, lessening the attraction of heterodox creeds and tantricism which adopted a liberal attitude towards the lower castes. Inasmuch as it encouraged the individual to work for the benefit of the masses by establishing works of public utility and charity, and shifted the emphasis from the performances involving slaughter of numerous animals to acts of benevolence, it was highly commendable even though side by side it also catered to the selfish interests of brāhmaṇas as they were projected as the most worthy donees for *dāna*.[4]

Advocates of *pūrtadharma*, who favoured excavation of wells and ponds, and free provision of water, were present in the court of king Dṛḍhavarman.[5] Manifold precious gifts including pearls, costly clothes, gold and silver utensils, and money were distributed freely amongst servants, dependents and the general populace by rulers in the course of birth and marriage festivities in the royal families,[6] as also on happy occasions such as the prince's successful recovery from his wounds.[7] Mention is also made of *mahādāna* (great charity) by a rich merchant on the birth of a son.[8] Distribution of alms to the poor and distressed also formed a part of preliminary worship of a deity.[9] Liberal charities were distributed amongst the poor and needy by wealthy traders, on their return from successful trade ventures,[10] and specially on occasions such as *Mahākārtika*[11] (the night of full-moon in the month of Kārtika). Those who failed to give charities out of self-earned wealth felt ashamed of themselves.[12] Provision for free food and water signified the liberal disposition of the towns-people.[13] It has already been noted that a large number of gifts were made to brāhmaṇas during this period. There are plenty of grants recording building of temples and gifts of land to brāhmaṇas. But as is evident from the account given by the Prākrit works, the practice of charity was by no means restricted to these fields and a large part of the money spent on charity went to poor relief and public works. The excavation of step-wells and tanks is corroborated by epigraphic as well as archaeological evidence.[14] Thus by impelling the rich to spend a part of their money on the poor and general public the practice served to remedy the economic inequities to a certain extent.

Excavation of wells, ponds etc. does not seem to have been much approved by the Jaina monks as it involved killing of souls (*jīvas*) existent in earth and water.[15] But *dāna* as such was an essential constituent of Jaina faith,[16] including *jñāna dāna, abhaya dāna* and *dharmopagraha dāna*.[17] *Jñāna dāna* was the gift of knowledge whereby one gained knowledge of bondage (*bandha*) and liberation, differentiated between virtues and sins, attained human and divine births, liberation and also omniscience.[18] *Abhaya dāna* involved non-violence towards all souls (*jīvas*) present in fire, earth, air, water and *vanaspati*, since all beings, even though suffering, wish to live on. A king gives up even his kingdom to save his life as one's life is one's dearest possession. By means of *abhaya dāna*, one gained long life, good looks and freedom from disease.[19] *Dharmopagraha dāna* involved gifts of food, drink, clothes, vessels, and medicine to the religious.[20] Given to a proper recipient with respect (*śraddhā*) it yielded much fruit, but given merely with the object of gaining fame without *śraddhā* it did not yield fruit just as a seed which had not been watered. Equally fruitless were the gifts made by one who killed beings. Improper *dāna* only dragged both the donee and the donor lower down in the world. Gifts given to a person observing the five great vows, in control of body, speech and mind, endowed with the qualities of patience, humility and forbearance were proper. Even good *dāna* bestowed on an unworthy recipient yielded only bad fruit just as milk fed to a serpent yielded only poison. On the other hand even insignificant *dāna* bestowed on a fit donee yielded good fruit, just as straw fed to a cow yielded milk.[21] The Jaina *dāna* was thus different in nature from brahmanical *dāna*, emphasising not gifts in the ordinary sense of the term but gifts of knowledge and safety to the people. *Dharmopagraha dāna* was apparently prescribed mainly to provide monks with articles of daily necessity as one following the Jaina way of life is projected as the most worthy donee.[22] Somadeva also refers to four kinds of gifts, viz., of *abhaya* or gift of protection, food, medicine and sacred lore in the *Yaśastilaka*.[23]

Tapas or penance was highly esteemed and those who practised it were highly revered, even though they were young in age.[24] Ascetics belonging to the brahmanical faith practised severe penance, fasting and emaciating the body.[25] *Tapas* also formed an important part of the Jaina monk's routine.[26] Sulaiman notes that he saw a man naked with the face turned towards the sun, having nothing on but a panther's skin and when he returned to that country sixteen years later he found the man in the same posture.[27]

Pilgrimage

Tīrthayātrā was a popular religious institution with great mass appeal and of considerable antiquity. The *Vanaparva* of the *Mahābhārata* gives an elaborate description of various *tīrthas* and the merits of *tīrthayātrā*,[28] which was further glorified by the Purāṇic literature. Long sections devoted to an account of the holy places and their glorification were added to the *Matsya Purāṇa, Kūrma Purāṇa, Varāha Purāṇa* and *Agni Purāṇa* during the eighth and ninth century AD.[29] The *Kuvalayamālā* mentions many important *tīrthas* and gives an idea of the purpose behind pilgrimages. *Tīrthas*, we learn, were believed to be invested with miraculous properties. While some went there hoping to gain absolution from their sins,[30] others went there believing that their diseases could be cured by a visit to these sacred places.[31] The poor would go there for spiritual solace.[32]

The river Ganga was the most popular spot for pilgrims. The *Kuvalayamālā* relates the story of a brāhmaṇa couple, who disenamoured with life because of their extreme poverty, set off on a pilgrimage to the Ganga, leaving the household in charge of their eldest son.[33] Elsewhere is an interesting context in which *piśācas* after deliberating over the merits and demerits of various attractive spots, gardens, rivers and mountains decide that the Ganga is the finest spot of all, because of its all-purifying nature. Regarded as the divine river, revered even by celestial beings, a bath in it was deemed to shatter even the most grievous sins into hundreds of fragments and annihilate them.[34] Reference is also found to the practice of consigning the bones of the dead to the Ganga.[35]

Pilgrimage to the Ganga and many other holy *tīrthas* had come to be prescribed as a means of expiation (*prāyaścitta*) by the brāhmaṇas. In the *Kuvalyamālā* a sinner, responsible for the death of his brother and sister, is advised to visit the various *tīrthas* of Gaṅgādvāra, Hemanta, Lalita, Bhadreśvara, Vīrabhadra, Someśvara, Prabhāsa and Pushkara.[36] Magical attributes were ascribed to the *tīrthas* by the people in general. Thus one would gather from the conversation of those suffering from various incurable diseases that leprosy was believed to be curable by bathing at Varanasi, a visit to the *Bhaṭṭāraka* of Mūlasthāna or a six months stay at *Mahākāla.*[37] Long accumulated sin could be washed off by suicide at the banyan tree of Prayaga (*Prayāgavaṭa*).[38] By bathing at the *Gaṅgāsāgarasaṅgama* and suicide by the deity Bhairava *Bhaṭṭāraka* one could wipe away even the most horrible sin of killing one's father and mother.[39]

Gaṅgādvāra is the well-known site of Haridvāra in U.P., where the river Ganga bursts through the Śivalik hills and descends upon the plains.[40] Varanasi and Prayaga are the two other sacred sites, Banaras and Allahabad, on the banks of the river Ganga. Gaṅgāsaṅgama is the holy confluence of the Ganga with the sea.[41] The special sanctity of the sites of Gaṅgādvāra, Prayaga and Gaṅgāsāgara is noted by various *Purāṇas* as the *Matsya, Kūrma, Garuḍa* and *Padma*[42] which declare that those who bathe therein reach heaven and those who die there are not born again.[43] Varanasi or Kāśī is lauded at great length by several Purāṇas such as the *Matsya, Kūrma, Liṅga, Agni* and *Skanda*, the *Kāśīkhaṇḍa* of the latter having about 15,000 verses on Banaras and its sub-*tīrthas*.[44] In keeping with the testimony of the *Kuvalayamālā* the *Kāśīkhaṇḍa* remarks that 'even incurable diseases, whether affecting the body outside or inside, are got rid by the touch with faith of the water (washing the image) of the deity'.[45] The *Prayāgavaṭa* is also mentioned by various Purāṇas.[46] From epigraphic evidence Bhillāditya, the father of Kakka, the Mandor Pratihāra ruler, is known to have proceeded to Gaṅgādvāra after bestowing the kingdom on his son.[47]

Pushkara is the famous Pushkara lake near Ajmer, the sanctity of which dates from an early period.[48] The *Vāyu* and *Brahmāṇḍa Purāṇas* hold *śrāddha* and *tapa* performed at Pushkara to be highly fruitful.[49] The *Padma Purāṇa* in its chapter dated between AD 600–800 also extols the merits of the holy waters of Pushkara.[50] Prabhāsa may either be Prabhāsa-Somanātha in Junagadh state, Kathiawar, or Prabhāsa-Kurukṣetra on the banks of the Sarasvatī.[51] In the time of Alberuni the *Śiva-liṅga* of Somanātha was famed to 'cure persons of every inveterate illness and heal every desperate and incurable disease'.[52]

As regards Lalita and Bhadreśvara, they may be identified as Laliteśvara of Prayaga and Bhadreśvara on the Kālī Sindh mentioned in the *Skanda Purāna* as *Jyotirliṅgas*.[53] Lakṣmīdhara, on the authority of the *Matsya Purāṇa*, speaks of Lalita at Prayaga as sacred to *Gaurī*.[54] The name of Someśvara occurs also in the *Matsya Purāṇa* and the *Kūrma Purāṇas* as the remover of all diseases.[55] Hemanta and Vīrabhadra have not been identified so far. The *Mūlasthāna Bhaṭṭāraka* appears to be the sun-god of Multān,[56] and *Mahākāla*, the famous Śiva temple at Ujjain,[57] mentioned as a *jyotirliṅga* in the *Śiva*[58] and *Skanda Purāṇa*.[59]

A pilgrim, according to the *Kuvalayamālā*, shaved off his hair, took an umbrella to ward off the heat and rain, suspended a gourd from the end of his staff, put on mineral-red garments, carried his small pot in a sling and travelled afoot, mostly living off alms and food provided by charity houses on the way.[60] This is in keeping with the injunctions of the Purāṇas. According to the *Matsya Purāṇa* one who travels to Prayaga in a conveyance drawn by bulls falls into hell and if a pilgrim because of riches or avarice or foolishness goes in a conveyance (not drawn by bulls) all his efforts become fruitless.[61] According to the

Padma Purāṇa one who uses a cart drawn by bulls is guilty of cow-slaughter[62] and the shaving off the hair by a pilgrim destroys the sins that have gone into the head.[63]

The practice of Hindu *tīrthayātra* has come in for much criticism at the hands of Jaina writers. Bathing at *tīrthas* is ridiculed by Uddyotana in these words: 'What good can external washing do when one bears a sinful mind? What are the properties that this water is blessed with? Does it remove sin or not? If it does, is the contact responsible for it or one's thoughts? If mere contact with water was so efficacious then the crocodile, fish and *cakravākas* ought to be first to attain heaven. Or if it was because of one's thoughts then why do people come to it from afar rather than merely meditate upon it and thereby attain heaven? If the waters are not themselves sin-removing but act thus for people endowed with special knowledge why then is the special knowledge not applied to the water in the wells? In reality this practice is a stupid custom.'[64] Similar ideas are expressed in the *Yaśastilaka* of Somadeva.[65]

To a person taking a close look at the Hindu *tīrthayātrās* however it will be clear that as a pilgrim underwent quite a few hardships whilst travelling afoot over long distances, a pilgrimage required considerable spiritual conviction, and therefore was somewhat an exercise in mental and physical discipline, very much as the performance of *tapas*, a necessary concomitant of both being purity of heart. The *Mahābhārata* and the *Purāṇas* promise the fruit of *tīrthayātrā* only to those who have faith, control over senses and purity of mind.[66] Properly performed thus, a pilgrimage did not merely consist of bathing at *tīrthas*, as the Jainas would have us believe, although its full implications may not have been realised by all. It cannot be gainsaid that the institution had considerable merits. Travelling broadened one's outlook and the mingling together of so many people from different parts of the country imbued with a common sense of purpose at these *tīrthas* must have created a wide awareness of the cultural unity of the vast Indian subcontinent.

The *Kuvalayamālā* shows that the pilgrimage was open to the poor as well as rich[67] and members of all the four castes, brāhmaṇas, kṣatriyas, vaiśyas and śūdras.[68] The *Matsya Purāṇa* and *Kūrma Purāṇa* also declare that *brāhmaṇas, vaiśyas, śūdras, varṇasaṃkaras* (persons born of mixed marriages) *mlecchas* etc. all who breathe their last at *Avimuktakṣetra* (Varanasi) attain the bliss of Śiva's abode.[69] The gathering of all these people at the *tīrthas* served to break down class and caste exclusiveness, at least temporarily. *Tīrthayātrā* provided even the poorest of poor, who could not afford to perform charity or other practices of *pūrtadharma*, with a practicable means of securing religious merit.

Women could also perform *tīrthayātra*,[70] as noted above and strive to attain merit. As it gave women an opportunity to travel and widen the horizons of their knowledge, it served as a valuable educational experience for them. The mingling of people of different religious persuasions at these *tīrthas* added to the catholicity of Hinduism. Pushkara which was a site sacred to Brahmā came to have a temple of *Ādivarāha* and the banks of all the three *puṣkaras* were studded with Śaiva temples built mainly by the Cāhāmāna rulers of Śakambharī and Ajmer.[71] An institution evolved by the brāhmaṇas in wake of the decline of the sacrificial ritual, it provided the masses, most of them not entitled to Vedic rites, with a simple and expedient means of attaining religious merit and salvation, and ensured their continued adherence to the brahmanical religion, thereby assuring the brāhmaṇas of a vast clientele. While the main beneficiaries of gifts at ancient *tīrthas* like Prayaga had been the *smārta* brāhmaṇas,[72] the growth of new *tīrthas* around Śaiva temples like Mahākāla and Somanātha must have benefited the *devalaka* (temple) brāhmaṇas as well. The popularity of the sites of Bhadreśvara, Mahākāla, Lalita etc., principally of a Śaivite character, as places of pilgrimage must have given a fillip to the popularity of Śaivism. Of these Mahākāla, as noted above,[73] had tantric associations and its rise into prominence is a reflection of the widespread acceptance of tantricism.

It is interesting to note that though they criticised the brahmanical practice of pilgrimage, the Jainas themselves appear to have associated holiness with certain places and visited them with great reverence. Thus in the *Kuvalayamālā* we come across a monk on his way to Mount Śatruñjaya to pay his homage to the *siddhas*[74] (emancipated souls). Elsewhere in the work we read of vidyādharas who go from Vaitāḍhya to Sammetaśikhara and thence to Śatruñjaya.[75] Reference is also found to a monk and his disciple proceeding to Sammetaśikhara to pay their respects, and knowing their end to be near, giving up their life there by *sallekhanā*.[76] Evidently Śatruñjaya and Sammetaśikhara had become famous as holy places by the time of Uddyotana. The *Kuvalayamālākathā* of Ratnaprabhasūri devotes many verses to the description of Śatruñjaya and refers to it as a *mahātīrtha* which shows that by the thirteenth century it gained even more fame and attracted many pilgrims.[77] The *Vividhatīrthakalpa* (fourteenth century) of Jinaprabhasūri mentions as many as 38 *tīrthas*.[78]

Śatruñjaya is in Kathiawar, seventy miles north-west of Surat and thirty-four miles from Bhownagar.[79] According to the Jaina canonical work (*Aṅga*) *Antagaḍadasāo*, prince Goyama renounced the world under Ariṭṭhanemi and attained salvation here.[80] According to the *Triṣaṣṭiśalākāpuruṣacarita* of Hemacandra, twelfth century, just as the blessed Ṛṣabha was the first tīrthaṅkara, so mount Śatruñjaya became the first *tīrtha*.[81] At Sammetaśikhara, identified with Pārasnāth hill in Bihar,[82] as many as twenty tīrthaṅkaras are reputed to have gained salvation.[83] Representations of Sammetaśikhara were also worshipped in later Jaina shrines, a famous example of which is available in the triple-Jaina shrine built by Vastupāla and Tejapāla on Mt. Girnār[84] in the thirteenth century. Aṭṭhāvaya or Aṣṭapada to which Uddyotana compares Jāvālipura because of its lofty Jaina temples[85] was also a celebrated Jaina pilgrimage site. Identified with the Kailāśa mountain, situated about 25 miles to the north of Mānasarovara beyond Gangri,[86] it is known as the place where Ṛṣabha gained salvation.[87] The *Niśītha Cūrṇi* considered visits to the places where tīrthaṅkaras were born, renounced the world, roamed about, achieved omniscience and salvation to be the means of purifying the vision and acquiring right faith in religion.[88] The practice of visiting these holy places indicates that pilgrimage had captured the popular imagination, the adherents of the Jaina faith also not remaining completely immune from its spell, though in this case *tīrthas* were places associated with the tīrthaṅkaras.

An unfortunate feature connected with *tīrthayātras* was the practice of religious suicide at these sacred spots, as can be seen above.[89] This was the offspring of a general belief that suicide at certain places led to expiation of sins. Motivated by such a belief, the *Kuvalayamālā* tells us, many would drown themselves in the ocean, fall down from a precipice, or enter fire.[90] Uddyotana saw little merit in these practices and denounced them as vehemently as the practice of pilgrimage. Fire, he stated, merely burnt the body, nor did water wash off sin. Falling off a mountain but smashed one's bones, the annihilation of sins being achievable only in course of time. The means by which the act of throwing one's self down was deemed to annihilate sins, he pointed out, was imperceptible, and commended instead the Jaina scriptures which laid emphasis on the cultivation of purity of mind whereby one could achieve annihilation of *karma* even while residing at home.[91] While Manu, Parāśara and Yama[92] disapproved of suicide, Medhātithi considered these modes of religious suicide quite desirable in case of old men suffering from incurable diseases, those who had lost all energy or were suffering from leprosy etc.[93] Ibn Khurdadba informs that persons who had grown very old and weak very often used to commit suicide in holy places either by drowning or burning themselves on auspicious days.[94] But it is evident that these practices had a wider application as people anxious to atone for their sins and gain merit resorted to these practices, regardless of their age.[95]

The practice of committing suicide at the *Prayāgavaṭa*[96] dates to a much earlier period, as evidenced by the *Matsya Purāṇa*,-which declared that one who gave up life near the *vaṭa* at Prayaga, attained the world of Rudra.[97] The *Kūrma, Padma*,[98] and *Agni Purāṇas*,[99] Kālidāsa[100] and Hieun Tsang,[101] attest to its popularity during the later period. Regarding suicide at Gaṅgāsāgara,[102] the *Kūrma Purāṇa* held that salvation was guaranteed at Gaṅgāsāgara whether one died in the water or the land or in the air.[103] Of historical instances of religious suicide pertaining to Rajasthan we have Jhoṭa of the Mandor Pratihāra family, great-grandfather of Bauka, who drowned himself in the Ganges,[104] and his son Bhillāditya, who after passing eighteen years at Haridvāra starved himself to death.[105] From the Sāmolī (Mewar) inscription (AD 646) we know of Jēntaka, who 'having seen the messengers of Yama' entered fire.[106]

Socio-religious Rites

Various socio-religious rites are performed in the life of a person from conception to death, to ward off evil spirits; attract favourable influences; obtain material gains such as progeny, wealth, long life, intellect; express joy, sorrow etc.; wash away physical impurities, confer social privileges and attain liberation.[107] Of these, the birth ceremonies, naming ceremony, *vivāha* and funeral ceremonies find mention in our works. These being the only four *saṃskāras* mentioned in epigraphs[108] as well shows their comparatively greater importance.

While the Dharmaśāstras are primarily concerned with the ritualistic aspects of these ceremonies, our works supply interesting details of the popular rites connected with them. At the birth of prince Kuvalayacandra, the *Kuvalayamālā* tells us, jewel lamps were lighted, strings of auspicious mirrors were suspended, *nandyāvarta* and *śatapatra* designs were drawn with white mustard and rice, protective rites performed with ashes, and a protective sword was placed near the mother and child.[109] The *nāmakaraṇa* ceremony was performed when he was twelve days old, in consultation with the mahābrāhmaṇas.[110]

Detailed descriptions of the customs and ceremonies connected with marriage, considered to be one of the most important *saṃskāras* in man's life, are available in our works. The auspicious day for the marriage was determined by the astrologer.[111] Once the suitable time had been ascertained, manifold preparations were set afoot at the bride's place. Among these activities at the palace of princess Kuvalaya-mālā, the *Kuvalayamālā* mentions the pounding of grain; preparation of various eatables and sweet-meats; testing of various jewels; preparation of the palace, pavilion and fire-altar; invitations to kings and relatives by sending messengers; decoration and whitewashing of houses; installation of canopies; sowing of barley-offshoots; making ornaments of gold; salutations to gods; decoration of streets; sewing of bodices; putting up of flags and making of beautiful fly-whisks.[112]

On the day of the wedding the mother of the bride, out of love for her future son-in-law, herself attended to the anointment of the bridegroom. Auspicious rites were performed with white mustard, rice (*akṣata*), and *svastika.* Then followed various ceremonies current in the couple's family and residential territory. Duly bathed and dressed in a clean pair of white garments, his body anointed with sandal, a *tilaka* mark of *gorocana* and white mustard seeds on his forehead, a garland of white fragrant flowers around his neck, the bridegroom proceeded to the marriage pavilion. Bedecked with pearl ornaments and attired in white garments, the bride, princess Kuvalayamālā, also arrived at the altar (*vedī*). When the auspicious moment (*lagna*) arrived, fire for the ceremony was brought from the *Agnihotraśālā* and made to burn brighter with the addition of ghee and sticks of the milky tree. Then in the presence of the elders of the family, the rulers attending the ceremony and brāhmaṇas proficient in the Vedas, customary rites and *śāstras*, the *lokapālas* (guardians of quarters) were invoked, the name of the bridegroom's father uttered and handfuls of fried rice (*lāja*) were given to the couple. Then followed the *pāṇigrahaṇa*, the hand of Kuvalayamālā being placed in the hands of the prince, whereupon unwidowed women sang, trumpets were blown, conches were sounded and cymbals were struck against each other. Brāhmaṇas recited, *mahāsāmantas* shouted '*Jaya, Jaya*' (victory, victory) and the elders showered blessings. The *lokapālas* and the fire were called upon to bear witness that the girl had been given in marriage and the couple circumambulated the fire four times, offering it handfuls of rice (*lājāñjali*) every time they did so. This done, even the old women in the family danced, and so did the mother of the bride. Manifold celebrations took place, and riches were freely distributed amongst the poor and the needy.[113]

Further details of the wedding ceremony can be had from the description of the marriage of princess Kusumāvalī in the *Samarāic-cakahā*. The date of wedding fixed, various charities were bestowed on the people. On the day of the wedding, the bride wearing a red coloured dress and facing eastwards sat on a raised platform covered with a *dukūla* sheet, in midst of a courtyard beautified with *raṅgāvali* patterns. Young unwidowed women dressed in red, with *dūrva* (grass) blades, curds and rice (*akṣata*) attended to her anoinment. After that followed a bath from a golden pitcher in the water of which were put flowers, tender sprouts, and leaves. The elders put *akṣata* on her head. At the moment fixed by the astrologers for the *pāṇigrahaṇa* ceremony, the bridegroom arrived in procession at the marriage pavilion (*vivāha-maṇḍapa*). At the entrance he was received by women who demanded the customary presents (*ācārimaka*) of him, after payment of which he alighted from the elephant. The ceremony known as *bhṛkuṭibhagna*, performed with a golden pestle to which was attached a jewelled girdle, then followed. Next the brideswomen took the bridegroom to the bride, and after their usual jokes and pranks (*kautukas*) asked for presents before giving him the first glimpse of the bride's face. This ceremony is referred to as *mukhachavisphoṭanikā*. Now the *pāṇigrahaṇa* was performed. The members of the bridegroom's party were lavishly entertained and presented with fragrant unguents, perfumes, betel-leaves, costly garments, ornaments, horses and elephants. Oblations of ghee, honey and rice were put into the fire and the bride and bridegroom started circumambulating the fire. When they took their first round the bride's father gave to the bridegroom a substantial amount of gold. In the second round, he gave necklaces and other ornaments. In the third round he gave silver utensils and in the fourth costly clothes.[114]

The observance of various ceremonies prescribed by the *Gṛhyasūtras* such as *maṇḍapakaraṇa* (erecting a pandal where ceremonies are to be performed), *vadhugṛhagamana* (bridegroom's going to the bride's home), *snāpana, paridhāpana* (making the bride bathe and put on new clothes), *parasparasamīkṣaṇa* (looking at each other), *kanyādāna* (gift of the bride), *agnisthāpana* (establishing the fire), *pāṇigrahaṇa* (taking hold of the bride's hand), *lājahoma* (offering of fried grain into the fire by the bride), *agnipariṇayana* (the bride and bridegroom going around the fire)[115] is evident from these accounts.

The *antyeṣṭi saṃskāra* was the last rite to be performed in the life of an individual. Cremation was the usual mode of disposal of the dead. The funeral bier, known as the *mṛtapātra* or *śavaśayana* was first prepared and the corpse was laid on it.[116] A poor man's bier consisted merely of an old cot with an old cloth serving as a covering for the dead body.[117] The relatives of the dead lifted the bier on their shoulders and carried it in procession to the cremation ground[118] to the accompaniment of the distinctive sound of the funeral drum.[119] There the funeral pyre was raised with wood, grass, ghee and flowers,[120] and the body was consigned to the flames. In the case of the rich, the pyre was prepared with fragrant aloewood and sandalwood[121] and manifold charities were distributed on the occasion.[122]

Libations of water and gifts to the brāhmaṇas also formed part of the funeral rites.[123] Reference is also found to the practice of immersing the bones of the dead in the Ganga.[124] The performance of *piṇḍadāna* (offering of balls of cooked food) too was a rite of great importance, which made the birth of a son appear absolutely essential.[125] *Śrāddhas* involving feasts to brāhmaṇas were in vogue as can be seen from the *Samarāiccakahā*, where a ruler has half of a huge Rohita fish cooked for the *śrāddhakarma* of his father and grandfather and sent to the brāhmaṇas.[126]

To sum up, the belief in charity, penance and pilgrimage made followers of different religious sects part of a common culture. The projection of *dāna* as an act of merit open not only to upper castes but śūdras as well reflected the improved material condition of the latter and considerably raised his religious status. Partly it worked to the advantage of the brāhmaṇas as it improved their economic condition by giving them an additional means of income and making them landowners through grants of land as they were regarded as the most worthy donees. But equally, if not more, it benefited the society as a whole as money was invested in the establishment of works of public utility and charity to the poor, not merely in sacrifices. The desire to earn religious merit impelled the richer sections to distribute alms to the poor and open hospitals which helped reduce economic inequities to a certain extent and provided welcome medical treatment to the poor. The providing of civic amenities like parks and wells benefited the masses and ensured easy supply of water for drinking as well as agriculture. The building of temples offered encouragement to architecture. The Jaina concept of charity was different in nature as it emphasised the gift of knowledge, protection and equipment to the religious. As knowledge implied true knowledge as conceived by Jainism and Jaina monks were projected as the worthy donees for gifts of equipment, the sphere of these gifts was rather limited and designed to further Jainism and provide for the need of Jaina monks. But the gift of protection was meant for all creatures and provided for the general good.

Tīrthayātrā was a means of gaining merit open to members of both sexes, rich as well as poor, and the śūdras along with members of the upper castes. As it enabled the less privileged sections of the society including people without money, women, a sizable section of the lower classes and sinners to aspire for religious merit it was an institution with considerable mass appeal. By promoting inter-regional contact and bringing people of different castes and customs together it at least temporarily broke down caste exclusiveness, contributed to cultural synthesis, and engendered a catholic outlook. For men and especially women, who may otherwise have not travelled much, it was an educative experience, for their geographical horizons widened and knowledge of the country increased. As the pilgrim traversed afoot long distances from one *tīrtha* to another living off alms, he cultivated considerable mental as well as physical discipline.

The location of brahmanical *tīrthas* in the sites around the river Ganges such as Prayaga, Banaras, Gaṅgādvāra, Gaṅgāsāgara and in Multan, Prabhāsa, Mahākāla etc. indicates the essential cultural unity of the period. The evolution of new *tīrthas* around the sites of Śaivite character and Śiva temples indicates the popularity of Śaivism to which it must have further contributed, besides benefiting temple brāhmaṇas as well. Tantric associations of *Mahākāla* which evolved as an important pilgrimage site indicates widespread acceptance of tantricism. Multan was a site sacred to the Sun god. The Jainas criticised the brahmanical practice of pilgrimage and bathing in rivers for removal of sins as irrational but they themselves attached great sanctity to places associated with the life of tīrthaṅkaras, such as Śatruñjaya, Sammetaśikhara and Aṭṭhāvaya. While some went there to pay their respects, others thought it to be the right place to end their life by *sallekhanā*. The current belief that suicide by drowning, falling from a precipice and entering the fire led to expiation of sins indicates superstitious beliefs current in society. Suicide at *Prayāgavaṭa* and Gaṅgāsāgara was deemed to be especially meritorious.

Various sacraments were performed to ward off evil influences and attract favourable ones. The birth, naming, marriage and funeral ceremonies were the most important of these. Placing of auspicious mirrors and designs around the mother and child, performing protective rites with ashes and sword and lighting lamps marked the birth ceremony. Various ceremonies such as the *maṇḍapakarana, agni-sthāpana, kanyādāna, pāṇigrahaṇa, lājahoma* and *agnipariṇayana* formed part of the marriage ceremony. Cremation, libations of water and *piṇḍadāna* were essential parts of the funeral ceremony. Bones of the dead were consigned to the Ganga, a practice considered to be stupid by the Jainas.

Notes and References

1. Kane, *HD,* II (i), p. 157.
2. See below, also śūdras.
3. *KM,* p. 65.
4. See brāhmaṇas, Supra, Chapter II.
5. खाणे कूव-तलाए बंधइ वावीओ देइ य पवाओ। *KM,* p. 205.
6. Ibid., pp. 18, 171; *SK,* p. 734.
7. *SK,* p. 527.
8. जाओ से दारओ . . . दवावियं च तेण महादाणं। Ibid., pp. 192–3.
9. दुग्गय-दुक्खिय-पंथ-कप्पडियादीणं मणोरहे पूरिऊणं। *KM,* p. 14.
10. *SK,* pp. 195, 235.
11. देसन्तराओ बहुयं दविणजायं विढविऊण महाकत्तिगीए दीणाणाहाणमणिवारियं महादाणं देन्तो। Ibid., p. 195.
12. Ibid., pp. 195, 409.
13. सूइज्जंति जत्थ पडिप्पवा-मंडवासत्तायारेहिं दाणवइत्तणाइं। *KM,* p. 31.
14. Infra, Chapter 9.
15. *KM,* p. 205.
16. *SK,* pp. 154–7; *KM,* p. 3.
17. *SK,* pp. 154–7.
18. Ibid., pp. 154–5.
19. *SK,* pp. 155–6.
20. Ibid., pp. 156 f.
21. Ibid., p. 158.
22. जाणह गाहगसुद्धं पंचमहव्वयधरो उ जो नियमा। गुरूसुस्सूसानिरओ जोगंमि समाहियप्पा य।। तह खन्तिमद्दवज्जवजुत्तो धणियं च विगयलोहो उ। मनवयणकायगुत्तो . . . । Ibid., p. 157.
23. K.K. Handiqui, *Yaśastilaka and Indian Culture,* p. 282.
24. *SK,* p. 13.
25. See above.
26. See above.
27. *ED,* I, p. 6
28. Chapter 81 f.
29. R.C. Hazra, *Studies in the Purāṇic Records on Hindu Rites and Customs,* Chapter IV.

30. *KM,* pp. 48, 55.
31. Ibid., p. 55.
32. Ibid., p. 45.
33. दूसह-दालिद्द-णिव्वेय-णिव्विण्णा गंगाए तित्थयत्ता-णिमित्तं विणिग्गया। Ibid., p. 45.
34. मित्त-वथ-कतानिं पि पातकानि सिन्नान-मेत्तकेनं येव सत-सक्करानि पनस्संति। . . . दिव्वाणं पि पूयणीया सव्व-पावहारी भगवई सुरसरिया। *KM,* p. 71.
35. जं पुण मयस्स अंगटिठ्याइं छुब्भंति जण्हवी-सलिले। Ibid., p. 49.
36. गंगा-दुवार-हेमंत-ललिय-भद्देस्सर-वीरभद्द-सोमेसर-पहास-पुक्खराइसु पिंडयं पक्खालयंतो परिभमसु। *KM,* p. 48.
37. अमुक्का वाणारसी-कोढिएहिं . . . मूलत्थाणु भडारउ . . . महाकाल-भडारयहं छम्मासे सेवण कुणइ। Ibid., p. 55.
38. चिर-परूढु पाव फिट्टइ . . . प्रयाग-वड-पडियहं। Ibid.
39. माइ-पिइ-वह-कयइं पि महापावाइं गंगा-संगमे ण्हायहं भइरव-भडारय-पडियहं णासंति। Ibid.
40. N.L. Dey, *Geographical Dictionary of Ancient and Medieval India,* pp. 62, 74.
41. D. Sharma, *RTTA,* p. 404; V.S. Agrawala, *KM,* pt. ii, p. 116.
42. *Matsya,* 106.54; *Kūrma,* I.37.34; *Garuḍa* (pūrva), 81.1–2; *Padma,* V.60.120.
43. The fame of Gaṅgāsāgara dates back to the time of the *Mahābhārata* which declares that a bath at the place yields the fruit of ten *aśvamedha* sacrifices. So does the name of Gaṅgādvāra, which is declared to be the gate (*dvāra*) to heaven and Varanasi, where a person who gives up life is said to attain salvation. *Vanaparva,* 84.27, 78-80; 85.4.
44. Kane, op. cit., p. 623.
45. Kane, op. cit., p. 641.
46. See below, religious suicide.
47. Jodhpur inscription of Bauka, *EI,* XVIII, pp. 87 f.
48. The *Mahābhārata* refers to it as a site sacred to Brahmā, where Gods as well as sages had attained perfection. *Vanaparva,* vv. 20–40. The Śaka ruler, Uṣavadāta, son-in-law of Nahapāna, is known to have bathed here and given in charity 3,000 cows and a village. *EI,* VIII, p. 78.
49. Vāyu, 77/40; *Brahmāṇḍa,* 3/13/40.
50. R.C. Hazra, *Studies in the Purāṇic Records on Hindu Rites and Customs,* pp. 121–3.
51. D. Sharma, *RTTA,* p. 403; N.L. Dey, *Geographical Dictionary of Ancient and Medieval India,* pp. 157–8.
52. Sachau, II, p. 104.
53. D. Sharma, op. cit., p. 403; cf. *Skanda Purāṇa, Kedārakhaṇḍa,* Chapter 7.31–3.
54. *Tīrthavivecana,* p. 172.
55. *Matsya,* 22.29; *Kūrma,* II.35.20.
56. See sun worship, Chapter 5.
57. See Śaivism, Chapter 5.
58. *Śiva Purāṇa,* Chapter I, 14–33; V.1.18, 21–4.
59. *Skanda Purāṇa, Kedāra Khaṇḍa* 7.31–3.

60. भिक्खं भमंतो कय-सीस-तुंड-मुंडणो करंका-हत्थो . . . तित्थसु पिंडयं पक्खालयंतो। *KM*, p. 48. कयाइं मुंडावियाइं सीसाइं। गहियाओ छत्तियाओ। लंबियं डंडयग्गे लावुयं। धाउ-रत्तयाइं कप्पडाइं। विलग्गाविया सिक्कए करंका। सव्वहा विरइओ दूर-तित्थयात्तिय-वेसो। Ibid., p. 58.
61. *Matsya Purāṇa*, 106.4–6.
62. *Padma*, IV 19.27.
63. शिरोगतानि पापानि यान्ति मुण्डनतो यत:। *Padma (Uttarakhaṇḍa)*, 237.45.
64. लोक-परंपरा-मूढा। *KM*, pp. 48–9.
65. Handiqui, *Yaśastilaka and Indian Culture*, pp. 253, 320.
66. *Mbh. Vana.*, 82, 9–12, *Anuśāsana*, 108.3–4; *Vāyu*, 77.125 and 127, qd. by *Tīrthakalpa*, pp. 5–6; *Skanda, Kāśīkhaṇḍa*, 56.52–3.
67. *KM*, p. 45.
68. Ibid., pp. 48, 55, 63, 71.
69. *Matsya*, 181, 19–21; *Kūrma*, 31.32–4.
70. *KM*, p. 45.
71. D. Sharma, *Lectures on Rajput History*, p. 96.
72. One who donates a kapila cow to a śrotriya brāhmaṇa, learned in the Vedas, at Prayaga attains heaven, *Matsya*, 105. 16–17; S.N. Roy, *Paurāṇic Dharma evaṃ Samāja*, p. 132.
73. See religion.
74. पट्ठिओ सेत्तुंजे महागिरिवरे सिद्धाणं वंदणा-णिमित्तं। *KM*, p. 80.
75. अम्हे वेयड्ढ-गिरिवराओ सम्मेय-सिहरं गया। तत्तो सत्तुंजयं चलिया। Ibid., p. 124.
76. सम्मेय-सेल-सिहरे वंदण-वत्तियाए संपत्तो। तत्थ य जाणिऊण अप्पणो कालं, कयं संलेहणा। Ibid., p. 216.
77. A.N. Upadhye, ed. *Kuvalayamālākathā*, 29; *Kuvalayamālā*, pt. II.
78. Singhi Jaina Granthamālā, Vol. X.
79. N.L. Dey, *Geographical Dictionary of Ancient and Medieval India*, p. 182.
80. *Antagaḍadasāo*, I, p. 6; J.C. Jain, *Life in Ancient India as Depicted in Jaina Canons*, p. 333.
81. J.C. Jain, op. cit., pp. 354 ff.
82. N.L. Dey, op. cit., p. 176.
83. *Āvaśyaka niryukti*, 307; *Nāyā.*, 8, p. 120; *Ācarāṅga Cūrṇi;* J.C. Jain, op. cit., p. 330.
84. U.P. Shah, *Studies in Jaina Art*, p. 117.
85. तुगमलघं जिण-भवण-मणहरं सावयाउलं विसमं। जावालिउरं अट्ठावयं व। *KM*, p. 282.
86. N.L. Dey, op. cit., pp. 12, 82.
87. J.C. Jain, op. cit., p. 268, It is referred to by ancient texts such as the *Jambudvīpaprajñapti*, *Ācarāṅga niryukti* and the *Vasudevahiṇḍi*. *Jambudvīpaprajñapti*, 33, *Ācarāṅga; Vasudevahiṇḍi*, p. 301; U.P. Shah, op. cit., p. 116.
88. *Niśītha Cūrṇi*, 3, p. 24.
89. *KM*, p. 55, see above, p. 150.
90. पडामि समुद्दे गिरि-टंके वाविसामि पायाले। जलणे व्व समारुहिमो। Ibid., p. 48.
91. जलणो डहइ सरीरं जलं पि . . . अंगट्ठियाइं भंजइ गिरी वि णवरं णिवडियाणं। Ibid., p. 72.
92. *Manu*, V. 89; *Parāśara* IV.1–2; *Yama*, 20–1.

93. *On Manu,* V. 88.
94. *ED,* I, p. 10.
95. *KM,* pp. 48, 55.
96. Ibid., p. 55, see above.
97. *Matsya*, Chapter 106, 11; P.K. Gode, 'The History of the Akṣayavaṭa at Prayaga and Gaya as revealed by some Sanskrit Texts', p. 382; *Studies in Indian Cultural History,* Vol. I.
98. *Kūrma.,* I. 37. 8–9; *Padma*, Ādikhaṇḍa, 43.11.
99. *Agni,* 111.13.
100. Kane, op. cit., p. 605.
101. Beal, I, p. 232.
102. *KM,* p. 55, see above.
103. जले स्थले अन्तरिक्षे च गंगायां गंगासागरसंगमे।। qd. D.C. Sircar, *Geography of Ancient and Medieval India,* p. 179.
104. Jodhpur Inscription of Bauka, verse 21; *EI,* XVIII, pp. 95 f.
105. Ibid., verse 23.
106. *EI,* XX, pp. 97 f.
107. R.B. Pandey, *Hindu Saṃskāras,* pp. 25–35.
108. V. Upadhyaya, *Socio-Religious Condition of Northern India,* p. 140.
109. विरएसु . . . मणि-पईवय-णिहाए . . . मंगल-दप्पण-मालाओ . . . भूइ-रक्खा परिहरंतए . . . णंदावत्त-सयवत्त-पत्तलेहाओ . . . बालयस्स देवीए य इमं रक्खा-मंडलग्गं। *KM,* p. 17.
110. Ibid., p. 21.
111. Ibid., p. 170; *SK,* pp. 74, 734.
112. *KM,* p. 170.
113. Ibid., pp. 170–1.
114. *SK,* pp. 47–80.
115. Kane, *HD,* II, (i), pp. 531 f.
116. *KM,* pp. 186, 224.
117. *SK,* p. 727.
118. *KM,* pp. 186, 224.
119. मयडिण्डिमसद्द। *SK,* p. 53.
120. *KM,* p. 48; Ibid., p. 186.
121. *SK,* p. 255.
122. Ibid.
123. तलए गंतूण देंति से वारिं . . . देंति गंतूण तस्स पुण्णेहिं बम्हण-कुलाणं। *KM,* p. 187.
124. अंगट्ठियाइं छुब्भंति जण्हवी-सलिले। Ibid., p. 49.
125. *KM,* p. 13.
126. एयस्स रोहियमच्छस्स पुच्छभायं तायं अज्जियं च उद्दिसिऊण माहणाणं रन्धावेहि। *SK,* p. 258. The use of the *Rohita* fish in *śrāddhas* had been sanctioned by Manu. *Manu,* V.16.

7

Toilet, Dress, Ornaments, Food and Drink

Toilet

GREAT CARE WAS taken to ensure personal hygiene and the toilet involved an elaborate process. The *Kuvalayamālā* mentions the following order of toilet: *abhyañjana*, or anointing the body with specially prepared oil (*śatasahasra-pāka tela*), massaging (*mardana* or *saṃvāhana*), rubbing with unguents (*udvartana* with *kaṣāyas*) to remove greasiness, *mārjana* or bathing with cool fragrant water and *vilepana* or smearing the body with perfumes.[1] Of *vilepanas* used by men we have reference to *candana* or sandal, *Haricandana*,[2] and *Malayacandana*.[3] Men would take great pains with toilet when going out. According to the *Kuvalayamālā* they would adorn themselves with chaplets of flowers, apply a *tilaka* on the forehead and collyrium to their eyes, and perfume their mouth with *tāmbūla* or betel leaf prepared from sweet smelling ingredients.[4]

The *Samarāiccakahā* gives an elaborate description of a bride's toilet. Her feet were dyed with red resin (*alaktaka*). On her thighs was put saffron (*kuṃkumarāga*) and on her breasts was inscribed a *patralekhā* (decorative pattern). Her face was washed with sandal water (*candana*) mixed with saffron (*kāleya*). Her lips were dyed and covered with bee's wax. On her forehead was put a *tilaka*. Her ears were dyed with saffron.[5] In the *Karpūramañjarī*, the heroine after her bath has her limbs anointed with saffron essence until they are yellow, her eyes adorned with collyrium, the wreath of curly locks fringing the crescent of her forehead arranged and her hair decorated with flowers.[6] The evidence of the *Kuvalayamālā* shows that in the summer women smeared their bodies with camphor powder, wore garlands of *pāṭala* flowers around their necks, put sandal on their forehead and adorned themselves with *mallikā* flowers.[7] In winter, sandalwood paste was not used, hair was braided, collyrium put in the eyes, and the face was smeared with oily substances.[8] As the month of Caitra set in and spring began, the cool season coming to an end, the *Karpūramañjarī* tells us, girls no longer put too much bee's wax (*madana*) on their lips, nor did they use perfumed oil for plaiting their hair, nor put large quantities of saffron on their faces, while they again set their heart on sandal-juice.[9] The *Kāvyamīmāṃsā* also refers to use of sandal, agallochum, saffron and musk in the rainy season, application of saffron with bee's wax on the mouth and fragrant oil to the hair in the cold season, application of crushed saffron on the bodies in winter and use of camphor powder in the summer season.[10] Women's toilet thus varied according to the season. Māgha speaks of the use of unguents of saffron, musk and sandal in general, or *kuṃkuma* and *lodhra* powders for the complexion[11] and *alaktaka*, the red resin for dyeing the lips and the soles of the feet.[12]

Of fashions peculiar to certain sections of society we learn of the application of black turmeric (*karcūra*) on the body by village women,[13] use of saffron paste on their cheeks, collyrium in their eyes[14] and turmeric on their bodies by Maratha women,[15] bathing, anointing, combing and parting the hair by *Lāṭas* whereby they made their limbs attractive.[16]

Dress

Garments made of various kinds of fabrics were in use. Various references to *kṣauma,*[17] *dukūla,*[18] *paṭṭāṃśuka,*[19] *raktāṃśuka,*[20] *kṛṣṇāṃśuka,*[21] *netrapaṭṭa,*[22] *gaṅgapaṭṭa.*[23] *citrapaṭṭa,*[24] *cīna* and *ardhacīna,*[25] *devadūṣya,*[26] *devāṅga,*[27] *valkaladukūla*[28] and *rallaka*[29] are to be found in our works.

Kṣauma is described in the *Kuvalayamālā* as a cloth of delicate and soft texture, garments of which were favoured in summer.[30] In the *Samarāiccakahā*, a bride wears a pair of *kṣauma* garments.[31] Elsewhere a prince is affectionately dressed in *kṣaumayugala* (pair of *kṣauma* garments) and taken to the king.[32] Lavish entertainment of a robber by a queen also includes present of *kṣaumayugala.*[33] On the basis of the evidence of the *Maitrāyanī Saṃhitā* and commentary of Kṣīrasvāmin on the *Amarakośa*, *kṣauma* has been identified as linen cloth made from the yarn of linseed flax, *kṣauma* or *atasī.*[34]

Numerous references to *dukūla* are to be found in our works. Members of the royal family wore garments of *dukūla* on the occasions of worship of deities,[35] wedding ceremonies,[36] and spring festivities.[37]

Dukūla garments are said to be given away along with precious gems at the birth of prince Kuvalayacandra.[38] They were also included among presents to the bridegroom's party.[39] *Dukūla* is also mentioned along with other auspicious objects among *abhiṣekamaṅgala* (auspicious objects for coronation).[40] These references leave no doubt about the popularity of *dukūla*, especially white, not only on ordinary but also important and auspicious occasions. Its adjectives such as *vara, pravara* (excellent), *vimala, manahara* (attractive)[41] show it to be a cloth of good quality. The *Amarakośa* identifies it with *kṣauma*.[42] But Kauṭliya differentiated between the two.[43] According to the *Niśītha Cūrṇi*, it was made from the bark of the *dukūla* tree.[44]

Various kinds of *aṃśuka* and *paṭṭa* fabrics are mentioned in our works. The king and queen are described as wearing *paṭṭāṃśuka*.[45] The heroine of the *Karpūramañjarī* was also dressed in a pair of *paṭṭāṃśuka* garments as blue as the tail-feathers of a king-parrot.[46] A bridegroom wore a *raktāṃśuka*[47] and so did a bride.[48] The night is compared to a woman wearing *kṛṣṇāṃśuka.*[49] *Netrapaṭṭa* and *citrapaṭṭa* are mentioned amongst valuable gifts.[50] A merchant is said to have gone to Cīna and Mahācīna and bought *gaṅgāpaṭṭa* and *netrapaṭṭa*.[51] Excellent garments (*pravara vastras*) of Cīna and Mahācīna are mentioned in the *Samarāiccakahā.*[52] On the basis of the *Anuyogadvārasūtra* which describes *aṃśuka* and *cīnāṃśuka* as worm products or *kīṭaja* and the *Bṛhatkalpasūtrabhāṣya*, *aṃśuka, paṭṭa* and *cīnāṃśuka* are identified as silken cloth.[53] *Cīnāṃśuka* was apparently Chinese silk imported from China which finds mention in the *Abhijñānaśākuntalam* and *Harṣacarita.*[54] *Cīna* is a generic name for Chinese silk,[55] *Ardhacīna* seems to have been gauze silk.[56] *Gaṅgapaṭṭa* was apparently a special variety of *cīnāṃśuka* imported from China.[57] It has been identified as a white silk known in India as *gaṃgājul.*[58] *Netrapaṭṭa* is a colour-silk mentioned for the first time in the *Raghuvaṃśa* of Kālidāsa.[59] Bāṇa describes *netra* as having variegated fine-looking designs of flowers and leaves.[60] The reference to it as a Chinese silk[61] is significant. Somadevasūri (tenth century) refers to *netra* as a superior silken fabric in use in the Rāṣṭrakūṭa empire.[62]

Devadūṣya and *devāṅga* were fabrics which the *Kuvalayamālā* associates with celestial beings. They are mentioned as divine enjoyments (*divyabhogas*), which one enjoys when born as a god.[63] Elsewhere, a celestial car (*devīvimāna*) is described as furnished above with a *devāṅga* cloth and an upper canopy of *devadūṣya* cloth.[64] The *Samarāiccakahā* refers to their use by affluent sections of society. A prince is described as wearing garments of spotless and patterned (*nirmalavicitra*) *devāṅga* on a visit to the park in springtime.[65] In the description of a king's bed chamber (*vāsagṛha*) we come across pillars decorated with *pravara devāṅga*.[66] *Devāṅga* clothes are presented to a Śabara chief who saved the king's life.[67] On the occasion of a royal wedding, the king gave orders to the keeper of garments to bring out *devāṅga* for display and distribute it amongst the attendants.[68] A bride in the royal family was covered with smooth *devadūṣya*.[69] The *Pāiasaddamahaṇṇavo* equates *devāṅga* and *devadūṣya*. Evidently they both represent some kind of costly cloth.[70] *Rallaka* and *kambala* were woollen clothes, the use of which the *Kuvalayamālā* notes in winter.[71]

The dress of men consisted of *vastra yugala*, a pair of garments,[72] which were probably the *uttarīya* and the *adhovastra*. Women wore an *uttarīya*,[73] and a *stanapaṭṭa*[74] or a *stanottariya*[75] as an upper garment which covered the breasts.[76] In winter they would wear *kūrpāsakas*,[77] which would be discarded at the advent of spring.[78] The stitching of *kūrpāsakas* on the occasion of the marriage of princess Kuvalayamālā is mentioned by Uddyotana.[79] The *kūrpāsaka*, according to the *Ṛtusaṃhāra* was the close-fitting bodice of women.[80] Kṣīrasvāmin explains *kūrpāsaka* etymologically as a women's garment, the sleeves of which came up to the *kurpāsa* (elbow).[81]

Dyed clothes were extensively used and we read of clothes coloured in blood-red, blue, black, and *kusumbha* red.[82] Red coloured garments were favoured by the bride[83] and the bridegroom.[84] White garments were also popular and seem to be considered pure and auspicious.[85]

Ornaments

Various ornaments were worn to enhance the beauty of one's person. 'Ornaments', says Kapiñjala in the *Karpūramañjarī*, 'cause the comeliness of even a person who is naturally handsome to unfold itself (to even greater beauty). A certain splendour results from adorning even precious stones with diamonds.'[86]

Not only women but men were inordinately fond of ornaments. Thus in the *Samarāiccakahā* we have the description of a prince whose ears were decorated with ear-rings (*śravaṇakuṇḍalas*), hands with bracelets (*māṇikya-kaṭaka*), arms with armlets (*keyūras*) studded with rubies, chest with a long necklace (*ratnaprālamba*), waist with a waistband (*bhuvanasāra kaṭisūtra*), and head with a bejewelled crown (*mukuṭa*).[87] Elsewhere we read of *ratnakuṇḍalas*,[88] crest jewel (*cūḍāmaṇi*),[89] signet ring (*nāmāṅkita mudrāratna*)[90] and emerald necklets (*markatamaṇi-kaṇṭhikās*)[91] worn by men. Abu Zaid (ninth century) has also noted that the kings of India were accustomed to wear ear-rings of precious stones, mounted in gold. They also wore necklaces of great value, formed of the most precious red and green stones.[92]

A good idea of the variety of ornaments worn by women can be had from the *Samarāiccakahā* which describes a bride decked with ornaments from head to feet. On her feet were put jewelled anklets (*maṇinūpuras*), and on her fingers rings set with jewels. A jewelled girdle (*maṇimekhalādāma*) was placed around the hips. *Bāhusārikās* ornamented her armpits. A *plavaṅgabandha* adorned her breast. A pearl-necklace reaching her hips encircled her neck. Her ears were decked with *ratnacakralatā*. A *dusurullaka* of pearls was placed round her neck and a *cūḍāratna* was placed on her forehead.[93] *Bāhusārikā, plavaṅgabandha* and *dusurullaka* are new names for ornaments not mentioned in earlier works.

Other ornaments of women mentioned are *maṇirasanā*,[94] *kāñcī*,[95] *kaṭisūtra*,[96] *kanakamahāśṛṃkhalā*[97] for the waist and *valaya*[98] (bracelet) for the wrist. We read of an extremely costly pair of jewelled bracelets (*māṇikyakaṭakayugala*) worn by a woman, to obtain which a robber cuts off her hands when unable to remove them.[99] Mention is also made of a pearl-necklace (*muktāphalamālā*) worth a hundred thousand *dīnāras*.[100] In the *Karpūramañjarī* the heroine is after bath adorned with ear-rings studded with gems (*ratna-kuṇḍala*), rows of bracelets (*valayāvalī*), a girdle bejewelled with rubies (*padmarāgamaṇikāñcī*), a necklace of monster pearls (*ṣaṇmāsikamauktikahāra*) and emerald anklets (*markata-mañjīra*).[101] While rich women wore gold, pearls and various jewels,[102] the poor village women sported *śaṃkha* bangles set with shining glass pieces.[103]

Flowers were also profusely used for decorating the body. They were woven into garlands and worn by a bridegroom,[104] used as chaplets,[105] and adorned the hair of women.[106] Śirīṣa flowers were put in the ears.[107] Village women used blue lotuses as ear-ornaments and tender lotus stalks as bracelets.[108]

Food

Various kinds of cereals, pulses, spices, fruits and meat formed part of the people's diet. Rice was a popular item of food and the *Kuvalayamālā* mentions the *śāli*[109] and *kalama*[110] varieties. Other food grains mentioned are *śyāmaka* and *kodrava* (kodo millet) eaten by wild rats,[111] and *yava*[112] (barley). Among pulses we have reference to *mudga.*[113] *Trikaṭu* spices (dry ginger or *sūṇṭha, marīca* or pepper, and *pīpala* or long pepper), salt (*lavaṇa*) and asafoetida (*hingu*) and turmeric (*haridra*) were used in preparation of food.[114] Besides these, cardamom (*elā*),[115] cloves (*lavaṅga*),[116] nutmeg (*jātiphala*)[117] and *kaṃkola (śītalacīnī)*[118] spices were also known.

Milk and milk-products were in use. The *Karpūramañjarī* refers to the *pañcagavyas.*[119] Our works also refer to food preparation such as *khīra,*[120] *pāyasa,*[121] *khaṇḍakhajjakas,*[122] *laḍḍukas,*[123] *kāsāra,*[124] *saktu*[125] and *maṇḍaka.*[126] *Khīra*, described as prepared with sugar and ghee[127] is a well-known dish. *Khaṇḍakhajjakas, laḍḍukas* and *saktu* are the preparations known as *khājās, laḍḍus* and *sattu. Khajjakas*, mentioned by *Jātakas* and Suśruta, were a preparation of wheat flour fried in ghee.[128] *Laḍḍukas* are the same as *modakas*, sweet balls prepared with the flour of rice or some pulse and sugar, referred to by the *Rāmāyana, Mahābhārata* and Suśruta.[129] *Saktu* was a parched barley meal which dates back to Vedic times.[130] *Kāsāra* is a new preparation of the period, made with wheat flour, milk, clarified butter, crystal sugar, cardamom and black pepper, according to the *Mānasollāsa.*[131] *Maṇḍaka*, according to the same work, was a loaf of bread prepared with wheat or rice flour mixed with salt, milk and clarified butter.[132]

Along with vegetarian dishes meat preparations were also quite popular. Not only were kings, for whom hunting was a favourite pastime, non-vegetarians, but the brāhmaṇas too appear to have had no hesitation in partaking of meat at religious ceremonies and *śrāddhas*. Uddyotana observes that when born as a rabbit, deer and buffalo, one's flesh was liable to be torn into pieces and eaten.[133] The *Samarāiccakahā* refers to the slaughter of fifteen buffaloes and preparation of buffalo's meat to provide a feast for brāhmaṇas on occasion of the worship of the *kuladevatā* by a ruler.[134] In another place a ruler is said to have sent cooked *rohita* fish to the brāhmaṇas for the *śrāddha* of his father and grandfather.[135] Elsewhere we read that when meat prepared for a festival in honour of a deceased father is snatched away by a cat, the cook, in want of other meat, secretly kills a pig.[136] Rulers ate fish,[137] the meat of buffalo[138] and sheep.[139] Regarding the preparation of fried fish, the *Samarāiccakahā* tells us that after the *rohita* was cut, the cook put into it *trikaṭu* spices, *hingu* and *lavaṇa*, immersed it in *haridra* water and fried it in boiling ghee.[140] Roasted preparation of mutton was known as *bhaṭitraka.*[141] Preparation of fried fish and roasted mutton are novelties and indicate an advance in the art of cooking meat. *Tāñtrikas* gave sanction to the use of meat.[142] Jainas tried to discourage the practice of meat-eating. The evil consequences of consuming animal flesh are amply stressed in Yaśodhara's tale in the *Samarāiccakahā*, where a ruler who has but eaten the so-called flesh of an artificial cock also acquires bad *karma* of long endurance.[143]

There is reference to a variety of fruits such as the mango variously known as *cūta,*[144] *āmra,*[145] and *sahakāra*;[146] jujube (*badara*);[147] plantain (*kadalī*);[148] orange (*nāraṅga*);[149] jackfruit (*panasa*);[150] hog-plum (*āmrātaka*);[151] pomegranate (*piṇḍīra*);[152] karaundā (*karamarda*);[153] lime (*jambīra*);[154] citron (*mātuliṅga*)[155] and coconut (*nālikera*)[156] which must have been extensively eaten.

Drinks

Intoxicating drinks, which were fairly common in Gupta times,[157] retained their popularity. In the *Kuvalayamālā* we read of the king after his bath, before he has taken his meals, visiting the *āpanaka bhūmi* or the drinking hall and partaking of wine, of which three varieties, *madhu, āsava* and *surā* flavoured with flowers, are mentioned in the context.[158] Elsewhere we have reference to *madirā.*[159] The *Samarāiccakahā* refers to the offering of *madhu,*[160] *āsava*[161] and *drakṣāpānaka*[162] to a thief being entertained by the queens at the palace. The *Karpūramañjarī* includes drinking of cool *surā* among the delights of summer.[163] It also mentions drinking of *vāruṇī.*[164]

Drinking was not confined to men alone. The evidence of the *Kuvalayamālā* shows that *surā* was taken by village women on festive occasions like the spring festival.[165] It also refers to drunken towns-women dancing on the occasion of the birth of prince Kuvalayacandra.[166] A similar reference is found in the *Samarāiccakahā.*[167] We also read of a woman enjoying wine in the company of her husband along with her friends.[168] The wide prevalence of drinking is attested by other sources. We learn from the Jodhpur inscription of Bauka that the children born of the brāhmaṇa Hariścandra were 'drinkers of wine'.[169] The Sīyaḍoṇi inscription mentions the *kallapāla* or distiller of liquor.[170] Of the three kinds of *surā*, viz. rice-flour, molasses and grapes or *madhūka* flowers, Medhātithi prohibits the use of all three to brāhmaṇas, but permits the use of the last two to the kṣatriyas and vaiśyas.[171] Elsewhere he observes that while brāhmaṇa women did not drink wine at festivals, kṣatriya and other women, to whom drinking was not forbidden, indulged in excessive drinking when they gathered on festive occasions.[172] Drinking of wine was an accepted practice of the *Kaula* sect.[173]

However there is no evidence of people becoming habituated to excessive drinking in our works. Sulaiman (AD 851) has observed that the Indian kings drank no wine as it was thought that a drunkard could not conduct the business of the kingdom.[174] Ibn Khurdadba (died AD 912) states that the kings and people regarded wine as unlawful[175] and that the kṣatriyas (*kataria*) drank no more than three cups of wine.[176] These statements confirm that Indians were not addicted to drinking.

Betel-chewing

Betel-chewing was a common practice and an honoured guest was welcomed with *tāmbūla.*[177] The rich offered it in a container of gold.[178] It was used to perfume the mouth before going for an outing.[179] Its description as *pañca-saugandhika tāmbūla*[180] shows that five ingredients were used in its preparation. Of these camphor (*karpūra*), cloves (*lavaṅga*) and śītalacīnī (*kaṃkola*) are mentioned in the context. Another ingredient nutmeg (*jātiphala*) is later named.[181] The *Samarāiccakahā* speaks of betel with camphor (*karpūravīṭakasanātha tāmbūla*), which was kept handy in the bed-chamber of a king.[182] The *Upamitibhavaprapañcākathā* (tenth century) also refers to *pañca-saugandhika tāmbūla* with cardamom, clove, camphor, nutmeg and mace.[183]

To conclude, the elaborate mode of toilet including anointment with oil, massaging, rubbing with unguents, bathing and smearing with perfumes indicates the care taken to maintain personal hygiene. A variety of perfumes, cosmetics and ornaments, differing according to climate and region, were used by both men and women. A wide range of textiles including *kṣauma, dukūla, devāṅga, devadūṣya*, indigenous and imported silken fabrics like *aṃśuka, paṭṭa, cīnāṃśuka, gangapaṭṭa* and *netrapaṭṭa*, were used for garments. New ornaments of the period indicate the fondness for ornaments and opulence of the rich. Women bedecked themselves with ornaments from head to feet and men also wore a variety of them.

The diet of the people was rich in variety, including various cereals, pulses, milk and milk preparations, spices and fruits. Meat of buffalo, sheep etc. and fish formed an important part of the diet of kṣatriyas. Brāhmaṇas also took meat on ceremonial occasions and *śrāddhas.* There was an advance in the art of cooking non-vegetarian dishes as indicated by new preparations of roasted mutton and fish. Intoxicating drinks were widely consumed, especially on festive occasions, in villages as well as cities. Betel-chewing was common. Offering of betel formed part of customary welcome.

Notes and References

1. *KM*, pp. 99, 105, 139, 157-8.
2. *SK*, p. 522. According to Arthaśāstra 2.11.45, *Haricandana* is of the colour of the feathers of a parrot and smells like mango fruit.
3. Ibid., p. 529. P.K. Gode notes the reference of Kālidāsa to the Candana plant on the Malaya mountain in his *Śākuntala* (Act IV) and Māgha's reference to the whiteness of the malaya born sandal (XI. 14); 'Some notes on history of Candana', pp. 314 f.; *Studies in Indian Cultural History,* Vol. I.
4. परिहिय मुंडे मालुल्लिया . . . पंच सोयंधियइं तंबोलह भरियइं गंडवासइं . . . विरइओ भालवट्टे तिलओ . . . अंजियइं अच्छिवत्तइं। *KM*, p. 84.
5. *SK*, pp. 75–6.
6. *Karpūra.*, II, 12-21.
7. कप्पूर-रेणु-रय-गुंडियओ . . . पाडला-दाम-सणाह-कंठओ मल्लिया-कुसुम-सोहओ . . . विइण्ण-चंदण-णेडालियओ। *KM*, p. 113.
8. अणायरिज्जंति चंदण-पंकयइं विरइंज्जंति वेणीओ, मक्खिज्जंति मुहइं, अंजिज्जंति अच्छिवत्तइं। Ibid., p. 169.
9. *Karpūra.*, I. 13-14.
10. *Kāvyamīmāṃsā*, XVIII.
11. Canto IX.7: VI.24; XVI.84 qd. D. Sharma, 'Gleanings from Sanskrit Literature', *JIH*, VIII, iii, p. 351.
12. IX.46; VII.63; D. Sharma, op. cit.
13. गाम-जुवईओ इव . . . कच्चूर-वयण-णिम्मंहत-परिमलाओ। *KM*, p. 8.
14. *Karpūra.*, I.16.
15. मरहट्ठिया इव उद्दाम-हलिद्दी-रय-पिंजराओ। *KM*, p. 8.
16. ण्हाओलित्त-विलित्ते कय-सीमंते सुसोहिय-सुगत्ते। Ibid., p. 153.
17. Ibid., p. 133; *SK*, pp. 519, 529, 786.
18. *KM*, pp. 11, 14, 18, 139; *SK*, pp. 78, 80, 125, 407, 522.
19. *KM*, pp. 10, 12, 74, 209; *Karpūra.*, II, 14.
20. *KM*, p. 51; *SK*, p. 75.
21. *KM*, p. 75.
22. Ibid., pp. 18, 66.
23. Ibid., p. 66.
24. Ibid., p. 18.
25. *SK*, p. 80.
26. *KM*, pp. 92, 94, 95, 275.
27. *SK*, pp. 80, 239, 629, 735.
28. *KM*, p. 128.
29. Ibid., p. 112.

30. कोमल-तणु-खोम-निवसणओ। Ibid., p. 113.
31. *SK*, p. 519.
32. Ibid., p. 529.
33. Ibid., p. 786.
34. *Maitrāyanī Saṃhitā*. III. 6.7; Kṣīrasvāmin's Commentary, II. 6:113; क्षुमाया: विकार: क्षौमम्, qd. B.P. Mazumdar, *Socio-Economic History of Northern India;* p. 194; B.N. Sharma, *Social Life in Northern India*, p. 271. In the days of Kauṭilya, Kāśī, and Puṇḍra were famous for *kṣauma.* In later days it was manufactured in Assam as well and we find bundles of *kṣauma* amongst the presents sent by Bhāskaravarman to Harṣa.
35. *KM*, pp. 14, 139.
36. *SK*, pp. 75, 78.
37. Ibid., p. 522.
38. *KM*, p. 18.
39. *SK*, p. 80.
40. Ibid., p. 125.
41. *SK*, pp. 68, 75, 78, 522.
42. *Amarakośa*, 2.6.113; qd. V.S. Agrawala, *Harṣacarita, Ek Sāṃskritika Adhyayana*, p. 76.
43. *Artha.*, II. 11. 102-6.
44. *Niśītha Cūrni*, II, p. 399; qd. Madhu Sen, *Cultural Study of the Niśītha Cūrṇi*, p. 151.
45. *KM*, pp. 10, 12, 209.
46. *Karpūra.*, II.14.
47. *KM*, p. 51.
48. *SK*, p. 75.
49. कसणंसुय-पाउया . . . राई रमणि व्व संयत्ता। *KM*, p. 75.
50. Ibid., p. 18.
51. Ibid., p. 66.
52. *SK*, p. 80.
53. V.S. Agrawala, op. cit., p. 78; Motichandra, *Costumes, Textiles, Cosmetics and Coiffure in Ancient and Medieval India*, p. 117.
54. *Abhijñanaśākuntalam*, I. 30; *Harṣacarita*, pp. 36, 167, 242.
55. Motichandra, op. cit., p. 116.
56. Ibid.
57. V.S. Agrawala in *Kuvalayamālā*, pt. II, p. 118.
58. Ibid.
59. 7.39; qd. V.S. Agrawala, *KM*, pt. II, p. 118.
60. *Harṣacarita*, p. 206; V.S. Agrawala, *Harṣacarita, Ek Sāṃskritika Adhyayana*, p. 79.
61. *KM*, p. 66.
62. Qd. V.S. Agrawala, *KM*, pt. II, p. 119.
63. *KM*, p. 275.
64. Ibid., p. 92.
65. *SK*, p. 522.

66. Ibid., p. 239.
67. *SK*, p. 799.
68. Ibid., p. 735.
69. Ibid., p. 519.
70. Mahāvīra is said to have joined the ascetic order wearing this cloth. Later, this piece was estimated as costing hundred thousand pieces of money. *Ācārāṅga Cūrṇi*, p. 268; qd. J.C. Jain, *Life in Ancient India as Depicted in the Jaina Canons*, p. 130.
71. *KM*, pp. 112, 169.
72. *KM*, pp. 11, 19, 84, 209; *SK*, pp. 529, 786, 799.
73. *SK*, pp. 348, 365, 407, 675, 704.
74. *KM*, p. 12.
75. Ibid., p. 25.
76. उत्तरीएण पच्छाइयपयोहरा। *SK*, p. 407.
    अन्नोन्नसमुक्खित्तुतरीयदीसन्तथणयवित्थारं। *SK*, p. 704.
77. णियसिज्जंति कुप्पासयइं। *KM*, p. 169.
78. *Karpūra.*, I. 13.
79. सीविज्जंति कुप्पासया। *KM*, p. 170.
80. Various Ajantā plates depict *kūrpāsakas* with sleeves and without sleeves. *Ṛtusaṃhāra*, V. 8; qd. Motichandra, *Costumes, Textiles, Cosmetics and Coiffure in Ancient and Medieval India*. p. 59.
81. On *Amarakośa*, II.6.118.
82. *KM*, pp. 51, 75, 82; *SK*, p. 75; *Karpūra.*, II.14.
83. *KM*, p. 26.
84. Ibid., p. 51.
85. See *dukūla*.
86. *Karpūra.*, II.25.
87. *SK*, p. 522.
88. *KM*, p. 11.
89. *SK*, p. 68; *KM*, p. 215.
90. Ibid., p. 108.
91. *KM*, p. 182.
92. *ED*, I, p. 11.
93. *SK*, pp. 76–7.
94. *KM*, p. 25.
95. Ibid., pp. 18, 104, 234.
96. Ibid., p. 25; *SK*, p. 80.
97. Ibid., p. 25.
98. Ibid., p. 1; *SK*, p. 523.
99. *SK*, p. 586.
100. दीनारसयसहस्समुल्लं मुत्ताहलमालं। Ibid., p. 418.
101. *Karpūra.*, II.13-18.
102. इब्भ-कुमारिया इव मुत्ताहल-सुवण्ण-रयणुज्जलाओ। *KM*, p. 7.
103. गाम-जुवईओ इव रीरिय-संख-वलय-काय-मणि-सोहाओ। Ibid., p. 8.
104. *KM*, p. 171.

105. Ibid., p. 84.
106. Ibid., p. 73.
107. Ibid., p. 112.
108. Ibid., p. 148.
109. *KM*, pp. 31, 45, 72.
110. Ibid., pp. 7, 31.
111. Ibid.
112. *KM*, p. 170.
113. Ibid., p. 186.
114. See below.
115. *KM*, pp.7, 33, 70, 106.
116. Ibid., pp. 7, 33, 70, 84, 104, 106.
117. Ibid., pp. 104, 134.
118. Ibid., p. 104.
119. *Karpūra.*, I. 20.
120. *KM*, p. 210.
121. Ibid.
122. *KM*, p. 170.
123. *SK*, pp. 103, 187, 189.
124. *KM*, pp. 187, 189.
125. *SK*, p. 253.
126. *KM*, p. 58.
127. खंड-घय-मीसियं पि हु खीरं। Ibid., p. 210.
128. Omprakash, *Food and Drinks in Ancient India*, p. 60.
129. Ibid., p. 289.
130. *Ṛgveda*, X.71.2; *Taittirīya brāhmaṇa*, III.8.14; Omprakash, op. cit., p. 291.
131. *Mānasollāsa*, III.1386-87.
132. *Mānasollāsa*, III.1375-81.
133. सस-संबर-महिस-पसुत्तणम्मि पुरिसेहिं मंस-लोहेणं। मंसं बहुसो खइयं फालेउं अंगमंगाइं।। *KM*, p. 40.
134. वावाइया पन्नरस महिसया। बंभणजणभोयणत्थं। *SK*, p. 260.
135. Ibid., p. 258.
136. पच्छन्नमेव वावाइऊण विससिओ कोलो। Ibid., p. 475.
137. Ibid., p. 258.
138. Ibid., p. 262.
139. Ibid.
140. Ibid., p. 258; D. Sharma, *RTTA*, p. 467.
141. Ibid., pp. 263-4.
142. See tantricism.
143. *SK*, pp. 245-50.
144. *KM*, p. 112; *SK*, p. 448.
145. *KM*, p. 119.
146. Ibid., pp. 32, 127; *SK*, pp. 70, 448.
147. *Dhū.*, III.17.
148. *SK*, pp. 71, 444, 797.

149. *KM*, pp. 106, 119; *SK*, p. 210.
150. *KM*, pp. 106, 119, 149; *SK*, p. 210, 797.
151. *KM*, p. 119.
152. Ibid., pp. 119, 122.
153. Ibid., p. 122.
154. *SK*, p. 797.
155. *KM*, pp. 106, 122.
156. Ibid., p. 149.
157. Cf. B.S. Upadhyaya, *India in Kālidāsa*, pp. 196-7; Chakladar, *Social Life in Ancient India*, p. 167.
158. *KM*, p. 20; According to Kauṭilya, *madhu* was wine from grapes and *āsava* was an extract of the wood-apple fruit (*kapittha*), inspissated juice of sugarcane and honey with some spices. *Arthaśāstra*, II, 25. *Surā*, generally produced with barley or rice flour, was the intoxicating drink of the common people in the Vedic period. *Ṛgveda*, VIII.2.12.24 c.
159. Ibid., p. 83. *Madirā*, mentioned by the *Mahābhārata* and Suśruta, was the cream of *surā*. *Mbh.*, Śāntiparva, 24.20; *Carakasūtrasthāna*, 27.178.
160. *SK*, p. 800.
161. Ibid., p. 786.
162. Ibid., *Drakṣāpanaka* was syrup prepared with grape juice. Omprakash, op. cit., p. 301.
163. गिम्हो . . . साअं सुरा सीअला। *Karpūra.*, IV.4.
164. वअणसीअला वारुणी। Ibid., IV. 6. *Vāruṇi* was a strong liquor prepared by fermenting the juices of palm fruit and dates, mentioned in the *Rāmāyaṇa*. *Rāmāyaṇa*, Ayodhyā, 14.20.
165. तस्य जाया सरिस-गाम-जुवई-तरुणीहिं जुण्ण-सुरा-पाण-मउम्मत। *KM*, p. 52.
166. मय-रस-वस-घुम्मिरं णच्चमाणाण . . . कामिणीणं। Ibid., p. 18.
167. सहरिसं वुड्ढाहि पिज्जमाणपवरासवाइं। *SK*, p. 602.
168. *KM*, p. 85.
169. Jodhpur Inscription of Bauka, *EI*, XVIII, verse 8.
170. *EI*, I, pp. 162 f.
171. *On Manu*, XI.97.
172. *On Manu*, IX.84.
173. *Karpūra.*, I.22 and 23.
174. *ED*, I, p. 7.
175. Ibid., p. 13.
176. Ibid., p. 16.
177. *KM*, p. 65; *SK*, pp. 64, 738, 741, 786.
178. *KM*, p. 64.
179. Ibid., p. 84.
180. Ibid.
181. Ibid., p. 104.
182. *SK*, p. 239.
183. V. 419.

8

Some Aspects of Daily Life

Recreations

PEOPLE AMUSED THEMSELVES with various pastimes. These included various sports and outside excursions which contributed to the well-being of their person; painting, dramas, dancing and music which were expressive of their refined and artistic tastes; various types of riddles which served as an intellectual exercise and sharpened the mental responses; and acrobatic shows and jugglery which provided simple entertainment to all and sundry. These did away with the monotony of life and made it more attractive. The *Samarāiccakahā* relates how when a prince showed himself averse to worldly pleasures, his friends sang songs, read out stories, played the *vīṇā*, discussed the *Kāmasūtra*, showed him paintings, took him to lakes and engaged in water-sports, went for excursions in gardens, put him on the swing and prepared beds of flowers to make him attached to the worldly ways of life.[1] In times of sorrow and distress, all entertainment was set aside. The *Samarāiccakahā* describes how when the king had a headache, the girls of the *antaḥpura* (inner apartments) gave up playing with the ball, painting, singing and dancing.[2] In the same book, there is the portrait of a love-stricken princess who would neither do any painting nor show any interest in the pet-birds, nor play the *vīṇā* (lute), nor cut designs on leaves, and not even play with the ball.[3]

Music, both vocal and instrumental, was popular amongst all sections of people. The arts of singing (*gīta*), instrumental music (*vādya*), knowledge of the seven notes (*svaragata*), playing the *puṣkara* or drum (*puṣkaragata*) and dancing (*nṛtya*) were cultivated even by princes.[4] Prince Kuvalayacandra had to his credit the mastery of musical instruments like the flute (*veṇu*) and tabor (*muraja*) as well as the sentiments (*rasas*) of love (*śṛṅgāra*), heroism (*vīra*), disgust (*bībhatsa*), pity (*karuṇā*) and humour (*hāsya*).[5] Ladies of royal families were generally proficient in playing the *vīṇā* (lute).[6] Among the various musical instruments played upon by the ladies of the town the *Kuvalayamālā* mentions the *vīṇā*, *vaccīsaka*, *muraja* (tabor), *triṣarika*, *vaṃśa* (flute) and *mukunda*[7] (drum). The *śaṃkha* (conch), *bherī* (kettle-drum), *tūrya* (trumpet), *kāhala*, *mṛdaṅga* (drum), *vaṃśa* and *vīṇā* are said to have been sounded at the departure of princess Kuvalayamālā from her parental home.[8] *Tūrya* was a popular musical instrument, played upon for auspiciousness at weddings,[9] other festivities,[10] and also at time of war.[11] The auspicious morning trumpet (*prabhātamaṅgala tūrya*) heralded the dawn for kings and princes.[12] Other instruments mentioned are *paṭaha* (drum),[13] *śṛṅga* (horn),[14] and *jhallarī*.[15]

Singing and dancing to the accompaniment of musical instruments was an essential part of every social and religious function. On the occasion of spring the sound of *carcarī* (song and dance) could be heard on all sides.[16] Specific dances such as *calli* and *daṇḍarāsa* performed at the time of the Banyan festival are described in the *Karpūramañjarī*. Thirty-two dancing girls are said to have taken part in the *daṇḍarāsa*, circling around with charmingly varied pose of hands and feet, their steps keeping in time with music.[17] With their shoulders and heads even, arms and hands even, other maidens with clear cut pose were rendering the *calli* dance, regulating its tempo by the beaten measure.[18] Auspicious songs were sung and musical instruments sounded at the time of marriage,[19] as well as when a ship departed on a voyage.[20] Temples are said to have reverberated with the sound of women's songs and musical instruments.[21] *Rāsanṛtyas* (Rāsa dances) of herdsmen were common features of the countryside and the sight of the lively songs and dances performed by these men and women left many a traveller spellbound.[22]

Dramatic performances were another popular form of recreation. Kings would entertain themselves with *nāṭakas*[23] (dramas). The *Kuvalayamālā* speaks of *prekṣaṇakas* or dramatic performances held as part of the public celebrations on the occasion of the coronation of the heir-apparent (*yauvarājyābhiṣekamahotsava*).[24] The *Samarāiccakahā* mentions *prekṣaṇakas* amongst pre-wedding festivities arranged by ministers acting on royal directives.[25] During autumn, parties of actors and dancers would move from village to village giving performances. The *Kuvalayamālā* graphically describes how such a programme was enacted at a village. The time of performance was placed in the first quarter of the night to suit the villagers who proceeded to the show after having secured their cattle and rounded up their work for the day. Some carried their shouting children and others their cots and sticks, irresistibly drawn towards the sound of music.[26] Of historical instances of the dramas we have the *Karpūramañjarī* and various other plays of Rājaśekhara. The *Karpūramañjarī* reveals that dramas were staged with elaborate preparation and a well planned set-up. There was hectic activity before the opening of the play *Karpūramañjarī.* Some actresses were putting together suitable costumes; others twining garlands of flowers; another putting the masks in order; some rubbing colours on a palette; the flute was being tuned; the lute was being strung; drums made ready; timbrels sounded and introductory stanzas were being rehearsed.[27]

Horse-riding was a favourite pastime of kings.[28] The *Kuvalayamālā* describes how the king along with prince Kuvalayacandra and other princes went to the horse-ground (*vāhyālī*) where the horse-keeper (*mahāśvapati*) gave them horses for riding. They then rode along the royal highway, passed through the town and the bazaar and came in the sight of the *vāhyālī* again. There both the king and the prince allowed their horses to race. The latter's horse overtook that of the former much to the jubilation of the entire gathering.[29] The kings also enjoyed hunting.[30] The *Kuvalayamālā* refers to prince Maṇiratha for whom it became such an obsession that it was his sole occupation. Armed with the sword, bow and arrows, he would incessantly roam about the forests teeming with deer, boars and rabbits, his extreme addiction to the chase attracting the disapprobation of all his elders.[31]

Some people kept pet birds and animals to amuse themselves. Pet swans,[32] peacocks,[33] parrots[34] and *sārikās*[35] are mentioned in our works. The *Samarāiccakahā* refers to a princess teaching parrots and *sārikās*.[36] The *Kuvalayamālā* describes how a princess instructed a royal parrot (*rājakīra*) in various *śāstras*.[37] Melodious pet birds were placed in cages around the house to add to its charm.[38] In the *Samarāiccakahā* a peacock is trained to dance by the headman of the village and presented to the king.[39] The king is said to have been so fond of his peacock and pet dog that when they died he buried them with the same pomp as his parents.[40] Another king grew so fond of a cock and hen that he ordered their keeper to bring them along with him wherever he went.[41] Cock and quail fights are mentioned among the arts studied by the prince in the *Kuvalayamālā*.[42]

Gambling held a fascination for certain people. Unprincipled people looked upon *dyūta* as a means of gaining wealth.[43] In the *Samarāiccakahā* we read of the king playing dice with a draught board (*akṣapāṭaka*).[44] Elsewhere we read of the king enjoying *akṣadyūtavinoda* (the gambling amusement) with his wives.[45] Reference is made to the sad plight of a merchant gambler who fled because of his inability to pay off the sixteen *suvarṇas* that he had lost at play, only to be relentlessly pursued by the other gamblers to whom he owed the amount.[46] Bathing at pools and water-sports were other popular pastimes. Playing in the bathing-pools until night-fall was one of the pleasures of summer.[47] Palaces were furnished with water tanks (*gṛhadīrghikās*), where princesses enjoyed bathing.[48] Reference is made to water-sports or *jala-krīḍā* in the *Samarāiccakahā*.[49] The *Kuvalayamālā* describes a celestial bathing-pool (*krīḍāvāpi, majjanavāpi*) furnished with a jewelled stairway, golden archway and banners, where the god enjoyed water-sports with nymphs.[50] Playing in water was a common sport for the village children.[51] Visiting parks and gardens,[52] and swinging[53] were common diversions on festive occasions. Princesses and ladies of the higher classes would enjoy playing with the ball.[54] Entertainment was also provided by conjurors or *indrajālikas*[55] and wrestlers with stout bodies giving demonstration of their art.[56]

Learned pastimes included various types of riddles of words and completion of unfinished verses. Of these, the *Kuvalayamālā* tells us, *prahelikā*, and *antyākṣarikā* were quite popular, and current even amongst the cowherd lads.[57] But the remaining intellectual exercises which are duly illustrated, *bindumatī, atthāviḍaya, praśnottara, pṛṣṭārtha, akṣaracyutaka, mātrācyutaka, binducyutaka, gūḍha-caturtha-pāda (bhāṇiyavviyā), bhaṇitavyatā, hṛdaya, padmagāthā, gāthārdha, saṃvidhānaka, gāthārākṣasa* and *prathamākṣara-racita* required considerable knowledge and practice.[58] *Bindumatī* required completion of a stanza in which all the alphabets (*akṣaras*) excepting the first and the last, had been replaced by *bindus* (dots), leaving only the *mātrās* (syllables).[59] When the entire verse was scattered and hidden in 32 squares, it was known as *atthāviḍaya*. In the provided illustration the reading of the squares in alternate order reveals the verse.[60] When two, three or four questions were put together and the answers to all was the same, the riddle was called *praśnottara*.[61] Of the many varieties of *praśnottara*, arising out of grammatical, dialectal and other variations,[62] an important one was *gūdhottara* where the answer was so skilfully concealed and enigmatic that one did not perceive it at one glance.[63] When the riddle itself stated the answer, it was known as *pṛṣṭārtha*.[64] The example given is a play on puns. When the pun (*śleṣa*) in a verse was disturbed by the lack of an alphabet (*akṣara*) and restored when the alphabet was restored, it was called *akṣaracyutaka*.[65] Similarly in *binducyutaka* a *bindu* and in *mātrācyutaka* a *mātrā* (syllable) was left out[66] from a verse. In *gūḍha-caturtha-pāda*, the last quarter of the verse lay hidden in the first three quarters of the verse and had to be sought accordingly.[67] The following literary exercises are not defined, but merely illustrated. In *bhaṇitavyatā* what was intended to be said was not apparently said.[68] In *hṛdayagāthā* the *hṛdaya* (heart) appears to have been the central theme.[69] In *saṃvidhānaka*, we see plans being cleverly laid out through a seemingly innocent verse.[70] *Gāthārākṣasa* provided the latter part of a stanza which could attach itself to any *gāthā*, just like a *rākṣasa* (demon) e.g., 'so saying the traveller fainted'.[71] In *prathamākṣara*, the first letters of the four quarters of the verse put together conveyed a message.[72] The *Samarāiccakahā* illustrates *praśnottaras*,[73] and *gūḍhacaturthaka*, in which the fourth quarter had to be supplied.[74] *Prahelikās* mentioned in the *Kuvalayamālā* are riddles which are listed among pastimes also by the *Kāmasūtra*.[75] *Antyākṣarikā* is the same as *pratimālā* as stated by the commentator Yasodhara in his commentary *Jayamaṅgalā*.[76] Mentioned among the 64 arts by Vātsyāyana, *pratimālā* included recitation of verses one after the other by a number of persons, the condition being that every reciter must repeat a verse commencing with the letter with which the previous speaker's verse ended.[77] Bāṇa in the *Kādambarī* refers to *akṣaracyutaka, mātrācyutaka, bindumatī* and *gūḍhacaturthapāda*.[78]

Painting was cultivated by both princes[79] and princesses.[80] In the *Samarāiccakahā* we read of a prince amusing himself with *ālekhyavinoda*[81] (pastime of painting) and drawing first an excellent representation of a vidyādhara couple[82] and later a life-like portrait of a princess.[83] The princess likewise inscribed a portrait of the prince.[84] In another place, a princess paints the picture of a female swan (*rājahaṃsikā*) mourning over the separation from her mate and sends it to her beloved.[85] Reference is also made to *citrakāras* (painters) who displayed their paintings before kings.[86] The *Kuvalayamālā* describes two huge painted scrolls (*citrapaṭas*), one depicting the various happenings in the human world, heaven and hell, and the other depicting the city of Campā and detailed account of one's past birth.[87] Vivid scenes of bird and animal life depicting various reptiles, insects, and birds as engaged in mutual conflicts, the weaker ones being attacked by stronger ones which in turn were seized by animals yet stronger were portrayed therein. The paintings are said to have been marked by purity of lines, richness of colours, beautiful seedling or stripling to show the effect of surroundings or high and low surfaces, and appropriate measurements.[88] Walls of palaces[89] and houses[90] were decorated with paintings. We read of *citraśālikās*[91] which appear to be rooms with frescoes on the walls, as the same room is also referred to as the *vāsagṛha*.[92] One of the *citraśālā* walls was adorned with a beautiful peacock.[93] There is a reference to paintings made with the powder of stones of different colours.[94] Mural paintings in residential houses were a common feature in the time of Kālidāsa who makes innumerable references to them.[95] The use of mineral colours in painting is known from the *Meghadūta*, *Nāgānanda* (seventh century) and may be discerned in the paintings of Ajantā.[96]

Another diversion was *patracchedya* or cutting designs on leaves.[97] In the *Kuvalayamālā*, princess Kuvalayamālā sends a female swan (*patracchedya rājahaṃsī*) cut on a *bhūrja* leaf as a love present to prince Kuvalayacandra[98] who reciprocates by inscribing with his nails the design of a water pond complete with water birds such as *haṃsa, sārasa* and *cakravāka* (swan, crane and ruddy goose) and a *gāthā* verse on a betel (*tambūla*) leaf.[99] In the *Samarāiccakahā* the prince asks for an instrument for cutting leaves (*patracchedyakartarī*) and cuts the design of a swan and fashions a *gāthā* out of *nāgavallī* leaves.[100] The art is listed among the subjects of the prince's curriculum, in the *Kuvalayamālā*,[101] as also in Bāṇa's *Kādambarī*.[102]

Festivities

Springtime was an occasion of great festivities and merriment.[103] The *Kuvalayamālā* describes vividly the coming of spring when the sound of *carcarī* (song and dance) and the drum (*paṭahika*) could be heard on all sides. Swings were attached to the branches of trees and young men and women gathered around, swinging, singing and dancing. There was a reckless abandonment about the atmosphere and wine seems to have been drunk freely.[104] The *madanamahotsava* (festival in honour of the god of love, Madana) was held on the *madanatrayodaśī* (thirteenth) day in the spring season when young men and women visited the outer gardens (*bahirodyāna*) where there was a temple of Kāmadeva.[105] From the *Samarāiccakahā* we learn that the festival was a time of rejoicement for all, high and low. *Nagaracarcarīs* (song and dance groups) of young people dressed in various apparels could be seen on the occasion.[106] Even the washermen felt impelled to take out a *carcarī* on the occasion.[107] Princes went to the park to join the spring revelries along with their retinue, attended by due pomp and splendour.[108] It is stated to be customary for the king also to participate in the spring festivities and pay a visit to the city to watch the *nagaracarcarīs*.[109] In the spring season again, in the month of caitra, was also celebrated the *hindolaka* or swing festival, described in the *Karpūramañjarī*. On the fourth day of the festival, women worshipped Pārvatī,[110] and dressed up in all their finery swung on highly decorated swings adorned with banners, chowries and bells.[111] Rājaśekhara in his *Kāvyamīmāṃsā* also observes that during the month of caitra women spent much of their time in singing, swinging and celebrating the deeds of Gaurī.[112] The *Upamitibhavaprapañcākathā* (tenth century) vividly describes how amidst songs and dances the spring revellers formed drinking bouts, and the king mounted on a huge elephant joined their revelries.[113]

On the full moon day, of jyeṣṭha, we learn from the *Karpūramañjarī*, the women observed the *Vaṭasāvitrīmahotsava*, the great banyan festival. On this day, the women performed various dances and sprinkled water on each other with water taken with jewelled cups. Some holding triple bows and adorned with peacock feathers paraded around as Pulindas, others wearing masks of ogresses enacted a cemetery-scene, and still others setting the people a-laughing by their dark dress, receded, bowed and laughed, further adding to the general merriment.[114]

The festivals of *Indramaha, Mahānavamī, Dīpāvalī, Baladevotsava* appear to have followed each other in succession after the rainy season.[115] Reference is made to human sacrifice being offered on *Navamī* day.[116] The *Niśītha Cūrṇi* (seventh century) mentions *Indramaha* as a great festival which was celebrated on the full moon day of āṣāḍha.[117] Earlier references to the festival are found in the *Mahābhārata*,[118] *Yājñavalkya Smṛti*[119] and *Bṛhatsaṃhitā*.[120] The *Kāvyamīmāṃsā* refers to the worship of weapons of war and waving of lights before horses, warriors and elephants of Mahānavamī day.[121] Alberuni states that at the festival holy to Mahānavamī, the sister of Mahādevī, offerings were made before an image called Bhagavatī, alms given before it and kids killed, and one who had nothing to offer sometimes pounced upon whomsoever he meets and kills him.[122] According to the *Kāvyamīmāṃsā*, rulers indulged in various sports and made ready for expeditions on *Dīpamālikā* day.[123] Siddharṣi Sūri (tenth century) also mentions *Dīpamālikā*.[124]

Śarat or autumn was a festive season when actors, dançers, boxers and bards started wandering around, entertaining the people.[125] The

Kuvalayamālā refers to the *Śaratpūrṇimāmahotsava* which was celebrated with great rejoicing and revelry, with the rich moving out (of their houses) to see the *nagarakaumudī*. In the city squares, actors (*naṭas*) would give performances.[126] Apparently the festival was identical with the *Kaumudīmahotsava* referred to in the *Samarāiccakahā* when people moved out into gardens to enjoy themselves[127] or the festival (*utsava*) celebrated on the *kaumudī* or full moon day.[128] In the Purāṇic literature the *Kaumudīmahotsava* is described as a festival falling on the full moon day in the month of āśvina, when houses were cleaned and whitewashed, flags were flown, lamps lit at night, and youthful couples sang danced and laughed.[129]

Besides the seasonal and religious festivals there were many other occasions of merry-making and social festivity. Uddyotana gives a graphic description of the celebrations attending the birth of prince Kuvalayacandra. Trumpets were blown. Camphor and musk powder was bestrewn all around. Women danced and the sound of their jingling anklets and girdles could be heard in all directions. Birds were freed from the cages. Elephants, horses, chariots, costly clothes and ornaments, etc. were distributed amongst different sections of people. The populace rejoiced everywhere.[130] On this day again, the *Samarāiccakahā* tells us, prisoners were freed, houses sported festive banners, special worship was offered at the sanctuaries, while the king himself went amongst the people to accept their felicitations.[131] Large-scale festivities were organised on occasions like the royal coronation. The *Kuvalayamālā* gives a vivid account of the *yauvarājyābhiṣekamahotsava* when the city put on a gala appearance by means of beautified streets, sprinkling of scented water on the roads, hanging of flower-garlands, putting up golden gates, adorning the palace, decorating the thresholds, making paintings on the walls of the royal court (*sabhā*), making offerings on the cross-roads, beginning of dramatic performances, hoisting of lion banners, installing canopies, hanging of *kaṭisūtra* ornaments from the ceiling of doorways and walls of houses, taking out of huge jewels to be put on show in the treasury, and the hanging of pearl-strings as festoons.[132] Detailed descriptions of such festivities are to be found also in Bāṇa's *Harṣacarita*[133] and *Kādambarī*.[134]

Superstitious Beliefs and Practices

A general belief in omens and portents, dreams and astrology prevailed during our period. That these had gained a strong hold on the people during a much earlier period is evidenced by the works of Kālidāsa,[135]

Varāhamihira's *Bṛhatsaṃhitā*[136] and Bāṇa's *Harṣacarita*.[137] In the seventh-century Rajasthan, the great astronomer Brahmagupta, whose home town was Bhillamāla, wrote the *Brahmasphuṭasiddhānta* and *Khaṇḍakhādyaka*, correcting the erroneous methods of Āryabhaṭa in the former work.[138] The *Kuvalayamālā* contains a brief exposition on various omens, good and bad. The sight of curds (*dadhi*), pitcher (*kalaśa*), conch-shell (*śaṃkha*), fly-whisk (*cāmara*), lotus (*padma*), *mahāvardhamāna* symbol and parasol was considered highly beneficial. Whatever was pleasing to sight, hearing, taste, smell and touch was auspicious, and otherwise, inauspicious. Thus the sight of bathed, anointed and well-clad people was auspicious while that of an unclean person was inauspicious. The sight of a *śramaṇa*, *sādhu*, pair of fish, earth and fruit was also a good omen. Sneezes of all kinds were considered inauspicious by some while others held only those from a certain quarter to be such. The movement of various animals and their sounds also indicated success or failure. While interpreting an omen, the particular quarter from which the omen appeared, styled *dīpta*, *aṅgārita* and *ādhūmita* (burning, sparkling and smoking) according to the position of the sun, was also taken into consideration.[139] For prince Kuvalayacandra, who was an expert at interpreting omens, the present of an umbrella presaged fulfilment of all desires.[140] The throbbing of the right eye and right arm of a man and left eye of a woman were considered auspicious.[141] The throbbing of the left eye of a man were considered inauspicious.[142] The throbbing of the head indicated gain of a kingdom, the throbbing of the arms presaged a meeting with someone held dear, the throbbing of the lip, ear, stomach also foreboding various auspicious and inauspicious events.[143] The unseasonal blossoming of flowers and sudden disappearance thereafter foretold a short change of government.[144] Abu Zaid also speaks of those who drew omens from flight of crows.[145] Alberuni refers to the art of taking auguries from the flights or cries of birds.[146]

According to the *Kuvalayamālā* the sight of curds, *akṣata*, gold, white mustard, *dūrva* offshoots, *rocanā, svastika, vardhamāna* and *nandyāvarta* symbols, leaves, parasol, fly-whisk, flowers, throne, barley offshoots, and lotus were considered auspicious at the commencement of the journey.[147] Among *abhiṣekamaṅgalas*, auspicious objects placed at the time of anointment, the *Samarāiccakahā* mentions a pair of fish (*matsya-yugala*), a full pitcher (*pūrṇa-kalaśa*), white flowers, *mahāpadma* (lotus), white mustard, clods of earth, bull, precious stones, *gorocanā*, lion's skin, white parasol, throne, chowries, *dūrva* grass, great banners, elephant's ichor (*gajamada*), grain (*dhānya*) and *dukūla*.[148] The Jainas considered objects associated with the tīrthaṅkaras to be especially auspicious and the *Kuvalayamālā* mentions chowries, parasol, *aśoka* tree, shower of flowers, halo as *maṅgalas*, concentration on which along with meditation on Jina was conducive to great merit.[149]

From ancient times[150] people believed that dreams foretold impending disasters and happy events. Dream interpretation was treated as a science and we read of *svapnaśāstrapāṭhakas*, those learned in the science of dreams in the *Kuvalayamālā*.[151] The queen saw in her dream a moon, to which clung a garland of fragrant lilies.[152] According to experts it indicated the birth of a great son to whom a beloved was attached from an earlier birth[153] and the prophecy was fulfilled in due course. The vision of a garland of fragrant lilies in the dream of another queen is taken to foretell the birth of a girl of immense beauty.[154] In the *Samarāiccakahā* the vision of a lion,[155] elephant,[156] moon,[157] goddess Śrī,[158] banner,[159] lake,[160] and sun[161] in the dreams of women herald the birth of sons who are destined to earn great fame. The dreams in which a snake enters the body on the other hand forebode the birth of an inauspicious issue.[162] Lord Mahāvīra himself is said to have interpreted a dream for the benefit of one of his followers.[163] Measures were also taken to counteract the evil effects of bad dreams. In the *Samarāiccakahā* where the dream of a fall from the top of the palace is believed to betoken some kind of disaster, its evil consequences are sought to be forestalled by performance of animal sacrifices to the tutelary deity.[164]

The people since early times[165] had a great faith in astrology. The *sāṃvatsara* or astrologer was a highly respected person whose services were employed even by kings. In the *Kuvalayamālā*, we have reference to a *mahāsāṃvatsara* who was called in by the king to cast the horoscope of the new-born prince.[166] Taking into consideration the month (*māsa*), date (*tithi*), week-days (*vāra*), asterism (*nakṣatra*), zodiacal signs (*rāśi*), *yoga* and *lagna*, he predicted that the prince would become either an emperor or an emperor-like king and was munificently rewarded in return.[167] There follows a detailed discourse on *rāśi-phalas* giving the traits and longevity of a child born in a particular *rāśi* on the authority of the *Vaṃgāla-Jāyaka* or *Jātaka* of Vaṃgāla-ṛṣi.[168] So great was the people's belief in astrology, the *Kuvalayamālā* tells us, that a marriage would be postponed for days together, notwithstanding the consternation and misgivings of the lovers, in case the astrologer declared a suitable *lagna* (auspicious moment) to be wanting in the near future,[169] as an auspicious marriage *lagna* was believed to confer a happy and prosperous long wedded life.[170] In the *Karpūramañjarī*, when the queen learns of the astrologer's prediction that the heroine's husband would be an emperor, she at once arranges the latter's marriage with her own husband, so that he may become an emperor, even though she is a very jealous wife otherwise.[171] Rulers would commence military operations against their foes,[172] members of royal families would undertake distant journeys,[173] and princes would be coronated as heir-apparents[174] at an auspicious moment determined by the astrologers. According to the *Samarāiccakahā*, astrologers took the measurement of the shade by the measuring rod to aid their predictions.[175] In the *Kuvalayamālā*, Lord Mahāvīra declares *nimittajñāna* (knowledge of omens) to be a branch of *śrutajñāna*; which enabled one to attain knowledge of the auspicious (*śubha*) and inauspicious (*aśubha*) of the past, present and future.[176] Some syllables, we learn, were considered auspicious, others inauspicious, and yet others of mixed effect. If the auspicious syllables came first in the speech, the outcome was deemed to be good, otherwise bad. A banner stood for success, smoke foretold failure, a lion signified gain through valour, a bull signified honour and so forth.[177]

There is reference also to the *samudraśāstra* or the science of interpretation of bodily marks of men and women and prognostication on basis of these bodily signs.[178] The knowledge of the *śāstra* enabled prince Kuvalayacandra to see through the disguise of the vidyādhara couple masquerading as Śabaras.[179] On the other hand, from the footprints of the prince which bore the figures of the lotus, conch-shell, *svastika*, discus, goad, parasol, and *toraṇa* (arch), the *yakṣa* maiden easily deduced the presence of a great man.[180] Uddyotana was well acquainted with the various signs (*lakṣaṇa*) and gives elaborate details covering more than two pages.[181] A detailed treatment of *aṅgavidyā* or science of prognostication on the basis of movement of bodily limbs is to be found in Puvvāyariya's Prākrit work, *Aṅgavijjāpaiṇṇayam*, assignable to about the fourth century AD.[182] Thus Jainas and non-Jainas both appear to have developed astrological sciences, excessive faith in which fed the credulity and superstitiousness of the people, though the practice cannot be said to have been universal. The evidence of the *Samarāiccakahā* indicates that there were some who did not set much by the augury of omens and placed their faith in God instead.[183] Medhātithi expressly states that destiny being incomprehensible 'it is not necessary to devote much attention to it' and stresses the importance of human activity.[184]

The superstitiousness of the people also expressed itself in belief in magic and the existence of ghouls (*vetālas*), goblins (*piśācas*) etc. The *Kuvalayamālā* relates the story of a robber who possessed a miraculous sword and a pill which when placed in the mouth bestowed added strength and lustre.[185] In the *Samarāiccakahā* a robber has a pill called *paradṛṣṭimohinī* (which deludes the sight of others) which when moistened with water rendered invisible anyone who rubbed his eyes with it.[186] A bracelet made of miraculous herb is said to have cured all wounds.[187] The goddess of a wishing-tree gives prince Sena a miraculous stone by which all diseases can be cured.[188] With this he succeeds in curing king Samaraketu, whom all his physicians had failed to cure.[189] In return for his services to his preceptor, a thief obtains the knowledge (*vidyā*) of opening locks and going through the air, on the condition that he is not to tell lies and is to perform penance if he inadvertently did so.[190] Ghouls (*vetālas*), spirits (*bhūtas*) and female goblins (*ḍākinīs*) were believed to roam around after dusk.[191] The cremation ground[192] and disasters[193] were associated with them. Representing evil spirits, they were believed to possess people and drive them insane.[194] It cannot be gainsaid that these superstitious beliefs exercised a far from healthy influence on society and constitute one of the irrational features of the period. But it has to be kept in mind that belief in magical practices and the supernatural is as old as the *Atharvaveda*. The fault of the people lay in not rising above such beliefs, which unfortunately were part of their past heritage.

Household Goods

Amongst furniture we have mention of *śayanīya*,[195] apparently representing the bed and bedstead as a whole, the *khaṭvā* or cot,[196] *paryaṅka* or couch used by the rich,[197] sometimes fashioned out of ivory,[198] or of reddish coral[199] and *āsana* or common seat.[200] Kings sat on the *siṃhāsana* or throne made out of gold[201] and studded with jewels.[202] Reference is also made to cotton mattresses and pillows.[203]

Other household articles included various utensils generally referred to as *pātra* or *bhāṇḍa*,[204] of which specific mention is made of *sthālas* or platters of silver[205] and gold[206] used in royal houses, *kaccolakas* or cups of silver,[207] *mallaka* (cup in common use),[208] *maṇivāraka* or jewelled cup,[209] *caṣaka* or goblet,[210] *madirābhājana* or *madirā-bhāṇḍaka*, cups for wine,[211] *tālikā*, a special container made of gold in which betel-leaf was served,[212] *ābharaṇakaraṇḍaka*, a jewellery box in which ornaments such as the ear-rings were kept,[213] *mañjūṣā* or casket for rubies,[214] *samudga* or casket,[215] *mahākaṭāha* or frying-pan,[216] *kuṭa* or pot used to draw water from the well,[217] *kalaśa* or water-pitcher,[218] *bhṛṅgāra* or golden water pitcher[219] *tāmramaya karaṇḍaka* or copper container,[220] and *ghaṭas* or clay pots.[221] Besides reference is also made to the *tāla-vrinta* or palm-fan,[222] lamp or *pradīpa*,[223] mirror known as *darpaṇa*,[224] *pañjara* or cage for birds,[225] parasol known as *ātapatra*,[226] royal umbrella or *puṇḍarīka*, studded with jewels and pearl-tassels, with a handle of gold[227] and *cāmara* or chowrie.[228]

Health and Diseases

Various references to diseases occur in the Jaina works which highlight men's vulnerability to manifold diseases to make their listeners aware of the harsh reality of worldly miseries. Thus we read of various physically handicapped persons such as the *kāṇa* or one-eyed,[229] *kubja* or humpbacked,[230] *paṅgu* or lame,[231] *andha* or blind,[232] *mūka* or dumb,[233] *badhira* or deaf,[234] *vāmana* or dwarf,[235] and *lalla* or stammerer.[236] Afflictions and diseases specifically mentioned are *jalodara* or dropsy,[237] *bhagandara* or fistula,[238] *kuṣṭha* or leprosy,[239] *śvāsa* or asthma,[240] *kāsa* or cough,[241] *arśas* or piles,[242] *lūtā*,[243] *śoṣa* or consumption,[244] *khasa* or itch,[245] *visphoṭaka* or boils,[246] *rudhirapravāha* or bleeding,[247] *śūla* or colic,[248] *pitta* or bile,[249] *jvara* or fever,[250] *mārī* or pestilence[251] *śīrṣavedanā* or headache,[252] *poṭṭaśūla* or stomachache,[253] *dantavedanā* or toothache,[254] *karṇaśūla* or ear-ache[255] and *akṣidukkha* or eye-trouble.[256] *Jalodara* is associated with emaciation of arms, swelling of feet, dulled eyes, numb tongue, sleeplessness, and intense pain,[257] and is described as a mortal disease which physicians could not cure. Reference is made to decadence of limbs in leprosy.[258] Spreading an infernal stench around, body covered with open sores upon which converged flies in hundreds, a leper aroused the pity of even of one who bore animosity towards him.[259] There were other incurable diseases too, marked by acute pain in the entrails, intense headache affecting even the eyes, shaking joints, chattering teeth and fast breathing, when the eyes closed and voice was arrested.[260] Headaches of rulers caused great disorder in the palace, when various physicians were called in, medicinal treatises were consulted, manifold medicines administered, ointments prepared from various jewels were applied, and priests performed purificatory rites.[261] The *Kuvalayamālā* records the current belief that one should not eat food, drink water or bathe immediately after one is over-exerted, hungry and thirsty, and quotes the *āyuśāstra* in this context. According to it the seven primary fluids of the human body (*dhātus*), chyle, blood, flesh, fat, bone, marrow and semen and the three humours, *vāta* (wind), *pitta* (bile) and *simbha* (phlegm) in such a person became temporarily deranged and if he ate or washed in such a state these became stationary in these positions, leading to *sannipāta* causing headache and other ailments.[262]

Thus the wealth, leisure and education of the urban rich had given rise to a distinctive urban ethos which was reflected in the cultivation of various artistic, literary and intellectual pastimes by the royalty and towns-men. Princes, princesses and towns-women were proficient in music, vocal as well as instrumental. Song and dance were an essential part of all social and religious festivals. *Calli* and *daṇḍarāsa* dances were performed at the banyan festival. The upper classes as well as service classes like washermen took out *carcarīs* (song and dance groups) on the occasion of spring.

Dramatic performances were a common feature of public celebrations on festive occasions in the city. Rulers enjoyed watching plays, which were staged with elaborate costumes, masks, music and rehearsal. Various kinds of riddles, completion of unfinished verses, painting and cutting designs on leaves were popular amongst princes as well as princesses, indicating their intellectual predilection and artistic sense. References to wall frescoes in houses as well as palaces, huge painted scrolls, use of powder of stones for painting, painting terminology such as *rekhā, varṇa* and *vartini* with mention of their fineness indicate the degree of perfection achieved in painting.

The royal pastimes of riding and hunting must have contributed to the physical well being of the royalty though the latter led to slaughter of animals and invited the censure of Jainas. But gambling, which appears to have been a popular sport amongst kings and merchants, was not so defensible as it led to loss to money and consequential debt. Towns-people were fond of keeping pet birds, the melodious notes of which added charm to their surroundings. Other pets included the dog, hen, cock and peacock. Cock and quail fights appear to have been another amusement.

Villagers were not skilled in the art of painting, drama and music. But they had a natural flair for music and dance and as a smooth routine of life was promoted by surplus production in agriculture it found expression in their cultural life in the form of their enthralling songs and dances in the countryside. Lively songs marked their celebrations at the advent of spring. They were appreciative of dramatic performances and when in the busy season of autumn parties of actors and dancers moved from village to village, villagers found time for their show at night.

Popular festivals included the *Madanamahotsava* in honour of Kāmadeva, *Hindolaka* or swing festival when women worshipped Parvatī, *Vaṭasāvitrīmahotsava* or banyan festival when women sprinkled water on each other, acted and danced, *Indramaha, Mahānavamī, Dīpāvalī, Baladevotsava* and *Kaumudīmahotsava*. The birth of a prince and royal coronation were also occasions of festivity; the city was decorated, gifts distributed and people made merry. While some festivals were held in honour of particular deities and served to popularise their cults others were related to special seasons and days. They gave people an opportunity to relax and enjoy themselves. Members of different castes from highest to lowest took part in these festivals and thus came together. Men and women mixed together freely on these occasions. The whitewashing of the city on festive occasions contributed to its cleanliness while its decoration provided employment to various artisans. An unfortunate practice connected with the spring and birth festivities was drinking.

There was a general belief that the future could be predicted through a study of omens, portents, dreams and astrology. The sight of various animate and inanimate objects, sneezes and throbbing of different limbs was classified as auspicious and inauspicious. Different sets of these objects were regarded as auspicious for commencement of a journey and anointment of a ruler. Jainas considered concentration on objects associated with tīrthaṅkaras along with meditation on Jina to be meritorious. There were specialists in dream interpretation who foretold future events and prescribed measures to counter the evil consequences presaged by bad dreams. Astrologers cast horoscopes of a new born child on the basis of the position of planets, time and date of the child's birth and prophesied his traits on the basis of the astrological treatise. They also decided auspicious moments for marriage and commencement of military campaigns, proceeding scientifically by taking the measurement of the shade by a measuring rod. The Jainas believed *nimittajñāna* or knowledge of omens to be a branch of their scriptural knowledge. *Samudraśāstra* or science of prognostication on the basis of bodily marks was another popular predictive science. Belief in efficacy of these sciences, magic and existence of ghouls reflects the superstitious beliefs current in society, among members of the brahminical faith, as well as Jainas.

A perusal of the household goods indicates that the rich collected many items of luxury which must have created a market for artisans and traders.

Notes and References

1. गायन्ति मणहरं, पढन्ति गाहाओ, पुच्छन्ति वीणापओए, पसंसन्ति नाडयाइं, वियारेन्ति कामसत्थं, दंसेन्ति चित्ताइं . . . दंसेन्ति सरवराइं, कारेन्ति जलकीडं, निवेसन्ति उज्जाणेसु . . . कीलन्ति डोलाहिं, रएन्ति कुसुमसत्थरे। *SK*, p. 707.
2. विरत्तकन्दुयकीलं परिचत्तचित्तयम्मवावारं विरयगीयनच्चणारम्भं। Ibid., p. 17.
3. नालिहइ चित्तयम्मं . . . पाढेइ ने य सुयसारियाण संघायं . . . सारेइ ने य वीणं पत्तच्छेज्जं पि न करेइ . . . न य कन्दुएण कीलइ। Ibid., p. 65. Music, staging of various plays, pleasure-baths in public tanks, playing dice, playing with a ball, swinging, story-telling, hunting were popular pastimes also in the time of Kālidāsa. The nāgaraka of Vātsyāyana entertained himself with literary compositions, painting, singing, instrumental music, garland-making etc. at social gatherings or *goṣṭhīs*.
4. *KM*, p. 22; *SK*, p. 602.
5. *KM*, p. 22.
6. *SK*, pp. 65, 309, 314.
7. एक्का वायइ वीणं अवरा वव्वीसयं छिवइ। . . . देइ मुरवम्मि पहरं अण्णा उण तिसरियं छिवइ। वंसं वायइ अण्णा छिवइ मउंदं पुणो। *KM*, p. 26.
8. संख-भेरी-तूर-काहल-मुइंग-वंस-वीणा। Ibid., p. 181.
9. *KM*, p. 171; *SK*, pp. 279, 519, 630.
10. *KM*, p. 18; *SK*, pp. 518, 527.
11. *SK*, p. 573.
12. *KM*, pp. 16, 198; *SK*, pp. 616–17.
13. *KM*, p. 16; *SK*, p. 573.
14. *SK*, p. 537.
15. *KM*, p. 171.
16. *KM*, p. 51; *SK*, pp. 42, 303, 521, 719.
17. *Karpūra.*, IV.11.
18. Ibid., IV.12.
19. *KM*, p. 171; *SK*, pp. 78, 519.
20. *KM*, p. 67.
21. Ibid., pp. 50, 83.
22. Ibid., pp. 7, 148, 238.

23. विविहणाडयछन्दनट्टियाइणा मणहरेण विणोएण। *SK*, p. 12.
24. पेच्छणए। *KM*, p. 199.
25. निउत्ताइं पेच्छणयाइं। *SK*, p. 734.
26. *KM*, p. 46.
27. *Karpūra.*, I.4.
28. *KM*, p. 23; *SK*, pp. 12–13, 618, 671, 740.
29. *KM*, pp. 23–6.
30. Ibid., pp. 185, 217 f.; *SK*, pp. 268, 797.
31. *KM*, pp. 217–23.
32. *Gṛha haṃsas*, *KM*, p. 8.
33. गृह मयूर, गृह शिखंडी। Ibid., pp. 8, 50.
34. Ibid., pp. 18, 123; *SK*, p. 65.
35. *KM*, p. 18; *SK*, p. 65.
36. *SK*, p. 65.
37. Ibid., p. 123.
38. *KM*, p. 83.
39. गाहिओ नट्टकलं। *SK*, p. 253.
40. Ibid., pp. 253–5.
41. Ibid., p. 265.
42. लावय-कुक्कुड जुद्धं। *KM*, p. 22.
43. जूयं खेल्लिमो . . . जहा अत्थ-संपत्ती होहिइ त्ति। Ibid., p. 57.
44. *SK*, pp. 254–5.
45. Ibid., p. 6, 785.
46. जूयवरवन्द्रपेल्लिओ भयकायरं भग्गओ पलोएमाणो आगओ जूययरो . . . रक्खउ अज्जओ। *SK*, pp. 198–9.
47. *Karpūra.*, IV. 4.
48. मज्जइ न य गेहदीहियाए। *SK*, p. 65.
49. Ibid., p. 707.
50. मज्जणं-वाविं . . . मणि-सोमाण . . . कलधोय-तुंग-तोरण-धवलद्धुत-धयवडाइल्ला। *KM*, p. 94.
51. गाम-डिंभरूय-सरिसइं जल-कीडा-वावडइं। Ibid., p. 121.
52. *KM*, p. 77; *SK*, pp. 63, 193, 522, 719.
53. *KM*, p. 51; *SK*, pp. 521, 719; *Karpūra.*, II. 30–40.
54. *SK*, p. 17, 65; *KM*, p. 232.
55. माया वंचणाइं णवरि दीसंति इंदियालिय-जणहं।। *KM*, p. 8.
56. मल्लो अप्फोडणं करेमाणो। सारीर-बलुम्मत्तो। Ibid., p. 187.
57. पहेलिया अंतिमक्खर-वूढाओ गोवाल-बालेसु वि पसिद्धाओ णज्जंति। Ibid., p. 174.
58. वियड्ढ-परिकप्पियाइं इमाइं विणोय-कारणाइं . . . महाकवियर-कप्पियाइं कवि-दुक्कराइं पओयाइं। Ibid.
59. जत्थक्खराइं कीरंति बिंदुणो आइमंतिमं मोत्तुं अत्थो उण साहिज्जइ सा बिंदुमइ त्ति णायव्वा। Ibid.
60. बत्तीस-घरऐसु वत्थ-समत्थेसु छुब्भइ सिलोओ। अहवा खप्परियासु। Ibid., p. 175.
61. चत्तारि दोण्णि तिण्णि व चउयाओ जत्थ पुच्छिया पण्हा। एक्केण उत्तरेण भणंति पण्हुत्तरं तमिह। Ibid.
62. लिंग-भिण्णं विभत्तिभिण्णं . . . सक्कयं, पाययं। Ibid.

63. पण्हं काऊण तओ गूढं जा उत्तरं पि तत्थेय। पर-मइ-वंचण-पडुयं तं चिय गूढुत्तरं। Ibid.
64. जं पुट्ठं तं दिज्जइ अंधो विय णेय जाणेय तह वि। तं पयड-गूढ-रइयं पट्ठट्ठं। Ibid.
65. जत्थ सिलेसो विहडइ चालिज्जंतेण अक्खरेणेय। घडिए पुण घडियं तं भणइ अक्खरच्चुययं। Ibid., p. 176.
66. Ibid.
67. गूढ-चउत्थय-पायं णामेणं चेय लक्खणं सिट्ठं। आइम-पएसु तीसुं गोविज्जइ जत्थ तुरिय-पयं। Ibid.
68. Ibid.
69. Ibid.
70. Ibid.
71. इमं च पच्छिमद्धं। जा कोइ भुयणे गाहा, तीय रक्खओ इव सव्वत्थेसु लगइ त्ति। Ibid.
72. तत्थ य पाय-पढमक्खराइं। Ibid., p. 177.
73. *SK,* pp. 610–12.
74. Ibid., pp. 617–18.
75. *Kāmasūtra,* I.3.33; qd. P.K. Gode, 'The Art of Capping Verses', *Dr. S.K. Belvalkar Felicitation Volume,* p. 171.
76. P.K. Gode, op. cit., p. 171.
77. H.C. Chakladar, *Social Life in Ancient India,* p. 164.
78. *Kādambarī,* p. 7.
79. *KM,* p. 185; *SK,* pp. 604 f.
80. *SK,* pp. 17, 65, 623–4.
81. Ibid., p. 604.
82. Ibid., p. 615.
83. Ibid., p. 619.
84. *SK,* pp. 623–4.
85. Ibid., p. 71.
86. Ibid., pp. 607 f.; *KM,* p. 233.
87. *KM,* pp. 185–93.
88. रेहा-विसुद्धं . . . सुविभत्त-वण्ण-सोहियं . . . वत्तिणी विरयणं . . . माण-जुत्तं . . . सुपइट्ठिय-अंगोवंगं। Ibid., p. 233; सुविहत्तज्जलेणं वणयकम्मेण . . . सुहुमरेहाए पयडदंसणेण निन्नुन्नयविभाएणं। *SK,* p. 615.
89. सयल-भवण-भित्ति-संकंत-कंत-चित्तयम्म-संकुलाओ। *KM,* p. 17.
90. पप्फोडेसु चित्त-भित्तीओ। Ibid., p. 83.
91. *SK,* pp. 254, 500.
92. Ibid., p. 512.
93. *SK,* pp. 500, 512.
94. णाणा-मणि-चुण्ण-विरइयालेक्खं। *KM,* p. 249.
95. B.S. Upadhyaya, *India in Kālidāsa,* p. 231.
96. V.S. Agrawala 'Painting Terminology from Sanskrit Literature', in *Dr C. Kunhan Raja Presentation Volume*, p. 496.
97. *KM,* pp. 22, 160, 169; *SK,* pp. 65, 73.
98. *KM,* p. 160.
99. Ibid., p. 169.

100. *SK*, p. 73.
101. *KM*, p. 22.
102. *Kādambarī*, p. 75.
103. *KM*, pp. 50–1; *SK*, pp. 62, 265, 303, 307, 408, 520 f., 719 f.
104. *KM*, pp. 50–2.
105. मयण-तेरसीए वट्टमाणे महामहे . . . कामदेवस्स बाहिरुज्जाण-देवउल-जत्तं पेच्छिउं . . . मयणूसवागएण। Ibid., p. 77.
106. मयणमहूसवे निग्गयासु विचित्तवेसासु नयरचच्चरीसु। *SK*, p. 42.
107. वत्थसोहगच्चचरि। Ibid.
108. Ibid., pp. 522–3.
109. Ibid., pp. 719–20.
110. *Karpūramañjarī*, II.6.
111. Ibid., II. 29, 30–40.
112. *Kāvyamīmāṃsā*, p. 105.
113. *Upamiti.*, pp. 590–603.
114. *Karpūra.*, IV. 9–18.
115. *KM*, p. 148.
116. इमाए णवमीए अम्हं च ओरद्धा देवयाराहणं काहिइ। तीए तुमं बली कीरिहिसि। Ibid., p. 59.
117. J.C. Jain, *Life in Ancient India as Depicted in the Jaina Canons*, p. 216.
118. Ādiparva, 63.1–29; Kane, *HD*, II, ii. p. 826.
119. *Yājñavalkya*, I.147.
120. The *Bṛhatsaṃhitā* describes in detail the mode of raising the flagstaff of Indra and its worship for four days, Kane, *HD*, II, ii, pp. 825–6; A.M. Shastri, *India as Seen in the Bṛhatsaṃhitā of Varāhamihira*, pp. 119–23.
121. *Kāvyamīmāṃsā*, p. 101.
122. Sachau, II, pp. 179–80.
123. *Kāvyamīmāṃsā*, p. 101.
124. D. Sharma, *ECD*, p. 299.
125. सरयागम . . . एरिसं पुहइं अवलोइऊण परितुट्ठा णड-णट्ट-मुट्ठिय-चारण-गणा परिभमउ समाढत्ता। *KM*, p. 46.
126. सरय-काले मत्त-पमत्ते णच्चिरे जणवए पुणणमासीए महंते ऊसवे णयरि-चच्चरे णडेण णच्चिउं पयत्तं। Ibid., p. 103.
127. कोमुइमहसवे उज्जाणगएसु नायरएसु। *SK*, p. 530.
128. कोमुईए अन्तेउराण जहिच्छापयारेण ऊसवपसाओ त्ति। Ibid., p. 783.
129. B.N. Sharma, *Social Life in Northern India*, p. 259.
130. *KM*, p. 18.
131. *SK*, p. 602.
132. *KM*, p. 199.
133. *Harṣacarita*, IV. 129 f.; Translation, Cowell, pp. 110 f. for birth ceremony.
134. *Kādambarī*, pp. 73–4 for birth festivaties, p. 110 for coronation ceremony.
135. B.S. Upadhyaya, *India in Kālidāsa*, pp. 329 f.
136. A.M. Shastri, *India as Seen in the Bṛhatsaṃhitā of Varāhamihira*, Chapter 4.

137. *Harṣacarita,* V.152–3; VI. 186; Translation, Cowell, pp. 134–5, 177.
138. P.C. Sengupta, 'Astronomy in Ancient India', in *Cultural Heritage of India,* Vol. VI, p. 80.
139. *KM,* pp. 183–4.
140. आयवत्त-रयणं उवणीयं ति ता सव्वहा भवियव्वं जहा-चिन्तिय-मणोरहेहिं । Ibid., p. 183.
141. *SK,* p. 101; *KM,* p. 157.
142. *SK,* pp. 570–1.
143. Ibid., pp. 157.
144. Ibid., pp. 515–16.
145. *ED,* I, p. 10.
146. Sachau, I, 158.
147. *KM,* p. 181.
148. *SK,* pp. 124–5.
149. *KM,* p. 184.
150. *Kalpasūtra,* II.4; III.32–46; IV. 65–86; *Harṣacarita,* V. pp. 150 f.
151. *KM,* pp. 16–17.
152. Ibid., p. 16.
153. Ibid., p. 17.
154. Ibid., p. 162.
155. *SK,* pp. 60–1.
156. Ibid., p. 192.
157. Ibid., p. 300.
158. Ibid., p. 407.
159. Ibid., p. 497.
160. Ibid., p. 601.
161. Ibid., p. 703.
162. Ibid., p. 117.
163. *KM,* p. 269.
164. *SK,* pp. 243 f.
165. The *Sūryaprajñapti* and *Candraprajñapti* are two *upāṅgas* of the Jaina canon dealing with astronomy. The *Joṇipāhuḍa* was an important work on *nimittaśāstra.* Its writer was Dharmasena *ācārya* who flourished in the middle of the first and second century AD.
166. महासंवच्छर . . . "साह कुमारस्स जम्म-णक्खत्तस्स गहाणं दिट्ठि" ति । *KM,* p. 19.
167. Ibid., pp. 19–20.
168. वंगाल-रिसिणो . . . वंगाल-जायगं । Ibid., p. 20.
169. गणिए गह-गोयरे गणएण ण ठवियं सुज्झमाणं लग्गं । Ibid., p. 158.
170. दीहाउ से भत्ता, चिरं अविहवा । Ibid., p. 170.
171. *Karpūra.,* IV. 18 f.
172. *SK,* p. 22. Harṣa commenced his military campaign at an hour carefully calculated by his astrologers. *Harṣacarita,* p. 202, Translation, Cowell, p. 197.
173. *KM,* p. 180.
174. Ibid., p. 199.

175. गहियसङ्कुच्छाएहिं सुणिय जोइससत्थपरमत्थेहिं भणियं जोइसिएहिं। *SK*, p. 22.
176. *KM*, pp. 268–9. Śrutajñāna or knowledge derived from sacred books is a branch of right knowledge according to Jaina canonical works of *Uttarādhyayana*, XXVIII, 4.
177. Ibid.
178. *KM*, pp. 116, 129–31.
179. Ibid., p. 129.
180. Ibid., p. 116.
181. Ibid., pp. 129–31.
182. J.C. Jain, *Life in Ancient India as Depicted in Jaina Canons*, p. 226. Varāhamihira devotes three chapters to the signs of men and women in general, and the five special types of men and women and their attendants *Bṛhatsaṃhitā*, LXVII, LXIX, LXVIII, A.M. Shastri, *India as Seen in the Bṛhatsaṃhitā of Varāhamihira*, p. 363.
183. *SK*, p. 571.
184. *On Manu*, VII. 205.
185. *KM*, pp. 250–3.
186. *SK*, p. 428.
187. Ibid., pp. 416, 425.
188. Ibid., pp. 564–8.
189. Ibid., p. 568.
190. Ibid., p.230.
191. किलकिलेंति वेयाला, पणच्चंति डाइणीओ, परिक्कमंति भूया। *KM*, p. 82.
192. Ibid., pp. 225, 247.
193. Ibid., pp. 66, 68.
194. Ibid., pp. 56, 78.
195. *SK*, pp. 66, 674, 738.
196. Ibid., p. 727.
197. *KM*, pp. 107, 161; *SK*, pp. 741, 760.
198. दन्तमय। *SK*, p. 800.
199. Ibid., p. 239.
200. Ibid., pp. 331, 364.
201. *KM*, p. 200.
202. Ibid., pp. 16, 200.
203. *SK*, pp. 239, 800; *KM*, p. 140.
204. *KM*, p. 48.
205. *SK*, p. 80; *KM*, p. 18.
206. *KM*, p. 18.
207. *SK*, p. 80.
208. *KM*, pp. 31, 117.
209. *Karpūra.*, IV.10, 13.
210. *KM*, p. 83; *Karpūra.*, IV. 19.
211. *KM*, p. 83.
212. *SK*, p. 80.

213. Ibid., p. 108.
214. *Karpūra.*, IV. 19.
215. *KM*, pp. 83, 140.
216. *SK*, p. 263.
217. *KM*, pp. 82, 150.
218. Ibid., pp. 132, 181, 200.
219. *KM*, pp. 93, 115–16.
220. Ibid., p. 259.
221. *SK*, p. 85.
222. *SK*, p. 66; *KM*, pp. 93, 113.
223. *KM*, pp. 17, 83; *SK*, p. 756.
224. Ibid., pp. 17, 93; *Karpūra.*, I.18.
225. *KM*, pp. 123, 127, 188.
226. Ibid., p. 93.
227. Ibid., p. 183.
228. Ibid., pp. 17, 93, 181.
229. *KM*, p. 2; *SK*, p. 286.
230. *KM*, p. 41; *SK*, p. 286.
231. Ibid.
232. *SK*, pp. 2, 40–1, 286.
233. *KM*, p. 41; *SK*, pp. 286.
234. *KM*, pp. 2, 40, 41.
235. Ibid., p. 41.
236. Ibid., pp. 2, 40.
237. Ibid., p. 41; *SK*, p. 480.
238. Ibid., pp. 41, 274.
239. *SK*, p. 261; *KM*, p. 274.
240. *KM*, p. 41.
241. Ibid., pp. 41, 274.
242. Ibid., p. 41.
243. Ibid., pp. 41, 274.
244. Ibid., p. 274.
245. *SK*, p. 480.
246. *KM*, pp. 41, 274.
247. Ibid., p. 274.
248. *SK*, p. 480.
249. *KM*, p. 210.
250. Ibid., pp. 41, 274.
251. Ibid., p. 274.
252. *SK*, pp. 17, 480; *KM*, p. 41, 274.
253. *KM*, p. 274.
254. Ibid.
255. Ibid.
256. Ibid.

257. संजायं जलोयरं, परिसुक्काओ भुयाओ, सूणं चलणजुयलं, मिलाणाइं लोयणाइं, जड्डिया जीहा, पणट्ठा निद्दा . . . समुब्भूया महावेयणा। *SK*, p. 480.
258. कत्थइ कुट्ठेण अहं सडिओ सव्वेसु चेय अंगेसु। *KM*, p. 274.
259. *SK*, p. 261.
260. Ibid., pp. 566–7.
261. सीसवेयणा . . . वेज्जा . . . उग्गाहेन्ति नाणाविहाओ,
चिगिच्छासंहियाओ, पीसिज्जंति बहुविहाइं ओसहाइं,
दिज्जंति सिरोवेयावहारिणो विचित्तरयणलेवा। Ibid., p. 17.
262. *KM*, p. 114. The concept of the three humours, the theory that diseases are generated by the derangement of the *dhātus* and stress on proper diet finds place in the works of Caraka assignable to the first century AD redacted by Dṛḍhabala in the eighth or ninth century AD and Suśruta, whose work was redacted by Nāgārjuna between the third and fourth century AD. Mitra Roy, 'Āyurveda', Chapter XI, *Cultural Heritage of India,* VI, pp. 152 f.; H.J.J. Winter, 'Science', Chapter XII, *A Cultural History of India*, ed., A.L. Basham, pp. 141 f.

9

Urban and Rural Life

THE PEACE AND political stability which Pratihāra rule gave Rajasthan brought in its wake general rural and urban prosperity. Contemporary literary works draw a picture of overwhelming opulence and plenty. We read of affluent villages,[1] some of them resembling big cities.[2] 'Decorated with many temples', Uddyotana says, 'The village Uccasthala bore resemblance to the heavenly city; full of manifold jewels, it looked like the nether-world; abundant in cattle, it resembled a cattle-shed (*goṣṭhāṅgana*); and full of riches, it appeared like the city of Kuvera (god of riches).'[3] Villagers are represented as happy and prosperous, and blessed with an abundance of wealth and grains,[4] cases of poverty being highly exceptional.[5] The agricultural prosperity is also evident from the references to luxuriant crops of rice and sugarcane,[6] and grand village feasts.[7] Wayfarers in the countryside were left spellbound by the lovely songs and dances of the gay farmer-folk tending their paddy fields.[8] We read of the land being tilled with bullocks, their nostrils pierced, a rope tied around their necks and a plough placed on their shoulders.[9] The ripe crops of pulse and paddy, after being harvested, were crushed with the help of bullocks tied to the middle of the post.[10]

That the reference to bountiful crops and prosperous cultivators are not mere conventional literary descriptions is evident from the testimony of other contemporary sources. The Ghaṭiyālā inscription of VS 918 tells us that Kakkuka, the Pratihāra ruler, had made the land 'fragrant with leaves of blue lotuses, and pleasant with groups of mango and *madhūka* trees, and covered it with the leaves of excellent sugarcane'.[11] Another Ghaṭiyālā record refers to his resettlement of the village of Rohinsakūpa which had been rendered uninhabitable by the Ābhīras.[12] This clearly indicates that some areas of Rajasthan had experienced an expansion of agrarian economy as a result of Kakkuka's initiative, a more advanced economy replacing the earlier primitive one, as tribal territory was taken over.[13] New areas must have been opened to advanced modes of cultivation also in other areas, where the tribals were subdued, as by Nāgabhaṭa and Caṇḍamahāsena of Dholpur,[14] contributing to a higher agricultural yield. Knowledge of rotation of crops[15] and procedure of rice cultivation[16] had been acquired much earlier in Rajasthan.

The mention of *araghaṭṭa*[17] attests to the existence of efficient techniques of irrigation, without which a high agricultural yield would hardly have been possible. The *araghaṭṭa* being a common simile employed in the *Kuvalayamālā*, its use must have been widespread. The unceasing cycle of births, old age and deaths is compared to an *araghaṭṭa* with hundreds of pots (*ghaṭīs*), one pouring water into the other.[18] In another instance, the beings (*jīvas*) are addressed thus, 'If thou desirest deaths, if thou are not disgusted with them, continue by all means in the *araghaṭṭa* of birth (*janma*) and death (*maraṇa*).'[19] Fields irrigated by *araghaṭṭas* find mention in the Ḍabok inscription of AD 644[20] and Pratāpgarh inscription of AD 946.[21] The technical nature of the *arahaṭṭa* or *araghaṭṭa*, generally translated as Persian wheel has been a matter of controversy, with Irfan Habib insisting on equating it with the *noriā*, i.e., a wheel carrying pots or buckets fixed on its rim, in which there is no chain carrying pots or gearing mechanism for continuous flow of water.[22] But the ninth century stone relief depicting a Persian wheel at work discovered at Mandor and a similar tenth century AD stone relief studded on the ceiling of Jageśvara at Sādaḍī in Pali district clearly show the pots tied to a rope in a row hanging below,[23] as pointed by Dr Chaṭṭopadhyaya.[24] There is no clear evidence of the gearing mechanism but the references to the continuous rotation of buckets in our works clearly suggest its use.

Excavation of wells (*kūpa*), tanks (*taḍāga*) and stepwells (*vāpī*) was considered meritorious[25] and this too must have helped ensure easy supply of water for irrigation purposes.[26] The reference to damming of water,[27] reservoirs bound with stones[28] bearing semblance to the ocean[29] and the cultivation of sugarcane in the arid zone of Rajasthan[30] also suggest harnessing of water for irrigation. The Guhilla ruler Dhanika is said to have constructed in VS 741 (AD 684) a step-well at Nagar

(Jaipur state) for the use of his subjects, for the performance of *abhiṣeka* of Śaṅkara and for the acquisition of religious merit.[31]

The Jodhpur inscription of Bauka (AD 837), tells us that his predecessor Śīluka had a tank excavated.[32] From the Mānasarovar inscription we learn that the Mānasarovar lake (near Chittor) was excavated in AD 713 by the Mori ruler Māna.[33] The Kāmān inscription of the Harṣa year 263 (AD 869) records the excavation of a step-well and temple by three brothers in memory of their father.[34] At Osia and Ābānerī we have huge step-wells built in the eighth-ninth century AD. The Osia step-well was about 125 feet long, 100 feet broad and 50 feet deep.[35]

Lack of rain, however, sometimes caused famines. The *Kuvalayamālā* describes a terrible drought and famine, extending over twelve years, when grains, fruits and vegetables failed to grow and the acute shortage of food led to the practice of *devārcana, atithisatkāra*, and *dāna* (worship of gods, entertainment of guests and alms-giving) falling into disuse.[36] Families came to the brink of extinction and the survivors migrated in the search of honourable means of sustenance.[37]

Villages were rich in cattle wealth,[38] which constituted an important source of rural prosperity because of its usefulness in agriculture and the value of dairy products. The prosperous rural settlement of Rāgaḍa is described as full of buffaloes like the vindhya forest and teeming with bulls like the abode of Śiva.[39] The countryside's richness in cattle could be ascertained from afar by the loud peal of their bells.[40] Pastoral products such as milk, curd and ghee were produced.[41] Pasturage which provides an important supplement to the resources of an arid zone was an important means of livelihood in Rajasthan from early times. The *Mahābhārata* states that the Matsyas were rich in cows.[42] According to Hieun Tsang the kingdom of Vairāṭa was famous for its sheep and oxen.[43]

The prosperity of villages was not totally dependent on an agrarian economy but had a wide economic base. *Vaṇiks* (traders) and market-roads (*Vīthis*) appear as a common feature of these villages.[44] Rich and enterprising *vaṇiks* and *sārthavāhas* residing in these villages are said to have departed to distant lands for trade and returned after earning much profit.[45] From the Ghaṭiyālā inscription we know that Kakkuka founded a market fit for traders, crowded with brāhmaṇas, soldiers and merchants 'at the village of Rohinsakūpa'.[46] It was decorated with variegated streets.[47] The operation of traders in the villages and the establishment of market places there was conducive to trade between the urban and rural areas, which must have facilitated the movement of agricultural surplus including commercial crops like surgarcane[48] and rural goods to the towns and the flow of urban goods into the villages, giving a stimulus to agriculture and contributing to rural prosperity.

The visit of a touring actor's troupe was a popular diversion for the villagers who flocked to the show even though their preoccupation with their fields, bullocks and ploughing operations in autumn left them with no time to spare during the day and the performance consequently had to be arranged during the first quarter of the night.[49] Spring time was a time of gay revelry for the village youth who gathered around the swings suspended from tree branches and sang merry ditties in praise of their beloveds.[50] The little children had their own amusements and in spring the villages reveberated with the sound of small drums (*paṭa-hikā*) beaten by them.[51] Playing in water was also a popular sport with them.[52]

Village elders known as *mahattaras* effectively participated in the judicial administration of the villages. In the *Kuvalayamālā* we read how a villager guilty of the sin of treachery towards his friend gathered the *grāmamahattaras*, confessed his crime before them and desired expiation by entering the fire. The *mahattaras* deliberated over the matter and by turns suggested alternative modes of expiation. In the end, the *jyeṣṭhamahāmahattara* (the chief *mahāmahattara*) who is described as the lord of the entire *draṅga*,[53] expressed his opinion that the guilty person should enter the sacred water of the Ganga. This suggestion won general approbation and the *mahattaras* unanimously advised the sinner to have a dip in the holy Ganga and fast unto death there.[54] The *mahattara* is mentioned among the officials and subjects to whom the Dhulev *agrahāra* grant of Mahārāja Bhetti of the Kiṣkindhā branch, AD 679, was addressed, besides the *kutuṃbins* or agriculturist householders.[55] The Dungarpur plate of Bābhaṭa of the same line, AD 689, mentions the *mahattara* as one of the three prominent persons who among others determined the boundaries of the two plots of land gifted to brāhmaṇas by Bābhaṭa.[56] *Mahattaras* are mentioned along with the *mahattamas* and *grāmagamika* in the Rajor (Old Alwar state) inscription, AD 959.[57] They are taken to represent the non-official element in the rural administration holding a position distinct from the *grāmagamika* or headman of the village who was a state employee.[58]

Besides villages with mixed population, consisting of various classes and castes, the *Kuvalayamālā* also mentions a brāhmaṇa *agrahāra* Saralapura, where resided the learned brāhmaṇa, Yajñadeva, surrounded by his numerous kin, and endowed with knowledge of the

Vedas (*Vedavidyā*).[59] Inscriptional evidence of *agrahāras* during the period is provided by the Daulatpurā (Jodhpur), AD 843,[60] and Barāh (U.P.),[61] (AD 836), grants of Bhoja which renewed *agrahāra* grants made in the times of Vatsarāja and Nāgabhaṭa II respectively.

Our works give a grandiloquent description of the splendour of contemporary towns, a part of which may be dismissed as conventional, another part brushed aside as poetic exaggeration, and yet its value as testimony to contemporary urban prosperity cannot be denied. Moats, high walls (*prākāras*), great gates (*gopuras*), arched gateways (*toraṇas*), beautiful mansions, market roads (*haṭṭamārgas*), temples, gardens and lakes were some of the outstanding features of the cities. Lofty *prākāras*, unsurmountable as the heart of faithful wives,[62] wide in expanse as the expanded hood of Śeṣa,[63] encircled the city closely as one lover embraces another,[64] with *gopuradvāras* adding to their beauty.[65] Around the walls were deep moats filled with water,[66] some adorned with red lotus (*tāmarasa*),[67] others concealed by the *nalinivana* (a wide expanse of lotuses)[68] and some full of lotuses as well as crocodiles.[69] Within the city were symmetrically placed triangles (*trikas*), quadrangles (*catuṣkas*) and crossings (*catvaras*).[70] The wide royal road (*rājapatha*) crossed the city, leading to the market road (*vipaṇimārga*) which passed through the busy market place.[71] The city abounded in lofty mansions. We read of abodes known as *bhavanas* which appeared like the peak of the Himālayas,[72] excelling even the splendour of Indra's mansion,[73] *prāsādas* which with their whiteness resembled masses of autumnal clouds[74] and *dhavalagṛhas* which shone as the conduct of the virtuous.[75] Thousands of banners could be seen fluttering over the city.[76] Market places were bustling with activity[77] and are described as full of precious stones (*māṇikya, muktā*), gold (*hiraṇya*) and grain (*dhānya*).[78] The bazaar of Vinītā is described by Uddyotana as having various streets, each displaying a different variety of goods, such as saffron (*kuṃkuma*), camphor (*karpūra*), aloewood (*aguru*), musk (*madana*) and perfumed powders like *abhivāsa* and *paṭavāsa*; cardamom (*elā*), cloves (*lavaṅga*), and *kaṃkola* spices; pearls, gold and precious gems (*ratna*); *netra* garments in different colours, red, white and black; *śaṃkha* bangles set with glass pieces; various weapons, bow and arrows and swords; conch-shells (*śaṃkha*), flywhisks (*cāmara*), bells (*ghaṇṭā*) and red lead (*sindūra*); various herbs and sandalwood; oil (*sneha*) victuals (*khādya*) and beverages (*peya*); turmeric (*haridra*); flesh (*māṃsa*), wines (*surā, madhu*) and salt (*viḍāo*).[79] A perusal of the above lists of articles sold in the market place indicates that they included both perishable commodities having limited markets such as eatables, flesh etc. as well as durable articles capable of wider circulation including grain, salt, cloth and luxury items like pearls, precious stones, perfumes etc. Mention of streets specialising in specific industrial items like perfumes, arms, *śaṃkha* ornaments reveal the picture of a town that was a centre of manufacture as well as exchange.

Lofty walls, moats and great gates etc. constitute traditional features of town-planning which find mention in the *Arthaśāstra*[80] and the *Purāṇas*.[81] As they find enumeration also in architectural treatises like the *Mānasāra*[82] (*c.* AD 700), and the *Samarāṅganasūtradhāra*[83] (*c.* eleventh century AD) besides our works, it may be reasonably presumed that they do not merely form part of conventional literary descriptions but actually indicate continued adherence to traditional patterns during our period. From the inscription of Bauka (AD 837), we know that his predecessors, the sons of Bhadrā, erected a high rampart around the fort of Mandor.[84]

A study of the epigraphic evidence of Rajasthan has revealed concentration of important merchant groups in the area of the former Jaipur state[85] as well as colonisation of new areas[86] in early medieval Rajasthan. The Sāmolī inscription (Udaipur) reveals that a group of *mahājanas* moved from Vasantgarh to Sirohi, AD 646, and explored the new area of Araṇyakūpagiri where they started a mine (*ākara*).[87] Kakkuka's initiative in establishing a market-place with variegated streets[88] has already been noted above. The existence of markets and streets specialising in separate commodities in contemporary cities is attested by the Āhār stone inscription (AD 864–905)[89] and the Sīyaḍoṇi inscription, AD 903.[90] Tenth-century inscriptions from Rajasthan testify to the sale of elephants, horses, agricultural produce, oil, betel leaves, cotton, copper, saffron, wheat, barley, salt etc. in the market places.[91]

The residents of the city are represented as highly righteous and possessing a high standard of living. Virtuous and prosperous, their only addiction, we are told, was to knowledge, while their pleasure lay in liberality and honour alone.[92] None amongst them was dirty, ill-clad, cowardly, greedy, foolish or jealous, we are told, but they were all well dressed, brave, liberal, virtuous, wise and trustworthy.[93] Water tanks, fountains, and pet animals added to the charm of their dwellings, of which we have a poetic description in the *Kuvalayamālā*. 'There the water lilies (*kumudas*) in the water-tanks (*gṛhavāpīs*) never ceased to bloom because of the moon-like radiance of the women's faces. With the fountains always showering the skies with water, the pet swans did not migrate to the Mānasa lake even during the rainy season. There the pet peacocks called out even in the summer, mistaking the sound of drums for the thunder of clouds. The domestic swans enraptured by the tinkling anklets of women followed after them, appearing like little children learning to walk.'[94] Mention is also made of jewelled ornamental arches or *toraṇas*,[95] floors[96] and walls.[97] The luxurious life of the rich is well brought out by Uddyotana's vivid description of the sleeping chambers (*vāsagṛhas*) of women being beautified for the reception of their husbands. The wall frescoes were unveiled; pieces of camphor dropped into the wine (*madirā*); flower garlands arranged in the house; leaf (*patralatā*) designs drawn on the floor; flower beds prepared; pots of incense lighted; cages of melodious pet birds placed around: clusters of betel leaves (*nāgavallī*) prepared, camphor sticks placed in caskets; globules of *kaṃkola* kept around; the bed-clothes and couches laid out in the latticed balconies; *śṛṅgāṭaka* and *valkala* necklaces, and *cakralatā* ornaments were put on; lamps lighted; wine brought in; the hair dressed; drinking cups handed over; and various eatables and drinks arranged besides the beds.[98]

In addition, we have the evidence of the *Karpūramañjarī*, according to which in the evening the jewelled roof-terraces (*maṇimayavallabhī*) and picture-galleries (*bhittiniveśa*) were opened for pleasure, the couches were hastily spread out by attendants and silks rustled as the fingers of the ladies-in-waiting moved over them.[99] At the rise of full moon we read that aloes were burnt as incense and lamps lighted at the pleasure-pavilions (*līlā-gṛhas*), where festoons of rare pearls were suspended, *pārāvata* birds (turtle-doves) let loose and charming pleasure-couches were prepared.[100]

From the *praśasti* of the *Kuvalayamālā* we learn that Jābālipura (Jalor) was economically prosperous, inhabited by rich Jaina laymen who contributed to the building of many Jaina temples.[101] The same was true of Gurjaradeśa as a whole.[102]

The description of the character of the towns-folk given in the Prākrit works is undoubtedly idealistic, though it is of some historical importance as an indication of the high ideals ever present before contemporary society. That the high standard of urban life presented in our works is not all poetic hyperbole is confirmed by the accounts of foreign writers, epigraphical sources, contemporary art pieces and architectural remains. The prosperity of Gurjaradeśa caused Sulaiman to observe: He (the king of Jurz) has great riches. Exchanges are carried on in his state with silver (and gold) in dust, and there are said to be mines (of these metals) in the country.[103] Epigraphic sources indicate that the period from the eighth century onwards saw the emergence of many new and prosperous towns in Rajasthan which grew around capitals, district headquarters, and places of religious and commercial importance.[104] Śīluka, the Mandor Pratihāra ruler is said to have established a city at the holy place called Tretā.[105] As markets sprung up to cater to the needs of the numerous people visiting these places they soon became prosperous urban centres and multifunctional in character.[106]

Craft specialisation and flourishing trade provided a sound economic basis to the prosperity of the urban centres, besides the agricultural productivity already noted above, which provided sufficient food surplus to support the growing urban population. The description of busy markets, lofty mansions, use of perfumes, garlands, jewellery, variety of textiles, costly utensils, musical instruments imply the existence of traders, masons, perfumers, garland-makers, jewellers, weavers, dyers and other craftsmen. The existence of a flourishing textile industry is borne out by the enumeration of different kinds of linen, silken and woollen fabrics such as *kṣauma, dukūla, aṃśuka, paṭṭa, devāṅga, rallaka* and *kambala.*[107] The reference to red, blue and black-coloured garments indicate the use of dyes.[108] The metal industry was another important industry. Uddyotana shows acquaintance with several metals, viz., lead (*nāga, sīsa*), copper (*śulba, tāmra*), bell-metal (*ghoṣa, kāṃsya*), gold (*hema, suvarṇa, kanaka*), silver (*tāra, rūpya*), iron (*tīkṣṇa, loha*), tin (*trapu*), and brass (*āra*).[109] We read of *suvarṇakāras*[110] (goldsmiths) and *lohāras*[111] (blacksmiths). The work of a goldsmith was a highly specialised one. Various processes were adopted by him to remove the impurity of gold, viz., testing it on the touch-stone, cutting, heating it under regulated fire, beating out into flat sheets, filing the sheets and the same process of beating it into a different shape, giving it the shape of a round bar and dividing it into several parts for final testing.[112] The jewel industry, closely allied to that of the goldsmith, was also quite advanced. Our works mention several precious stones, viz., *sphaṭika*[113] (rock-crystal), *padmarāga*[114] (ruby), *markata*[115] (emerald), *karketana*[116] (crysoberyl), *indranīla*[117] (sapphire), *vajra*[118] (diamond), *muktā*[119] (pearl), *sūryakānta*[120] (sun-stone), and *vidruma*[121] (coral). These were used in necklaces, ear-rings and other ornaments along with gold. Sometimes gold was also used for making platters and utensils.[122] Amongst the manufactures of the blacksmith we have mention of iron-fetters (*lohaśṛṃkhalā*),[123] iron vessel (*lohakumbhī*),[124] iron club (*lohamayalakuṭam*),[125] iron pegs (*khūnṭī*),[126] iron rods (*loha-śalākā*)[127] and iron nails (*lohakīlaka*).[128]

Workers in stone had acquired high proficiency and fashioned colossal images of white marble.[129] The widespread use of perfumes and their liberal besprinkling on occasions of joy[130] indicates that perfumes were commodities of common consumption and products of a class of specialists. The various references to wine-drinking are sufficient evidence of a liquor industry.[131] The oil industry was well developed. Oil (*sneha*) is mentioned as one of the products sold in the market-place.[132] We read of the use of linseed oil for lighting a fire[133] and a special variety known as *sahasrapāka*[134] for massaging the body and applying on the hair. Reference is also made to potters (*kumbha-kāras*).[135] Working in bronze, iron, ivory and gold; knowledge of jewels and perfumery was included in the list of subjects to be studied by a prince.[136]

Contemporary epigraphic evidence available from Rajasthan does not give a detailed account of these crafts but coupling it with archaeological evidence enables us to partly confirm the evidence presented by our sources. Industrial development had started early in Rajasthan as revealed by the excavations at Rairh, Nāliāsar, Bairat[137] and Noh.[138] Beautiful seventh-century Jaina bronze images have been discovered at Piṇḍavāḍa-Sirohī.[139] In an inscription dated VS 741 the Bhīnamāla *śilpīs* (artisans) who constructed a *vāpī* (step-well) at Nagara, are described as expert sculptors and architects.[140] The Kāmān inscription (AD 786–905) refers to the guilds of potters and artisans.[141] The remains of the Osia Harihara temples, Buckalā temple as well as various idols of gods and goddesses belonging to the Pratihāra period testify to the skill of its architects and sculptors.[142] A tenth-century stone relief from Āhār (near Udaipur), depicts three blacksmiths at work, one using the bellows, the second pressing an iron bar on an anvil and the third about to pound the metal with his hammer.[143]

Some aspects of the widespread internal and external trade have been noted earlier.[144] In the *Kuvalayamālā*, Sopārā is described as a big emporium of traders, the mercantile activities of which extended to the far off regions of Kośala, Uttarāpatha, eastern India, Dvārakā, Babbarkūla and foreign countries like China, Suvarṇadvīpa and Ratnadvīpa. Horses were procured from Uttarāpatha in exchange of betel-nut, yak-tails from eastern India in exchange of pearls, ivory from *Barbarakūla* or Barbaricum in exchange of textiles, and conch-shells from Dvārakā, *Gaṅgapaṭṭa* and *Netrapaṭṭa* were obtained from China, gold from

Suvarṇadvīpa and jewels from Ratnadvīpa.[145] The mention of export of horses from Uttarāpatha in general to Sopārā[146] and specific mention of a merchant of Taxilā in Uttarāpatha taking horses and selling them in the south[147] indicates that horses were imported through the north-western route. The mention of *Vollāha, Keyāha* and *Serāha* horses,[148] which are Arabic names for horses,[149] further indicate that they were imported from Arab countries. Merchants from as many as eighteen different regions, Gollas, Madhyadeśa, Magadha, Antarvedī, Kīra, Dhakkas, Sindhu, Maru, Gurjaras, Lāṭa, Mālava, Karṇāṭaka, Tāiyā or Tājika, Kośala, Maharashtra, Āndhra and the *Khasa, Pārasa* and *Babbara* people are said to have gathered at the market place of Vijayāpurī in the south.[150]

Other literary and epigraphic sources corroborate this evidence. Sopārā has been identified as the Sūbāra of foreign writers[151] and located with modern Sopārā in the district of Thana, 37 miles north of Bombay.[152] The accounts of the Arab travellers Al Masudi[153] (*c.* AD 956), Alberuni[154] and Al Idrisi (eleventh century)[155] confirm that the port which carried on a flourishing trade in the time of Periplus and Ptolemy[156] retained its importance in later times. That there was a well organised horse trade in the Pratihāra empire is evident from the Pehoā inscription (AD 882–83) which records the activities of a guild of horse dealers.[157] Sale of horses is also recorded in the inscription of Allaṭa of Mewār, AD 953,[158] Bayānā inscription of Cittralekhā (AD 955)[159] and the Harṣa inscription (AD 973).[160] Sulaiman noted that the king of Jurz had numerous horses.[161]

Sulaiman and Masudi noted that the kingdom of Ruhmi (Bengal) produced *samara* (yak-tail) hair from which fly-whisks were made[162] which confirms the import of yak-tails from eastern India mentioned by the *Kuvalayamālā*. Barbaricum, a flourishing port in the time of Periplus, has been taken to have been so named because of its trade with Berber or East Africa.[163] In the light of this the statement of Cosmas that Ethiopian elephants had large tusks which were exported by sea to India, besides the mention of export of many other articles of merchandise from Barbaria in Ethiopia[164] is significant inasmuch as it suggests that the ivory exported to other parts of India by Barbaricum, which the *Kuvalayamālā* speaks of, might have been of African origin.

The Prākrit works draw a picture of brisk Indian trade with Sri Lanka, South-east Asia and China. The *Kuvalayamālā* speaks of a trader having left Kośala for Laṅkāpurī.[165] We learn from the *Samarāiccakahā* that one of the routes to Sri Lanka was via Śripura in Suvarṇadvīpa, from where ships are said to have left for Sri Lanka practically everyday.[166] Mention has already been made of import of jewels from Ratnadvīpa,[167] which has been identified with Sri Lanka.[168] Trade with Ceylon, which is known to have existed as early as the Jātaka period,[169] had increased considerably in the Gupta period[170] and Varāhamihira[171] refers to imports of pearls from Ceylon. An eighth-century Sanskrit inscription from Sri Lanka informs us that the caravan of Indian merchants was skilled in sea travel and was expert in buying and selling and careful in loading cargoes.[172]

The *Samarāiccakahā* describes the sea voyages of Indian merchants from Tāmralipti to Mahākaṭāha[173] (Kedah in western Malaya) and Suvarṇadvīpa[174] (Sumatra). The merchant Dharaṇa is said to have brought ingots of gold from Suvarṇadvīpa.[175] The *Kuvalayamālā* also speaks of import of gold from Suvarṇadvīpa.[176] In the seventh century, I-tsing is known to have actually sailed in the ship of the king of Śrīvijaya from Keddah to Tāmralipti.[177] The Pālas had intimate contact with the Śailendra empire[178] and the art of Java reveals Pāla influence.[179] Abu Zaid (AD 916) noted that the town of Kalah was the most important commercial centre for trade in aloe, camphor, sandalwood, ivory, tin and many other articles.[180] The statement of Rājaśekhara that in describing Dvīpāntara one should be faithful to its dress, costume etc.[181] also attests to the intimate contact with South-east Asia. Import of gold is also suggested by the epithet 'the produce of Suvarṇadvīpa' applied to gold by the *Vaijayantī*[182] (eleventh century). Alberuni also speaks of Suvarṇadvīpa as the 'gold islands' where one could obtain much gold as deposit by washing only a little of the earth of that country.[183] Tāmralipti was an ancient celebrated port of eastern India, represented by modern Tamluk, known to be the place of embarkation for Ceylon, Java and China in the days of the Chinese pilgrims Fa-hien, Hieun Tsang, I-tsing and Daṇḍin, the author of the *Daśakumāracarita* as well.[184] The Dūdhapāni inscription of Udayamāna (Bihar) assigned paleographically to eighth century AD reveals that merchants from distant places like Ayodhya frequented the port of Tāmralipti for trade.[185]

A large variety of silken fabrics appear to have been imported from China. Besides reference to voyages to China for *gaṅgāpaṭṭa* and *netrapaṭṭa*,[186] we have mention of fabrics apparently of Chinese origin, such as *cīnāṃśuka, cīna* and *ardhacīna*.[187] In the *Samarāiccakahā* we read of a *sārthavāha* proceeding with a mighty caravan to the port of Vaijayantī on the eastern coast and taking a ship of China.[188] The exchange of embassies which took place between the Pallavas and

China in AD 720 presupposes close trade relations.[189] A Chinese account of AD 749 refers to the Canton river as full of vessels from India, Persia and Arabia and says that in Canton itself there were three brāhmaṇa temples where Indian brāhmaṇas lived.[190] Sulaiman and Al Masudi noted that horns of rhinoceros were exported from Rahma (Bengal) to China.[191] Al Masudi further noted that ships from India, Basra, Siraf and Oman ascended the river Khanfu to reach Khanfu[192] (Canton). China was known as the land of silk in the time of Cosmas[193] and the reference to *cīnāṃśuka* in the literature of this period as in the time of Kālidāsa and Bāṇa[194] as well as later works as the *Upamitibhavaprapañcākathā*[195] (tenth century) indicates that the import of this variety continued. Rashiddudin who quoted from Alberuni stated that large ships brought choice merchandise and clothes from China and Mahachina.[196]

Uddyotana gives a vivid description of the preparations made for a sea voyage, including arrangements of boats or ships; loading of merchandise; bringing together other sailors; calculation of the duration of the journey both inward and outward; fixation of the date and time of departure; observations of portents whether favourable or vice versa; making announcements about the journey; prayers to popular deities; feeding the brāhmaṇas; paying respect to select persons; worshipping of the deities; arrangement of sails, raising of the mast; fitting the furniture for sitting and sleeping; collecting loads of timber for plank and fuel and filling containers with sweet, fresh water,[197] which clearly attests to the existence of well organised seaborne trade. The *Samarāiccakahā* states that a ship from Tāmralipti reached Suvarṇabhūmi in two months.[198] This has been taken to indicate that the speed of Indian ships had fallen behind those of the foreigners[199] since a Chinese ship normally took one month to reach Ku-lin (Quilon) from Lan-li (extreme north-west coast of Sumatra)[200] and an Arab ship took one month to reach Kalah Bār (Kedah) from Kūlam Mali (Quilon).[201] But it has been convincingly pointed out that the Arab and Chinese sources are referring to journeys along the direct sail winds in the open sea and therefore the journeys were certainly much shorter than those in the sheltered waters or in the bay.[202] The early Bengali *Cāryapadas* frequently refer to boats, including sea-going vessels and mention their component parts, viz., helm, oars, instruments for bailing water, ropes both for towing and fixing it to a wooden post on the land, sails, mast and wheels.[203] According to the Khalimpur inscription, the bed of the Ganga was covered by the mighty fleet of Dharmapāla.[204]

Reference to various varieties of coins, *dīnāra, suvarṇa, rūpaka* and *varāṭikā* in literature shows the prevalence of money economy, an important feature of urbanisation and concomitant of widespread trade. *Dīnāras* and *rūpakas* are said to have been given away as rewards to astrologers,[205] gardeners,[206] and painters[207] etc. and as gifts at the time of a prince's birth.[208] A trader is given goods worth five lakhs of *dīnāras* as an investment to acquire riches by trade.[209] A gambler flees because he owed sixteen *suvarṇas* to others.[210] Traders who proceed from Kāśī to Daksiṇāpatha (South India) earn 5,000 *suvarṇas* each.[211] The reference to the plight of the poor who picks a *varāṭikā* from the ground[212] indicates that the cowrie was the currency of the poor.

Dīnāra, the name of which was derived from the Roman *dinarius*,[213] was according to Haribhadra's *Dharmabindu*,[214] the costliest coin of the period. A slightly earlier reference to it comes from the *Niśītha Cūrṇi*[215] and later from the *Upamitibhavaprapañcākathā* (tenth century).[216] According to the *Niśītha Cūrṇi*[217] it was a gold coin which was common in eastern India. Abu Zaid's[218] statement that aloes from Kāmarūpa, valued sometimes at 200 *dīnāras* per maund, were brought to the sun temple of Multān, where merchants bought it from the priest of the deity, indicates that *dīnāras* of Sind were frequently brought into India.[219] The Arab accounts also speak of horns of rhinoceros exported from Rahma to China to be made into fashionable and costly girdles which sometimes fetched 2,000 or even 4,000 *dīnāras*.[220] Various Gupta epigraphs[221] testify to the use of *dīnāras* in the Gupta period and the Gupta coins up to the time of Kumāragupta follow the Kuṣāṇa standard of 120 or 121 grains, based on the weight of *Dinarius*.[222] It is not unlikely that these gold coins were also unearthed and used.[223]

Suvarṇa was an ancient gold coin mentioned by Kauṭilya and Manu, denoting a gold coin weighing 80 *rattis* or about 144 to 146 grains.[224] *Rūpaka*, taken basically to denote a silver coin,[225] finds mention in various inscriptions of Rajasthan, such as the Āhār Sāraneśvara inscription of Allaṭa, AD 953,[226] Hastikuṇḍin inscription of Dhavala, AD 996,[227] and Nāḍol grant, AD 1156.[228] From the charge of one *dramma* on the sale of an elephant and two *rūpakas* on that of a horse in the Āhār Sāraneśvara inscription,[229] it is obvious that *rūpaka* was lower in value than *dramma*.

The wide provenance of silver-coins issued by Raṇahastin, which have been attributed to Vatsarāja,[230] viz. in U.P., Rajasthan and Saurashtra, though few, suggest their wide circulation as a result of trade. *Drammas*, which are mentioned in various Pratihāra inscriptions,[231] are known to have been in use in Rajasthan from references to them in the seventh-century Goth Manglod (Jodhpur) inscription of Dadhimātā,[232] and the inscription of Allaṭa of Mewar, VS 1010.[233] The *Ādivarāha drammas* mentioned in the Sīyaḍoṇi inscription and identified as coins of Bhoja are found both in silver and copper,[234] usable both in long distance and day to day transactions. Uninscribed coins of the Indo-Sassanian type, known as *gadhaiyā* coins, with rude imitation of the Sassanian bust, assignable to the seventh-twelfth centuries have been found in Rajasthan and Gujarat.[235] The *Dravyaparīkṣā* of Thakkura Pheru describes *Gurjarī mudrās* issued by the Pratihāras.[236]

Besides the traders and artisans, a large number of people following service occupations such as the garland-makers,[237] washermen,[238] and cooks[239] also lived in these cities. There were also priests, various administrative personnel such as the *kāraṇikas*,[240] *daṇḍapāśikas*[241] and *ārakṣikas*,[242] prostitutes,[243] painters,[244] musicians and actors.[245] The cities thus became centres of multifarious activities and provided outlets to people desirous of quick economic gain.[246] The consequent intermingling of people from various stratas of society and different regions, following the most diverse occupations could not but invest the urban residents with a broad outlook. The religious tolerance and syncretism of the period[247] were in consonance with their liberal spirit. The materialistic environment of the cities engendered the evolution of a secular outlook and a distinct urban culture. Secular sciences such as *arthaśāstra, dhātuvāda, khanyavāda, āyuśāstra* and *aśvaśāstra* flourished.[248] The rich utilised their wealth and leisure in the cultivation of artistic and intellectual pursuits,[249] besides building lofty temples in honour of various deities. The *Karpūramañjarī* indicates the development of secular drama.

In towns lived also the royalty, whose splendour and luxury was even greater than the rich towns-folk. From the *Samarāiccakahā* we learn that prince Guṇasena had different palaces in different cities, the palace Vimānacandaka in Vasantapura and palace Sarvatobhadra in Kṣhitipratiṣṭhita.[250] The palace Vimānacandaka held all the enchantment of the rainy season with the smoke arising from black *agaru* wood casting a shade like clouds on a rainy day; jewel necklaces (*ratnāvalīs*) flashing like lightening; necklaces of pearls (*muktāvalīs*) bearing semblance to streams of water; lines of chowries appearing like rows of cranes; suspended garlands of *paṭṭāṃśuka* surpassing the beauty of rain; the ground, washed with scented water, bearing a sweet odour; and humming bees swarming around the flower arrangements.[251] The king's sleeping chamber (*vāsagṛha*) was furnished with auspicious jewelled lamps; pavements bestrewn with the most fragrant flowers; jewelled walls besmeared with musk; pillars of gold adorned with exquisite *devāṅga* cloth; a canopy of resplendent patterned cloth; bedsteads of reddish coral, covered with splendid mattresses and pillows; receptacles of gold; festoons of flower-garlands, incense issuing forth from pitchers of gold; pairs of beautiful *pārāvata* and *kalahaṃsa* birds; betel (*tāmbūla*) with camphor and *vāruṇī* wine served in golden cups.[252] In the morning the king was awakened from his sleep by the sound of the *tūrya* instrument whilst women sang auspicious songs, and bards sang the glories of the dawn and panegyrics.[253] The other apartments in the royal residence included an *āpanabhūmi*, where sweet drinks were served,[254] a *bhojanamaṇḍapa*, where food was served,[255] and a *kopagṛha*, where the queen retired when she was angry.[256]

The assembly (*sabhā*) of the king held in the *bahiropasthānamaṇḍapa* or outer audience hall was a grand affair. Here the king sat on a golden throne studded with jewels, surrounded by his *mantrins, mahābrāhmaṇas, mahākavis, mahāśvapatis* (head of cavalry), *mahāsenāpatis* (military commander), and *mahāpurohita*. Seated there were also good reciters of Sanskrit, Prākrit and Apabhraṃśa; scholars proficient in *Bharata-śāstra* (dramatic science); characteristics of elephants and horses; specialists in the use of the dagger, bow and arrow, discus, spear, sling and noose; experts in cutting designs on leaves (*patracchedya*), painting, alchemy, astrology, *śakunaśāstra* (science of omens), science of dreams and *nimitta*. No art or science, we are told, remained unrepresented there.[257] It was also the venue for religious discussions.[258] Into the *ābhyantaropasthānmaṇḍapa* the king admitted only a select few, such as his queen, ministers, and trusted followers, with a female door-keeper (*pratihārī*) standing guard at the door and allowing entry only with express royal permission.[259] The *bahiropasthānamaṇḍapa* corresponds to the *vāhyasthānamaṇḍapa* or *mahāsthānamaṇḍapa* of Bāṇa where public appearances, discussions and meetings were held.[260] The *ābhyantaropasthānamaṇḍapa* corresponds to the *bhuktasthānamaṇḍapa* of Bāṇa where the king is said to have sat with a few chosen princes, ministers and friends.[261]

Visits to parks and gardens formed an important part of city life. Luxuriously laid out gardens known as *bhavanodyāna* were attached to the palaces of kings as well as the houses of the rich,[262] while public gardens known as *bahirodyāna* were situated outside the city.[263]

Haribhadra dwells at length on the beauty of the *bhavanodyāna* with its vine arbour resonant with the sound of birds (*gṛhasārikā*); the clump of *aśoka* trees adorned with red leaves like a bridegroom attired in red; the water tank (*bhavanadīrghikā*) with lotus plants and sportive *kalahaṃsa* birds; the mango grove resonant with the notes of cuckoos; the *mādhavīlatā* bower attended by swarms of bees intoxicated by the nectar of its blossoms; clusters of betel-nuts entwined with masses of *nāgavallī*; bunches of saffron filling the skies with their sweet fragrance and the attractive plantain arbour gently swaying with the wind.[264] Uddyotana gives an equally picturesque description of the *bahirodyāna* visited by king Purandaradatta. 'With its arm-like creepers swaying in the wind, it seemed to dance; resonant with the notes of various birds, it seemed to sing; and echoing with the cries of cuckoos it appeared to be giving shouts of "victory, victory". The *raktāśoka* shoots seemed to beckon, and the bending crests of *śāla* trees appeared to bow. With the blooming of fresh blossoms the garden appeared to laugh and with the fading flowers falling off it seemed to be shedding tears. The gaze of the king, passing over the *mādhavī* bower, *bakula* tree, *raktāśoka*, mango, *sindhuvāra, candana* and *elā* forest, remained arrested there for long.'[265]

In the towns, as in the villages, the people had a considerable say in administration and we find that the king worked in close co-operation with the town elders known as *nagaramahallakas* or *nagaramahantakas*, and the *pañcakula*, both representatives of the popular element. In the *Samarāiccakahā* we read of the king ordering his officials, the *kāraṇikas*, to take the *nagaramahantakas* with them to search the house of a suspect for stolen property.[266] As the *kāraṇikas* are later described as *pradhānanagarajanādhiṣṭhita*,[267] i.e., supervised by the chief elders of the town, it may be assumed that the *mahantakas* enjoyed more authority than the former. An interesting episode in the *Kuvalayamālā*[268] describes how when a sudden spate of thefts rocked the city, the *nagaramahallakas* called upon the king to draw his attention towards the same and remind him that it was the ruler who was the strength of the weak. The king, on being informed by the *pratihārī* that the elders stood at the door seeking audience with him is said to have anxiously instructed her to make haste and usher them in. Prompt measures to catch the criminal were initiated by the king after his meeting with the elders. It is evident that the king appreciated the representative character of the *mahallakas*. Their part in judicial proceedings is brought out in the story where when a mock quarrel takes place between newly weds the friends declare that the case ought to be put before the ruler and the *nagaramahallakas*.[269] Preservation of peace was another important function of these elders. In the *Samarāiccakahā* we read how when a dispute arose between two vain *śreṣṭhiputras*, an assembly of *mahantakas* deliberated over the issue and despatched four representatives, who were proficient in *dharma* and *artha*, eloquent in speech, old in age and highly respected by all citizens to rebuke them for their ill-placed vanity. As their wishes carried weight as commands, a peaceful settlement was soon achieved.[270]

The *pañcakula* or committee of five assisted in the administration of justice. In the *Samarāiccakahā* when the king's treasury is looted, a joint committee of the *kāraṇikas* and *pañcakulas* carries out judicial investigations,[271] the former representing the official element, and latter seemingly the popular element. Elsewhere in the same work when a king is faced with the problem of establishing the ownership of certain gold ingots it is the *pañcakula* which is sent forth to fetch a sample of the ingots in question. The identity of the owner being established, the king accompanied by the *pañcakula* proceeds to the spot where the ingots lie, and they are restored to their rightful owner after being duly counted by the *pañcakula*.[272]

Epigraphic evidence of active public participation in the municipal administration during the period is not wanting. From the *Vaillabhaṭasvāmin* inscription of Gwalior dated AD 876 we learn that the civil affairs of the town were entrusted to a non-official body, consisting of two *śreṣṭhins* and one *sārthavāha*, known as *vara*.[273] The Sīyaḍoṇi inscription indicates that in the times of Mahārāja Dūrbhaṭa and *Mahārājadhirāja* Niṣkalaṅka, the affairs of the town were managed by the *pañcakula*, the executive of which consisted of two members, who changed from time to time.[274] References to *pañcakulas* occurs in various post-Pratihāra inscriptions belonging to Rajasthan.[275] As the *pañcakulas* of the Pratihāra period have been merely described as *tadadhiṣṭhita* (supervised or presided over by ruler) and not as *tanniyukta* (appointed by the ruler) as in the later records their status is likely to have been better.[276]

Adequate attention to means of irrigation, flourishing agriculture, industry and trade, abundant cattle wealth and healthy participation in civic administration were bound to produce results beneficial to the society. The high standard of living and luxury of town life depicted in our works leave no doubt that the people in general enjoyed high prosperity. But it has to be recognised that not all sections of society were equally prosperous. There are references in our works, albeit few, which indicate that standards of living differed radically from person to person and poverty was not unknown. In the *Samarāiccakahā* we read of a poor man Saddhaḍa, who lived with his wife Candrā and his son Sarga. On his death, his wife earned a living by doing odd jobs in other houses such as carrying water and her son Sarga by collecting fuel etc. in the woods, the hard life lead by them leading to frayed tempers.[277] From the *Kuvalayamālā* we learn that whereas in the winter the rich enjoyed the luxuries of chambers laden with the perfume of black aloewood and saffron, straw and husk from the threshing floor were the only recourse of farmers, while the children of the poor took to fire of chaff and cow-dung.[278] The ornaments of the rich and poor differed radically.[279] Mention is also made of a beggar asking for food, and his poverty.[280] Nevertheless the poor were relatively well off in the sense that the people were philanthropic in spirit, and in normal times there was plenty of food around and no cause for anyone to starve. *Pūrta-dharma* being highly popular, free eating places (*satrāgāra*) and hospitals (*ārogyaśālā*) were provided by the rich who also took pleasure in distributing alms to the poor.[281] In the *Kuvalayamālā*, we read of an *anāthamaṇḍapa* at Mathura where the various diseased and disabled, poor and helpless people gathered.[282]

In conclusion, villages were affluent. Fields tilled with the help of oxen drawn ploughs produced a high agricultural yield. The cultivation of sugarcane which requires water and reference to *araghaṭṭa* indicates the use of advanced techniques of agriculture. The belief in the acquisition of merit by excavation of wells, tanks and step-wells also helped ensure easy supply of water for irrigation. The richness in cattle wealth, by providing cattle for agriculture as well as pastoral products, made an important contribution to rural economy. The existence of rural traders must have facilitated exchange of agricultural surplus and cash crops like sugarcane with urban goods. Villagers had a lively vibrant culture expressed in their spellbinding songs and dances while tending their fields and gay revelry at the advent of spring as they sang and swung on swings suspended from the branches of trees. The performance of a touring actor's troupe was avidly watched by them. Village councils consisting of *mahattaras* or village elders administered justice which indicates considerable village autonomy in judicial matters. Besides villages with mixed populations there were *agrahāra* villages, peopled by brāhmaṇa families.

Towns were surrounded by moats, high walls and gateways. The market places had various streets displaying different commodities, including perishable commodities having limited markets as victuals, flesh etc. as well as durable articles capable of wider circulation and industrial items which reveals that towns were centres of manufacture as well as exchange. The rich towns-people had a luxurious standard of living with flowers, tanks, fountains, paintings, jewels, ornaments, and other items of luxury, lending a magnificence to their surroundings and providing a market for craftsmen, traders and artists who supplied these goods. A large number of specialist craftsmen, including weavers, workers in various metals, jewellers, perfumers, potters etc. lived in these cities. There resided also traders who engaged in widespread internal and external trade. Traders from different regions gathered at centres of inter-regional trade such as Sopārā and Vaijayantī. Traders from Vaijayantī, Tāmralipti and Sopārā embarked on sea voyages to China, South-east Asia and Ceylon. They exchanged distinctive regional products like betel-nuts, yak-tails, and conch-shells, high value goods like horses, silk and jewels and essential commodities like salt, and grain. Other residents of the city included people following service occupations such as garland-makers, washermen, cooks, priests, and various administrative personnel. The consequent intermingling of people of various strata and regions endowed the urban dwellers with a broad outlook, characterised by religious tolerance, syncretism, and secular outlook. A distinct urban culture evolved, the rich utilising their leisure in the cultivation of artistic and intellectual pursuits. Patronage of scholars by the ruler and urban elite made cities centres of learning and literary activity.

A ruler had different residences in different cities where he lived in even greater splendour than the townsmen. His establishments included the outer audience hall where his royal assembly was attended by ministers, military commanders, poets and experts in various arts and sciences, the inner audience hall where only a select few gained admission, the sleeping chamber, eating place, drinking hall etc. Beautifully laid gardens attached to the palace of the king, and houses of the rich as well as public gardens speak of the aesthetic sense of the urban people. The people of the town participated in their administration through the town elders known as *nagaramahallakas* who maintained public peace and were closely associated with judicial proceedings by the rulers as also the popular committee of five known as the *pañcakula*. Despite the general prosperity, the standards of living differed, the poor led a hard life, and beggars existed. But there was a definite attempt to improve their position by providing eating places, orphanages for the diseased and disabled, hospitals as well as distributing of alms.

Notes and References

1. *KM*, pp. 45, 50, 65.
2. महाणयर-सरिसं। Ibid., p. 50.
3. उच्चत्थलं णाम गामं, सग्ग-णयरं पिव सुर-भवणेहिं, पायालं पिव विविह-रयणेहिं, गोट्ठंगणं पिव गो-संपयाए, धणय-पुरी विय धण-संपयाए त्ति। Ibid., p. 65.
4. Ibid., pp. 50, 56.
5. Ibid., p. 56.
6. Ibid., pp. 7, 31, 45, 72.
7. Ibid., pp. 31, 56.
8. Ibid., p. 7.
9. एए वि एत्थ जुत्ता परयत्ता कड्ढिऊण णत्थासु।
   खंधारोविय-जूया गलय-णिबद्धा बलीवद्दा।। Ibid., p. 186.
10. . . . मुग्ग-सालीओ। चमढेहि बइल्लेहिं गलए मेढी-णिबद्धेहिं। Ibid., p. 186.
11. णीलुप्पलदलगन्धा रम्मा मायन्दमहूअविन्देहिं।
    वरइक्खुपण्णपच्छण्णा एसा भूमिकया जेण। Ghaṭiyālā inscription no. 2, vs 918; *JRAS*, 1896, pp. 513–21.
12. Ghaṭiyālā inscription no. 1, vs 918; *EI*, IX, pp. 279–81.
13. B.D. Chattopadhyaya, 'Origin of Rajputs: The Political, Economic and Social Processes in Early Medieval Rajasthan', *IHR*, III, no. 1, July '76, pp. 62–4.
14. See *mlecchas*, pp. 97–8.
15. The Ḍabok (Udaipur) inscription of AD 644 refers to *Śāradyagraiṣmika* fields (fields that could be tilled in autumn as well as summer), *EI*, XX, p. 122.
16. Rice was cultivated at Rangamahal, known to have been inhabited between the second to sixth or seventh century AD. Rydh, Hanna, *Rangmahal* Hieun Tsang had noted that grain was abundant in Pariyātra, identified with Bairat. Late wheat was grown there and a strange variety of rice, which ripened after sixty days. *Beal* (i), p. 179.
17. *KM*, pp. 30, 229, 232, 263, 277.
18. भव-सय-रहट्ट-घड़ी-सरिसेणं जम्म-जरा-मरण-णिरंतरेण। Ibid., p. 229.
19. अह इच्छसि मरणाइं मरणेहि य णत्थि तुज्झ णिव्वेओ। ता अच्छसु वीसत्थो जम्मण-मरणारहट्टम्मि।। Ibid., p. 277.
20. Ḍabok inscription, AD 644; *EI*, XX, pp. 122–5.
21. *EI*, XIV, pp. 176 f.
22. Presidential address, *PIHC*, XXXI, pp. 148–55.

23. R.C. Agrawala, 'Rājasthān kī Prācīna Mūrtikalā me Rahaṭa', *Maru Bhāratī*, XIV, p. 4.
24. Chattopadhyaya, B.D., 'Irrigation in Early Medieval Rajasthan', *JESHO*, XVI, pp. 293–316.
25. *KM*, pp. 65, 205.
26. According to Dr. R.S. Sharma the word *vāpī*, is derived from the sanskrit root *vap* which means 'to sow' and therefore it is clear that step-wells were meant for irrigating the fields; 'How Feudal was Indian Feudalism' in D.N. Jha ed. *Feudal Social Formation in Early India*, p. 189.
27. जलं पि बंधंति। *KM*, p. 35.
28. दोण्णि व तलायइं जाइं ण घण-घडिय-कसण-पत्थर-णिबद्धइं। Ibid., p. 50.
29. महा-समुद्र-सच्छमेहिं तलाय-बंधेहिं जणवय-विहवइं। Ibid., p. 31.
30. Kuva.; Ghaṭiyālā inscription 2; see above, p. 200.
31. *Bhārata Kaumudī*, I, p. 269.
32. *Puṣkariṇī kārita*, *EI*, XVIII, pp. 87 f.
33. Tod, *Annals and Antiquities of Rajasthan*, II, pp. 919–22.
34. *EI*, XXXVI, pp. 52–5.
35. R.C. Agrawala, 'Rājasthān ke Katipaya Prācīna Sarovar aur Vāpī', *Varadā*, VI, (iv), pp. 59–60.
36. *KM*, p. 117.
37. Ibid., p. 118.
38. Ibid., pp. 45, 65.
39. Ibid., p. 45.
40. Ibid., p. 31.
41. Ibid., p. 206.
42. B.C. Law, 'The Ancient Town of Bairāta', *Jadunath Sircar Commemoration Volume*, p. 219.
43. *Beal*, I, 179.
44. *KM*, pp. 50, 57, 65, 72.
45. Ibid., pp. 57 f., 65 f.
46. Ghaṭiyālā inscription no. 2; *JRAS*, 1895, pp. 513–21.
47. Ghaṭiyālā inscription no. 1 of Kakkuka; *EI*, IX, pp. 279–81-विचित्रवीथिसंपूर्ण हट्टं।
48. See pp. 200–1 above.
49. *KM*, p. 46.
50. Ibid., p. 52.
51. Ibid., p. 51.
52. Ibid., p. 121.
53. V.S. Agrawala explains draṅga as a village, an encampment (*KM*, pt. II, 137) of an itinerant tribe like the gūrjaras.
54. 'जलणं पविसामि' त्ति चिंतयंतेण मेलिया सव्वे गाम-महत्तरा . . . अहो गाम महत्तरा, महापावं मए कयं। *KM*, p. 63.
55. D.C. Sircar, *Guhilas of Kiṣkindhā*, p. 62.
56. Ibid., p. 66.

57. *EI,* III, pp. 265–7.
58. B.N. Puri, *History of the Gūrjara Pratihāras,* p. 113.
59. बंभणाणं अग्गाहारं। तत्थ जण्णदेवो . . . बहु-सयण-वेय-विज्जा-धण-परिवारियस्स वच्चंति दियहा। *KM,* p. 258.
60. *EI,* V, pp. 208–13.
61. *EI,* XIX, pp. 15–19.
62. *SK,* p. 299.
63. Ibid., p. 496.
64. Ibid., p. 702.
65. *KM,* pp. 50, 124.
66. Ibid., pp. 31, 45, 64, 124; *SK,* pp. 7, 299, 702.
67. *KM,* p. 31.
68. *SK,* p. 7.
69. Ibid., p. 299.
70. Ibid., pp. 7, 702.
71. *KM,* pp. 24–6.
72. *SK,* p. 496.
73. Ibid., p. 7.
74. Ibid., p. 299.
75. *KM,* p. 117.
76. Ibid., pp. 31, 103.
77. Ibid., p. 190.
78. माणिक्कमुत्ताहलहिरणधन्नाउलरून्दहट्टमग्गा। *SK,* p. 702.
79. *KM,* pp. 7–8.
80. *Arthaśāstra*, part II.
81. S.N. Roy, *Paurāṇic Dharma aur Samāj,* pp. 347 f.
82. P.K. Acharya, *Indian Architecture According to the Mānasāra-Śilpa-śāstra,* pp. 40, 144.
83. Ibid., pp. 40–1.
84. *EI,* XVIII, pp. 87 f.
85. Sakrāi inscription, AD 822, *EI,* XXVI, pp. 27 f.; Khaṇḍelā inscription, AD 807; *EI*, XXXIV, pp. 159–63; Mandkila inscription, AD 896; *EI*, XXXIV, pp. 77 f.; B.D. Chattopadhyaya, 'Markets and Merchants in Early Medieval Rajasthan', *Social Science Probings,* II, 1985, p. 415.
86. The Chittorgarh inscription of sixth century suggests that the family of Viṣṇudatta, described as 'vaṇijam śreṣto' moved from Mandasor to Chittor; B.D. Chattopadhyaya, op. cit., p. 416.
87. *EI,* XX, pp. 97 f.; B.D. Chattopadhyaya, op. cit., p. 416.
88. Ghaṭiyālā ins. no. 1 of Kakkuka; *EI,* IX, pp. 279–81.
89. It refers to the main bazaar roads (*haṭṭamārga*), main streets (*bṛhadrathyās*) and small streets (*ku-rathyās*) and houses mostly constructed of burnt bricks in existence at the town of Tattānandapura where resided wealthy merchants of the *varkkaṭavaṇik* community migrated from Rajasthan. *EI,* XIX, pp. 52 f.

90. Separate markets and streets dealing with different classes of commodities, the *dosihaṭṭa* (textile market), *prasannahaṭṭa* (liquor market), *kaṅsārakavīthi* (street of braziers), *catuṣkahaṭṭa, mahattakahaṭṭa* and sellers of salt (*nemakavaṇik*), sellers of betel (*tāmbolikas*), wine-merchants (*kallapālas*) and sellers of sweets are mentioned. *EI*, I, pp. 162 f.
91. Cf. Inscription of Allaṭa of Mewar, AD 953, *Indian Antiquary*, LVIII, pp. 161 f.; Rājor inscription of Mathanandeva, AD 959, *EI*, III, pp. 263 f.; Hastikuṇḍi inscription of Dhavala, AD 997; *EI*, X, pp. 20 f.
92. *KM*, p. 8.
93. Ibid., p. 64.
94. Ibid., p. 8.
95. Ibid., p. 7.
96. Ibid., pp. 24, 107.
97. Ibid., pp. 7, 17.
98. Ibid., p. 83.
99. *Karpūra.*, I. 36.
100. Ibid., III. 27.
101. *KM*, p. 282.
102. Ibid.
103. *Elliot and Dowson*, I, p. 4.
104. Bhillamāla, Mandor, Rājor, Cāṭsū, Chittor developed as capitals under the various branches of the Pratihāras and Guhillas. Didwana (Jodhpur state) was a district headquarter. Āhār and Shergarh (Kota) were centres of commerce. Pushkara, Sakrāi and Nāgdā etc. were centres of pilgrimage. K.C. Jain, *Ancient Cities and Towns of Rajasthan*, pp. 66 f., 496 f.
105. *EI*, XVIII, pp. 87 f. त्रेतातीर्थे च पत्तनम्।
106. K.C. Jain, op. cit.
107. See chapter on dress.
108. Ibid.
109. *KM*, pp. 195, 198.
110. *SK*, p. 460.
111. *KM*, p. 48.
112. Ibid., p. 2.
113. Ibid., p. 92.
114. Ibid., pp. 92, 127, 156.
115. Ibid., pp. 92–3, 171.
116. Ibid., pp. 92–3.
117. Ibid., p. 93.
118. Ibid.
119. Ibid., pp. 7, 18.
120. Ibid., p. 50.
121. *SK*, p. 239.
122. *KM*, p. 18; *SK*, pp. 239–40.
123. *SK*, pp. 171, 263; *KM*, p. 154.

124. *SK*, p. 173.
125. Ibid., p. 254.
126. Ibid., p. 263.
127. Ibid., p. 543.
128. Ibid., p. 760.
129. *KM*, pp. 115, 119, 120, 128.
130. See chapter on toilet.
131. See food and drinks.
132. *KM*, pp. 8, 117.
133. *SK*, p. 788.
134. *KM*, pp. 84, 157.
135. Ibid., p. 48.
136. Ibid., p. 22; see education.
137. The excavations at Rairh, Naliāsar and Bairat reveal the presence of potters, goldsmiths, weavers, jewellers, blacksmiths, cobblers, carpenters and stone-cutters. K.C. Jain, *Ancient Cities and Towns of Rajasthan*, pp. 85 f., 112 f., 121 f., 197.
138. A well preserved smelting furnace with a large quantity slag, shell bangles, potter's stamps form part of the material relics at Noh indicating the industrial richness of the site in the Kuṣāṇa period. Kameshwar Prasad, *Cities, Crafts and Commerce Under the Kuṣāṇas*, p. 42.
139. Umakant Shah, *Lalit Kalā*, 1–2.
140. *Bhārata Kaumudī*, I, pp. 269 f.
141. *EI*, XXIV, pp. 329 f.
142. R.C. Agrawala, 'Pratihāra Yugīn Mandira aur Mūrtiyān', *Varadā*, VI, (i), pp. 16 f.
143. R.C. Agrawala, 'Rājasthān ke do Mahatvapūrṇa Prastara Phalaka', *Maru Bhāratī*, XIV, pt ii, pp. 4–6.
144. See vaiśyas.
145. *KM*, pp. 66–7. Barbarakūla is identified by V.S. Agrawala as Barbaricum, the region along the sea coast of Sindh (*KM*, Part II, p. 118).
146. Ibid., p. 65.
147. Ibid.
148. Ibid., p. 23.
149. V.S. Agrawala, *KM*, part II, p. 116.
150. *KM*, pp. 152–3; see 'Literature', p. 239, fn. 203.
151. Hodivala, *Studies in Indo-Muslim History*, p. 66; Motichandra, *Trade and Trade Routes in Ancient India*, p. 202.
152. N.L. Dey, *Geographical Dictionary of Ancient and Medieval India*.
153. Al Masudi, *c.* AD 956 refers to it as a town. *ED*, I, p. 24.
154. Alberuni (eleventh century) mentions it as a port on the western coast. Sachau, I, p. 209.
155. According to Al Idrisi (eleventh century) it was a populous and busy town, considered one of the entrepots of India. *ED*, I, p. 85.

156. Motichandra, *Trade and Trade Routes in Ancient India,* p. 104.
157. *EI,* I, pp. 184 f.
158. *Indian Antiquary,* Vol. 58, p. 161.
159. *EI,* XXII, pp. 120 f.
160. *EI,* II, pp. 116 f.
161. *ED,* I, p. 4.
162. Ibid., I, p. 5.
163. V.S. Agrawala, Introduction to Motichandra's *Trade and Trade Routes in Ancient India,* p. xiii.
164. Cosmas, XI, p. 372.
165. *KM,* p. 74.
166. *SK,* p. 328.
167. *KM,* p. 66.
168. Motichandra, *Trade and Trade Routes in Ancient India,* pp. 60, 146–7, etc.
169. *Mahājanaka Jātaka,* 539; *Valahasyasa Jātaka,* Vol. 2, pp. 127 ff. qd. Motichandra, *Trade and Trade Routes in Ancient India,* pp. 62–3.
170. According to Cosmas (AD 535–47) elephants, horses, silk, aloes, cloves and sandalwood were exported from India to Ceylon. *Cosmas,* XI, 363–5, 371–2.
171. *Bṛhatsaṃhitā,* LXXX 23. qd. A.M. Shastri, *India as Seen in the Bṛhatsaṃhitā of Varāhamihira,* p. 322.
172. *Journal of Asiatic Society of Bengal,* Part I, 1935.
173. *SK,* pp. 205, 585.
174. Ibid., p. 327.
175. Ibid., pp. 444 f.
176. *KM,* p. 66.
177. R.C. Majumdar, *Suvarṇadvīpa,* I. 7, II.350; I-tsing, pp. xxv, xxxiv. Trade with South-east Asia is as ancient as the Jātaka period, cf. Motichandra, *Trade and Trade Routes in Ancient India*, pp. 60–1.
178. An inhabitant of Gauḍa, Kumāraghosha was the preceptor of the Śailendra emperor, Dharaṇīndravarman in AD 782. R.C. Majumdar in R.C. Majumdar (ed.), *Age of Imperial Kannauj,* p. 414. About the middle of ninth century, Bālaputradeva of the Śailendra dynasty, built a monastery at Nalanda and requested Devapāla to grant five villages for its upkeep. Nalanda copper plate, qd. R.C. Majumdar in R.C. Majumdar (ed.), *History of Bengal,* pp. 9, 122–3.
179. R.C. Majumdar and D.C. Ganguly in R.C. Majumdar (ed.), *History of Bengal,* p. 671.
180. Qd. by R.C. Majumdar in R.C. Majumdar (ed.), *Comprehensive History of India,* Vol. III, Part II, p. 1296.
181. *Kāvyamīmāṃsā,* p. 10.
182. *Vaijayantī,* p. 42. 1.21.
183. Sachau, II, p. 106.

184. H.C. Rayachaudhari in R.C. Majumdar (ed.). *History of Bengal*, pp. 29–30.
185. *EI*, II, 345.
186. *KM*, p. 66.
187. See chapter on textiles; *SK*, pp. 80, 360.
188. Ibid., p. 443.
189. Adhir Chakravarti in 'Some Aspects of Indo-China Maritime Trade' in B.D. Chattopadhyaya (ed.), *Essays in Early Economic History*, p. 161.
190. K.A.N. Shastri, Foreign notices.
191. Qd. U.N. Ghoshal in R.C. Majumdar (ed.), *Age of Imperial Kannauj*, p. 403.
192. Qd. U.N. Ghoshal, in *Age of Imperial Kannauj*, p. 401.
193. Cosmas., II, p. 47.
194. *Kumārasambhava*, VII.3; *Śākuntalam*, I, p. 838. *Harṣacarita*, pp. 36, 167, 242.
195. *Upamitibhavaprapañcākathā*, p. 154.
196. *ED*, I, p. 69.
197. *KM*, p. 67.
198. *SK*, p. 327.
199. A.L. Basham, 'Note on Seafaring in India', in *Arts and Letters*, XXIII, p. 69; L. Gopal, *Economic Life in Northern India*, pp. 125–6.
200. *Chau Ju-Kua*, p. 101, n. 11 qd. L. Gopal, *Economic Life in Northern India*, p. 126.
201. Hourani, *Arab Seafaring*, p. 75.
202. V.K. Jain, *Trade and Traders in Western India*,. p. 88.
203. R.C. Majumdar, *History of Bengal*, p. 617. The *Cāryapadas* are assignable to the period AD 950–1200, Ibid., p. 384.
204. Khalimpur inscription, Regnal year 32, no. 1.
205. *KM*, p. 20.
206. Ibid., p. 32.
207. *SK*, p. 614.
208. *KM*, p. 18.
209. *SK*, p. 410.
210. Ibid., p. 199.
211. *KM*, p. 57.
212. Ibid., p. 43.
213. D. Sharma, *RTTA*, p. 9; L. Gopal, *Economic Life in Northern India*, p. 497.
214. *Dharmabindu*, p. 154; D. Sharma, *RTTA*, p. 497.
215. *Nisitha Cūrṇi*, 3, pp. 111, 388.
216. *Upamiti*., p. 353.
217. *Niśītha Cūrṇi*, 3, p. 111.
218. *ED*, I, p. 11.
219. P. Niyogi, *Economic History of Northern India*, p. 140.
220. Ferrand, Textes, pp. 44, 105.

221. Gadhwā Stone inscription of Candragupta II; Gadhwā stone inscription of Skandagupta; Koṭivarṣa inscription, AD 443–4; Baigram inscription, AD 447–8.
222. A.S. Altekar, *The Coinage of the Gupta Empire,* pp. 294–6.
223. D. Sharma, *RTTA,* p. 497.
224. U.N. Ghoshal in *Age of Nandas and Mauryas,* p. 279; A.S. Altekar, *The Rāṣṭrakūṭas and Their Times,* p. 365. According to Viṣṇugupta, as quoted in Hemādri's *Vratakhaṇḍa,* 70 *rūpakas* = 1 *suvarṇa* and 28 *rūpakas* = 1 *dīnāra* implying the ratio of *dīnāra* and *suvarṇa* as 2:5. Kane, *HD,* III, p. 122, fn., 1.2; R.C. Agrawala, 'Rūpaka, a coin denomination', *JNSI,* XIX, p. 116. But Nārada and Bṛhaspati regard *dīnāra* and *suvarṇa* as synonymous. cf. S.K. Maity, *Economic Life in Northern India,* p. 221; L. Gopal, *Economic Life in Northern India,* p. 209.
225. R.C. Agrawala, 'Rūpaka, a coin denomination' in *JNSI,* XIX, pp. 115 f.
226. *Indian Antiquary,* Vol. 58, p. 161.
227. *EI,* X, pp. 24 f.
228. *Indian Antiquary,* xli, pp. 202–3.
229. *Indian Antiquary,* Vol. LVIII, p. 161; D. Sharma, *ECD,* p. 340; Idem, *RTTA,* p. 503.
230. D. Sharma, 'Identification of Raṇahastin with Vatsarāja Pratihāra', *JNSI,* XVIII, pp. 222–3; P.L. Gupta, 'The Attribution of the Coins of Raṇahastin', *JNSI,* XX, pp. 189–91.
231. Āhār inscription, Harṣa Saṃvat 258; *EI,* XIX, pp. 52 f.; Pehoa inscription, AD 882; *EI,* I, pp. 184 f.; Sīyaḍoṇi inscription, tenth century, *EI,* I, pp. 162 f.
232. AD 608, *EI,* XI, pp. 299 f.
233. *Indian Antiquary,* Vol. 58, p. 161.
234. R.C. Agrawala, 'Dramma in Ancient Indian Epigraphs and Literature', *JNSI,* XVII, p. 64.
235. V.N. Reu, *Coins of Marwar,* pp. 2 f.; Cunningham, *Coins of Medieval India,* p. 48; Altekar, *Comprehensive History of India,* Vol. III, ii, p. 1400.
236. D. Sharma, *RTTA,* p. 499.
237. *SK,* p. 228.
238. Ibid., pp. 42, 286.
239. Ibid., p. 264.
240. Ibid., pp. 91, 222.
241. Ibid., p. 93.
242. Ibid.
243. Supra, p. 63.
244. *SK,* p. 607.
245. *KM,* pp. 103, 199.
246. Ibid., p. 57.
247. See religion.
248. See education.

249. See amusements.
250. *SK*, pp. 12, 35.
251. Ibid., p. 15.
252. Ibid., pp. 239–40.
253. *KM*, pp. 91, 141, 161, 173, 198.
254. Ibid., p. 20.
255. Ibid., pp. 15, 20.
256. Ibid., p. 12.
257. Ibid., p. 16.
258. Ibid., p. 203.
259. Ibid., p. 9.
260. V.S. Agrawala, *Harṣacarita, Ek Sāṃskritika Adhyayana*, pp. 205–6.
261. Ibid., p. 205.
262. *SK*, pp. 67, 70–1; *KM*, pp. 165–6.
263. *KM*, p. 77.
264. *SK*, pp. 70–1.
265. *KM*, p. 33.
266. *SK*, p. 91.
267. Ibid.
268. *KM*, p. 247.
269. अहो, महंतो एस ववहारो, जइ परं सिरिविजयसेण-नरवइणो णयर-महल्लयाणं च पुरओ णिव्वडइ त्ति। Ibid., p. 172.
270. *SK*, pp. 409–10.
271. Ibid., p. 222.
272. Ibid., pp. 460–1.
273. *EI*, I, pp. 154 f. Altekar suggests that the name vara was given to the executive because it used to change by turn. *State and Government in Ancient India*, p. 222.
274. *EI*, I, pp. 162 f.
275. The Lālarāī stone inscription of Kelhaṇadeva (vs 1233) records a grant made in the presence of the village *pañcakula*. The Bhīnmāla stone inscription of Udaisiṃha, vs 1306 and Sāñchor inscription of Sāmantasiṃha, vs 1345 refer to *pañcakulas* appointed by the rulers exercising local authority. *EI*, XI, pp. 49, 55, 57 f.
276. D. Sharma, *RTTA*, p. 351.
277. *SK*, p. 583.
278. *KM*, p. 169.
279. See ornaments.
280. *KM*, p. 188.
281. Ibid., pp. 31, 58, 65; *SK*, p. 195.
282. Ibid., p. 55.

10

Education, Language and Literature

EDUCATION

THE IMPORTANCE OF education was well realised. The curriculum of study was comprehensive and aimed at an all round development of personality. Instruction in diverse subjects such as the scriptures, philosophical subjects, literary sciences, military arts, commerce, fine arts and handicrafts was imparted to ensure the proper growth of physical, mental and intellectual faculties. For this purpose, children from rich families, sons of rich merchants,[1] and princes[2] were entrusted to the care of a teacher known as *lekhācārya* or *upādhyaya*. Prince Kuvalayacandra is said to have resided with the *lekhācārya* in utter seclusion, unseen even by his parents, from the age of eight, for a period of twelve years, gaining mastery over the various arts.[3] After completion of his education, he was duly tested by his father who took his son out for a practical display of the art of horse-riding and questioned him about the characteristics of various horses.[4]

Detailed lists of the subjects studied by princes occur in both the *Kuvalayamālā* and the *Samarāiccakahā*, the former enumerating as many as 72 subjects and the latter 89. These include writing (*lekha*)[5] and arithmetic (*gaṇita*);[6] grammar (*vyākaraṇa*),[7] lexicon (*nighaṇṭu*)[8] and etymology (*nirukta*);[9] religious scriptures including the *Rāmāyaṇa, Mahābhārata* and *Vedas*;[10] philosophical subjects such as *Sāṅkhya, Yoga* and *Hetuśāstra* or logic;[11] medicine (*āyurjñāna*);[12] *Arthaśāstra* (*arthapada*);[13] poetics comprising *kāvyam*,[14] metrics (*chanda*),[15] *āryā, śloka* and *gīti*[16] verses; story-telling (*ākhyāyikā*), composition of stories (*kathā-nibandha*),[17] and knowledge of riddles (*prahelikā*);[18] fine arts, viz. music (*gāndharva*)[19] comprising singing (*gīta*),[20] knowledge of seven *svaras* or notes (*svaragata*),[21] instrumental music (*vādita*)[22] and beating time in music (*samatāla*),[23] dancing (*nṛtya*)[24] as well as drama (*nāṭaka*)[25] and painting (*ālekhya*);[26] astrology (*jyotiṣa*,[27] *horā*,[28] *varṣaguṇahorā*[29]) and astronomy (*candracarita, sūryacarita, rāhucarita, grahacarita*);[30] martial arts, fighting with arms, sticks, fists and bones, fighting, wrestling, heavy fighting (*bāhuyuddha, daṇḍayuddha, muṣṭiyuddha, asthiyuddha, yuddha, niyuddha, yuddhaniyuddha*),[31] archery (*dhanurveda*),[32] knowledge of arrows (*iṣvastra*),[33] array and counter array (*vyūha, prativyūha*);[34] signs (*lakṣaṇa*) of men, women, elephants, cows, cocks, sheep, discus, parasol, sticks, swords, gems and leather (*puruṣa, strī, gaja, go, kukkuṭa, meṣa, cakra, chatra, daṇḍa, asi, maṇi, carma*);[35] manufacturing articles of gold (*suvarṇakarma*,[36] *suvarṇavāda*[37]), silver (*hiraṇyavāda*),[38] iron (*kālāyasakarma*),[39] ivory (*dantakarma*),[40] and copper (*tāmrakarma*);[41] domestic arts, including culinary science (*sūpaśāstra*),[42] the art of preparing food (*annavidhi*)[43] and drink (*pānavidhi*),[44] tailoring (*vastrakarma*),[45] art of making a bed (*śayanāvidhi*),[46] proper mode of sleeping and sitting (*śayanāsanavidhi*),[47] garland-making (*mālākarma*),[48] flower arrangement (*puṣpavidhi*);[49] toilette, *gandhayukti*[50] (perfumery), rules relating to ornaments (*ābharaṇvidhi*,[51] *ālaṅkārikakarma*[52]), art of decorating a maiden (*taruṇīprītikarma*);[53] architectural arts (*vastu*),[54] survey, measurement and planning of camps, cities and building (*skandhāvāramāna, nagaramāna, vastumāna, skandhāvāraniveśa, nagaraniveśa* and *vastuniveśa*);[55] games such as *sūtrakrīḍā* (playing with strings), *vastrakrīḍā* (playing with clothes), *vāhyakrīḍā* (riding), *nālikākrīḍā* (a kind of dice),[56] gambling (*dyūta*),[57] cock and quail fights (*lāvaka-kukkuṭayuddha*),[58] sciences of alchemy (*dhātuvāda*),[59] dreams (*svapnaśāstra*),[60] omens (*śakunaśāstra*),[61] occult sciences such as *avasvāpini* (art of putting to sleep),[62] *taludghāṭana* (art of opening locks),[63] *tantra*,[64] *mantra*[65] and similar arts and sciences.

Though it is difficult to believe that a prince actually mastered all these subjects within the short span of a few years, and as a study of the list of the *kalās* given in the Jaina canonical literature[66] reveals, the courses of study enumerated are largely conventional, they nevertheless are of importance as they acquaint us with the ideal curriculum of the period. It is hard to gainsay the fact that they were studied by some section or other of the Rājasthānī society in our period, in light of the evidence presented by these Prākrit works themselves, other literary and epigraphic evidence, contemporary as well as posterior,[67] and the account of Alberuni.[67a] Uddyotana shows good knowledge of *aśvaśāstra*,[68] *rāśi-phala,*[69] *khanyavāda,*[70] *lakṣanaśāstra,*[71] *samudraśāstra,*[72] *dhātu-vāda,*[73] *nimittajñāna,*[74] earlier literary works,[75] and contemporary religious and philosophical tenets[76] in his *Kuvalayamālā*. That some princes were quite well read can be seen from the Jodhpur inscription of Bauka, AD 837, which refers to his predecessor Kakka's extraordinary knowledge of prosody (*chanda*), grammar (*vyākarṇa*), logic (*tarka*), astronomy (*jyotiṣa*), various *kalās* and poetry in all languages.[77] The Ghaṭiyālā inscription, AD 861, contains a verse written by the Pratihāra ruler Kakkuka, which testifies to his skill in versification.[78] Rājaśekhara refers to the fourteen *vidyāsthānas*, including the four *Vedas*, six *Vedāṅgas*, and four *śāstras* comprising the *Purāṇas, Ānvīkṣikī, Mīmāṃsā* and *Smṛtis*, the number of which arose to eighteen by the addition of *Vārtā, Kāmaśāstra, Śilpaśāstra* and *Daṇḍanīti.*[79] *Sāhityavidyā* or the science of literature was also a *vidyā* according to him.[80]

Brāhmaṇas must have paid special attention to the study of religious scriptures and we read in the *Kuvalayamālā* not only of brāhmaṇas learned in the Vedas but also acquainted with the works of Vyāsa, Vālmīki, Manu, Mārkaṇḍeya, and the *Gītā*.[81] Epigraphic evidence attests to this.[82] There were brāhmaṇas who studied secular subjects as well. Brāhmaṇas who were employed in royal service as ministers may be presumed to have been well-versed in polity. Haribhadra's wide knowledge may partly be ascribed to the fact that he was a brāhmaṇa by birth and *purohita* by profession[83] before he became a convert to Jainism and therefore had the customary upbringing and education of a brāhmaṇa. Rājaśekhara, the brāhmaṇa preceptor of Mahendrapāla,[84] the author of the *Kāvyamīmāṃsā* and secular dramas, was evidently a distinguished scholar with wide intellectual learning and secular interests. Abu Zaid (ninth century) speaks of the brāhmaṇas as men devoted to religion and men of science.[85]

Vaiśyas too were well educated. The *Samarāiccakahā* refers to the sons of *seṭṭhis* who received education from a *lekhācārya* and mastered the various arts.[86] In the *Kuvalayamālā* we read of the son of a *mahā-seṭṭhi* who put to good use the lore of mining (*khanyavāda*) studied by him.[87] Following Manu, Medhātithi expects the vaiśyas to possess a knowledge of the economic products of different countries and their prices, arithmetic and various alphabets.[88] It is quite natural that vaiśyas who were prosperous traders, temple trustees and acted as patrons of learning[89] went in for literary education as well.

Our works contain no direct reference to the education of śūdras. But the evidence that certain members of the śūdra class took up trade as their vocation,[90] clearly suggests that some of the śūdras were quite literate. This alone would have enabled them to understand the intricacies of business and successfully accumulate wealth.[91] Medhātithi observed that śūdras were sometimes teachers of grammar and other sciences.[92] The artisan and craftsmen members of the vaiśya and śūdra class must have received technical education through the apprentice system, with master artisans, as laid down by Yājñavalkya and Nārada.[93] These and other classes of society such as the ploughmen do not appear to have received a formal literary education. But as their specialised crafts and agricultural competence[94] shows that they were well trained in their fields, whether by master craftsmen or relatives, and though they may have been largely illiterate, it would be improper to call them uneducated also. Their attendance at public narrations of religious and philosophical *kathās* by Jaina *sādhus* which gave them a moderately good understanding of these works was also highly educative.

Large educational establishments known as *maṭhas* were in existence and served as great centres of learning. The *Kuvalayamālā* gives a vivid description of a huge *maṭha* situated near the city of Vijayā on the southern coast.[95] Its external appearance was that of a temple. It seems to have had residential accommodation and included students from different parts of India such as Lāṭa, Karṇāṭaka, Mālava, Kannauj, Maharāṣṭra, Saurāṣṭra, Śrīkaṇṭha and Sindha,[96] who received instruction in diverse subjects such as archery (*dhanurveda*), manoeuvring with a shield (*phalakakrīḍā*), use of sword and bow (*asi dhanu praveśa*), fighting with a spear (*kuntayuddha*), fighting with clubs (*lakuṭiyuddha*), fighting with arms (*bāhuyuddha*), wrestling (*niyuddha*), painting (*ālekhya*), singing (*gīta*), instrumental music (*vādya*) and *Bhāṇa, Dombilika* and *Sṛṅgāṭaka* (various forms of plays).[97] At one place, prince Kuvalayacandra came across lecture groups (*vyākhyānamaṇḍalīs*), where lectures were delivered on advanced branches of learning such as grammar and the various philosophies, viz., Buddhism, *Sāṅkhya, Vaiśeṣika, Mīmāṃsā, Naiyāyika,* Jainism and *Lokāyata*.[98] In another place, he saw persons who cultivated the various arts and sciences, such as *nimitta, mantra, yoga, añjana, kuhaka* (black magic), *dhātuvāda, yakṣiṇīsiddhi, kṣātra* or military science, *yogamālā, yantramālā, jyotiṣa, rasabandha, rasāyana, chanda, patracchedya, dantakarma* (ivory work), *lepakarma* (modelling), *kanakakarma* (work in gold) etc.,[99] making him marvel at the extraordinary mastery of the preceptors over 72 *kalās* and 64 *vijñanas*. Some pupils there, again, were given solely to Vedic studies, and Uddyotana, who as a Jaina probably saw not much sense in this, gives a caricature of these students, committing to memory Vedic texts, of robust bodies, with well developed muscles, leading a carefree life, having violent dispositions. They are said to be a set of fools, and bereft of upright morals.[100] The accompanying remark that they subsisted on the food given by others[101] indicates that free food was provided at these *maṭhas*.

Endowed with a liberal and comprehensive character, these *maṭhas*, where the philosophies of different sects and different branches of learning could be studied by one must have made an invaluable contribution to contemporary education. There was nothing very original about the establishment of these brahmanical organised educational institutions, as they but followed the pattern of the Buddhist University of Nālandā, which had a wide curriculum, consisting of Buddhist and non-Buddhist religious and philosophical works, as well as secular subjects like medicine and astronomy.[102] But now the benefits of contacts with students from different states and teachers engaged in teaching diverse disciplines which widened the horizons of the pupil's knowledge and provision of free food which brought education within the reach of even the poor, would appear to have extended to a larger number of students. The *Upamitibhavaprapañcākathā* (tenth century) also refers to *vidyāmaṭhas* established by the rich where the pupils received free food and education.[103] Many south Indian inscriptions dating from tenth century onwards record instances of colleges endowed by temple charities.[104] An inscription dated AD 975 records the grant of land to a *maṭha*, where students were fed and taught, at Hebbal in Dhārwār district.[105] The evidence of our work is important as it provides one of the earliest descriptions of such a *maṭha*.

The youth of Vārāṇasī in the country of Kāśī are said to have studied the various kalās and the *Cāṇakyaśāstra*,[106] the latter evidently the *Arthaśāstra* of Kauṭilya. Vārāṇasī or Kāśī, established as a centre of learning by the time of the *Jātakas*[107] and noted by Hieun Tsang[108] is known to have retained its renown in the latter period from Alberuni as well.[109] That the treatise of Kauṭilya alone has been singled out for mention indicates that it was an important subject of study at Vārāṇasī. It is a subject included in the curriculum for princes in the *Samarāiccakahā*[110] as also in the earlier work of Daṇḍin.[111]

While the subjects of study mentioned in our works include for the most part the traditional curriculum set down in the Jaina canonical texts,[112] there are significant variations indicating that many new branches of study had come into prominence by our period. *Tantra* became the subject of study for princes[113] as well as Jaina monks.[114] The various *siddhis* figure among the subjects dealt with in the *maṭhas* as do other occult subjects such as *yantramālā* and *yogamālā*.[115] Reference has already been made above to the popularity of tantricism during the period.[116] The Vikramaśilā University of Bihar, founded by the ruler of Bengal, Dharmapāla (eighth century), had tantric *ācāryas* and was associated with the composition and translation of many tantric works.[117] Tārānātha writes that Nālandā also had become a prominent centre of tantricism in eighth century AD.[118]

The occult sciences of *dhātuvāda* were assiduously cultivated by all sections of society, including princes[119] and merchants.[120] Alchemical experiments are described in detail in the *Kuvalayamālā* which speaks of three specific classes of *dhātuvādins*, viz., *Kriyāvādins*, *Narendras* and *Dhātuvādins* who employed the techniques of *yogayukti* (use of powder), *rasabandhana* (use of mercury) and *kṣārayukti* (use of alkali) respectively.[121] Certain alchemists, we learn, believed the red colour of the flame to be indicative of the making of copper, yellow of gold, white of silver, black of iron and colourless of bronze. According to others, the true technique was an unknown secret. If the fire was of lower heat, lead was produced, but if the heat became excessive, then granular gold was manufactured. If the fire was of moderate heat, the contents of the crucible just drained in liquid form. If the flame was greasy, the contents turned black. To turn baser metal into gold, it was put into the crucible and heated, after which some kind of herbal powder was added to it.[122]

Such was the popularity of *dhātuvāda* that the hero of the *Kuvalayamālā* asserts unequivocally that it is not to be dismissed as a mere belief[123] and quotes the authority of the *Joṇīpāhuḍa* 'wherein whatever was written could never be wrong, though mountains may move and the heavenly river may change its course'.[124] The dismal state of so many alchemists who were forced to go abegging because of their failure to manufacture gold, according to him, was to be ascribed to their ignorance of the *āgamas*, non-observance of celibacy, greed, selfishness, pride and other vices, and the science was not to be discredited on that account.[125] *Sarvajña* (the omniscient, i.e. Jina) was the presiding deity who had given out the *Joṇīpāhuḍa*,[126] said prince Kuvalayacandra and demonstrated how by saluting the Jinas and the *siddhas* and adding the power (*cūrṇa*) as prescribed in the *Joṇīpāhuḍa*, gold could be successfully manufactured.[127] The uttering of the correct *mantras* was deemed to be highly efficacious. The provision for salutations to Jinas and observance of celibacy etc.[128] in the preparation of gold indicate the association of religious mysticism with alchemy.

Joṇīpāhuḍa was an ancient Jaina text and its association with *dhātu-vāda* expresses the deep belief people had in its efficacy. The detailed description of the practice of alchemists well illustrates that *dhātuvāda*, which finds mention in the list of *kalās* in the *Kāmasūtra*[129] and is associated with the *Dhārmikadraviḍa* in the *Kādambarī*,[130] had become an important subject of study. The earliest available book on alchemy, *Rasaratnākara*, attributed to Nāgārjuna belongs to the seventh or eighth century.[131]

An allied subject that gained in popularity was the *khanyavāda*, the knowledge of which enabled one to perceive hidden treasures. The secondary branches of the malūra tree, it was held, indicated the presence of wealth below. The extent, nature, and depth of the wealth was determined by the size, juice and height of the tree.[132] The sciences of *rasabandha* and *rasāyana* also gained a place in the educational system.[133] The sciences of alchemy and *rasāyana* are noted by Alberuni (eleventh century) amongst sciences that preyed on the ignorance of the people.[134] *Rasāyana*, he observed, was a word composed with *rasa*, i.e., gold, which denoted an art which restored health to the ill and youth to the aged.[135] Nāgārjuna's *Rasaratnākara* was followed by many later Indian works like the *Rasārṇava* (*c*. AD 1200) and *Rasaratnasamuccaya* (AD 1300) which deal with the metallic preparations calculated to give perpetual youth, invisibility etc.[136] In a way these sciences were beneficial as they encouraged the growth of chemistry by arousing interest in quicksilver etc. but when they got entangled with religious mysticism and *mantravāda* the rational approach could not but be slowed down and Alberuni's remarks appear to be quite justified on these grounds.

A praiseworthy feature of education during this period was that equal importance appears to have been attached to vocational and non-vocational courses. Training in the fine arts and industrial arts were regarded as much of education as mastery of the literary arts and therefore included even in a prince's curriculum. Thus the ideally educated person was one who was proficient not only in one but all branches of knowledge. The *Kuvalayamālā* shows that experts in the *Bharataśāstra*, evidently the *Nāṭyaśāstra* of Bharata, arts like *patracchedya* (cutting designs on leaves) and painting were as much a part of the king's court as poets and experts in various languages.[137] Rājaśekhara also visualises the king poet as surrounded by Sanskrit poets, *Vaidikas*, logicians, *Paurāṇikas* etc. (those proficient in *Vedas*, philosophy, *Purāṇas* etc.) as well as actors, dancers, jewellers, goldsmiths, rope-dancers, jugglers and so on.[138] By retaining interest in subjects like philosophy, the quest for the eternal truth continued, representing the pursuit of knowledge for its own sake, and it must have been duly impressed on the pupil that material considerations were not all that mattered in one's life, though perhaps not always with the same effect. Other necessary sciences such as the *Arthaśāstra* were also not neglected.

The educational system had its defects as well. Mention has already been made of the immense popularity of the different sciences of prognostication such as astrology, *samudraśāstra, svapnaśāstra, śakunaśāstra*, and *nimitta*,[139] the results of which were hardly beneficial as they encouraged growth of superstitions, as did the development of the occult sciences. Vedic studies continued during this period, but the evidence of Uddyotana would make us believe that it consisted mainly of a mere recitation of Vedic texts by memory whereby its pupils gained neither any learning nor any mental or moral discipline.[140]

The Jainas attached great importance to *svādhyāya* or self-study. This included not only the study of the Jaina scriptures, but various secular subjects as well. Thus the preceptor Dharmanandana, the *Kuvalayamālā* tells us, was surrounded by a multitude of *sādhus* who were engaged in the study of the Aṅgas, viz. *Sūtrakṛtāṅga, Sthānāṅga, Samavāyāṅga, Ācārāṅga, Vyākhyāprajñapti, Jñātṛdharmakathā, Upāsakadaśā, Antakṛddaśā, Anuttaraupapātikadaśā, Praśnavyākaraṇa, Dṛṣṭivāda*, i.e., all the Aṅgas, except the *Vipākaśruta* which has been somehow left out; the three Upāṅgas viz., the *Sūryaprajñapti, Candraprajñapti* and the *Prajñāpanā*; five and ten limbed syllogism, *nimitta* which disclosed to one the visible and invisible world (*loka* and *aloka*), remote objects and minute objects; the *Joṇīpāhuḍa* which contained knowledge about the origin of various beings and combinations of various jewels, metal and gold; *kāvya, tantra* and *mantra*.[141]

Jaina *ācāryas* like Haribhadra Sūri and Uddyotana were not only thoroughly conversant with the various Jaina scriptures, but had good knowledge of the various lores and sciences,[142] which reflects their deep erudition and wide learning. They were adepts in poetics, solving of riddles and completion of unfinished verses.[143] Classical and non-classical literature was also studied by them. Uddyotana was fully acquainted with the contributions made by earlier authors, Jaina as well as non-Jaina, in the field of *kathā* (narrative) literature.[144] Complimentary references are made in the *Kuvalayamālā* to Pādalipta, Chappaṇṇaya and Sātavahana.[145] Pādalipta is identified as the author of the *Taraṅgavatī*, with an allusion to its central theme figuring around a couple of ducks.[146]

Sātavahana or Hāla had a great hold on the village folk and his *kośa* was an inexhaustible thesaurus.[147] Chappaṇṇaya connoted a group of poets adept in wise sayings.[148] The *Vaḍḍakahā* or *Bṛhatkathā* of Guṇāḍhya was like a veritable mirror for poets and is likened to Sarasvatī.[149] Vyāsa and Vālmīki to whom we owe the *Bhārata* and *Rāmāyaṇa* are mentioned as unsurpassed models.[150] The *Kādambarī* of Bāṇa is admired for its exquisite expression.[151] Reference is made to Vimala, identifiable with the author of the *Paumacariya* and his Prākrit language is called *sarasa* (tasteful) like nectar.[152] Devagupta, a royal saint of the Gupta family was well known for his *Supuruṣacarita.*[153] Harivarṣa, the author of the *Harivaṃśauppatti* is complimented for his popularity and spotless expression.[154] *Sulocanā* was a well-narrated Jaina *dharmakathā.*[155] The royal saint Prabhañjana was famous for his *Yaśodharacarita.*[156] The *Varāṅgacarita* and *Padmacarita* are referred to as charming works composed by praiseworthy poets, Jaḍiya i.e. Jaṭila and Raviṣena respectively.[157] Uddyotana mentions also the author of the *Samarāiccakahā* (Haribhadra) as his guru in scriptural instruction.[158] The works of other poets known as Abhimānāṅka, Parākramāṅka and Sāhasāṅka are also mentioned as worthy of note.[159]

It is evident that the Jaina monks did not restrict their study to Jaina literature alone but read and admired most of popular non-Jaina Sanskrit literature as well. Of the authors mentioned by Uddyotana, Vyāsa and Vālmīki are well known. *Taraṅgavatī* is a famous Prākrit work written by Pādalipta, whom Uddyotana appears to put as a contemporary of Hāla, placed in the beginning of the Christian era. Its original is now lost and we have only a shorter Prākrit digest known as the *Taraṅgalolā*, written 1,000 years later.[160] The *Sattasaī* of Hāla is an extant anthology of 700 verses in Mahārāṣṭrī Prākrit, the themes of which, as indicated by the *Kuvalayamālā*, are drawn primarily from rural life.[161] An anthology of *Chappaṇṇaya-gāhāo*, allied to the work of Hāla, has also come to light.[162] The *Bṛhatkathā* of Guṇāḍhya, composed in *Paiśācī* Prākrit, which is assigned by legend to the Sātavāhana period,[163] is lost. We possess however three Sanskrit versions.[164] Bāṇa's *Kādambarī* is a celebrated work even now.

The *Paumacariya* of Vimala is the Jaina version of the Rāmāyaṇa, written in Mahārāṣṭrī Prākrit, composed according to the author 530 years after Mahāvīra's nirvāṇa, i.e. VS 60,[165] The *Padmacarita* of Raviṣeṇa in Sanskrit which follows closely Vimala Sūri's work, was composed in VS 733.[166] *Sulocanā kathā* by Mahāsena finds mention in Jinasena's *Harivaṃśa* (AD 783) as well as in Dhavala's *Harivaṃśa* in

Apabhraṁśa (*c.* eleventh century AD).[167] *Varāṅgacarita* is a Jaina text composed in Karnataka, referred to by the *Harivaṃśa* of Jinasena as the work of Jaṭāsiṃhanandi[168] and tentatively placed at the close of the seventh century AD.[169] The work of Prabhañjana has been respectfully referred to by Vāsavasena (earlier than AD 1308), a later writer on the *Yasodharacarita*.[170] The story of Yasodhara is incorporated in the fourth *bhava* of Haribhadra's *Samarāicchakahā*.[171]

LANGUAGE AND LITERATURE

Language

Prākrit was a sacred language for the Jainas since their āgamas were composed in it and the eighth and ninth century belonged to the Jaina polymaths Haribhadra and Uddyotana who made significant contributions to Prākrit literature. It however appears that Apabhraṃśa was, at this time, a literary language much closer to the spoken form of speech than the standardised Prākrit.[172] In the *Kuvalayamālā*, those learned in Apabhraṃśa are represented as attending the royal assembly along with the reciters of Prākrit and Sanskrit.[173] Passages of Apabhraṃśa are introduced into the *Kuvalayamālā* itself, as the author himself also informs us in the introductory opening. These include conversational passages of the inmates of an *anāthamaṇḍapa* (home for destitutes),[174] *grāmamahattaras,*[175] and boys belonging to a residential school,[176] passages where Uddyotana evidently thought it befitting to reproduce the colloquial speech faithfully. Even the Prākrit passages in the *Kuvalayamālā* quite often use what are looked upon as forms special to Apabhraṃśa.[177] The layers of society that favoured Apabhraṃśa most are indicated by the use of Apabhraṃśa forms by the king while addressing the *aśvapati* (horse-keeper),[178] the song of the *grāma-naṭī* (village actress) in Apabhraṃśa,[179] and the Apabhraṃśa verse of the Gurjara traveller[180] in the *Kuvalayamālā*.

As a living language, Apabhraṃśa must have held universal appeal and Uddyotana's observations regarding the style and structure of Sanskrit, Prākrit and Apabhraṃśa, which he recognises as the three major languages of the time are noteworthy in this context. In his opinion, Sanskrit, with its manifold vocabulary, compounds, indeclinables, prepositions, cases and genders, was full of difficulties, and dangers like a villain's heart crowded with hundreds of bad thoughts. The association with Prākrit like that with the words of good people, was a happy one; it was an ocean of worldly information crowded with the waves of discussions about various arts, it was full of nectar-drops that were oozing out on account of its being churned by great persons and it was composed with a variety of nice arrangement of words. Apabhraṃśa was a balanced and pleasing admixture of the waves of pure and impure Sanskrit and Prākrit words; it was even (or smooth) as well as uneven (or unsmooth); it flowed like a mountain river flooded by fresh rains; and it captivated the mind like the words of a beloved when she was coquettishly angry.[181] The author's liking for Apabhraṃśa is quite obvious here. The gradual development of Apabhraṃśa as a popular literary language is confirmed by Rājaśekhara, who places Apabhraṃśa poets on the western side of the literary court of the king-poet.[182] According to him, the people living in Marwar were fond of Apabhraṃśa.[183]

Prākrit had its own charms and besides the Jaina writers, Rājaśekhara also undertook to compose a work in Prākrit. To put it in his own words, 'Sanskrit poems are harsh, but a Prākrit poem is very smooth, the difference between them in this respect as great as that between men and women.'[184] In the *Bālarāmāyaṇa* too, he describes Prākrit as elegant and possessing natural sweetness.[185] In the *Kāvyamīmāṃsā* he refers to Prākrit poets.[186] While in earlier dramas, the use of Prākrit was generally reserved for women and persons of inferior rank,[187] his play *Karpūramañjarī* is written entirely in Prākrit. Centering around a fictitious amour of court-life, obviously designed for the pleasure of a court audience, and known to have been actually staged, it attests to the cultivation of Prākrit at the royal court, of which evidence comes also from Chittor where Māhuka, a descendant of Māgha, wrote the Prākrit work, *Haramekhalā* at the court of Dharaṇīvarāha in VS 887, i.e. AD 830–31.[188] The Prākrit compositions of Haribhadra and Uddyotana being primarily meant for recitation in public indicate on the other hand that a large number of Jaina laity were well conversant with Prākrit.

With Prākrit no longer the spoken language of the common people, however, Sanskrit had gained ground as the literary language of the learned. Haribhadra himself wrote Sanskrit commentaries on the Jaina canonical texts (Āgamas), which before him had been generally explained by Prākrit commentaries,[189] such as the *Nandisūtra, Āvaśyakasūtra, Anuyogadvārasūtra* and *Daśavaikālika.*[190] The *Kuvalayamālā* too has Sanskrit passages, from which we learn that Sanskrit morning prayers (*suprabhātastotras*) addressed to the *Jinas*[191] as well as the five exalted ones[192] and verses (*ślokas*) glorifying the doctrine of the Jina (*Jinaśāsana*)[193] were current among the Jaina laity. A *Yakṣa* maiden (*yakṣakanyā*) offering worship to Ṛṣabha is described as singing a dvipadī verse (*dvipadīkhaṇḍa*) in Sanskrit in his praise.[194] Besides we come across a poet reciting a Sanskrit *subhāṣita*[195] and brāhmaṇas quoting Sanskrit quotations from the scriptures.[196] Sanskrit was the language mostly employed in epigraphs and the Pratihāra ruler Kakkuka is known to have composed a verse in Sanskrit.[197]

Besides Sanskrit, Prākrit and Apabhraṃśa, Uddyotana also recognises the existence of a fourth *bhāṣā* (language), Paiśācī,[198] which he duly illustrates in the *Kuvalayamālā*, but attributes it therein to the *piśācas* (goblins) who dwell in the cavity of the banyan tree.[199] As seen above, he makes complimentary references to the *Bṛhatkathā*, the famed Paiśācī work of Guṇāḍhya. Rājaśekhara also speaks of *Paiśāca* or *Bhūtabhāṣā* poets.[200]

Deśībhāṣās or local dialects were gaining prestige. Uddyotana's mention of *Deśī* among the subjects to be studied by a prince[201] is an index of their growing popularity. They appear to have represented territorial spoken forms of speech, as distinguished from the literary languages having cultivated styles of their own.[202] Uddyotana shows a good knowledge of these *deśībhāṣās*. Eighteen of these dialects spoken by the merchants of different territories meeting in the market-place are referred to in the *Kuvalayamālā* of which sixteen are duly illustrated, viz. those of the Gollas, Madhyadeśa, Magadha, Antarvedī (area between Ganga and the Yamunā), Kīras, Ḍhakkas, Saindhavas, Mārukas (marudeśa or Marwar), Gurjaras, Lāṭas, Mālavas, Karṇāṭaka, Tājikas, Kośala and Mahārāṣṭra and Āndhras.[203]

Literature

The *kathā* literature of the period was rich and varied. Haribhadra refers to three divisions of subject-matter (*kathāvastus*), viz., *divya* (concerned with gods), *divya-mānuṣa* (concerned with gods and men), and *mānuṣa* (concerned with men)[204] and four kinds of *kathās, dharmakathā, arthakathā, kāmakathā* and *saṃkīrṇakathā* dealing with the topics of *dharma, artha, kāma* and the first three combined respectively.[205] Of these *dharmakathā* is declared to be the highest type of narrative, illustrating as it does such virtues as forbearance, leniency, straightforwardness, austerities, truthfulness, the *anuvratas* and other vows.[206] The *Samarāiccakahā*, he tells us, is a *dharmakathā* with *divya-mānuṣa vastu.*[207] In addition to these three varieties, Uddyotana mentions the divisions of *sakala, khaṇḍa, ullāpa, parihāsa* and *vara kathās*, classifying the *Kuvalayamālā* as primarily a *dharmakathā* which has become a *saṃkīrṇakathā* because it combines the characteristics of all these five and embraces topics of *artha* and *kāma* along with *dharma*, besides being endowed with the merits of various narratives, amorous sentiment, well arranged sub-plots, and exposition of various arts and branches of knowledge.[208] He also further subdivides the *dharmakathā* into four kinds—*ākṣepiṇī* or pleasant, *vikṣepiṇī* or unpleasant, *saṃvegajananī* or enlightening, and *nirvegajananī* or leading to renunciation.[209] By means of the first, the mind of the hearer is first captivated; by the second, the mind of the hearer which had already come under the teacher's grip was now to be distracted from its attachment or addiction; by the third, the mind of the hearer was made receptive to religious ideas; by the last the mind developed positive detachment.[210] The disquisition on the nature of different *kathās*, classified variously according to their subject-matter, topics and style of writing is very illuminating and amply shows the richness of contemporary *kathā* literature. *Khaṇḍakathā* and *sakalakathā* are noted by Hemacandra. According to him in the former the main event took place at the middle or end of the composition while in the latter one acquired all the fruits at the end as in the *Samarāiccakahā*.[211] *Ullāpa* primarily means 'sweet' and coaxing conversation, while, *parihāsakathā* denotes an 'amusing' story.[212]

The *Samarāiccakahā* and *Dhūrtākhyāna* are the two principal Prākrit works of the Jaina *ācārya* Haribhadra Sūri who flourished in Rajasthan during the eighth century. Written in Mahārāṣṭrī Prākrit, the *Samarāccakahā*, an independent didactic tale in the tradition of earlier extensive fictional Jaina religious narratives such as the *Taraṅgavatī* and *Vasudevahiṇḍī*, traces the inimical behaviour of two souls over a circle of nine births as the evil consequence of their *karma*. Samarāditya in a former life was inadvertently negligent thrice towards an invited ascetic guest, who consequently forced to go hungry for three consecutive months, conceived an inveterate hatred for him, which reappearing unabated in their later births as father and son, son and mother, twice husband and wife, cousins, prince and vidyādhara and in the end prince and caṇḍāla, caused the latter to pursue the former and seek revenge from him. Written in simple and conversational prose, interspersed with verses here and there, and free from any unnecessary ornamentation, the work astutely combines an interesting narrative with dogmatic teachings and didactic episodes, its style well adapted to the understanding of an audience of some culture rather than that of great learning.[213]

The *Dhūrtākhyāna*, narrated for the benefit of the pious residents of Chittor (Citrakūṭa),[214] is a satire unique in Indian literature. Written entirely in verse, it is the story of five rogues, four men and a woman, who hold a contest in relating imaginary personal experiences. The absurd and fantastic tales of each rogue were confirmed as credible by others who brought forward parallel stories from the epics and *Purāṇas*; thus the Purāṇic legends are satirised. Ultimately the female cheat confounded the others with the tale that they were her runaway slaves. The conception and construction of the composition is exemplary; its approach is intellectual so that neither religious didacticism or eroticism mars the beauty of this work, and there is a delightful intermingling of fantasy and reality, making it a product far ahead of its times.[215] Like the *Samarāiccakahā*, its style is simple and fluent, and well suited for an audience of mediocre understanding. The characters employed in the *Dhūrtākhyāna* were well known in popular Indian tales. Śaśa and Mūladeva are referred to in Bāṇa's *Kādambarī* and the *Bhāṇa Padmaprābhṛtaka*.[216] The story of the four rogues Śaśa, Elāṣāḍha, Mūladeva and Khaṇḍapānā occurs in brief in the *Niśīthasūtrabhāṣya*, believed to have written by Saṃghadāsagaṇi, a contemporary of Haribhadra.[217] But Haribhadra's ingenuity alone weaved these motifs together and transformed them into a satire by the addition of parallel epic and Purāṇic episodes in a skilful manner.

Sanskrit literature has very little of satire or satirical verses in the proper sense. Some amount of vivid realism and satirical portraiture is to be found in the early Bhāṇas, as well as in Daṇḍin's *Daśakumāracaritam*,[218] but they 'seldom reach the proportion and propriety of real satire'.[219] The earliest datable Sanskrit satire is the *Kuṭṭanīmata* or 'advice of a procuress' by Dāmodaragupta, the minister of Jayapīḍa of Kashmir (AD 779–813), which is more erotico-comic than satiric.[220] The other notable satirist is the Kashmiri poet Kṣemendra (eleventh century).[221] Later writers were unable to produce such satires.[222] In the light of this, the *Dhūrtākhyāna* assumes all the more importance, as it illustrates the creative genius of Haribhadra, who broke away from traditional stereotyped plots and composed a distinctive and original satire, free from both the erotico-comic tendency of Dāmodaragupta and heavy didacticism of Kṣemendra. Though the story undoubtedly has a religio-moral purpose, the writer refrains from the temptation to load it with preachings. He is content with merely stating at the conclusion that the popular scriptures do not contain any attractive stuff and one should follow the path preached by *sarvajña*[223] (the omniscient).

Haribhadra's pupil Uddyotana Sūri's *Kuvalayamālā* is distinct from earlier Jaina romance inasmuch as it is an early example of the *campū* form, which is characterised by a natural blending of prose and verse both of which flow out spontaneously for the poetic effect of the narration.[224] The verses here are not specially reserved for an important idea, poetic description, or impressive speech etc. but come sometimes to continue the narration, now and then by way of an effective description, at times as gnomic, religious or didactic sermons and at times by way of clarificatory elaboration. In this way it differs radically from the primitive prose and verse narrative found in the Pāli *Jātaka* or fable literature, in which the verse is chiefly of a moralising or recapitulatory character.[225] It dates earlier than the oldest extant Sanskrit *campūs*.[226]

The principal language employed in the *Kuvalayamālā*, is Mahārāṣṭrī Prākrit, but as noted above, some portions are written in Apabhraṃśa, and even in Paiśācī. The story illustrates the evil consequences of the five passions, anger, deceit, vanity, greed and infatuation through a biography of five souls passing through several births. It is a prominent example of continuous composition in Prākrit, a massive work dealing not only with a number of lives, but also embodying a large number of sub-stories, its narration uninterrupted by any division like the *ucchvāsa* or *pariccheda* etc. The author exhibits significant poetic talent. Strings of similes (*upamās*)[227] and puns (*śleṣas*)[228] add to the beauty of his work. The *śrṃkhalā-yamaka* is often used.[229] The verses for the most part are written in *gāthā* metre but the *anuṣṭubh, toṭaka, daṇḍaka, dvipadī, gītikā, duvalaya, gīti, saṃkulaka, sragdharā* are also used frequently.[230] Uddyotana himself refers to the use of the *ullāla, kulaka, gāthā, dvipadī, gītikā, duvalaya, cakkalaya, tiyalaya, daṇḍaka, nārācaka, taraṅgaka, toṭaka* and *vrittạ* in the introduction to the *Kuvalayamālā*.[231]

It cannot be gainsaid that both Haribhadra and Uddyotana have consciously or sub-consciously inherited from earlier writers certain contexts and motifs and echo many a dogmatic detail from the canonical texts.[232] The numerous entertaining and instructive pieces inserted in Jaina canonical texts such as the *Jñātṛdharmakathā, Vipākaśruta, Uttarādhyayanasūtra, Niryuktis* etc. undoubtedly served as models for their works[233] as did Sanskrit classical works which Uddyotana respectfully refers to.[234] Narration of earlier births is a recurrent theme to be found in the Jaina canonical works, Buddhist *Jātakas*, later Jaina narrative literature and Bāṇa's *Kādambarī*.

But there are significant points of difference between earlier works and the narratives of Haribhadra and Uddyotana. As observed by Jacobi, while in the *Taraṅgalolā, karma,* remembrance of a previous birth and its consequences serve to motivate the story, in the *Samarāic-cakahā* the story serves to illustrate those ideas and to impress the hearers with certain moral principles.[235] The same is true of the *Kuvalayamālā*. Both are eminently *dharmakathās*. While *Kādambarī* shows through successive births and rebirths the steadfastness of love and its eventual fulfilment through persistence these works illustrate the enduring consequences of past and present action (*karma*), good as well as bad, in manifold subsequent births. Deft handling of highly complex plots, with a large number of characters involved passing through a series of births, with many sub-tales, parallel episodes and apalogues, well knit together and presented in a lucid manner is their speciality. Though parallel motifs and literary devices may be adduced, it is undeniable that the subject-matter presenting a vivid picture of characters drawn from all layers of society and contemporary life is primarily derived from direct observations of social types and contemporary practices. The ingenuity and originality of the authors shines through in the mingling of romantic situations, humorous episodes and poetic descriptions with a religious theme, which make their works entertaining as well as instructive.

The *Karpūramañjarī* of Rājaśekhara, a play in four acts, composed entirely in Prākrit, is the earliest example of *saṭṭaka* that has come down to us. According to the author, the *saṭṭaka* is the name of a play which resembles a *nāṭikā*, excepting that only the connecting scenes (*praveśakas* and *viṣkambhakas*) and *aṅkas* do not occur.[236] The acts are called *yavanikāntara.*[237] '*Saṭṭaka* is to be danced', says the *Karpūramañjarī*,[238] and as the word *sāḍika* which is regarded as an equivalent of *saṭṭaka* occurs with the Bharhut bas-relief of a dance[239] it appears that dancing formed an essential part of this form of drama. The *Karpūramañjarī* is a comedy relating the manipulations which bring about the marriage of king Caṇḍapāla with Karpūramañjarī, the cousin of the queen miraculously brought to the palace by a magician, despite the queen's jealousy and her imprisonment of the heroine. Though Rājaśekhara does not rank high as a playwright, in the *Karpūramañjarī* he displays some real poetic talent.[240] He turns out harmonious verses in the swing scene.[241] He skilfully handles elaborate metres like the *śārdūlavikrīḍita* and *sragdharā* and displays as many as seventeen varieties of metres in the *Karpūramañjarī*.[242] He is fond of proverbial expressions such as 'a bangle on a wrist needs no mirror',[243] 'musk is not sold in a petty hamlet or a jungle, nor is gold tested without a touchstone'[244] etc. and is a keen observer of local customs and practices.[245]

The term *saṭṭaka* or *sāḍika* is very old[246] but it is not mentioned in the *Nāṭyaśāstra* of Bharata.[247] Sections of *Agnipurāṇa* dealing with dramaturgy refer to it.[248] Abhinavagupta, the commentator on Bharata's *Nāṭyaśāstra* (*c.* tenth century AD), observed that it was similar to a *nāṭikā*.[249] This type of composition was known also to Hemacandra[250] but no other early *saṭṭaka* has yet been found. It was the *Karpūramañjarī*, which served as an inspiration for the subsequent extant Prākrit *saṭṭakas*, which come from much later dates and are evidently modelled after the work of Rājaśekhara.[251]

In conclusion, education was given great importance. Princes and sons of rich merchants were handed over to teachers to study in complete seclusion for a number of years. The curriculum of a prince, including diverse subjects like writing, arithmetic, grammar, scriptures, philosophy, medicine, *arthaśāstra*, poetics, arts and crafts, astrology, martial arts, architecture, games, sciences of dreams and omens and occult sciences, indicates that the ideal curriculum was comprehensive. Brāhmaṇas paid special attention to scriptures but secular subjects were also not neglected. Vaiśyas mastered the various arts, knew the lore of mining and acted as patrons of learning. Śūdras who took up trade were evidently literate. Specialised crafts indicate that artisan members of the śūdra class must have received technical education.

Brahmanical *maṭhas* emerged as centres of higher learning drawing pupils from all over India. They imparted secular education comprising not only Vedic studies but martial arts, fine arts, dramas, crafts, poetics and occult lores. These *maṭhas* which provided residence and free food brought education within the reach of the poor, promoted inter-regional contacts and bestowed a secular outlook on their pupils. Rulers also promoted education by grant of villages to brāhmaṇas.

The *arthaśāstra* continued to be an important object of study at Vārāṇasī. Tantra and occult subjects like *yantramālā* and *yogamālā, siddhis* like *añjana* and *yakṣiṇīsiddhi*, alchemy, and *khanyavāda*, gained, popularity as subjects of study. *Rasabandha* and *rasāyana*, the latter indicating the science which restored youth etc., gained a place in the curriculum. These and alchemy encouraged the growth of chemistry, but the association of religious mysticism and magical words with these sciences, retarded meaningful scientific advance.

The equal importance attached to vocational and non-vocational subjects and the absence of favoured treatment to literary learning as compared to training in fine arts and industrial arts were commendable features of education. The continued study of philosophy indicates that the materialistic environment and luxuries had not extinguished the quest for spiritual knowledge. The practical science of *arthaśāstra*, more relevant in urban surroundings, was also not neglected. But the growth of various sciences of prognostication and occult sciences encouraged the growth of superstitions. Vedic studies appear to have been commonly reduced to mere memorisation of the texts. The Jainas studied various religious and secular subjects including Jaina canonical texts, Sanskrit classical texts, earlier Jaina narrative and didactic literature, *tantra* and various lores and sciences which accounts for their deep erudition that was reflected in their works, whereby the masses gained knowledge of diverse aspects of learning they would have otherwise remained unaware of.

Apabhraṃśa and not Sanskrit or Prākrit was the commonly spoken form of speech which was developing into a literary language. Uddyotana introduced Apabhraṃśa passages in his work and described the language as captivating. That Prākrit found favour amongst not only Jaina writers like Haribhadra and Uddyotana but also Rājaśekhara, whose plays were designed for the pleasure of a court audience, indicates the cultivation of Prākrit in royal courts besides amongst the Jaina monks and laity. The inclusion of Sanskrit morning prayers and verses glorifying Jina in the *Kuvalayamālā* by Uddyotana and the writing of the first Sanskrit commentaries on Jaina canonical texts by Haribhadra indicates that Sanskrit had become the literary language of the learned. Paiśācī, as a literary language, was known but its attribution to the goblins indicates that it was not much in use. *Deśībhāṣas* or local dialects used by the common people were gaining prestige and their importance was being recognised by the upper classes of society, as indicated by their inclusion in curriculum of a prince and their illustration in the *Kuvalayamālā*.

Jaina Prākrit literature was rich, with varied subject matter, topics and style of writing. The *Samarāiccakahā* of Haribhadra was a didactic tale which illustrated the evil consequences of bad *karma* over a cycle of nine births, weaving in simple prose an interesting narrative together with dogmatic teachings. The *Dhūrtākhyāna* of the same author was a unique satire, which satirised the purāṇic legends in a rational and logical manner, and not with fanatical unbalanced criticism. The *Kuvalayamālā* of Uddyotana, an early example of *campū*, which entails a smooth admixture of prose and verse, effectively illustrated the evil consequences of passions. These works, though they may have derived certain motifs and literary devices from earlier works, were independent compositions, and their originality shone through their ingenious blending of humorous and romantic plots with a religious theme. The Prākrit *Karpūramañjarī* of Rājaśekhara is the earliest extant *saṭṭaka* form of drama. It is a comedy centring around a court amour, written for a court audience, replete with elaborate metres and proverbial expressions and permeated with the court atmosphere.

Notes and References

1. समप्पिया य लेहायरियस्स । *SK*, p. 105.
2. लेहाहरियस्स उवणीओ । *KM*, p. 21.
3. Ibid., p. 21.
4. Ibid., pp. 23–4.
5. *SK*, p. 602.
6. *KM*, p. 22.
7. Ibid.
8. Ibid.
9. Ibid.
10. Ibid.
11. Ibid.
12. Ibid.
13. *SK*, p. 602.
14. Ibid.
15. *KM*, p. 22.
16. *SK*, p. 602.
17. *KM*, p. 22.
18. *SK*, p. 602.
19. *KM*, p. 22.
20. *SK*, p. 602.
21. Ibid.
22. Ibid.
23. Ibid.
24. *KM*, p. 22.
25. Ibid., Nāṭya, *SK*, p. 602.
26. *SK*, p. 602; *KM*, p. 22.
27. *KM*, p. 22.
28. *SK*, p. 602.
29. *KM*, p. 22.
30. *SK*, p. 603.

31. Ibid.
32. *KM*, p. 22.
33. *SK*, p. 603.
34. Ibid.
35. Ibid.
36. *KM*, p. 22.
37. *SK*, p. 603.
38. Ibid.
39. *KM*, p. 22.
40. Ibid.
41. Ibid.
42. Ibid.
43. *SK*, p. 602.
44. Ibid.
45. *KM*, p. 22.
46. *SK*, p. 602.
47. *KM*, p. 22.
48. Ibid.
49. Ibid.
50. *KM*, p. 22; *SK*, p. 603.
51. *SK*, p. 603.
52. *KM*, p. 22.
53. *SK*, p. 603.
54. *KM*, p. 22.
55. *SK*, p. 603.
56. Ibid.
57. *KM*, p. 22; *SK*, p. 603.
58. *KM*, p. 22.
59. Ibid., p. 22; *SK*, p. 603.
60. *KM*, p. 22.
61. Ibid.
62. Ibid.
63. Ibid.
64. Ibid.
65. *Mantrāgatam*, *SK*, p. 603.
66. J.C. Jain, *Life in Ancient India as Depicted in Jaina Canons*, pp. 172 f.
67. Cf. *Agni*, 225, 1–4, Kane, *History of the Dharmaśāstra,* Vol. III, p. 50. *Upamiti.*, Prastāva 3, Chapter 1; Prastāva 4, Chapter 2; D. Sharma, *Early Chauhan Dynasties,* pp. 322–3.

67a. Sachau, I, pp. 125–33, 159, 187–9.

68. *KM*, pp. 23–4.
69. Ibid., p. 20.
70. Ibid., p. 104.
71. Ibid., pp. 116, 129.

72. Ibid., p. 129.
73. Ibid., pp. 195–8.
74. Ibid., pp. 268–9.
75. Ibid., pp. 3–4.
76. Ibid., pp. 150–1, 203–7.
77. (छंदो) व्याकरणं तर्क्को ज्योतिःशास्त्र कलान्वितं। सर्वभाषाकवित्वंच विज्ञातं सुविलक्षणम्।। v. 25, *EI*, XVIII, pp. 87 f.
78. Ghaṭiyālā Inscription no. 1; *EI*, IX, pp. 279 f.
79. *Kāvyamīmāṃsā*, pp. 3–4.
80. Ibid., p. 4.
81. *KM*, p. 48.
82. See chapter on brāhmaṇas.
83. Jacobi, Introduction to *SK*, pp. vii–viii.
84. *Karpūra.*, I.5, I.9.
85. *ED*, I, p. 10.
86. गहिओ कलाकलावं समप्पिया य लेहायरियस्स। *SK*, pp. 105, 407.
87. *KM*, p. 104.
88. *On Manu*, IX. 329–32.
89. See vaiśyas.
90. *KM*, p. 65.
91. Ibid.
92. *On Manu*, III. 156.
93. *Yājñavalkya*, II. 184; *Nārada* (abyupetyasusrūṣā) [illegible]6–20 qd. Kane, *HD*, II, i, p. 365.
94. See urban and rural life.
95. महंतं मढं। *KM*, pp. 150–2.
96. लाडा कण्णाडा वि य मालविय-कणुज्ज-गोल्लया केइ। मरहट्ठ य सोरट्ठा ढक्का सिरिअंठ-सेंधवया।। Ibid., p. 150.
97. Ibid., p. 150.
98. Ibid., pp. 150–1.
99. Ibid., pp. 151–2.
100. Ibid.
101. Ibid., p. 152.
102. Life, pp. 112, 121.
103. D. Sharma, 'Dasvīm Śatābdī me Rājasthānī Sikṣā Paddhati', *Maru Bhāratī*, VII, 3, p. 7; *Upamiti.*, p. 624.
104. R.K. Mookerji, *Ancient Indian Education*, p. 367.
105. *EI*, IV, p. 358; Altekar, *Rāṣtrakūṭas and Their Times*, p. 402.
106. सिक्खविज्जंति जुवाणा कला-कलावइं चाणक्क-सत्थइं च। *KM*, p. 56.
107. R.K. Mookerji, *Ancient Indian Education*, p. 490.
108. Beal, Si-yu-ki, II, p. 44.
109. He observed that Varanasi and Kashmir were the high schools of Hindu sciences in his times. Sachau, I, p. 173.

110. *SK*, p. 602.
111. *Daśakumāracaritam*, pp. 21–2.
112. J.C. Jain, *Life in Ancient India*, pp. 172–3.
113. *KM*, p. 22.
114. Ibid., p. 34.
115. Ibid., p. 151.
116. See religion.
117. R.C. Majumdar, *History of Bengal*, Chapter XI; N.K. Dutt in *Age of Imperial Kannauj*, pp. 270 f.
118. N.K. Dutt, op. cit., p. 267.
119. *KM*, p. 22.
120. Ibid., p. 191.
121. Ibid., p. 197.
122. Ibid., pp. 195–7; V.S. Agrawala, *KM*, pt. ii, p. 127.
123. तीए भणियं अज्जउत्त, किर एत्थ णत्थि फलं, वादो चेय केवलं। कुमारेण भणियं 'मा एवं भणह'। Ibid., p. 197.
124. अवि चलइ मेरु-चूला सुर-सरिया अवि वहेज्ज विवरीया।
ण य होज्ज किं चि अलियं जं जोणी-पाहुडे रइयं।। Ibid.
125. Ibid.
126. भगव सव्वण्णू जेण एयं सव्वं जोणीपाहुडं भणियं। Ibid.
127. णमोक्कारिया सव्व-जय-बंधवो जिणवरिंदा, पणमिया सिद्धा। *KM*, p. 196.
128. J.C. Jain, *Prākrit Sāhitya kā Itihās*, p. 673.
129. *Kāmasūtra*, I.3.16.
130. *Kādambarī*, p. 227.
131. P.C. Ray, *History of Hindu Chemistry*, Introduction, pp. xxxix–xl.
132. *KM*, p. 104.
133. Ibid., p. 151.
134. Sachau, I, pp. 187 f.
135. Ibid., p. 188.
136. Devasthali in *Age of Imperial Kannauj*, p. 198; *Struggle for Empire*, p. 328.
137. पायय-पाढया . . . सक्कय पाढया . . . अण्णे भारह-सत्थ-पत्तट्ठा . . . पत्त-छेज्ज-पत्तट्ठा . . . चित्तयम्म-कुसला। *KM*, p. 16.
138. *Kāvyamīmāṃsā*, pp. 54–5; Introduction, pp. xxxvi–xxxvii.
139. See popular beliefs and superstitions.
140. Supra, p. 232. Alberuni also states that the brāhmaṇas recited the Vedas without understanding its meaning. Sachau, I, p. 125. The *Dharmaśāstra* writers did not approve of such a practice and various authorities such as Manu, Śabara, Dakṣa, Viśvarūpa and Aparārka condemn the mere memorisation of the Vedas and insist on comprehension of its meaning. Cf. Kane, *HD*, II (i), p. 357.
141. *KM*, p. 34.
142. See above.
143. See Chapter 8.

144. *KM*, pp. 3–4.
145. पालित्तय-सालाहण-छप्पण्णय-सीह-णाय-सद्देहिं ।
संखुद-मुद्ध-सारंगओ व्व मह ता पयं देमि ।। Ibid., p. 3.
146. Ibid.
147. Ibid.
148. Ibid.
149. Ibid.
150. Ibid.
151. Ibid.
152. Ibid.
153. Ibid.
154. Ibid.
155. Ibid.
156. Ibid.
157. Ibid., p. 4.
158. Ibid.
159. Ibid.
160. Pādalipta's work enjoyed great reputation, and is mentioned by various works such as the *Anuyogadvārasūtra* (fifth century), *Niśītha Cūrṇi* (AD 676), *Daśavaikālika Cūrṇi*, Dhanapāla, author of *Tilakamañjarī* (tenth century), and *Prabhāvakacarita* (thirteenth century). J.C. Jain, *Prākrit Sāhitya kā Itihās*, pp. 376–7.
161. A.N. Upadhye, 'Prākrit Language and Literature', in *Cultural Heritage of India*, Vol. V, p. 173. Bāṇa evidently refers to the work when he says that Sātavāhana made an immortal treasure (*kośa*) of songs adorned with fine expressions of character like jewels. *Harṣacarita*, Introductory verse 13; Translation Cowell, p. 2.
162. A.N. Upadhye, op. cit., *Cultural Heritage of India*, Vol. V, p. 174.
163. Keith, *History of Sanskrit Literature*, pp. 267–8.
164. These are the *Bṛhatkathāślokasaṃgraha* (*c.* eighth century AD) *Bṛhatkathāmañjarī* of Kṣemendra (eleventh century) and *Kathāsaritasāgara* of Somadeva (eleventh century). Respectful references to Guṇāḍhya's *Bṛhatkathā* by Subandhu, Bāṇa and Daṇḍin attest to the importance attached to it in the seventh century. Keith, *History of Sanskrit Literature*, pp. 266, 272 f.
165. N.R. Premi, *Jaina Sāhitya aur Itihās*, p. 88.
166. Jinasena also praises the *Padamcaritā* of Raviṣeṇa in his *Harivaṃśapurāṇa* (vs 840), five years after Uddyotana. Ibid.
167. Ibid., p. 420; A.N. Upadhye, *KM*, pt. II, p. 126.
168. N.R. Premi, *Jaina Sāhitya aur Itihās*, pp. 123, 138.
169. Introduction to *Varāṅgacarita*, ed. Upadhye, Bombay, 1983.
170. N.R. Premi, op. cit., p. 421; Upadhye, *KM*, pt. II, p. 126.
171. In the tenth century Somadeva narrates the story in his *Yaśastilaka* and Puṣpadanta in his Apabhraṃśa work *Jasaharacariu*, which indicates its

popularity amonst the Jainas. Handiqui, *Yaśastilaka and Indian Cutlure*, Chapter III.

172. A.N. Jpadhye, *KM*, pt. II, p. 79.
173. *KM*, p. 16.
174. Ibid., p. 55.
175. Ibid., p. 63.
176. Ibid., pp. 151–2.
177. A.N. Upadhye, *KM*, pt. II, p. 79.
178. *KM*, p. 23.
179. Ibid., p. 47.
180. Ibid., p. 59.
181. *KM*, p. 71; A.N. Upadhye, *KM*, pt. II, p. 77.
182. पश्चिमेनापभ्रंशिन: कवय: । *Kāvyamīmāṃsā*, p. 55.
183. सापभ्रंशप्रयोगा: सकलमरू । Ibid., p. 51.
184. *Karpūra.*, I. 7.
185. *Bālarāmayaṇa*, Act I, 10; qd. p. xliii, Introduction to *Kāvyamīmāṃsā*.
186. पूर्वेण प्राकृता: कवय: । *Kāvyamīmāṃsā*, p. 54.
187. A.B. Keith, *Sanskrit Drama*, p. 335.
188. D. Sharma, *RTTA*, p. 517.
189. Jacobi, Introduction to the *SK*, pp. xi–xii.
190. Ibid.
191. *KM*, p. 214.
192. Ibid., p. 198.
193. Ibid., p. 175.
194. Ibid., p. 116.
195. Ibid., p. 103.
196. Ibid., p. 48. In the tenth century, Siddharṣi Sūri composed the *Upamitibhava-prapañcākathā* in Sanskrit because it had found a place 'in the hearts of vain people' who thought slightingly of Prākrit and 'one should delight as many people as possible'. *Upamiti.*, I.51–2.
197. Ghaṭiyālā inscription no. 1 of Kakkuka, vs 918; *EI*, IX, pp. 279 f.
198. *KM*, p. 4.
199. Ibid., p. 71.
200. *Kāvyamīmaṃsā*, p. 55.
201. *KM*, p. 22.
202. A.N Upadhye, *KM*, pt. II, p. 77.
203. *KM*, pp. 152–3.4. V.S. Agrawala (*KM*, pt. II, p. 124) and J.C. Jaina (*Prākrit Sāhitya ka Itihās*) identify Golla as the region of Godāvarī. But A.N. Upadhye takes Gollas to be in itenerant tribe. Upadhye (*KM*, pt. II, p. 144) identifies Dhakka as Ṭakka or Punjab but V.S. Agrawala would identify it with Dacca. Tājikas are identified as Persians or Arabs by Upadhye (op. cit.) but Tāpti by V.S. Agrawala (op. cit.) Kīras are identified as Kashmiris by Upadhye (op. cit.) but Kulu and Kangra by V.S. Agrawala.
204. दिव्वं दिव्वमानुसं मानुसं च । *SK*, p. 2.

205. अत्थकहा, कामकहा, धम्मकहा, संकिणकहा च। Ibid., pp. 3–4.
206. Ibid., p. 3.
207. दिव्वमानुसवत्थुगयं धम्मकहं। Ibid., p. 4.
208. *KM*, p. 4.
209. अक्खेवणी मणोणुकूला, विक्खेवणी मणो-पडिकूला, संवेग-जणणी णाणुप्पत्ति-कारणं, णिव्वेय-जणणी उण वेरग्गुप्पत्ती। Ibid.
210. Ibid., pp. 4–5.
211. *Kāvyānuśāsana*, pp. 463–5, qd. A.N. Upadhye, *KM*, pt. II, p. 127.
212. *Kāvyānuśāsana*, op. cit.
213. Jacobi, Introduction to *SK*, pp. xxii ff.
214. *Dhū.*, V. 23.
215. A.N. Upadhye, Introduction to the *Dhū.*, pp. 12–25.
216. Ibid., pp. 20, 22.
217. J.C. Jain, *Prākrit Sāhitya kā Itihās*, pp. 211–13, 416.
218. The *Daśakumāracaritam* pictures hypocritical ascetics, fraudulent priests, cunning bawds and Buddhist nuns acting as procuresses.
219. S.K. De, *History of Sanskrit Literature*, Vol. 1, pp. 197, 207 f.
220. S.K. De, op. cit., p. 197; A.B. Keith, *History of Sanskrit Literature*, pp. 236–7.
221. His novels *Kalāvilāsa, Darpadalana, Narmamālā, Deśopadeśa* and *Samayamātrikā* are bitter satires on corrupt bureacracy and successful deceit and vice, as practised by bawds, quacks, dishonest traders, and so forth. A.K. Warder, 'Classical Literature' in Basham ed. *Cultural History of India*, p. 192; S.K. De, op. cit., pp. 404 f.
222. S.K. De, *History of Sanskrit Literature*, Vol. 1, p. 410.
223. *Dhū.*, V. 120–2.
224. A.N. Upadhye, *KM*, pt. II, pp. 84, 110.
225. S.K. De, op. cit., p. 434.
226. These include the *Nalacampū* of Trivikrama bhaṭṭa, whom we know as the author of the Nausari inscription of Rāṣṭrakūṭa Indra III, AD 915, and the *Yaśastilaka* of Somadeva, the Digambara saint, AD 959. A.B. Keith, *History of Sanskrit Literature*, pp. 332–3.
227. *KM*, pp. 66, l.19 f.; 82, l.12 f.; 214, l.6 f., etc.
228. Ibid., pp. 7, 26 f.; pp. 8, l.8 f.; pp. 121, l.1 f.
229. Ibid., pp. 7, 17 f.; pp. 14, l.26 f., pp. 69, l.16 f.; pp. 73, 1.3 f.
230. Upadhye, *KM*, pt. II, p. 85.
231. *KM*, p. 4.
232. A.N. Upadhye, *KM*, pt. II, pp. 86 f.
233. Nemichandra Shastri, *Haribhadra kā Prākrit Kathā Sāhitya*, pp. 195–6.
234. A.N Upadhye, *KM*, pt. II, p. 87.
235. Jacobi, Introduction to the *SK*, p. xx.
236. सो सट्टओ त्ति भणइ दूरं जो णाडिआइ अणुहरइ।
किं उण पवेसविक्खम्भङ्काई केवलं ण दीसन्ति। I.6.

237. *Karpūra.*; A.B. Keith, *Sanskrit Drama*, p. 232.
238. सट्टअं णच्चिदव्वं। *Karpūra.*, I.4.
239. Hultzsch, *ZDMG*, XL, 66, no. 50; qd. A.B. Keith, *Sanskrit Drama*, p. 350; Konow, *Karpūra.*, p. 195; C. Chakravarti 'Characteristics of the *saṭṭaka* form of drama', *IHQ*, VII, i, p. 169.
240. Keith, *Sanskrit Drama*, p. 238.
241. *Karpūra.*, II, 30 f.
242. Keith, *Sanskrit Drama*, pp. 236 f.; Konow, Introductory essay in *Karpūra.*, pp. 205–7.
243. *Karpūra.*, I. 18.
244. Ibid., I. 18.
245. See festivals.
246. See Bharhut stūpa above.
247. J.C. Jain, *Prākrit Sāhitya kā Itihās*, p. 627.
248. *Agni*, 338.2.
249. J.C. Jain, *Prākrit Sāhitya kā Itihās*, p. 627; C. Chakravarti, op. cit., p. 170.
250. *Kāvyānuśāsana*, p. 444.
251. Those are the *Candralekhā* by Rudradāsa, resident of Calicut (seventeenth century), *Ānandasundarī* by Ghanashyāma, born at Tanjore (eighteenth century), and *Śṛṅgāramañjarī* of Viśvesvara, resident of Almora (*c.* eighteenth century.) J.C. Jain, op. cit., pp. 630–3; A.N. Upadhye, Prākrit Language and Literature, *Cultural Heritage of India*, V, p. 168.

11

Conclusion

RAJASTHAN HAD MUCH in common with other parts of India, in terms of broad patterns of social and cultural development. It shared with them the growing character of feudal polity, tantric influences, popularity of pilgrimages, beliefs in omens and superstitions and traditional features of social life such as the caste system, the joint family structure, dependence of women, love of ornaments, etc. Part of this social and cultural affinity was derived from their inheritance of a common historical heritage. The earliest Aryan civilisation had flourished along the banks of the river Sarasvatī. Later, as a part of the Mauryan empire as well as under the sphere of Śaka, Kuṣāṇa and Gupta influence successively, the socio-cultural contacts continued, fostering evolution of similar social values and traditions. The coming of the Pratihāras led to a long lasting political unification with other parts of northern India. The sense of belonging to a larger entity, transcending the local unit, was thus never lost. The acquaintance of Uddyotana with the works of Hāla, Bāṇa as well as the *Padmacarita* and *Varāṅgacarita*, written as late as the seventh century in Karnataka, indicate flourishing inter-regional cultural contacts.

Nevertheless geographical features, relative isolation and differences of historical experience had invested the region with a uniqueness of its own. As already pointed above, the harsh climate bred a people hardy, vigorous and mentally alert. The undependable character of agriculture made sole dependence on agrarian economy unpracticable and encouraged them to adopt additional means of employment and subsistence such as trade and industry from early times. The geographical position of Rajasthan between northern India and Gujarat as well as its natural resources also facilitated the growth of trade and industry, to which the peace and order under the Pratihāras gave a further stimulus. Rajasthan, with the establishment of territorial monarchy in place of disunited republican states, was more united and more progressive than ever before and consequently, though urbanism has been deduced to have declined in various other parts of the country, Rajasthan saw a fresh wave of urbanism. Many of the ancient towns had declined by the eighth century. Some like Rangmahal were probably evacuated because of the disappearance of the river Sarasvatī. Rairh and Nagara lost their importance when they no longer remained centres of administrative power as the tribal power of the Mālavas declined. Archaeological excavations and local traditions suggest that many areas in Rajasthan including Mādhyamikā, Pushkara, Rairh, Naliāsar and Nagara suffered greatly due to Hūṇa invasion. But in their place arose new towns, some as administrative headquarters and capitals of the various ruling dynasties which now came to the fore and grew to be multifarious in character, centres of educational, religious and commercial activity as Bhīnmāl, Mandor, Ḍīḍwānā, Cāṭsū and others. Agricultural prosperity generated by improved irrigational facilities and encouragement by the ruler, as well as extension of cultivation by rehabilitation of land previously rendered uninhabitable by the predatory activities of tribals, produced food surplus capable of supporting an urban population. The distant ventures of an enterprising class of traders and the activities of artisans who turned out specialised craft products, contributed to urban prosperity. The disapproval of agriculture by Haribhadra indicates that Jainism, with its strict insistence on non-violence from early times, was even now a religion more acceptable to the traders than the agriculturists, and the flourishing state of Jainism is symptomatic of a thriving mercantile economy.

In Rajasthan because of the constant influx of foreigners from the north-west which threatened to disturb the social order and due to closer contact with the villages and towns caused by the expansion of territorial states a greater need might have been felt to preserve the essentials of the ancient social structure by adherence to the fourfold caste system. Social stability seems to have been maintained by incorporating non-aryans into the society and keeping the avenues of social mobility open in a bid to assimilate diverse social groups. The miscellaneous composition of the Rajput class shows that the people of Rajasthan rose above caste rigidity and lived in a mobile society. Their assimilative and liberal attitude had its roots in the past, when Rajasthan had successfully absorbed the various republican tribes such as the Mālavas, Yaudheyas and Arjunāyanas which had immigrated therein in the wake of Alexander's invasion.

Another distinctive feature of Rajasthan was the popularity of Jainism, which had declined in other parts of northern India. Under the leadership of reformers like Haribhadra and Uddyotana, it set a high moral tone for its followers and disapproved of caste pride. While Digambara Jainism, which flourished in the south, had come to hold śūdras ineligible for initiation the *ācāryas* of Rajasthan gave initiation to the śūdras. Literature received an impetus from them. Works of great literary value were composed in Prākrit. Rationalism was encouraged. Haribhadra rejected the brahmanical religious myths because they were irrational and upheld Jainism on the ground that it was rational, not merely because it was preached by Jina. The grosser practices of tantricism could not make headway into Jainism. Jainism encouraged monogamy. These healthy features must have had a beneficial effect on society as a whole.

In certain fields, developments in earlier centuries, some common to various parts of India, some peculiar to Rajasthan, especially the seventh-century Rajasthan, had already set in motion forces which manifested themselves in full form in the eighth and ninth centuries. The establishment of Cāpa, Pratihāra, Guhila and Maurya kingdoms in the seventh-century Rajasthan indicates the process of expansion of a territorial polity into tribal areas.[1] Epigraphic references to feudatory titles held by Devagaṇa, Bhāvihita and Bābhaṭa, rulers of the Kiṣkindhā line of the Guhilas,[2] as well as Rajjila, chief of Aṛbudadeśa, feudatory of Varmalāta,[3] all belonging to the seventh century, indicate the emergence of feudalism. The rise of urbanism was facilitated by use of artificial irrigation as indicated by use of *araghaṭṭa*,[4] activities of merchants as recorded by the Sāmolī inscription, Vasantgarh inscription and Dūṅgarpur plate,[5] and exploitation of mineral resources as recorded by the Sāmolī inscription,[6] all again of the seventh century. Though knowledge of early Rājasthānī society is inadequate, many unhealthy features such as caste exclusiveness, low position of women and neglect of their education, evils of polygamy, pitiable position of widows, beliefs in omens and superstitions were present in earlier periods in India. Other features such as syncretism, toleration, charity, pilgrimage, idol worship, temple worship, popularity of purāṇic deities and improvement in the position of the śūdras characterised the Gupta period.

Surveying the social and cultural history of the period as a whole we find that the ancient social framework of caste system was retained, presumably to keep away social chaos, ensure observance of social duties and the continuity of cultural values, while various social adjustments were made to suit the changing conditions. Brāhmaṇas continued to hold the foremost position in society, in their roles as scholars, ministers, and custodians of the sacred law, though their special legal privileges and political influence of the priest appears to have suffered a diminution in the urban milieu. Land grants, which formed an important constituent of the popular practice of charity providing them with a substantial means of subsistence, made them landholders and associated them with agriculture. A privileged status was claimed for the caste as a whole but in actual practice it appears to have been accorded largely only to those who were learned and deserving. Kṣatriyas who wielded royal power naturally enjoyed a high status in society, rivalling that of the brāhmaṇas, but the composition of the ruling class appears to have been miscellaneous, with non-kṣatriyas including vaiśyas and tribals gaining a place in the order of warriors. Members of the warrior class known as *rājapūtras* and *ṭhakkuras* emerged as members of the landed aristocracy as rulers bestowed land grants on them in return for their services. The vaiśyas of Rajasthan who largely turned to trade as their vocation enjoyed an influential position in society and even political authority by virtue of their wealth, entrepreneurship, education and beneficence notwithstanding their low ritual status. They sometimes deviated from traditional vaiśya duties by taking up feudal military service. Some śūdras took up trade and gained wealth, thereby attaining a respectable status in society as well as gaining the valuable religious right to perform *pūrtadharma*. Peasant and artisan members of the śūdra community appear to have been relatively well off with the agricultural prosperity and flourishing state of arts and crafts. The *antyajas* stood lowest in the social scale, with the higher classes treating them with contempt and regarding them as untouchables. Aboriginal members of the *mleccha* class who lived by brigandry and followed a cruel, unethical way of life were feared, despised and kept at a distance. But the process of socio-religious assimilation of the *mlecchas* was on with their being variously absorbed as military commanders, subordinate feudal chiefs, members of the royal court and *antyajas* in accordance with their capability whilst bloody rituals and tantric practices current amongst them gained a place in Hinduism.

Tantricism and Jainism, which did not recognise caste distinctions in matters of religion, and feudalism, which overrode caste prejudices in development of feudal ties, were conducive to a partial amelioration in the position of the lower orders. Marriages were generally arranged within the same caste, but instances of *anuloma* marriages indicate that caste rules regarding intermarriage were not very rigid. In the liberal atmosphere of towns, the qualifications of the bridegroom rather than the caste were at times regarded to be the decisive factors for settling a marriage. Rules regarding inter-dining were not very strict and the brāhmaṇas partook the food of śūdras on ceremonial occasions.

Sāmantas, constituting an influential section of society rendered military service and tribute to the ruler, attended his court and participated in his socio-religious activities. They played a decisive role in royal succession. Some became very powerful and revolted. Bonds of feudal kinship developed between landlord and vassals as well as between co-vassals, bringing together kṣatriyas, vaiśyas and tribals in a close feudal bond that set aside caste prejudices. The class of vassals included *ṭhakkura* and *rājapūtras* who received grants of land in lieu of military service as well as defeated rulers. *Olagā*, a new term, indicating feudal military service, marked an important stage in feudal development. Rewarded by hereditary grants of land entailing hereditary service at times, it was sometimes adopted because of economic compulsion.

The joint family headed by its patriarch was generally prevalent. It served a useful purpose by providing socio-economic security to the younger members and widows. The son had a special position in the family as he served to perpetuate the family and was considered to be a religious necessity. Women held a respected position as wives and mothers. The birth of a daughter was not so welcome as that of a boy, but she was well brought up. Princesses and women serving in royal courts were highly accomplished in fine arts, had well developed literary skills and cultural interests but the education of women in general declined. References to royal *svayaṃvaras*, post-puberty arranged marriages and love marriages side by side with mention of vaiśya child widows and pre-puberty marriages amongst brāhmaṇas indicate that the age of marriage was variable. The evils of polygamy and *satī* flourished. Widow remarriage was not in vogue and the life of a widow who lived on after her husband's death was miserable. The theory of perpetual tutelage held ground. Women who left the world and joined the brahmanical and Jaina monastic orders were highly revered. Exemption from capital punishment was an important legal privilege held by women.

Toleration was one of the marked features of religious life. Religious competition though present was not acrimonious. Criticism of other faiths did not go to fanatical limits. Even as Vedic sacrifices continued to form a part of brahmanical religion, the Vedic gods receded to the background. Viṣṇu, visualised as the consort of Lakṣmī, conceived as a redeemer in his Varāha and Vāmana forms, as well as Kṛṣṇa, whose marvellous deeds and youthful life while appealing to the popular imagination facilitated the assimilation of tribals, enjoyed considerable popularity. So did Śiva, worshipped in the Umāpati, *ardhanārīśvara, liṅga* and terrific forms. The absorption of tantric elements by Śaivism as expressed in the association of tantricism with the famed temple of Mahākāla, and the development of the Kāpālika sect which acquired prominence as well as respectability while holding out the prospect of the attainment of miraculous powers, served to further popularise Śaivism amongst both the lower and higher strata of society. Śakti, visualised as the manifestation of supreme power, was widely worshipped in some form or the other as Lakṣmī, Śrī, Durgā, Kātyāyanī, Mahiṣāsuramardinī, Gaurī, Caṇḍikā and Cāmuṇḍa. Bloody rituals attending her worship as Caṇḍikā and Kātyāyanī by the aryanised people indicate the assimilation of the fierce cult of the non-aryans, amongst whom she was popularly worshipped with offerings of human and animal flesh. Goddesses occupied a pre-eminent position in Jainism as well. Tantric ideas found universal acceptance. Mystic practices acquired special significance and were believed to be conducive to success and attainment of supernatural powers. They were widely practised by various sects, brahmanical as well as Jaina. The development facilitated the absorption of tribals into the brahmanical fold. But it also set an unhealthy trend as it encouraged people to attach less importance to religious and moral observances as a means of attainment of spiritual and temporal goals and rely instead on mystic practices. The grosser practices of *pañcatattva* worship also made their appearance in the extremist sect of the Kaulas but society by and large remained free from erotic rites and their detrimental influences. Jainism flourished due to the dedicated efforts of its *ācāryas* who condemning the luxurious life of the *caityavāsins*, led an itinerant monastic life, thereby establishing widespread contact with the masses whom they edified through simple religious tales. Zealous Jaina monks performed severe penances and observed the practice of *sallekhanā*, which must have won them the respect and admiration of the people. The absorption of theistic traits as expressed in the belief in the accrual of rich rewards through devotion to Jina and worship of his idol, as well as appearance of tantric elements such as the conception of yakṣiṇīs, attendant spirits of tīrthaṅkaras as bestowers of occult powers, who were propitiated by tantric rites, further helped in popularising Jainism.

The provision of *pūrtadharma* for higher castes as well as śūdras as a means of securing spiritual progress by the brahmanical religion was a commendable feature, encouraging the establishment of works of public utility and charity. People of all four castes engaged themselves in acts of benevolence, distributing liberal charities and excavating wells and ponds. Jaina *dāna*, consisting of the gifts of knowledge, security and gifts of useful things to the religious was different in character. Pilgrimage had an important place in contemporary socio-religious life. A visit to *tīrthas* was believed to bring absolution from sins and cure incurable diseases. By bringing together people of different regions, castes and classes at the *tīrthas*, pilgrimages promoted social, cultural and regional integration. To those who visited it with devotion it granted spiritual solace. Beside the ancient *tīrthas* of long standing sanctity new *tīrthas* with Śaivite and tantric associations had come into existence. The discreditable practice of religious suicide at *tīrthas* was current during this period, as in the earlier. Great significance was attached to socio-religious rites performed at the time of birth, marriage and death. They were regarded as auspicious and beneficial for this world as well as the other and deemed to lend sanctity to a marriage.

The high standard of cleanliness and elaborate toilet cultivated in Gupta times was maintained during our period. People decorated themselves with manifold unguents, flowers and ornaments. A wide variety of textiles was in use. Society was partly vegetarian and partly non-vegetarian. The kṣatriyas enjoyed taking meat. Brāhmaṇas also took meat at *śrāddhas*. New meat dishes such as fried fish and roast mutton are mentioned in our works. Men and women both drank wine especially on festive occasions, but there appears to be no addiction to drinking. Betel-chewing was common. The people had a lively spirit and liked to enjoy life. There were many occasions of social and religious festivity when members of both sexes sang, danced, visited gardens and made merry. The rich cultivated fine arts like painting and drama, amused themselves with riddles and played with the dice. There was a general belief in various sciences of prognostication.

Villages and towns were equally prosperous. The prosperity of villages emnated from their agricultural productivity, efficient techniques of irrigation such as the *araghaṭṭa*, cattle wealth and rural traders. Craft specialisation, widespread internal and external trade and the prevalence of money economy contributed to urban affluence. A broad and secular outlook characterised the urban people who utilised their leisure time in the cultivation of artistic and literary pursuits. Rich towns-folk lived in great luxury. Amidst even greater grandeur dwelt the ruler who was a patron of learning and surrounded himself with experts from different fields. People exercised a say in their administration, in villages through *grāmamahattaras* and in towns, through *nagaramahallakas* and the *pañcakula.*

The system of education was comprehensive and aimed at imparting knowledge of vocational as well as non-vocational subjects. New subjects of study such as *tantra, dhātuvāda* and *rasāyana* and other occult subjects had made way into the educational curriculum. Brahmanical *maṭhas* providing secular education became great centres of education to which students flocked from far and wide. Sanskrit enjoyed the distinction of being the language of the learned. In recognition of this development, Jaina scholars adopted the Sanskrit language as a medium for reaching the educated circles. They also incorporated forms of Apabhraṃśa and whole passages in Apabhraṃśa, the living language, in their narration of popular Prākrit tales keeping in mind the interests of the unlettered people of the countryside who could not read or understand the literary language of scholars. Even illiterate men and women could thus imbibe information and ideas. Various regional dialects had become part of the spoken speech.

Thus the period was characterised by the growth of feudalism, Jainism and tantricism as powerful forces which operating against the backdrop of urbanisation transcended caste distinctions in matters of religion and feudal ties. They aided the liberal and assimilative forces in society, working against the oppressiveness of caste rules, and facilitating the absorption of tribals; the latter process was also promoted by the incorporation of various tribal cults by the Purāṇic sects as well. The reformist activity of Jaina saints who laid emphasis on the observance of ethical values rather than observance of caste rules and sought to eradicate the corruption of the church set a healthy trend which subsequently bore fruition in the *vidhicaitya* movement of the *Khartaragaccha* spearheaded by Jineśvarasūri, Abhayadevasūri (eleventh century), Jinavallabhasūri (twelfth century) and Jinadatta Sūri (twelfth century), purging the Jaina church of many evil practices. The Jaina teachers' appeal to rationalism rather than blind faith, the religious toleration, advocacy of *pūrtadharma*, the establishment of brahmanical centres of learning endowed with a catholic outlook, the recognition of the merit of non-vocational courses of study were commendable features. So was the output of imaginative literature, which in touch with common life was instructive as well as entertaining, while incorporating forms, vocabulary and expressions drawn from Apabhraṃśa and *deśī* stock so that it appealed not only to intellectuals but catered to the tastes and sentiments of the masses as well. The territorial polity of the Pratihāras, practices like *tīrthayātrā* (pilgrimage), use of Sanskrit as a literary language in intellectual circles, existence of centres of education to which students from different regions flocked, as well as flourishing trade centres in which traders from far flung areas gathered served as integrating forces, promoting inter-regional contacts.

There were disturbing trends as well. Tantricism inculcated belief in the efficacy of mystic practices. Feudalism encouraged centrifugal tendencies when the centre was weak. Devotion was conducive to blind faith. Belief in astrology, omens etc. bred a fatalistic outlook. The practice of *sati*, polygamy, absence of widow remarriage and neglect of women's education kept the position of women low. The continuance of the association of untouchability with certain sections of society was most unfair.

Notes and References

1. Cf. B.D. Chattopadhyaya, 'Origin of the Rajputs: The Political Economic and Social Processes in Early Medieval Rajasthan', *IHR,* No. I, p. 63.
2. The inscription of Bhāvihita, AD 653 describes Devagaṇa as *avāpta-aśeṣa-mahāśabda* Devagaṇa and Bhāvihita as *samadhigata-pañca-mahāśabda.* The Dungarpur plate of AD 689 describes Bābhaṭa as *samupārjita-pañca-mahāśabda*; D.C. Sircar, *Guhilas of Kiṣkindhā,* p. 58.
3. Vasantgarh inscription of Varmalāta, AD 625; *EI,* IX, p. 191.
4. Ḍabok inscription, AD 644; *EI,* XX, pp. 122 f.
5. Sāmolī inscription, AD 646; *EI, XX,* pp. 97 f.; Vasantgarh inscription, AD 625, *EI,* IX, p. 191; Dungarpur plate of Bābhaṭa, AD 689.
6. Sāmolī inscription mentions that the mahajana community started an *āgara* (mine), which became a source of livelihood for the people: *EI,* XX, pp. 97 f.

Bibliography

ORIGINAL SOURCES

Abhijñāna Śākuntalam of Kālidāsa, with Rāghavabhaṭṭa's Gloss, 12th edn., NSP, Bombay, 1958.

Ācārāṅga Sūtra, ed. with English translation by H. Jacobi, Sacred Books of the East, Vol. XXII.

Agni Purāṇa, Eng. trans. M.N. Dutt, Calcutta, 1903.

Amarakośa or Nāmaliṅgānuśāsana of Amara Singh, ed. with commentary of Bhaṭṭakṣīrasvāmin by A.D. Sharma and N.G. Sardesai, Poona, 1941.

Aṅgavijjā, ed. Muni Puṇyavijaya, Banaras, 1957.

Arthaśāstra of Kauṭilya, ed. R.P. Kangle, part I, text, Bombay, 1960; part II, ed. R.P. Kangle, English translation with notes, Bombay, 1963.

Aupapātika Sūtra, with Abhayadevasūri's vritti, pub. by Nirnayasagara, Bombay, 1916.

Bhagavatī Ārādhanā of Ācārya Śivārya, ed. K.C. Shastri, Sholapur, 1978, 2 Vols.

Bṛhaspati Smṛti, trans. J. Jolly, SBE, Vol. XXIII, Oxford, 1889, rep. Delhi, 1965.

Bṛhatsaṃhitā of Varāhamihira, ed. with Eng. trans. and notes by V. Subrahmanya Sastri and M. Ramakrishna Bhatt, 2 Vols., Bangalore, 1947.

Bṛhatkathākośa of Hariṣeṇa, ed. A.N. Upadhye, Bombay, 1943.

Bṛhatkathāmañjarī of Kṣemendra, ed. Śivadatta and K.P. Parab, Bombay, 1931.

Caṇḍakauśika of Kṣemīśvara, ed. Jivananda Vidyanagara Bhattacharya, Calcutta, 1931.

Daśakumāracaritam of Daṇḍin, 2nd edn., Chowkhamba Series, Varanasi, 1958.

Devīmāhātmya, ed. and translated by V.S. Agrawala, Varanasi, 1963.

Dhūrtākhyāna of Haribhadra Sūri, ed. Jinavijaya Muni, Bombay, 1944.

Harṣacarita of Bāṇa, ed. K.P. Parab, Bombay, 1925; English translation by E.B. Cowell and F.W. Thomas, Motilal Banarsidass, Delhi, 1961.

Kādambarī of Bāṇa, ed. Peterson, part I, text, Bombay, 1900; Hindi translation by R. Shastri, Kāśī, 1959.

Kalpa Sūtra, English translation by H. Jacobi, Sacred Books of the East, Vol. XXII, Delhi, 1980.

Kāmasūtra of Vātsyāyana with commentary Jayamangala, ed. D.L. Goswami, Banaras, 1929; Eng. trans. by Dr B.N. Basu, revised by R.L. Ghosh, 5th edn., Calcutta, 1944.

Karpūramañjarī of Rājaśekhara, ed. Sten Konow, translated by Lanman, 2nd issue, 1963.

Kaulajñānanirṇaya, ed. P.C. Bagchi, Calcutta, 1934.

Kāvyamīmāṃsā of Rājaśekhara, ed. C.D. Dalal and R.A. Sastri, 3rd edn., Bombay, 1934.

Kṛtyakalpataru of Lakṣmīdhara, ed. K.V.R. Aiyangar, 14 Vols., Gos., Baroda.

Kūrma Purāṇa, ed. N. Mukhopadhyaya, Calcutta, 1890.

Kuvalayamālā of Uddyotana Suri, ed. A.N. Upadhye, part I, Prākrit text, Bombay, 1959; ed. A.N. Upadhye, part II, Introduction, Cultural note and Ratnaprabha Sūri's *Kuvalayamālākathā*, Bombay, 1970.

Mahābhārata, 6 Vols., published Gita Press, Gorakhpur.

Mālatīmādhava of Bhavabhūti, with Sanskrit and Hindi commentaries by Sesrajasarmasastri, Chowkhamba Sanskrit Series, Banaras, 1954.

Mānasāra, trans. P.K. Acharya, Allahabad, 1933.

Manu Smṛti, trans. Sir William Jones, Calcutta, 1974.

Medhātithi's commentary on *Manu*, translated by Ganganath Jha, 1922–29.

Mitākṣara (Commentary by Vijñāneśvara on Yajñavalkya), ed. J.R. Gharpure, Bombay, 1914; trans. J.R. Gharpure, Bombay, 1936 ff.

Nārada Smṛti, trans. J. Jolly, SBE, Vol. XXIII, rep. Delhi, 1965.

Prabhāvakacaritā of Prabhācandra, ed. H.M. Sharma, Bombay, 1909; ed. Muni Jinavijaya, SJS, Calcutta, 1940.

Prabodhacandrodaya of Kṛṣṇamiśra, ed. Misra, Banaras, 1955.

Pṛthvīrājavijaya of Jayānaka, ed. by G.H. Ojha and C. Guleri, Ajmer, 1941.

Raghuvaṃśa of Kālidāsa with Mallināthaś Commentary, ed. N.R. Acarya; N.S.P., Bombay, 1948; ed. with Eng. trans. by G.R. Nandargikar, 3rd edn., Bombay, 1897.

Rājataraṅgiṇī of Kalhaṇa, ed. Durga Prasad, Bombay, 1892; Eng. trans. by M.A. Stein, London, 1900; rep. Delhi, 1961.

Rāmāyaṇa of Vālmīki, Eng. trans. by M.N. Dutt, 3 Vols., Calcutta, 1892–93.

Ratnakaraṇḍaka Śravakācāra of Samantabhadra, ed. J.K. Mukhtiar, Vīra Sevā Mandir, Delhi, 1955.

Ṣaḍdarśana-samuccaya of Haribhadra, ed. by Goswami Damodara Sastri, Banaras, 1957.

Samarāiccakahā of Haribhadra Sūri, ed. Dr H. Jacobi, Vol. I, text and introduction, Calcutta, 1926; ed. Pandit Bhagwandas with Sanskrit chāyā, part I, 1938; ed., Paṅdit Bhagwandas with Sanskrit chāyā, part II, 1942.

Samarāṅganasūtradhāra, ed. T. Gaṇapati Sastri, Baroda, 1924–25.

Sarvārthasiddhi of Pujyapāda, ed. and trans. by Phūlchand Śāstri, Bhāratīya Jñānapītha, Kāśī, 1955.

Śiśupālavadha of Māgha, ed. Durgaprasad, Bombay, 1957.

Skanda Purāṇa, Hindi trans., Lucknow, 1908–10.

Smṛtisandarbha, Vol. I; Manu Smṛti, Nārada Smṛti, Atri Smṛti, Atrisaṃhitā, Viṣṇu Smṛti, Saṃvarta Smṛti, Dakṣa Smṛti, Aṅgiras Smṛti, Śatātapa Smṛti, Calcutta, 1952.

Smṛtisandarbha, Vol. II; Parāśara, Bṛhatparāśara, Laghuhārita and Vṛddhahārita Smṛtis.

Smṛtisandarbha, Vol. III, Yājñavalkya, Kātyāyana, Āpastamba, Laghuśaṃkha, Śaṃkha, Likhita, Śaṃkhalikhita, Vasiṣṭha, Auśnas Saṃhitā, Auśnas Smṛti and Bṛhaspati Smṛtis.

Sthānāṅga, ed. and commented by Muni Nathmal, pub. by Jaina Viśvabhāratī, Lāḍnū, 1976.

Sūtrakṛtāṅga, English translation by H. Jacobi, Sacred Books of the East, Vol. XLV, Delhi, 1980.

Tattvārthasūtra, ed. by Phulachanda siddhāntaśāstri, Banares, VS 2476.

Upamitibhavaprapañcākathā of Siddharṣi Sūri, ed. P. Peterson and H. Jacobi, Calcutta, 1899.

Uttarādhyayana Sūtra, English translation by H. Jacobi, Sacred Books of the East, Vol. XLV, Delhi, 1980.

Varāṅgacarita of Jaṭāsiṃhanandi, ed. A.N. Upadhye, Bombay, 1938.

Vasudevahiṇḍī of Saṃghadāsagaṇi, ed. Caturvijaya Muni and Puṇyavijaya Muni, Vols. I–II, Bhavnagar, 1930–31.

Vāyu Purāṇa, ed. R. Mitra, Calcutta, 1880–88.

Viṣṇu Purāṇa, trans. H.H. Wilson, rep. Calcutta, 1972.

Yājñavalkya Smṛti, Eng. trans. by J.R. Gharpure, Bombay, 1936.
Yaśastilaka of Somadeva, ed. and trans. into Hindi by Sunder Lal Sastri, Varanasi, 1960.

FOREIGN ACCOUNTS

Beal, Samuel, *Si-yu-ki, Buddhist Records of the Western World*, translated from the Chinese of Hieun Tsang, 2 Vols., London, 1906.
Elliot, H.M. and Dowson, J., *The History of India as Told by Its Own Historians*, Vol. I, Kitabmahal.
Legge, J., *A Record of Buddhistic Kingdoms*, Delhi, 1991.
McCrindle, J.W., trans. and ed. *Ancient India as Described in Classical Literature*, Westminster, 1901, rep. Delhi, 1979.
Sachau, F.C., *Alberuni's India*, 2 Vols., London, 1910.
Schoff, W.R., trans. and ed. *The Periplus of the Erythraean Sea*, London, 1912, rep. Delhi, 1974.
Takakusu, J., trans. *A Record of the Buddhist Religion as Practised in India and Malaya Archipelago, AD 671–95*, by I-tsing, Oxford, 1896, rep. Delhi, 1982.

SECONDARY WORKS

Acharya, P.K., *Indian Architecture According to the Mānasāra-Śilpa-śāstra*, Allahabad, 1927.
———, *A Dictionary of Hindu Architecture*, Delhi, 1981.
Adhya, G.L., *Early Indian Economics*, Bombay, 1966.
Agrawala, V.S., *Harṣacarita: Ek Sāṃskṛtika Adhyayana*, Patna, 1953.
———, *Kādambarī: Ek Sāṃskṛtika Adhyayana*, Banaras, 1958.
Aiyangar, K.V.R., *Aspects of the Social and Political System of Manusmṛti*, Lucknow, 1949.
Allan, J., *Catalogue of Coins of Ancient India*, 1975.
Altekar, A.S., *State and Government in Ancient India*, 3rd edn., Delhi, 1958.
———, *The Coinage of the Gupta Empire*, B.H.U., 1957.
———, *The Position of Women in Hindu Civilisation*, 2nd edition, Banares, 1956.
———, *The Rāṣṭrakūṭas and their Times*, Poona, 1934.
———, *The Village Communities in Western India*, OUP, 1927.
Awasthi, A.B.L., *Studies in Skanda Purāṇa*, part I, Lucknow, 1966.
Baden-Powell, *Indian Village Community*, London, 1896; rep. Delhi, 1975.

Bagchi, P.C., *India and China*, Bombay, 1944.

———, *Studies in the Tantras*, Calcutta, 1939.

Banerjee, A.C., *Aspects of Rajput States and Society*, Delhi, 1981.

———, *Lectures on Rajput History*, Calcutta, 1962.

Banerjea, J.N., *Paurāṇic and Tantric Religion*, Calcutta, 1966.

———, *The Development of Hindu Iconography*, Calcutta, 1956, rep. Delhi, 1974.

Banga, Indu (ed.), *The City in Indian History*, Delhi, 1991.

Barnett, L.D., *Antiquities of India*, Calcutta, 1964.

Barodia, U.D., *History and Literature of Jainism*, Bombay, 1909.

Basham, A.L. (ed.), *A Cultural History of India*, Oxford, 1975.

———, *Origins and Development of Classical Hinduism*, Delhi, 1992.

———, *The Wonder that was India*, 3rd edn., London, 1967.

Begde, P.V., *Ancient and Medieval Town Planning in India*, Delhi, 1978.

Bhandarkar, R.G., *Vaiṣṇavism, Śaivism and Minor Religious Systems*, Poona, 1928.

Bhargava, D., *Jaina Ethics*, Delhi, 1968.

Bhatia, P., *The Paramāras*, Delhi, 1970.

Bhattacharya, B.C., *The Jaina Iconography*, 2nd edn., Delhi, 1974.

Bhattacharya, H. (ed.), *The Cultural Heritage of India*, Vol. IV, Calcutta, Revised edn., 1956, rep. 1969.

Bhattacharya, N.N., *Ancient Indian History and Civilisation*, Delhi, 1938.

———, *Ancient Indian Rituals and Social Contents*, Delhi, 1975.

———, *The Indian Mother Goddess*, Delhi, 1977.

Bhattacharya, S. and Thapar, Romila (ed.), *Situating Indian History*, Oxford University Press, 1986.

Bhattacharya, S.C., *Some Aspects of Indian Society: From c. 2nd Century* BC *to c. 4th Century* AD, Calcutta, 1978.

Bhattacharya, Tarapad, *Cult of Brahmā*, Varanasi, 1969.

Bhattacharya, U.C., *Catalogue and Guide to Rajputana Museum*, Ajmer, Jaipur, 1960–61.

Bloch, Marc, *Feudal Society*, Vol. II, London, 1965.

Bose, A.N., *Social and Rural Economy of Northern India (c. 600* BC–AD *200)*, 2 Vols., 2nd edn., Calcutta, 1961–67.

Brown, Percy, *Indian Architecture* (Buddhist and Hindu), 4th edn., Bombay, 1959.

Buhler, G., *The Indian Sect of the Jainas*, trans. J. Burgess, 2nd edn., Calcutta, 1963.

Burgess, J., *Digambara Jaina Iconography*, Bombay, 1904.

Chakladar, H.C., *Social Life in Ancient India*, Calcutta, 1929.

Chakrabarti, H.P., *Trade and Commerce of Ancient India* (200 BC–AD 650), Calcutta, 1956.

Chakravarti, Chintaharan, *Tantras: Studies on their Religion and Literature*, Calcutta, 1972.

Chakravarti, P.C., *Doctrine of Śakti in Indian Literature*, Calcutta, 1940.

Chatterji, B.R., *India and Java*, Calcutta, 1933.

Chatterji, S.K., *The Cultural Heritage of India*, Vol. V, Calcutta, Revised edn., 1978.

Chattopadhyaya, B.D. (ed.), *Essays in Ancient Indian Economic History*, Delhi, 1987.

———, *Aspects of Rural Settlement and Rural Society in Early Medieval India*, Calcutta, 1990.

Chattopadhyaya, D.P. (ed.), *History and Society: Essays in Honour of Professor Niharranjan Ray*, Calcutta, 1978.

Chattopadhyaya, S., *Early History of North India*, Calcutta, 1950.

———, *Social Life in Ancient India (in the background of the Yajñavalkya Smṛti)*, Calcutta, 1965.

Coomaraswamy, A.K., *Jaina Art*, Delhi, 1994.

Coulborn, R. (ed.), *Feudalism in History*, Princeton University Press, 1956.

Cunningham, A., *Ancient Geography of India*, Calcutta, 1914.

———, *Coins of Medieval India*, Delhi, 1967.

Das, S.K., *Economic History of Ancient India*, Calcutta, 1925.

Dasgupta, S.N., *History of Indian Philosophy*, 5 Vols., Cambridge, 1922–55.

Dasgupta, S.N. and De, S.K., *History of Sanskrit Literature*, Calcutta, 1947.

Deo, S.B., *History of Jaina Monachism*, Poona, 1956.

Derret, J.D.M., *Religion, Law and State in Ancient India*, London, 1968.

Desai, M.D., *Jaina Sāhitya no Saṃkṣipta Itihāsa* (in Gujarati), Bombay, 1933.

Desai, P.B., *Jainism in South India and Some Jaina Epigraphs*, Sholapur, 1957.

Deshpande, C.D., *Western India—A Regional Geography*, Dharwar, 1948.

Devahuti, D., *Harsha*, Oxford, 1970.

Dey, N.L., *Geographical Dictionary of Ancient and Medieval India*, London, 1927.

Deyell, J.S., *Living without Silver: The Monetary History of Early Medieval North India*, Delhi, 1990.

Drekmeier, C., *Kingship and Community in Early India*, Stanford, 1962.

Dumont, Louis, *Homo Hierarchius: The Caste System and its Implications*, Eng. trans. by Mark Sainsbury, London, 1970.

Dutt, B.B., *Town Planning in Ancient India*, Calcutta, 1925, rep. Delhi, 1977.

Dutt, B.N., *Studies in Indian Social Polity*, Calcutta, 1944.

Dutt, N.K., *Origin and Growth of Caste in India*, Vol. I, Calcutta, 1968.

Dutt, R.C., *A History of Civilization in Ancient India*, first Indian rep. 1972, Vishal Pub., Delhi.

———, *Later Hindu Civilization*, AD 500–1200, 4th edn., Calcutta, 1965.

Dwivedi, R.C., *Contribution of Jainism to Indian Culture*, Varanasi, 1975.

Faraquhar, J.N., *An Outline of the Religious Literature of India*, first Indian rep. 1967, Delhi.

Fick, R., *Social Organisation in North Eastern India in Buddha's Time*, Delhi, 1972.

Getty, Alice, *Ganesha*, Delhi, 1991.

Ghosh, A., *The City in Early Historical India*, Delhi, 1990.

———, ed. *Jaina Art and Architecture*, 3 Vols., Delhi, 1974.

Ghoshal, U.N., *A History of Indian Political Ideas*, Oxford, 1959.

———, *Studies in Indian History and Culture*, Delhi, 1965.

Ghurye, G.S., *Caste and Race in India*, 5th edn., Bombay, 1979.

Gode, P.K., *Studies in Indian Cultural History*, Vol. I, Hoshiarpur, 1961.

———, *Studies in Indian Literary History*, 3 Vols., Vols. I and II, Bombay, 1953–54, Vol. III, Poona, 1956.

Goetz, H., *The Art and Architecture of Bikaner State*, Oxford, 1960.

Gonda, J., *Aspects of Early Viṣṇuism*, Utrecht, 1954.

Gopal, L., *Aspects of History of Agriculture in Ancient India*, Varanasi, 1980.

———, *Early Medieval Coin—Types of Northern India*, Varanasi, 1966.

———, *Economic History of Northern India* (AD 700–1200), Varanasi, 1965.

Gupta, Chitralekha, *The Brāhmaṇas of India*, Delhi, 1983.

Habibullah, A.B.M., *The Foundation of Muslim Rule in India*, Lahore, 1945.

Handa, D., *Osian: History, Archaeology, Art and Architecture*, Delhi, 1984.
Handiqui, K.K., *Yaśastilaka and Indian Culture*, Sholapur, 1949.
Hazra, R.C., *Studies in the Purāṇic Records on Hindu Rites and Customs*, Calcutta, 1940.
———, *Studies in the Upapurāṇas*, Vol. II, Calcutta, 1963.
Hiriyana, M., *Outlines of Indian Philosophy*, London, 1931.
Hodivala, S.H., *Studies in Indo-Muslim History*, Bombay, 1939.
Hopkins, E.W., *Epic Mythology*, Delhi, 1974.
Hutton, J.H., *Caste in India*, 3rd edn., Oxford University Press, 1961.
Jain, C.R., *Fundamentals of Jainism*, Meerut, 1974.
Jain, J.C., *Life in Ancient India as Depicted in Jaina Canons*, Bombay, 1947.
———, *Prakrit Jaina Kathā Sāhitya*, Ahmedabad, 1971.
———, *Prakrit Narrative Literature, Origin and Growth*, Delhi, 1981.
Jain, J.L., *Outlines of Jainism*, Oxford, 1940.
Jain, J.P., *Jaina Sources of the History of Ancient India*, Delhi, 1964.
Jain, K.C., *Jainism in Rajasthan*, Sholapur, 1963.
———, *Ancient Cities and Towns of Rajasthan*, Delhi, 1972.
Jain, P.C., *Labour in Ancient India*, Delhi, 1971.
Jain, Prem Suman, *Kuvalayamālākahā kā Sāṃskṛtika Adhyayana*, Bihar, 1975.
Jain, V.K., *Trade and Traders in Western India*, Delhi, 1990.
Jaiswal, Suvira, *The Origin and Development of Vaiṣṇavism*, Delhi, 1967.
Jha, D.N., *Economy and Society in Early India*, Delhi, 1993.
———, (ed.), *Feudal Social Formation in Early India*, Delhi, 1987.
Jolly, J., *Hindu Law and Customs*, Calcutta, 1928.
———, *Indian Medicine*, Delhi, 1977.
Kalghatgi, T.G., *Jaina View of Life*, Sholapur, 1970.
Kane, P.V., *History of the Dharmaśāstra*, 5 Vols., Poona, 1930–62,
Kangle, R.P., *Kautiliya Arthaśāstra—A Study*, Bombay, 1965.
Karve, Irawati, *Kinship Organization in India*, Poona, 1953.
———, *Hindu Society: An Interpretation*, 1961.
Kautawala, G.K., *Cultural History from the Matsya Purāṇa*, Baroda, 1964.
Keith, A.B., *A History of Sanskrit Literature*, Oxford, 1920.
———, *The Sanskrit Drama*, Oxford, 1924.
Ketkar, S.V., *History of Caste in India*, New York, 1909, London, 1911.

Kosambi, D.D., *An Introduction to the Study of Indian History*, 2nd edn., Bombay, 1975.

———, *The Culture and Civilization in Ancient India*, Delhi, 1987.

———, *Myth and Reality*, Bombay, 1962.

Lal, B.B., *Indian Archaeology since Independence*, Delhi, 1964.

Law, B.C., *India as Described in Early Texts of Buddhism and Jainism*, rep. Delhi, 1980.

———, *Tribes in Ancient India*, Poona, 1943.

Lorenzen, David, *The Kāpālikas and Kālamukhas*, Delhi, 1972.

Macdonell, A.A., *History of Sanskrit Literature*, London, 1900; rep. Delhi, 1971.

Maity, S.K., *Economic Life in Northern India in the Gupta Period (c. AD 300–550)*, 2nd edn., Delhi, 1970.

Majumdar, A.K., *Concise History of India*, Vol. III, Delhi, 1983.

Majumdar, B.P., *Socio-Economic History of Northern India (AD 1030–1194)*, Calcutta, 1960.

Majumdar, R.C., *Corporate Life in Ancient India*, 3rd edn., Calcutta, 1969.

———, ed., *Comprehensive History of India*, Vol. III, part II.

———, *History of Bengal*, Dacca, 1943.

———, *Suvarṇadvīpa*, parts 1 and 2, Dacca, 1937–38.

———, ed., *The Age of Imperial Kannauj*, Bombay, 1955.

———, ed., *The Age of Imperial Unity*, Bombay, 1951.

———, ed., *The Classical Age*, Bombay, 1954.

———, ed., *Vākāṭaka-Gupta Age*, Lahore, 1946.

———, ed., *Vedic Age*, London, 1951.

Mehta, M.L., *Jaina Culture*, Varanasi, 1969.

Mirashi, V.V., *Studies in Indology*, 4 Vols., 1960–66.

Misra, V.C., *Geography of Rajasthan*, Bombay, 1967.

Monier-Williams, M., *Religious Thought and Life in India*, London, 1891; rep. Delhi, 1975.

Mookerji, R.K., *A History of Indian Shipping and Maritime Activity*, London, 1912.

———, *Ancient Indian Education*, 2nd edn., rep. Delhi, 1974.

———, *Local Government in Ancient India*, Oxford, 1919.

Motichandra, *Costumes, Textiles, Cosmetics and Coiffure in Ancient and Medieval India*, Delhi, 1973.

———, *Trade and Trade Routes in Ancient India*, Delhi, 1977.

Mumford, Lewis, *The City in History*, London, 1961.

Munshi, K.M., *The Glory that was Gurjaradeśa*, part III.

———, *The Imperial Gurjaras*, Bombay, 1944.

Nahar, P.C. and Ghosh, K.C., *Epitome of Jainism*, Calcutta, 1917.

Nandi, R.N., *Religious Institutions and Cults in the Deccan*, Delhi, 1973.

———, *Social Roots of Religion in Ancient India*, Delhi, 1986.

Nath, Vijaya, *Dāna: Gift System in North India, A Socio-Economic Perspective*, Delhi, 1987.

Niyogi, Pushpa, *Contributions to the Economic History of Northern India from the Tenth to the Twelfth Century* AD, Calcutta, 1962.

Ojha, G.H., *Dūṅgarpur Rājya kā Itihās*, Ajmer, VS 1992.

———, *Jodhpur Rājya kā Itihās*, Vol. I, Ajmer, VS 1938.

———, *Rājpūtāne kā Itihās*, Ajmer, VS 1982, 1st edn.; VS 1993, 2nd edn.

———, *Udaipur Rājya kā Itihās*, Ajmer, VS 1985.

Omprakash, *Food and Drinks in Ancient India*, Delhi, 1961.

Pande, B.M. and Chattopadhyaya, B.D. (eds), *Archaeology and History*, 2 Vols., Delhi, 1987.

Pande, G.C., *Foundations of Indian Culture*, 2 Vols., Delhi, 1990.

Pandey, L.P., *Sun Worship in Ancient India*, Delhi, 1971.

Pandey, Rajbali, *Hindu Saṃskāras*, 2nd edn., rep. Delhi, 1982.

Parasher, Aloka, *Mlecchas in Early India*, Delhi, 1991.

Pathak, V.S., *Śaiva Cults in Northern India*, Varanasi, 1960.

Patil, D.R., *Cultural History from the Vāyu Purāṇa*, Poona, 1946.

Payne, E.A., *The Śāktas*, Calcutta, 1933.

Prabhu, P.H., *Hindu Social Organisation*, 4th edn., Bombay, 1963.

Prasad, Kameshwar, *Cities, Crafts and Commerce under the Kuṣāṇas*, Delhi, 1984.

Premi, N.R., *Jaina Sāhitya aur Itihās*, Bombay, 1956.

Puri, K.N., *Excavations at Rairh (AD 1938–39)*, Jaipur.

Puri, B.N., *History of the Gurjara Pratihāras*, Bombay, 1957.

Rai, Jaimal, *The Rural-Urban Economy and Social Changes in Ancient India (c. 300 BC–AD 600)*, Delhi, 1974.

Rai, S.N., *Paurāṇic Dharma evaṃ Samāja*, Allahabad, 1968.

Rai, U.N., *Prācīna Bhārat men Nagar tathā Nagar Jīvan*, Allahabad, 1965.

Randhawa, M.S., *A History of Agriculture in India*, Vol. I, Delhi, 1980.

Rao, T.A.G., *Elements of Hindu Iconography*, Madras, 1914, 1916; rep. ed. K.K. Dasgupta, Varanasi, 1972.

Ray, Aniruddha and Bagchi, S.K., *Technology in Ancient and Medieval India*, Delhi, 1986.

Ray, H.C., *Dynastic History of Northern India*, 2 Vols., Calcutta, 1931, 1936.

Ray, P. and Sen, S.N. (eds), *The Cultural Heritage of India*, Vol. VI, Calcutta, rev. edn., 1986.

Ray, P.C., *History of Chemistry in Ancient and Medieval India*, Calcutta, 1956.

Rayachaudhari, H.C., *Early History of the Vaiṣṇava Sect*, Calcutta, 1920.

———, *Political History of Ancient India*, Calcutta, 1950.

Renou, Louis, *Civilisation of Ancient India*, Delhi, 1987.

Reu, B.N., *Coins of Marwar*, Jodhpur, 1946.

Rydh, Henna, *Rang Mahal: The Swedish Archaeological Expedition to India (1952–4)*, Lund, 1959.

Sahni, D.R., *Archaeological Remains and Excavations at Bairāṭ*, Jaipur.

Saletore, B.A., *Medieval Jainism*, Bombay, 1938.

Saletore, R.N., *Early Indian Economic History*, Bombay, 1994.

Sastri, K.A.N., *A History of South India*, 4th edn., OUP, 1966.

———, *Development of Religion in South India*, Madras, 1963.

———, (ed.), *Comprehensive History of India*, Vol. II, Calcutta, 1957.

Satish Chandra (ed.), *Essays in Medieval Indian Economic History*, Delhi, 1988.

Schubring, Walther, *The Doctrine of the Jainas*, 1st edn., 1962, rep. Delhi, 1978.

Sen, A., *Schools and Sects of the Jaina Literature*, Calcutta, 1931.

Sen, Madhu, *A Cultural Study of the Niśītha Cūrṇi*, Amritsar, 1975.

Senart, A., *Caste in India*, London, 1930; rep. Delhi, 1975.

Shah, C.J., *Jainism in North India, 800 BC–AD 526*, London, 1932.

Shah, U.P., *Studies in Jaina Art*, Banares, 1955.

Sharma, B.N., *Social Life in Northern India (AD 600–1000)*, Delhi, 1966.

———, *Social and Cultural History of Northern India, c. AD 1000–1200*, Delhi, 1972.

Sharma, D., *Early Chauhan Dynasties*, 2nd edn., Delhi, 1975.

———, *Lectures in Rajput History and Culture*, Delhi, 1970.

———, (ed.), *Rajasthan Through the Ages*, Bikaner, 1966.

Sharma, G.N., *Social Life in Medieval Rajasthan, AD 1500–1800*, Agra, 1968.

Sharma, Mathura Lal, *Rajasthan*, Delhi, 1972.

Sharma, R.S., *Indian Feudalism, c. 300–1200*, Calcutta, 1965.

———, *Material Culture and Social Formations in Ancient India*, Delhi, 1983.

———, *Perspectives in Social and Economic History of Early India*, Delhi, 1983.

Sharma, R.S. and Jha, V.N. (eds), *Indian Society: Historical Probings*, Delhi, 1974.

Sharma, R.S., *Śūdras in Ancient India*, 2nd edn., Delhi, 1980.

———, (ed.), *Survey of Research in Economic and Social History of India*, Delhi, 1986.

———, *Urban Decay in India*, Delhi, 1987.

Sharma, Ramashraya, *A Socio-Political Study of the Vālmīki Rāmāyaṇa*.

Sharma, S.R., *Jainism and Karṇāṭaka Culture*, Dharwar, 1940.

Shastri, A.M., *India as Seen in the Bṛhatsaṃhitā of Varāhamihira*, Delhi, 1969.

Shastri, Nemichandra, *Haribhadra ke Prākrit Sāhitya kā Ālocanātmaka Pariśīlana*, Bihar, 1965.

Shrimali, K.M. (ed.), *Essays in Indian Art, Religion and Society,* Delhi, 1987.

Sikdar, J.C., *Studies in the Bhagavatīsūtra*, Bihar, 1964.

Singh, R.B.P., *Jainism in Early Medieval Karṇāṭaka (c.* AD *500–1200)*, Delhi, 1975.

Singh, R.L., *India: A Regional Geography*, Delhi, 1990.

Sinha, Surjit, *Caste in India: Its Structural Pattern and Socio-Cultural Integration*, 1967.

Sircar, D.C., *Land System and Feudalism in Ancient India*, Calcutta, 1966.

———, *Select Inscriptions*, Vol. I, Calcutta, 1942.

———, *Studies in the Geography of Ancient and Medieval India*, Delhi, 1960.

———, *Studies in the Political and Administrative Systems in Ancient and Medieval India*, Delhi, 1974.

———, *The Guhilas of Kiṣkindhā*, Calcutta, 1965.

———, *The Śakta Pīṭhas*, rep. Delhi, 1973.

———, (ed.), *The Śakti Cult and Tārā*, Calcutta, 1967.

Southeimer, G.D., *The Joint Hindu Family* (Its Evolution as a Legal Institution), Delhi, 1977.

Stein, Burton, *Peasant, State and Society in Medieval South India*, Delhi, 1980.

Stevenson, Sinclair, *Heart of Jainism*, Delhi, 1970.

Tatia, Nathmal, *Studies in Jaina Philosophy*, Banaras, 1951.
Thakur, V.K., *Historiography of Indian Feudalism*, Patna, 1989.
———, *Urbanisation in Ancient India*, Delhi, 1981.
Thapar, Romila, *Ancient Indian Social History*, Delhi, 1978.
———, *From Lineage to State, Social Formations in the Mid-First Millennium* BC *in the Ganga Valley*, OUP, 1984, rep. 1993.
Tod, James, *Annals and Antiquities of Rajasthan*, ed. Crooke, Delhi, 1971, 1st Indian rep.
Tripathi, R.S., *History of Kannauj*, Banares, 1937.
Upadhyaya, B.S., *India in Kālidāsa*, Allahabad, 1947.
Upadhyaya, G.P., *Brāhmaṇas in Ancient India (c. 200* BC–AD *500)*, Delhi, 1979.
Upadhyaya, V., *The Socio-Religious Conditions of Northern India (*AD *700–1200)*, Varanasi, 1964.
Vaidya, C.V., *History of Medieval Hindu India*, Vol. I, Poona, 1921; Vol. II, Poona, 1924.
Wagle, N.K., *Society at the Time of the Buddha*, Bombay, 1966.
Warmington, E.H., *The Commerce between the Roman Empire and India*, Cambridge, 1928.
Weber, Max, *The Religion of India*, Delhi, 1992.
Winternitz, M., *History of Indian Literature*, Vol. II, 2nd edn., 1972, rep. 1977, Delhi.
Wiser, W.H., *The Hindu Jajmānī System*, Lucknow, 1936.
Wittfogel, K., *Oriental Despotism*, New Haven, 1957.
Woodroffe, John, *Śakti and Śāktas*, Madras, 1969.
Yadava, B.N.S., *Society and Culture in Northern India in the Twelfth Century*, Allahabad, 1973.
Yadava, Jhinkoo, *Samarāiccakahā: Ek Sāṃskritika Adhyayana*, Varanasi, 1977.

COMMEMORATION AND FELICITATION VOLUMES GRAMMARS AND DICTIONARIES

Ācārya Bhikshu Commemoration Volume, Calcutta, 1961.
Bhāratīya Purātatva. Muni Jinavijaya Felicitation Volume, Jaipur, 1971.
Dr S.K. Belvalkar Felicitation Volume, Banares, 1957.
Jadunath Sircar Commemoration Volume, Panjab University, 1958.
Rajasthan: A Symposium, Government of Rajasthan, 1951.
Rājendra Sūri Commemoration Volume, Rajasthan, 1957.
Shri Hazārīmala Commemoration Volume, Rajasthan, 1965.

Prākrit Mārgopadeśikā by Jivaraj Doshi, Delhi, 1968, 1st edn.
Prākrit Vijñāna Pāthamālā by Vijayakastūrasūri, 3rd edn., Ahmedabad, 1962.
Pāia-Sadda-Mahaṇṇavo: A Comprehensive Prākrit-Hindi Dictionary, Vol. I by Hargovind Das Seth, Calcutta, 1923.
A Concise Sanskrit-English Dictionary by V.V. Bhide, Poona, 1926.
The Practical Sanskrit-English Dictionary by V.S. Apte, Bombay, 1924.

JOURNALS AND PERIODICALS

Ancient India, New Delhi.
Anekāntā, Delhi.
Annals of the Bhandarkar Oriental Research Institute, Poona.
Annual Report of the Archaeological Survey of India.
Bhārata Kaumudī, Allahabad.
Bhāratīya Vidyā, Bombay.
Epigraphia Indica.
Indian Antiquary, Bombay.
Indian Culture, Calcutta.
Indian Historical Quarterly, Calcutta.
Jaina Antiquary, Bihar.
Journal of the Asiatic Society of Bengal, Calcutta.
Journal of the Bihar Research Society, Patna.
Journal of the Bihar and Orissa Research Society, Patna.
Journal of the Economic and Social History of the Orient, Leiden.
Journal of the Ganganath Jha Research Institute, Allahabad.
Journal of Indian History, Trivandrum.
Journal of the Numismatic Society of India, Banares.
Journal of the Oriental Institute, M.S. University of Baroda.
Journal of the Royal Asiatic Society of Great Britain and Ireland, London.
Maru Bhāratī, Pilani.
Proceedings and Transactions of the All-India Oriental Conference.
Proceedings of the Indian History Congress.
Proceedings of the Rajasthan History Congress.
Rajasthan Bhāratī, Bikaner.
Researcher, Jaipur.
Social Science Probings, Delhi.
The Indian Historical Review, Delhi.
Varadā, Rajasthan.

Index